A Charlton Standard Catalogue

Canadian Coins

Volume Two

Collector and Maple Leaf Issues

SECOND EDITION, 2011

W. K. Cross

The Charlton Press

TORONTO, ONTARIO • PALM HARBOR, FLORIDA

COPYRIGHT NOTICE

TRADEMARK NOTICE

DISCLAIMER

While every care has been taken to ensure accuracy in the compilation of the data in this catalogue, the publisher cannot accept responsibility for typographical errors.

Library and Archives Canada Cataloguing in Publication

Canadian coins (Charlton Press)
Canadian coins : a Charlton standard catalogue. volume two: collector coins

Annual
59th ed. (2005) -
Continues: Charlton standard catalogue of Canadian coins, ISSN 0706-0424
ISSN 1716-0782
ISBN 978-0-88968-342-6

1. Coins, Canadian--Catalogs. 2. Coins, Canadian--Prices--Periodicals. and collecting. I. Title

CJ18610.S82 59- 2005- 737.4971'029 C2005-902187-X

Printed in Canada
in the Province of Quebec

EDITORIAL

Editor	W. K. Cross
Editorial Assistant	Jean Dale
Editorial Assistant	Mark Drake
Graphic Technician	Davina Rowan
Photography	Scott Cornwell

VERY SPECIAL MENTION

Jim Charlton must be given special credit for all his work over the years which made this catalogue and the Charlton "Series of Catalogues" possible.

SPECIAL MENTION

We would like to thank all contributors for submitting prices, answering requests or supplying information which assisted in building the many past editions of this catalogue.

We would like to thank the following for their contributions to the 2nd edition of Canadian Coins, Volume Two: **Randy Ash**, Alberta; **Dawn Bell**, New Brunswick; **Trevor Bishop**, Ontario; **Sandy Campbell**, Nova Scotia; **Marc and Mary Dolph**, Ontario; **Jamie Flamenbaum**, Ontario; **Dan Gosling**, Alberta; **Ian Laing**, Manitoba; **Kevin Mosher**, Alberta; **Todd Sandham**, Ontario; **Terry Stark**, Alberta; **Michael Thomas**, Nova Scotia; **Paul Waldie**, Ontario

The Charlton Press

Editorial Office
P.O. Box 820, Postal Station Willowdale B
North York, Ontario M2K 2R1
Tel.: (416) 488-1418 Fax: (416) 488-4656
Tel.: (800) 442-6042 Fax.: (800) 442-1542
www.charltonpress.com email: chpress@charltonpress.com

Colonial
Acres Coins
www.colonialacres.com
Visit us online today!
We Buy Coins!
One of the Largest Selections of coins &
Royal Canadian Mint Products in Canada!
300 Victoria St. North
Unit #7
Kitchener, ON,
N2H 6R9
Toll Free: 1-888-255-4565
Fax: 519-579-0532
email: info@colonialacres.com
web: www.colonialacres.com
We want to purchase Canadian Coins, USA Coins & Banknote Collections. We will provide
FREE appraisals for Individuals & Estate Collections. You can also mail your items to us for a free
appraisal. We will travel to purchase any major deal of Canadian or U.S. Coins.
All transactions held in the strictest confidence.

THE COIN CABINET
We are always looking to purchase estates, collections, and individual coins, paper money, military
medals, bulk gold and silver (bars, rings, etc.), and all related bullion and numismatic material.
506-642-2646
E-mail: coins118@hotmail.com
84 King St., Saint John, NB E2L 1G4
506-857-9403
E-mail: coincbnt@nb.aibn.com
118 Cameron St., Moncton, NB E1C 5Y6

APPLICATION FOR MEMBERSHIP/SUBSCRIPTION

Applications for membership/subscription in **The Royal Canadian Numismatic Association** may be made by any reputable party upon payment of the required dues.

❑ Mr. ❑ Mrs. ❑ Ms.

❑ Regular ❑ Family ❑ Junior
❑ Club / Corporate ❑ Life Membership

❑ Renewal ❑ Reinstatement ______
(old member #)

Name: (Also list name of spouse if family membership)

Street/Mailing Address:

City: Province/State: Country: Postal Code/Zip:

Telephone Number: E-mail Address:

W.K.CROSS
Signature of applicant: Sponsored by:

Juniors (under 18 years of age) must provide Birth date: ______________

Numismatic Speciality (optional): ______________

❑ I would like to be contacted by a mentor who also has my speciality (optional)

Dues

Dues shown are in Canadian dollars to Canadian addresses and in U.S. dollars to all other addresses. Payment may be made by money order, bank draft or personal cheque. We regret that we are unable to offer credit card services at this time. Postage stamps are not acceptable. Currency (U.S. or Canadian only) is acceptable and should be sent by security registered mail only. Membership is not Goods and Services taxable.

Regular - Canada and USA Applicants 18 years of age or over $35.00
Regular - Foreign (non-USA) US$ please $50.00
Junior - Applicants under 18 years of age $16.50
Persons under 18 must be sponsored by a parent or guardian
Family - Member, spouse & children at home under age 18, one *CN Journal* only .. $44.00
Corporate - Clubs, Societies, Libraries and other non-profit organizations ... $35.00
Life Membership $595.00
Life Membership Senior (65 years of age and older) $395.00
(After one year of regular membership. Details on payment plan available on request.)

Please mail application and payment to:

The Royal Canadian Numismatic Association
5694 Highway #7 East, Suite 432
Markham ON Canada L3P 1B4
Tel: 647-401-4014; Fax: 905-472-9645;
E-mail: *info@rcna.ca* Web site: ***www.rcna.ca***

Apply for membership in the RCNA online at: *www.rcna.ca/paydues.php*

Application must be complete and accompanied by full dues to be accepted.

TABLE OF CONTENTS

PLATINUM COINS

COLLECTOR SETS

MAPLE LEAF BULLION COINS

75th Anniversary of the First Bank Notes Issued by the Bank of Canada
Ten Dollars, 2010

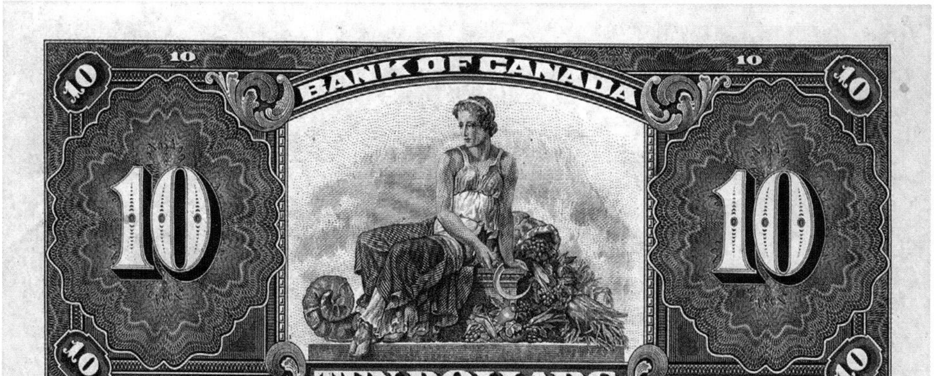

BC-8 Bank of Canada $10 English Issue - 1935
Back Design: —/Harvest allegory: Seated female with fruits of harvest/—

INTRODUCTION

The first non-circulating legal tender coin (NCLT) struck in Canada was a 1908 Edward VII gold sovereign. This coin was struck at the Ottawa Branch Mint in specimen quality along with specimen examples of the other five denominations (one cent, five cents, ten cents, twenty-five cents and fifty cents) that made up the circulating coins of the day. The difference between the five subsidiary coins and the gold sovereign was that the latter, being struck only in specimen quality, had no circulating counterpart. While the 1908 gold sovereign was not a commemorative issue, the current thinking is that it was struck to establish a series. There are still a few questions regarding this NCLT coin that have yet to be answered. One is "How was it distributed?"

Modern Canadian NCLT coinage began with the issue of the 1967 centennial anniversary specimen gold set. This set contained seven coins, the most important being a $20 gold coin. This coin was similar to the 1908 sovereign in that there was no circulating counterpart. This coin set also the stage for the next forty years. The Royal Canadian Mint sold 334,288 gold sets in 1967, creating a production bottleneck that was not cleared until well into 1968. The sales volume of 1967 collector coins was not lost on the organising officials of the Montreal 1976 Olympics games, for 1972 saw the beginning of the greatest issue of NCLT coins in Canadian history.

Canadian Coins, Volume Two: Collector Issues, 2011, second edition, records and lists over forty years of non-circulating legal tender coins issued by the Royal Canadian Mint in Canada.

COMMEMORATIVE COINS

Commemorative coins are issued to commemorate a particular personage, event, either historic or current, or a place. Such coins have a distinct design with reference to the occasion for which they are issued. Many coins of this category are collector items only, but a great number were issued for circulation to promote a major national event, such as the Vancouver 2010 Olympic Winter Games.

Vast numbers of thematic coins highlighting monuments, sites, historical personalities, endangered species, or just wild species common to a specific area, are now being inserted into this commemorative mix. The line between commemorative and thematic coins is blurred, and probably intentionally so.

Types of Commemoratives

We shall include thematic coins among the commemoratives. Commemorative/thematic coins can be divided into two categories:

1. **Commemorative/thematic legal tender circulating issues.**

These are the everyday coins used in commerce which bear a design commemorating an event. They are issued at face value, without a premium, within a certain time frame. Usually, the concept is centred on one denomination, but may encompass all denominations for an event of outstanding national significance such as the Centennial of Confederation. This category of commemorative is issued in "business strike" or circulation finish.

2. **Non circulating legal tender commemorative/ thematic issues.**

NCLT coins are deemed legal tender by a mint, but there is no expectation that they will be released into circulation. In theory, they may be used in commerce to purchase goods and services, but their recognition as a medium of exchange, and their acceptance by the modern day public, is questionable. In this category we will find single coins and sets, depending on how the issuing authorities developed their marketing strategies. The selling price has no relationship either to the face value or the intrinsic value. The selling price, intrinsic value and face value diminish in that order. The issuing authorities generally have no intention ever to redeem commemorative or thematic issues.

The earlier issues may command a substantial market price increase over the original issue price because of the increased intrinsic value of precious metals. Modern commemorative coins usually need time and additional increases in intrinsic value to return a profit.

FINISHES

Sales of modern collector coins are basically driven by the finish on the coins. The Royal Canadian Mint currently uses nine different finishes. See the next page for an outline of the different finishes used. A collector should be well versed in the different finishes as they will, at times, greatly affect the value of the issue.

FRATERNAL AFFILIATION

Over the years, coin clubs have sprung up in many Canadian Communities. In addition, both Canada and the United States have national organisations which hold annual conventions. Coin clubs constitute one of the most attractive features of present-day collecting. They offer beginning collectors the opportunity for good fellowship and the encouragement and knowledge of more experienced collectors. The larger groups maintain lending libraries and publish a journal or newsletter on a regular basis, Memberships and other information can be obtained from:

Royal Canadian Numismatic Association
5694 Highway # 7 East, Suite 432
Markham, Ontario
Canada L3P 1B4
Tel.: (647) 401-4014 Fax: (905) 472-9645
Email: info@rcna.ca

Ontario Numismatic Association
P.O. Box 40033, Waterloo Sq. P.O.
75 King Street South
Waterloo, Ontario
Canada N2J 4V1
www.ontario-numismatic.org/index.html

COLLECTOR COINS

Finishes 1953 to Date

Introduction: A coin finish simply means the surface quality imparted to a blank during the striking process. At the striking stage the main factors influencing the quality of the finish are: (1) The quality of the blanks, (2) The finish of the dies, (3) The speed and pressure of the press, and (4) The number of times the blank is struck.

The loading and unloading of the striking chamber, or press is another factor in maintaining the quality of the finish on coins.

The finish (quality) order from lowest to highest is: circulation, uncirculated, proof-like/brilliant uncirculated, specimen, proof.

Coins with Circulation : *Brilliant Relief Against a Satin Background*. This is the most common finish found on all business strikes, from the one cent to the two dollar coins. These are production coins struck at the rate of 700 to 800 per minute. They are allowed to tumble into waiting hoppers, then put through counting and wrapping machines before being sent to the Banks.

Coins with Uncirculated Finish: ***Brilliant Relief Against a Satin Background.*** This process is very similar to the circulation finish above with common dies being used, but with slower striking speeds and definitely more care in the loading and unloading of the press. There are far less handling marks than the circulation variety, but still marks may be found.

The Uncirculated finish is used by the Numismatic Department of the Mint on singles and sets offered to collectors, or sold into the giftware market.

Coins with Proof-Like Finish: *Frosted to Semi-Mirror Relief Against a Semi-Mirror Background*. These coins are produced on a slow moving press with reasonably high pressure. The planchets and dies are polished with each coin being removed from the press individually. Large coins may be struck more than once.

The following die states are found on proof-like coins:

(1) Ultra Heavy Cameo (UHC): Full frosting across the relief of the coin, both effigy and legend, when viewed from all directions under full lighting conditions.

(2) Heavy Cameo (HC): The frosting is neither full nor evenly applied across the relief of the coin. In fact, some areas may appear bright when viewed under full lighting conditions.

(3) Cameo (C): Touches of frosting may appear on the relief of the coin. There will be bright areas when the coin is viewed under full lighting conditions.

(4) No Cameo. No frosting, all relief areas will appear bright. There is no difference in contrast between the bright field and a bright relief. The majority of coins are from this die state.

Nickel has a hardness higher than silver making the striking of coins more difficult. In 1968 with the change from silver to nickel coinage came the need for a new finish on numismatic items. That finish is:

Brilliant Uncirculated Finish: *Brilliant Design, Legends and Dates Against a Brilliant Background.* Coins are struck by a slow moving press using high pressure, and polished dies. Blanks are inserted, and coins removed by hand. This finish was used on all packaged singles and sets offered by the Mint from 1968 to 2004. In 2004 production of sets was divided between Uncirculated and Brilliant Uncirculated.

Specimen Finish: From 1968 to 2010 there have been three different finishes used by the Mint on specimen coinage.

1968 to 1995: *A Brilliant Relief Against a Brilliant Background.* A double-struck coin on a polished blank, by a highly polished die.

1996 to 2009: *A Brilliant Design, Frosted Legends and Date Against a Line Background.* As above, but instead of a brilliant background there is a parallel lined background. This finish was first used by the Bullion Department on maple leaf coinage.

2010: *A Brilliant Design, Frosted Legends and Date Against a Laser Lined Background.* As above, but the background is now a frosted lined background which is produced by laser etching.

Proof Finish: *Frosted Relief Against a Mirror Field.* This is the highest quality finish used by the Royal Canadian Mint on Canadian coinage. By definition, all coins with this finish are designated Ultra Heavy Cameo (UHC). They are identified in the pricing tables by PR/UHC (proof/ultra heavy cameo).

Reverse Proof Finish: *Mirror Relief Against a Frosted Background.* This type of finish is at times called "satin matte" because of the background texture. All elements of the design that are in relief have a highly reflective finish.

Bullion Finish: *Brilliant Relief Against a Parallel Lined Background.* This finish was first used in 1979 on gold maple leafs for the bullion program. The finish is found on gold, platinum, palladium and silver maples. As this finish is the standard used on the maple leaf issues the grading designation is Mint State (MS).

Bullion-Specimen (Reverse Proof): *Brilliant Relief Against a Satin Background.* A finish not often used, it can be found on special edition bullion singles and sets.

Bullion-Proof: ***Frosted Relief Against a Mirror Background.*** This finish is the same as that found on all numismatic proof issues.

All of the above finishes are now embellished with special effects created with technologies such as holograms, enamelling, selective plating, painting and laser enhancements. All are noted in *Canadian Coins, Volume One*, 64th edition under the description, with the type of specialty added.

ONE CENT

ONE CENT, 90TH ANNIVERSARY OF THE ROYAL CANADIAN MINT, 1908-1998.

Issued to commemorate the opening of the Royal Canadian Mint, a five-coin set featuring the same reverse designs as the original 1908 coins, except for the double date 1908-1998, was struck. The set was issued in two finishes, matte and mirror proof. The matte set cent does not carry the country of origin, "Canada." This error was corrected on the mirror proof issues.

Matte Proof Issue Without "CANADA" on Obverse

Mirror Proof Issue Reverse

Mirror Proof Issue With "CANADA" on Obverse

Designers and Engravers:
Obv.: Dora de Pédery-Hunt
Rev.: Ago Aarand, G. W. DeSaulles
Composition: Copper plate, 92.5% Ag, 7.5% Cu
Silver content: 5.24 g, 0.169 tr oz
Weight: 5.67 g
Diameter: 25.4 mm
Thickness: 1.5 mm **Die Axis:** ↑↑
Edge: Plain **Finish:** See below
Case: See Special Issue Proof Sets, page 285

DATE	DESCRIPTION	QUANTITY SOLD	ISSUE PRICE	FINISH	PR-67 UHC	PR-68 UHC
1998 (1908-)	Without "CANADA"	18,376	N.I.I.	Matte Proof	40.	45.
1998 (1908-)	With "CANADA"	24,893	N.I.I.	Mirror Proof	25.	30.

ONE CENT, 50TH ANNIVERSARY OF THE CORONATION OF QUEEN ELIZABETH II, 1953-2003.

This one cent coin, which carries the double date 1953 2003, is from the Special Edition Proof Set issued in 2003 to commemorate the 50th anniversary of the Coronation of Queen Elizabeth II.

Designers and Engravers:
Obv: Mary Gillick, Dora de Pédery-Hunt
Rev.: G. E. Kruger-Gray
Composition: Copper
Weight: 2.50 g
Case of Issue: See Special Issue Proof Sets, page 286
Diameter: 19.05 mm
Thickness: 1.25 mm
Edge: Plain
Die Axis: ↑↑
Finish: Proof

DATE	DESCRIPTION	QUANTITY SOLD	ISSUE PRICE	FINISH	PR-67 UHC	PR-68 UHC
2003 (1953-)	50th Anniv. Coronation Queen Elizabeth II	21,537	N.I.I.	Proof	20.	25.

ONE CENT, ROYAL CANADIAN MINT ANNUAL REPORT, SELECTIVELY GOLD PLATED, 2003.

This one cent coin is the first of a series of six coins, one of which was to be included each year with the Annual Mint Report, leading up to the Royal Canadian Mint's centennial in 2008. However, this series was discontinued with the issue of the 2006 Annual Mint Report. See the One Cent Derivatives listed below.

Designers and Engravers:
Obv.: Dora de Pédery-Hunt, Ago Aarand
Rev.: G. E. Kruger-Gray
Composition: Copper plated zinc
Weight: 2.25 g
Finish: Proof, Selectively gold plated
Case of Issue: See Derivatives below
Diameter: 19.05 mm
Thickness: 1.45 mm
Edge: Plain
Die Axis: ↑↑

DATE	DESCRIPTION	QUANTITY SOLD	ISSUE PRICE	FINISH	PR-67 UHC	PR-68 UHC
2003	Copper plated zinc, Selectively gold plated	7,746	N.I.I.	Proof	55.	85.

ONE CENT DERIVATIVES

DATE	DESCRIPTION	QUANTITY SOLD	ISSUE PRICE	ISSUER	FINISH	MARKET VALUE
2003	**2003 Annual Mint Report**, One cent coin, selectively gold plated	7,746	19.95	RCM	PR-67	75.
2003	**Coronation Coin and Stamp Set**, two one cent coins, 1953 and 2003; two fifty cent coins, 2002 Jubilee and 2003 Uncrowned Portrait; two mint and two cancelled stamps of Her Majesty's Jubilee and Coronation; Presentation Case	14,743	22.95	RCM, CP	MS-65	35.

THREE CENTS

THREE CENTS, 150TH ANNIVERSARY OF CANADA'S FIRST POSTAGE STAMP, 2001.

Sir Sandford Fleming's (1851) Three Pence Beaver was Canada's first postage stamp and a symbol of the transfer of postal authority from Britain to Canada.

Designers and Engravers:
Obv.: Dora de Pédery-Hunt
Rev.: Sir Sandford Fleming, Cosme Saffioti
Composition: 92.5% Ag, 7.5% Cu, 24-karat gold plate
Silver content: 4.95 g, 0.159 tr oz
Weight: 5.35 g
Edge: Plain
Diameter: 21.3 mm
Die Axis: ↑↑
Thickness: 1.9 mm
Finish: Proof
Case of Issue: See Derivatives below

DATE	DESCRIPTION	QUANTITY SOLD	ISSUE PRICE	FINISH	PR-67 UHC	PR-68 UHC
2001	3 Cent Beaver	59,573	N.I.I.	Proof	25.	35.

THREE CENT DERIVATIVES

DATE	DESCRIPTION	QUANTITY SOLD	ISSUE PRICE	ISSUER	FINISH	MARKET PRICE
2001	**Three Cents,** Medallion, Stamp set, Maroon leatherette case, COA	59,573	39.95	RCM, CP	PR-67	30.

SPECIAL NOTE ON FINISHES

It is very important to understand the different finishes the Royal Canadian Mint uses on their various issues. These finishes are altered from time-to-time as the Mint develops new products.

For example, the brilliant relief against a parallel lined background finish first used on bullion coins was carried forward in 1996 to be used on the coins contained in the specimen set.

In 2006 this finish was used on giftware coins such as the twenty-five cent coin issued to celebrate the 80th birthday of Queen Elizabeth II.

Now, in 2010, we have a new specimen finish (brilliant relief against a laser-lined background) which is used for the coins contained in the specimen set. There are now two different specimen finishes being utilised on Canadian coinage.

Circulation, uncirculated, and brilliant uncirculated (proof-like) finishes are another very confusing mixture of finishes, see page xxiv for a further explanation.

FIVE CENTS

FIVE CENTS, 90TH ANNIVERSARY OF THE ROYAL CANADIAN MINT, 1908-1998.

Issued to commemorate the opening of the Royal Canadian Mint, a five-coin set featuring the same reverse designs as the original 1908 coins, except for the double date 1908-1998, was struck. The set was issued in two finishes, matte and mirror proof.

Designers and Engravers:
Obv.: Dora de Pédery-Hunt
Rev.: Ago Aarand, G. W. DeSaulles
Composition: 92.5% Ag, 7.5% Cu
Silver content: 1.08 g, 0.035 tr oz
Finish: Matte Proof, Mirror Proof
Case of Issue: See Special Issue Proof Sets, page 285
Weight: 1.167 g
Diameter: 15.494 mm
Thickness: 1.0 mm
Die Axis: ↑↑
Edge: Reeded

DATE	DESCRIPTION	QUANTITY SOLD	ISSUE PRICE	FINISH	PR-67 UHC	PR-68 UHC
1998 (1908-)	90th Anniv. Royal Canadian Mint, Matte Proof	18,376	N.I.I.	Proof	20.	30.
1998 (1908-)	90th Anniv. Royal Canadian Mint, Mirror Proof	24,893	N.I.I.	Proof	20.	30.

FIVE CENTS, LES VOLTIGEURS DE QUEBEC, 2000.

Les Voltigeurs regiment was formed in March 1862, and was headquartered in Quebec. In 1942 it provided an armoured regiment for the Canadian Forces in World War II.

Designers and Engravers:
Obv.: Dora de Pédery-Hunt
Rev.: RCM Staff
Composition: 92.5% Ag, 7.5% Cu
Silver content: 4.90 g, 0.158 tr oz
Weight: 5.3 g
Diameter: Round: 21.3 mm
Thickness: 1.85 mm
Edge: Plain
Die Axis: ↑↑
Finish: Proof
Case of Issue: Black leatherette clam style case; green insert and sleeve; encapsulated coin

DATE	DESCRIPTION	QUANTITY SOLD	ISSUE PRICE	FINISH	PR-67 UHC	PR-68 UHC
2000	Les Voltigeurs de Québec	34,024	16.95	Proof	20.	30.

FIVE CENTS, ROYAL MILITARY COLLEGE OF CANADA, 2001.

The Royal Military College was established by an act of Parliament on May 26th, 1874. The college is located in Kingston, Ontario.

Designers and Engravers:
Obv.: Ago Aarand, G. W. DeSaulles
Rev.: G. T. Locklin, Susan Taylor
Composition: 92.5% Ag, 7.5% Cu
Silver content: 4.90 g, 0.158 tr oz
Weight: 5.3 g
Diameter: Round: 21.3 mm
Thickness: 1.85 mm
Edge: Plain
Die Axis: ↑↑
Finish: Proof
Case of Issue: Black leatherette clam style case; green insert, encapsulated coin, multicoloured sleeve

DATE	DESCRIPTION	QUANTITY SOLD	ISSUE PRICE	FINISH	PR-67 UHC	PR-68 UHC
2001	Royal Military College of Canada	25,834	16.95	Proof	20.	30.

FIVE CENTS, 85TH ANNIVERSARY, BATTLE FOR VIMY RIDGE, 2002.

Vimy Ridge, France was the location of one of the major battles of World War I. It was taken and held by Canadian troops from April 9th to 12th, 1917.

Designers and Engravers:
Obv.: Dora de Pédery-Hunt
Rev.: S. A. Allward, Susan Taylor
Composition: 92.5% Ag, 7.5% Cu
Silver content: 4.90 g, 0.158 tr oz
Weight: 5.3 g
Diameter: Round: 21.3 mm
Thickness: 1.85 mm **Edge:** Plain
Die Axis: ↑↑ **Finish:** Proof
Case of Issue: Black leatherette clam style case; maroon insert, encapsulated coin, multicoloured sleeve

DATE	DESCRIPTION	QUANTITY SOLD	ISSUE PRICE	FINISH	PR-67 UHC	PR-68 UHC
2002	85th Anniv. Battle for Vimy Ridge	22,646	16.95	Proof	35.	50.

FIVE CENTS, 50TH ANNIVERSARY OF THE CORONATION OF ELIZABETH II, 1953-2003.

Elizabeth II was crowned Queen on June 2nd, 1953, in Westminster Abbey, London.

Designers and Engravers:
Obv.: M. Gillick, D. de Pédery-Hunt
Rev.: G. E. Kruger-Gray, T. Shingles
Composition: 92.5% Ag, 7.5% Cu
Silver content: 4.90 g, 0.158 tr oz
Weight: 5.3 g
Diameter: 12-sided: 21.3 mm
Thickness: 1.85 mm **Edge:** Plain
Die Axis: ↑↑ **Finish:** Proof
Case of Issue: See Special Issue Proof Sets, page 286

DATE	DESCRIPTION	QUANTITY SOLD	ISSUE PRICE	FINISH	PR-67 UHC	PR-68 UHC
2003 (1953-)	50th Anniv. Coronation Queen Elizabeth II	21,537	N.I.I.	Proof	20.	40.

FIVE CENTS, 60TH ANNIVERSARY, D-DAY LANDING, 1944-2004.

On June 6th, 1944, over 175,000 troops landed on the beaches of Normandy, along a fifty mile front.

Designers and Engravers:
Obv.: Susanna Blunt, Susan. Taylor
Rev.: Thomas Shingles, RCM Engravers
Composition: 92.5% Ag, 7.5% Cu
Silver content: 4.90 g, 0.158 tr oz
Weight: 5.3 g
Diameter: 12-sided: 21.3 mm
Thickness: 1.85 mm **Edge:** Plain
Die Axis: ↑↑ **Finish:** Proof
Case of Issue: See Derivatives, page 5

DATE	DESCRIPTION	QUANTITY SOLD	ISSUE PRICE	FINISH	PR-67 UHC	PR-68 UHC
2004 (1944-)	60th Anniv. D-Day, 1944-2004	20,019	N.I.I.	Proof	60.	85.

FIVE CENTS, 60TH ANNIVERSARY OF VE-DAY, 1945-2005.

These coins were issued to celebrate the 60th anniversary of the victory over Nazi Germany in Europe. Peace was declared May 8th, 1945.

The selectively gold plated Victory five cent coin was issued in conjunction with the 2005 Annual Mint Report. This is the third coin in what was to be an annual series ending in 2008. The series was discontinued with the issue of the 2006 annual report. See the Five Cent Derivatives listed below.

Common Obverse

1945-2005 Victory

2004-2005 Victory Gold plated

Designers and Engravers:
Obv.: T. H. Paget, Thomas Shingles
Rev.: Thomas Shingles, Christie Paquet
Composition: 92.5% Ag, 7.5% Cu
Silver content: 4.90 g, 0.158 tr oz
Weight: 5.3 g
Diameter: 12-sided: 21.3 mm
Thickness: 1.85 mm **Edge:** Plain
Die Axis: ↑↑ **Finish:** Proof
Case of Issue: See Derivatives below

DATE	DESCRIPTION	QUANTITY SOLD	ISSUE PRICE	FINISH	PR-67 UHC	PR-68 UHC
2005 (1945-)	60th Anniv. VE-Day, 1945-2005	42,792	N.I.I.	Proof	45.	55.
2005 (1945-)	60th Anniv. VE-Day, Selectively gold plated	6,065	N.I.I.	Proof	75.	85.

FIVE CENT DERIVATIVES

DATE	DESCRIPTION	QUANTITY SOLD	ISSUE PRICE	ISSUER	FINISH	MARKET VALUE
2004 (1944-)	**D-Day Five Cents**, 1944-2004; Bronze medallion, CD, Folder	20,019	29.95	RCM	PR-67	65.
2005 (1945-)	**VE-Day Five Cents**, 1945-2005; Bronze medallion, Booklet	42,792	29.95	RCM	PR-67	50.
2005 (1945-)	**2005 Annual Mint Report**, Five cent coin, selectively gold plated		24.95	RCM	PR-67	
	English	5,213				80.
	French	852				100.

TEN CENTS

TEN CENTS, 500TH ANNIVERSARY OF CABOTO'S FIRST TRANSATLANTIC VOYAGE, 1997.

Giovanni Caboto (c.1450-c.1508) was an Italian navigator and explorer whose 1497 discovery of North America is commonly held to be the first voyage to the continent since those of the Vikings.

Designers and Engravers:
Obv.: Dora de Pédery-Hunt
Rev.: Donald H. Curley, Stan Witten
Composition: 92.5% Ag, 7.5% Cu
Silver content: 2.22 g, 0.071 tr oz
Finish: Proof
Case of Issue: Clear plastic case with black insert, white sleeve.
See Derivatives, page 7

Weight: 2.40 g
Diameter: 18.00 mm
Thickness: 1.20 mm
Edge: Reeded
Die Axis: ↑↑

DATE	DESCRIPTION	QUANTITY SOLD	ISSUE PRICE	FINISH	PR-67 UHC	PR-68 UHC
1997	500th Anniv. of Caboto's Voyage	49,848	10.95	Proof	20.	30.

TEN CENTS, 90TH ANNIVERSARY OF THE ROYAL CANADIAN MINT, 1908-1998.

First opened on January 2nd, 1908, the Ottawa Branch of the Royal Mint became the Royal Canadian Mint in 1931.

Designers and Engravers:
Obv.: Dora de Pédery-Hunt
Rev.: G. W. DeSaulles
Composition: 92.5% Ag, 7.5% Cu
Silver content: 2.15 g, 0.069 tr oz
Finish: Matte Proof, Mirror Proof
Case of Issue: See Special Issue Proof Sets, page 285

Weight: 2.32 g
Diameter: 18.03 mm
Thickness: 1.70 mm
Edge: Reeded
Die Axis: ↑↑

DATE	DESCRIPTION	QUANTITY SOLD	ISSUE PRICE	FINISH	PR-67 UHC	PR-68 UHC
1998 (1908-)	90th Anniv. Royal Canadian Mint, Matte Proof	18,376	N.I.I.	Proof	20.	40.
1998 (1908-)	90th Anniv. Royal Canadian Mint, Mirror Proof	24,893	N.I.I.	Proof	20.	50.

TEN CENTS, 100TH ANNIVERSARY OF THE BIRTH OF THE CREDIT UNIONS IN NORTH AMERICA, 2000.

The first credit union in North America, The Caisse Populaire de Lévis in Quebec, began operation on January 23rd, 1901, with a ten cent deposit.

Designers and Engravers:
Obv.: Dora de Pédery-Hunt
Rev.: Jean-Guy Lebel, W. Woodruff
Composition: 92.5% Ag, 7.5% Cu
Silver content: 2.22 g, 0.071 tr oz
Finish: Proof
Case of Issue: Green printed card folder with encapsulated coin

Weight: 2.40 g
Diameter: 18.00 mm
Thickness: 1.20 mm
Edge: Reeded
Die Axis: ↑↑

DATE	DESCRIPTION	QUANTITY SOLD	ISSUE PRICE	FINISH	PR-67 UHC	PR-68 UHC
2000	100th Anniv. Birth of Credit Unions in N.A.	69,791	9.95	Proof	10.	15.

Note: 1. For the ten cent font varieties of 2007 (Curved and Straight 7) see page 258.
2. For the ten cent Finish variety from the 2010 Special Edition Specimen Set, see page 281.

TEN CENTS, INTERNATIONAL YEAR OF THE VOLUNTEERS, 2001.

The United Nations declaration of International Year of the Volunteers gave cause for celebration for over 7.5 million Canadian volunteers.

Designers and Engravers:
Obv.: Dora de Pédery-Hunt
Rev.: R.C.M. Design, Stan Witten
Composition: 92.5% Ag, 7.5% Cu
Silver content: 2.22 g, 0.071 tr oz
Finish: Proof
Case of Issue: Multicoloured printed card folder with encapsulated coin

Weight: 2.40 g
Diameter: 18.00 mm
Thickness: 1.20 mm
Edge: Reeded
Die Axis: ↑↑

DATE	DESCRIPTION	QUANTITY SOLD	ISSUE PRICE	FINISH	PR-67 UHC	PR-68 UHC
2001	International Year of the Volunteers	40,634	14.95	Proof	10.	15.

TEN CENTS, 50TH ANNIVERSARY OF THE CORONATION OF QUEEN ELIZABETH II, 1953-2003.

Elizabeth II was crowned Queen June 2nd 1953; her 50th anniversary was June 2nd, 2003.

Designers and Engravers:
Obv.: Dora de Pédery-Hunt
Rev.: Emanuel Hahn
Composition: 92.5% Ag, 7.5% Cu
Silver content: 2.15 g, 0.069 tr oz
Finish: Matte Proof, Mirror Proof
Case of Issue: See Special Issue Proof Sets, page 286

Weight: 2.32 g
Diameter: 18.03 mm
Thickness: 1.70 mm
Edge: Reeded
Die Axis: ↑↑

DATE	DESCRIPTION	QUANTITY SOLD	ISSUE PRICE	FINISH	PR-67 UHC	PR-68 UHC
2003 (1953-)	50th Anniv. Coronation Queen Elizabeth II	21,537	N.I.I.	Proof	15.	25.

TEN CENTS, 100TH ANNIVERSARY OF THE CANADIAN OPEN GOLF CHAMPIONSHIP, 2004.

The Canadian Open Golf Tournament was first played on the Royal Montreal Golf Club course in 1904. The tournament was won by the English player, John H. Oke.

Designers and Engravers:
Obv.: Susanna Blunt, Susan Taylor
Rev.: Cosme Saffioti
Composition: Nickel plated steel
Weight: 1.75 g
Case of Issue: See Derivatives below

Diameter: 18.03 mm
Thickness: 1.22 mm
Edge: Reeded
Die Axis: ↑↑
Finish: Circulation

DATE	DESCRIPTION	QUANTITY SOLD	ISSUE PRICE	FINISH	MS-65 NC	MS-66 NC	MS-67 NC
2004	100th Anniv. of Canadian Open Golf Championship	39,486	N.I.I.	Circulation	15.	25.	50.

TEN CENT DERIVATIVES

DATE	DESCRIPTION	QUANTITY SOLD	ISSUE PRICE	ISSUER	FINISH	MARKET VALUE
1997	**John Caboto Ten Cents,** Sterling;. Canada 45¢ stamp; Italy 1300 Lira stamp; Set in multicoloured card folder	N/A	19.95	RCM, CP	PR-67	25.
2000	**Bluenose Ten Cents**, Sterling; Two 46¢ stamps; Blue presentation case	15,000	19.95	RCM, CP	PR-67	15.
2001	**International Year of the Volunteers Ten Cents**, Thank You card and envelope	N/A	N/A	RCM	MS-65	10.
2004	**Ten Cent and Five Dollar Coins,** (10th Anniv. Canadian Open Golf Championship); Framed with two 48¢ circular stamps	18,750	49.95	RCM, CP	MS-65, PR-67	30.
2004	**Canadian Open Championship Ten Cents,** Framed with two circular commemorative stamps, and a divot repair tool	20,736	21.49	RCM, CP	MS-65	15.
2004	**Canadian Open Championship Ten Cents**, Canister also contains four commemorative stamps, a divot repair tool, three golf balls, five golf tees and a T-shirt	N/A	39.95	RCM, CP	MS-65	20.

TWENTY-FIVE CENTS

125TH ANNIVERSARY OF CANADA, SILVER PROOF AND NICKEL UNCIRCULATED SETS, 1992.

Issued by the Royal Canadian Mint, in silver and nickel, the twelve different designs represent a familiar scene from each of the twelve provinces and territories of Canada. This is the first issue of sterling silver twenty-five cent coins since 1919.

Also, a collection of nickel brilliant uncirculated coins mounted in a coloured map of Canada, with each twenty-five cent coin placed in the province or territory commemorated by its design was released October 7th, 1992. The Canada Day dollar which is the central point of a compass is listed on page 90.

1867-1992
Obverse

Designers and Engravers:
Obv.: Dora de Pédery-Hunt, Ago Aarand
Rev.: See reverse illustration

	Silver	Nickel
Composition:	Silver	Nickel
Silver content:	5.458 g	—
	0.175 tr oz	—
Weight:	5.90 g	5.05 g
Diameter:	23.8 mm	23.88 mm
Thickness:	1.7 mm	1.6 mm
Edge:	Reeded	Reeded
Die Axis:	↑↑	↑↑
Finish:	Proof	Circulation

Issue Price:
Individual proof silver: $9.95
13-coin proof silver set: $129.45
13 coin nickel set, "Map" holder: $17.25

Quantity Sold: Total individual silver coins: 651,812
Total silver sets: 84,397
Nickel sets, "Map" holder: 448,178

Case: (A) Royal blue flocked single coin case
(B) Royal blue flocked case, 13 coins. Twelve 25¢ coins; one $1.00 coin

New Brunswick
January 9, 1992
Ronald Lambert
Sheldon Beveridge

Northwest Territories
February 6, 1992
Beth McEachen

Newfoundland
March 5, 1992
Christopher Newhook

Manitoba
April 7, 1992
Muriel Hope
Ago Aarand

Yukon
May 7, 1992
Libby Dulac
William Woodruff

Alberta
June 4, 1992
Mel Heath
William Woodruff

DATE	DESCRIPTION	PROOF STERLING SILVER		UNCIRCULATED NICKEL		
		PR-67 UHC	PR-68 UHC	MS-65 NC	MS-66 NC	MS-67 NC
1992	New Brunswick	15.	30.	10.	15.	30.
1992	North West Territories	15.	30.	10.	15.	30.
1992	Newfoundland	15.	30.	10.	15.	30.
1992	Manitoba	15.	30.	10.	15.	30.
1992	Yukon	15.	30.	10.	15.	30.
1992	Alberta	15.	30.	10.	15.	30.

125TH ANNIVERSARY OF CANADA, SILVER PROOF AND NICKEL UNCIRCULATED SETS, 1992. (cont.)

Prince Edward Island
July 7, 1992
N. Roe, S. Beveridge

Ontario
August 6, 1992
Greg Salmela
Susan Taylor

Nova Scotia
September 9, 1992
Bruce Wood
Terry Smith

Quebec
October 1, 1992
R. Bukauskas
Stanley Witten

Saskatchewan
November 5, 1992
Brian Cobb
Terry Smith

British Columbia
November 9, 1992
Carla Egan
Sheldon Beveridge

DATE	DESCRIPTION	PROOF STERLING SILVER		UNCIRCULATED NICKEL		
		PR-67 UHC	PR-68 UHC	MS-65 NC	MS-66 NC	MS-67 NC
1992	Prince Edward Island	15.	30.	10.	15.	30.
1992	Ontario	15.	30.	10.	15.	30.
1992	Nova Scotia	15.	30.	10.	15.	30.
1992	Quebec	15.	30.	10.	15.	30.
1992	Saskatchewan	15.	30.	10.	15.	30.
1992	British Columbia	15.	30.	10.	15.	30.
1992	13 Coin Silver Proof Set	100.	—	*	*	*
1992	13 Coin Nickel Set with "Map" Holder	*	*	10.	—	—

125TH ANNIVERSARY MULE, 1867-1992.

1867-1992 obverse is muled with a Caribou reverse. The coin was reportedly issued in a Brilliant Uncirculated set of 1993.

Designers and Engravers:
Obv.: Dora de Pédery-Hunt
Rev.: Emanuel Hahn
Composition: Nickel
Weight: 5.05 g
Diameter: 23.88 mm
Thickness: 1.6 mm **Edge:** Reeded
Die Axis: ↑↑ **Finish:** Circulation

DATE	DESCRIPTION	MS-65
1992 (1867-)	Mule	Only one known

90TH ANNIVERSARY OF THE ROYAL CANADIAN MINT, 1908-1998.

Issued to commemorate the opening of the Branch Mint in Ottawa, a five-coin set was struck featuring the same reverse designs as the original 1908 coins, except for the double date 1908-1998. The set was issued in two finishes, matte and mirror proof.

Designers and Engravers:
Obv: Dora de Pédery-Hunt
Rev.: Ago Aarand, W. H. J. Blakemore
Composition: 92.5% Ag, 7.5% Cu
Silver content: 5.374 g, 0.173 tr oz
Weight: 5.81 g
Diameter: 23.62 mm
Thickness: 1.7 mm **Edge:** Reeded
Die Axis: ↑↑ **Finish:** See below
Case: See Special Issue Proof Sets, page 285

DATE	DESCRIPTION	QUANTITY SOLD	ISSUE PRICE	FINISH	PR-67 UHC	PR-68 UHC
1998 (1908-)	90th Anniv. R.C. Mint	18,376	N.I.I.	Matte Proof	15.	40.
1998 (1908-)	90th Anniv. R.C. Mint	24,893	N.I.I.	Mirror Proof	15.	50.

MILLENNIUM SILVER PROOF AND NICKEL UNCIRCULATED COMMEMORATIVE SETS, 1999.

The twelve 25-cent nickel coins (circulation finish) of 1999 were issued along with a 1999 millennium medallion, inserted in a replica of a 1785 map of Canada. Two different medallions were issued, one with a maple leaf obverse, the other carried the Nestlé logo; both have the common Royal Mint logo reverse. They were only available in the millennium set. The set of twelve coins was also issued in sterling silver with a proof finish.

1999
Obverse

Designers and Engravers:
Obv.: Dora de Pédery-Hunt
Ago Aarand
Rev.: See reverse illustration

Composition:	Silver	Nickel
Silver content:	5.458 g	—
	0.175 tr oz	—
Weight:	5.90 g	5.05 g
Diameter:	23.88 mm	23.88 mm
Thickness:	1.7 mm	1.6 mm
Edge:	Reeded	Reeded
Die Axis:	↑↑	↑↑
Finish:	Proof	Circulation

Issue Price:
Individual proof silver: $14.95
12 coin proof silver set: $149.45
12 coin unc. nickel / RCM set: $24.95
12 coin unc. nickel / Nestlé set: $24.95

Quantity Sold: Total individual silver coins: 111,414
Total silver sets: 60,245
Total nickel sets: 1,499,973

Case: (A) Gold plastic single hole, oval case, royal blue flocked insert
(B) Gold plastic 12-hole, oval case, royal blue flocked insert

January
P. Ka-Kin Poon
Cosme Saffioti

February
L. Springer
José Osio

March
M. Lavoie
Stan Witten

April
Ken Ojnak Ashevac
Sheldon Beveridge

May
S. Minenok
William Woodruff

June
G. Ho
William Woodruff

July
M. H. Sarkany
Stan Witten

August
A. Botelho
Cosme Saffioti

September
C. Bertrand
Stanley Witten

October
J. E. Read
Sheldon Beveridge

November
B. R. Bacon
Stan Witten

December
J. L. P. Provencher
Stan Witten

DATE	DESCRIPTION	PROOF STERLING SILVER PR-67 UHC	PROOF STERLING SILVER PR-68 UHC	UNCIRCULATED NICKEL MS-65 NC	UNCIRCULATED NICKEL MS-66 NC	UNCIRCULATED NICKEL MS-67 NC
1999	January, A Country Unfolds	15.	30.	10.	15.	30.
1999	February, Etched in Stone	15.	30.	10.	15.	30.
1999	March, The Log Drive	15.	30.	10.	15.	30.
1999	April, Our Northern Heritage	15.	30.	10.	15.	30.
1999	May, The Voyageurs	15.	30.	10.	15.	30.
1999	June, From Coast to Coast	15.	30.	10.	15.	30.
1999	July, A Nation of People	15.	30.	10.	15.	30.
1999	August, The Pioneer Spirit	15.	30.	10.	15.	30.
1999	September, Canada Through a Child's Eye	15.	30.	10.	15.	30.
1999	October, A Tribute to the First Nation	15.	30.	10.	15.	30.
1999	November, The Airplane Opens the North	15.	30.	10.	15.	30.
1999	December, This is Canada	15.	30.	10.	15.	30.
1999	12 Coin Silver Proof Set plus RCM Medallion	100.	—	*	*	*
1999	12 Coin Nickel Set plus RCM Medallion	*	*	12.	—	—
1999	12 Coin Nickel Set plus "Nestlé" Medallion	*	*	12.	—	—

Note: Prices for individual twenty-cent coins are for examples that are certified. The set prices are for raw coins.

TWENTY FIVE CENT MILLENNIUM MULES OF 1999.

It is in the 1999 millennium nickel set that the "No Denomination" coins of September and November are found. During the Fall of 1999, a Queen Elizabeth II obverse die became paired with the reverse dies of September and November millennium twenty-five cents coins creating two mules. The interesting result of these pairings is that for the first time Canada has a non-denominated legal tender coin.

Queen Elizabeth II
No denomination
Obverse

1999 September
Reverse Mule

1999 November
Reverse Mule

DATE	DESCRIPTION	MS-63 NC	MS-64 NC	MS-65 NC	MS-66 NC
1999	September, no denomination, Mule	85.	125.	150.	200.
1999	November, no denomination, Mule	85.	125.	150.	200.

TWENTY-FIVE CENT SOUVENIR MEDALLIONS OF 1999.

Along with the nickel souvenir sets two different medallions were issued: A Royal Canadian Mint medallion and a Nestlé Canada Inc. medallion.

1999 RCM
Medallion Obv.

1999 RCM
Medallion Rev.

1999 Nestlé
Medallion Obv.

1999 RCM
Medallion Rev.

DATE	DESCRIPTION	MINTAGE	ISSUE PRICE	FINISH	MS-65 NC	MS-66 NC	MS-67 NC
1999	RCM Medallion	N/A	N.I.I.	Circulation	10.	15.	30.
1999	Nestlé Medallion	N/A	N.I.I.	Circulation	10.	15.	30.

TWENTY-FIVE CENT STERLING SILVER SOUVENIR MEDALLION OF 1999-2000.

The 24-coin sterling silver set which was issued for the Chinese market in Hong Kong contains a 1999-2000 sterling silver medallion.

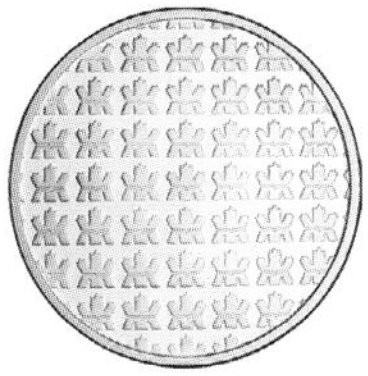

DATE	DESCRIPTION	MINTAGE	ISSUE PRICE	FINISH	PR-67 UHC	PR-68 UHC
1999-2000	Stirling silver Medallion	N/A	N.I.I.	Proof	75.	125.

MILLENNIUM SILVER PROOF AND NICKEL UNCIRCULATED COMMEMORATIVE SETS, 2000.

The 2000 Souvenir set was issued in sterling silver with a proof finish and in nickel with a circulation finish. The nickel set features 12 coins plus the 2000 commemorative medallion which was only issued with the souvenir set. The coins are displayed on an easel featuring an aerial photograph of Canada.

2000
Obverse

Designers and Engravers:
Obv.: Dora de Pédery-Hunt
Ago Aarand
Rev.: See coin

	Silver	Nickel
Composition:	Silver	Nickel
Silver content:	5.458 g	—
	0.175 tr oz	—
Weight:	5.90 g	5.05 g
Diameter:	23.88 mm	23.88 mm
Thickness:	1.7 mm	1.6 mm
Edge:	Reeded	Reeded
Die Axis:	↑↑	↑↑
Finish:	Proof	Circulation

Case of Issue:
Silver: (A) Black plastic single-hole, oval case, royal blue flocked insert
(B) Black plastic 12-hole, oval case, royal blue flocked insert
(C) Red plush presentation case, light brown insert, 24 coins, a 1999 and 2000 medallion. Issued for the Chinese market.
Nickel: (A) 13 hole, Map of Canada. (B) 13 hole, plastic case

Issue Price:
Individual proof silver: $14.95
12 coin proof silver set: $149.45
12 coin unc. nickel/RCM set: $24.95
12 coin unc. nickel set/plastic case: $49.55
Quantity Sold: Total silver sets: 37,940
Total nickel sets: 876,041

January
Donald F. Warkentin
José Osio

February
John Jaciw
William Woodruff

March
Daryl Dorosz
Stan Witten

April
Annie Wassef
Stan Witten

May
Randy Trantau
José Osio

June
Haver Demirer
José Osio

July
Laura Paxton
Stan Witten

August
W. S. Baker
Susan Taylor

September
Cezar Serbanescu
Cosme Saffioti

October
Jerik (Kong Tat) Hui
Susan Taylor

November
Kathy Vinish
William Woodruff

December
Michelle Thibodeau
José Osio

DATE	DESCRIPTION	PROOF STERLING SILVER		UNCIRCULATED NICKEL		
		PR-67 UHC	PR-68 UHC	MS-65 NC	MS-66 NC	MS-67 NC
2000	January, Pride	15.	30.	10.	15.	30.
2000	February, Ingenuity	15.	30.	10.	15.	30.
2000	March, Achievement	15.	30.	10.	15.	30.
2000	April, Health	15.	30.	10.	15.	30.
2000	May, Natural Legacy	15.	30.	10.	15.	30.
2000	June, Harmony	15.	30.	10.	15.	30.
2000	July, Celebration	15.	30.	10.	15.	30.
2000	August, Family	15.	30.	10.	15.	30.
2000	September, Wisdom	15.	30.	10.	15.	30.
2000	October, Creativity	15.	30.	10.	15.	30.
2000	November, Freedom	15.	30.	10.	15.	30.
2000	December, Community	15.	30.	10.	15.	30.
2000	12 Coin Silver Proof Set	100.	—	*	*	*
2000	12 Coin Nickel Set, RCM Medallion	*	*	12.	—	—
2000	12 Coin Nickel Set, Nestlé Medallion	*	*	12.	—	—

TWENTY-FIVE CENT SOUVENIR MEDALLIONS OF 2000.

Again in 2000 the nickel souvenir sets contained souvenir medallions. Two types were issued: The Royal Canadian Mint and Nestlé Canada Inc.

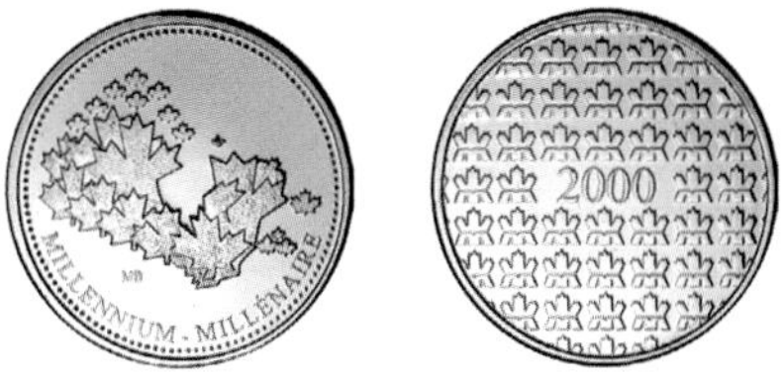

2000
Royal Canadian Mint Medallion

2000
Nestle Medallion

TWENTY-FIVE CENT MEDALLION MULE OF 2000.

In 2000 two dies were mismatched creating another mule. The obverse die of the February twenty-five cents is paired with the obverse die of the 2000 medallion. The mule is found in the February position of the 13-hole, Map of Canada Brilliant Uncirculated Set of 2000.

February Reverse

February Obverse

=
Mule

Medallion Obverse

Medallion Reverse

DATE	DESCRIPTION	QUANTITY SOLD	ISSUE PRICE	FINISH	MS-63 NC	MS-64 NC	MS-65 NC	MS-66 NC	MS-67 NC
2000	R.C.M. Medallion	N.I.I.	—	Circulation	—	—	5.	10.	20.
2000	Nestlé Medallion	N.I.I.	—	Circulation	—	—	5.	10.	20.
2000	Coin / Medallion Mule	N.I.I.	—	Circulation	400.	700.	1,000.	2,000.	—

TWENTY-FIVE CENTS, CANADA'S FIRST COLOURISED COIN, 2000.

Issued to celebrate the year 2000, this was the first colourised coin issued by the Royal Canadian Mint.

Designers and Engravers:
Obv.: Dora de Pédery-Hunt
Rev.: Donald F. Warkentin, José Osio
Composition: Nickel
Weight: 5.05 g
Diameter: 23.88 mm **Edge:** Reeded
Thickness: 1.6 mm **Die Axis:** ↑↑
Finish: Circulation, Colourised
Case of Issue: Blister packed on information card.

DATE	DESCRIPTION	QUANTITY SOLD	ISSUE PRICE	FINISH	MS-65 NC	MS-66 NC	MS-67 NC
2000	Millennium, Colourised	49,719	8.95	Circulation	20.	25.	50.

TWENTY-FIVE CENTS, CANADA DAY SERIES, 2000-2008.

The following series of twenty-five cent coins were issued to celebrate the Canada Day celebrations that took place during the last week of June, leading up to July 1st.

In 2004, four thousand six hundred and fifteen "Moose"" coins were given to new Canadians during Canada Week Celebrations, June 25th to July 1st. Of the initial offering of 27,000, only 16,028 were sold in a "walking bundle" (see page 36).

Years:	2000	2001 to 2008
Composition:	1.00 nickel	Nickel plated steel
Weight:	5.05 g	4.4 g
Diameter:	23.88 mm	23.88 mm
Thickness:	1.6 mm	1.58 mm
Edge:	Reeded	Reeded
Die Axis:	↑↑	↑↑
Finish:	Circulation, Painted	2001 to 2008: Circulation, Painted 2004: Circulation

Cases of Issue: 2000: Blister packed on information card.
2001: Encapsulated coin fastened to an information card
2002 to 2008: Folder
2004: See Derivatives, page 36

2000

Designers and Engravers:
Obv.: Dora de Pédery-Hunt
Rev.: Laura Paxton, Stan Witten

2001

Designers and Engravers:
Obv.: Dora de Pédery-Hunt
Rev.: Silke Ware, William Woodruff

2002

Designers and Engravers:
Obv.: Dora de Pédery-Hunt, Ago Aarand
Rev.: Judith Chartier, Stan Witten

2003

Designers and Engravers:
Obv.: Dora de Pédery-Hunt, Ago Aarand
Rev.: Jade Pearen, Stan Witten

2004

Designers and Engravers:
Obv.: Susanna Blunt, Susan Taylor
Rev.: Cosme Saffiotti, Stan Witten

2004

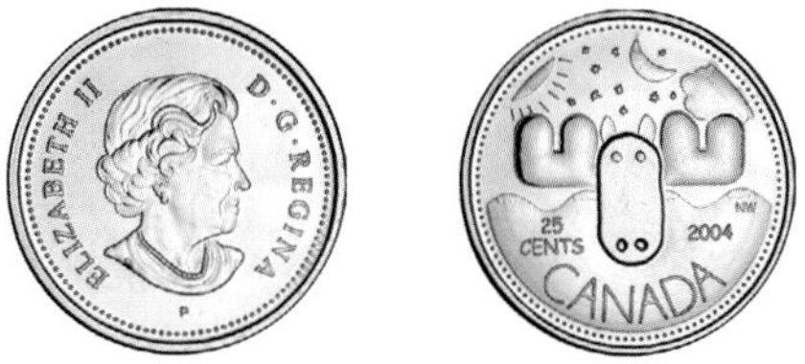

Designers and Engravers:
Obv.: Susanna Blunt, Susan Taylor
Rev.: Nick Wooster, William Woodruff

TWENTY-FIVE CENTS, CANADA DAY SERIES, 2000-2008 (cont.)

2005

Designers and Engravers:
Obv.: Susanna Blunt, Susan Taylor
Rev.: Stan Witten, Stan Witten

2006

Designers and Engravers:
Obv.: Susanna Blunt, Susan Taylor
Rev.: Stan Witten, Stan Witten

2007

Designers and Engravers:
Obv.: Susanna Blunt, Susan Taylor
Rev.: José Osio

2008

Designers and Engravers:
Obv.: Susanna Blunt, Susan Taylor
Rev.: RCM Staff

DATE / COMP. MARK	DESCRIPTION	QUANTITY SOLD	ISSUE PRICE	FINISH	MS-65 NC
2000	Canada Day, Colourised	26,106	8.95	Circulation	100.
2001P	Canada Day, Colourised	96,352	9.95	Circulation	15.
2002P (1952-)	Canada Day, Colourised	49,901	9.95	Circulation	20.
2003P	Canada Day, Colourised	63,511	9.95	Circulation	20.
2004P	Canada Day, Colourised	44,752	9.95	Circulation	15.
2004P	Canada Day, Citizenship	16,028	N.I.I.	Circulation	40.
2005P	Canada Day, Colourised	58,370	9.95	Circulation	20.
2006P	Canada Day, Colourised	30,328	9.95	Circulation	20.
2007	Canada Day, Colourised	27,743	9.95	Circulation	20.
2008	Canada Day, Colourised	11,538	9.95	Circulation	20.

TWENTY-FIVE CENTS, CANADA DAY SERIES, 2009, (GIFTWARE).

In 2009 the Royal Canadian Mint discontinued the standard Canada Day colourised twenty-five cent piece, changing it to a crown size coin, with no relation to the standard twenty-five cent denomination.

Designers and Engravers:
Obv.: Susanna Blunt, Susan Taylor
Rev.: RCM Staff
Composition: Nickel plated steel
Weight: 12.59 g
Diameter: 35.0 mm
Thickness: 2.0 mm
Edge: Plain
Die Axis: ↑↑
Finish: Specimen, Painted
Case of Issue: Folder

DATE	DESCRIPTION	QUANTITY SOLD	ISSUE PRICE	FINISH	MS-65 NC
2009	Canada Day, Churchill	11,091	14.95	Specimen	20.

TWENTY-FIVE CENTS, 50TH ANNIVERSARY OF THE CORONATION OF QUEEN ELIZABETH II, 1953-2003.

This twenty-five cent coin is from the Special Edition Proof Set issued in 2003 to commemorate the 50th anniversary of the Coronation of Queen Elizabeth II.

Designers and Engravers:
Obv: Mary Gillick, Thomas Shingles
Rev.: Emanuel Hahn, Thomas Shingles
Composition: 92.5% Ag, 7.5% Cu
Silver content: 5.458 g, 0.175 tr oz
Weight: 5.90 g
Diameter: 23.88 mm
Thickness: 1.6 mm
Edge: Reeded
Die Axis: ↑↑
Finish: Proof
Case of Issue: See Special Issue Proof Sets, page 286

DATE	DESCRIPTION	QUANTITY SOLD	ISSUE PRICE	FINISH	PR-67 UHC	PR-68 UHC
2003 (1953-)	50th Anniv. Coronation Queen Elizabeth II	21,537	N.I.I.	Proof	40.	60.

TWENTY-FIVE CENTS, CHRISTMAS DAY SERIES, COLOURISED, 2004-2010.

The twenty-five cent coloured Christmas Day coins are issued as part of the Holiday Gift Set series, see page 269. The quantity sold figures shown are from the number of Holiday Sets sold for that year.

Designers and Engravers:
Obv.: Susanna Blunt, Susan Taylor
Rev.: See coin

Composition: Nickel plated steel
Weight: 4.40 g
Diameter: 23.88 mm
Finish: Circulation, Decal
Case of Issue: See Holiday Gift Sets page 269

Edge: Reeded
Thickness: 1.58 mm
Die Axis: ↑↑

Obverse
With Mint Mark "P"
2004-2006

2004
Santa Claus
José Osio

2005
Christmas Stocking
José Osio

2006
Santa in Sleigh
and Reindeer
M. Hallam, J. Osio

Obverse
With RCM Logo
2007-2009

2007
Christmas Tree
RCM Staff

2008
Santa
RCM Staff

2009
Santa Claus and
Maple Leaves
RCM Staff

Obverse
Without RCM
Logo 2010

2010
Santa Claus and
Christmas Tree
RCM Staff

DATE / COMP. MARK	DESCRIPTION	SOURCE	QUANTITY SOLD	ISSUE PRICE	FINISH	MS-65 NC
2004P	Santa Claus		62,777	N.I.I.	Circulation	30.
2005P	Christmas Stocking	Available	72,831	N.I.I.	Circulation	20.
2006P	Santa in Sleigh and Reindeer	only from	99,258	N.I.I.	Circulation	20.
2007	Christmas Tree	Holiday	66,267	N.I.I.	Circulation	20.
2008	Santa	Gift Sets	42,344	N.I.I.	Circulation	20.
2009	Santa Claus and Maple Leaves		32,967	N.I.I.	Circulation	20.
2010	Santa Claus and Christmas Tree		N/A	N.I.I.	Circulation	20.

TWENTY-FIVE CENTS, SILVER POPPY, ROYAL CANADIAN MINT ANNUAL REPORT, SELECTIVELY GOLD PLATED, 2004.

This coin is the second in the Royal Canadian Mint Annual Report series. This series was cancelled in 2007.

Designers and Engravers:
Obv.: Susanna Blunt, Susan Taylor
Rev.: Cosme Saffioti, Stan Witten
Composition: 92.5% Ag, 7.5% Cu
Silver content: 5.458 g, 0.175 tr oz
Weight: 5.90 g
Diameter: 23.88 mm **Edge:** Reeded
Thickness: 1.7 mm **Die Axis:** ↑↑
Finish: Proof, Selectively gold plated
Case of Issue: See Derivatives, page 36

DATE	DESCRIPTION	QUANTITY SOLD	ISSUE PRICE	FINISH	PR-67 UHC	PR-68 UHC
2004	Poppy, selectively gold plated	12,677	N.I.I.	Proof	30.	40.

TWENTY-FIVE CENTS, POPPY, COLOURISED, 2005, (GIFTWARE).

This coin was issued to commemorate Remembrance Day 2005. It is encased in a plastic bookmark.

Designers and Engravers:
Obv.: Susanna Blunt, Susan Taylor
Rev.: Cosme Saffioti, Stan Witten
Composition: Nickel plated steel
Weight: 4.40 g
Diameter: 23.88 mm **Edge:** Reeded
Thickness: 1.58 mm **Die Axis:** ↑↑
Finish: Circulation, Colourised
Case of Issue: See Derivatives, page 36

DATE / COMP. MARK	DESCRIPTION	SOURCE	QUANTITY SOLD	ISSUE PRICE	FINISH	MS-65 NC
2005P	Poppy, Colourised	Bookmark	29,975	N.I.I.	Circulation	20.

Note: A colourised circulation Poppy coin was issued in 2004 to commemorate Remembrance Day 2004. See Volume One, 65th Edition, page 161.

TWENTY-FIVE CENTS, 60TH ANNIVERSARY OF THE LIBERATION OF THE NETHERLANDS, 2005.

The Canadian Armed Forces played a leading role in the liberation of the Netherlands that was completed May 5th, 1945. This coin was issued in an eight-coin, Brilliant Uncirculated set, by the Netherlands Mint.

Designers and Engravers:
Obv.: Susanna Blunt, Susan Taylor
Rev.: Peter Mossman, José Osio
Composition: 92.5% Ag, 7.5% Cu
Silver content: 5.458 g, 0.175 tr oz
Weight: 5.90 g
Diameter: 23.88 mm **Edge:** Reeded
Thickness: 1.7 mm **Die Axis:** ↑↑
Finish: Specimen
Case of Issue: See Derivatives, page 36

DATE	DESCRIPTION	QUANTITY SOLD	ISSUE PRICE	FINISH	SP-66	SP-67	SP-68
2005	60th Year of Liberation	3,500	N.I.I.	Specimen	100.	125.	200.

TWENTY-FIVE CENTS, QUEBEC WINTER CARNIVAL, 2006 (GIFTWARE).

The Quebec Winter Carnival, the largest in North America, is held each year in Quebec City, Quebec.

Designers and Engravers:
Obv.: Susanna Blunt, Susan Taylor
Rev.: RCM Staff
Composition: Nickel plated steel
Weight: 4.40 g
Diameter: 23.88 mm **Edge:** Reeded
Thickness: 1.58 mm **Die Axis:** ↑↑
Finish: Circulation, Painted
Case of Issue: See Miscellaneous Gift Sets, page 276

DATE / COMP. MARK	DESCRIPTION	SOURCE	QUANTITY SOLD	ISSUE PRICE	FINISH	MS-65 NC
2006P	Quebec Winter Carnival, Painted	Promo Gift Set	8,200	N.I.I.	Circulation	20.

TWENTY-FIVE CENTS, BREAST CANCER AWARENESS, 2006 (GIFTWARE).

This coin was issued to promote awareness for breast cancer. It is identical to the circulation issue, except the three outer ribbons, plus the central ribbon are painted pink. This variety was issued encased in a plastic bookmark. Removal of the coin from the encased plastic is very difficult and may result in the Awareness ribbons being damaged.

Designers and Engravers:
Obv.: Susanna Blunt, Susan Taylor
Rev.: RCM Staff
Composition: Nickel plated steel
Weight: 4.40 g
Diameter: 23.88 mm **Edge:** Reeded
Thickness: 1.58 mm **Die Axis:** ↑↑
Finish: Circulation, Painted
Case of Issue: See Derivatives, page 36

DATE / COMP. MARK	DESCRIPTION	SOURCE	QUANTITY SOLD	ISSUE PRICE	FINISH	MS-65 NC
2006P	Breast Cancer Awareness, Painted	Bookmark	40,911	N.I.I.	Circulation	15.

NOTE FOR COLLECTORS

NC – Non-circulating, in the data table signifies the coin was struck as a collectors item and was never meant for circulation.

TWENTY-FIVE CENTS, QUEEN ELIZABETH II COMMEMORATIVES, 2006-2007 (GIFTWARE).

Designers:
Obv.: Susanna Blunt
Rev.: See reverse illustration
Composition: Nickel plated steel
Weight: 12.61 g
Diameter: 35.00 mm
Finish: Specimen, Decal
Case of Issue: Blistered packed on information card

Engravers:
Obv.: Susan Taylor
Rev.: See reverse illustration
Thickness: 3.40 mm
Edge: Plain
Die Axis: ↑↑

2006 80TH BIRTHDAY OF QUEEN ELIZABETH II

2006 Obverse

Designer: Cosme Saffioti
Engraver: Cecily Mok

2007 60TH WEDDING ANNIVERSARY ELIZABETH II AND PRINCE PHILIP

2007 Obverse

Designer: R. R. Carmichael
Engraver: RCM Staff

DATE	DESCRIPTION	QUANTITY SOLD	ISSUE PRICE	FINISH	MS-65 NC
2006 (1926-)	80th Birthday of Queen Elizabeth II	24,977	19.95	Specimen	25.
2007 (1947-)	60th Wedding Anniversary Elizabeth II and Prince Philip	15,235	21.95	Specimen	25.

TWENTY-FIVE CENTS, NHL HOCKEY SERIES (GIFTWARE), 2006-2007.

The nine coloured twenty-five cent coins listed below are found in the NHL Team Gift Sets of 2006 and 2007, see page 270.

Designers:
Obv.: Susanna Blunt
Rev.: RCM Staff
Composition: Nickel plated steel
Weight: 4.40 g
Diameter: 23.88 mm
Finish: Circulation, Decal
Case of Issue: See NHL Team Gift Sets, page 270

Engravers:
Obv.: Susan Taylor
Rev.: RCM Staff
Thickness: 1.58 mm
Edge: Reeded
Die Axis: ↑↑

2006 HOCKEY SEASON, 2005-2006.

Common Obverse

Montreal Canadiens

Ottawa Senators

Toronto Maple Leafs

DATE / COMP. MARK	DESCRIPTION	SOURCE	QUANTITY SOLD	ISSUE PRICE	FINISH	MS-65 NC
2006P	Montreal Canadiens Logo	NHL Team	11,765	N.I.I.	Circulation	20.
2006P	Ottawa Senators Logo	Gift	Included	N.I.I.	Circulation	20.
2006P	Toronto Maple Leafs Logo	Sets	Included	N.I.I.	Circulation	20.

2007 HOCKEY SEASON, 2006-2007

Common Obverse

Calgary Flames

Edmonton Oilers

Montreal Canadiens

Ottawa Senators

Toronto Maple Leafs

Vancouver Canucks

DATE / COMP. MARK	DESCRIPTION	SOURCE	QUANTITY SOLD	ISSUE PRICE	FINISH	MS-65 NC
2007	Calgary Flames Logo	Available	1,082	N.I.I.	Circulation	15.
2007	Edmonton Oilers Logo	only from	2,214	N.I.I.	Circulation	15.
2007	Montreal Canadiens Logo	NHL	4,091	N.I.I.	Circulation	15.
2007	Ottawa Senators Logo	Team	2,474	N.I.I.	Circulation	15.
2007	Toronto Maple Leafs Logo	Gift	5,365	N.I.I.	Circulation	15.
2007	Vancouver Canucks Logo	Sets	1,526	N.I.I.	Circulation	15.

OCCASIONS SERIES, 2007-2010

TWENTY-FIVE CENTS, OCCASIONS SETS, 2007-2010 (GIFTWARE).

In 2007 the Royal Canadian Mint continued their expansion into the giftware market with an issue of three new Occasion Gift Sets. The sets contain seven circulation finish coins with the Caribou twenty-five cent coin being replaced with a coloured twenty-five cent coin representing the occasion.

Common Obverse 2007-2008

Designers and Engravers:
Obv.: Susanna Blunt, Susan Taylor
Rev.: RCM Staff
Composition: Nickel plated steel
Weight: 4.40 g
Thickness: 1.58 mm
Diameter: 23.88 mm
Die Axis: ↑↑
Edge: Reeded
Finish: Circulation, Decal
Case of Issue: See Gift Sets, pages 266-268, 274-275

OCCASIONS - 2007

Balloons Birthday Set

Bouquet Wedding Set

Fireworks Congratulations Set

Maple Leaf Oh! Canada Set

Rattle Baby Set

DATE	DESCRIPTION	SOURCE	QUANTITY SOLD	ISSUE PRICE	FINISH	MS-65 NC
2007	Balloons, Birthday Gift Set	Available	24,531	N.I.I.	Circulation	20.
2007	Bouquet, Wedding Gift Set	only from	10,318	N.I.I.	Circulation	20.
2007	Fireworks, Congratulations Gift Set	Occasions	9,671	N.I.I.	Circulation	20.
2007	Maple Leaf, Oh! Canada Gift Set	Gift	24,096	N.I.I.	Circulation	25.
2007	Rattle, Baby Gift Set	Sets	30,090	N.I.I.	Circulation	20.

OCCASIONS - 2008

Cake Wedding Set

Canadian Flag Oh! Canada Set

Party Hat Birthday Set

Teddy Bear Baby Set

Trophy Congratulations Set

DATE	DESCRIPTION	SOURCE	QUANTITY SOLD	ISSUE PRICE	FINISH	MS-65 NC
2008	Cake, Wedding Gift Set	Available	7,407	N.I.I.	Circulation	15.
2008	Canadian Flag, Oh! Canada Gift Set	only from	30,567	N.I.I.	Circulation	15.
2008	Party Hat, Birthday Gift Set	Occasions	11,376	N.I.I.	Circulation	15.
2008	Teddy Bear, Baby Gift Set	Gift	29,636	N.I.I.	Circulation	15.
2008	Trophy, Congratulations Gift Set	Sets	6,821	N.I.I.	Circulation	15.

OCCASIONS SERIES, 2007-2010 (cont.)

TWENTY-FIVE CENTS, OCCASIONS SETS, 2007-2010 (GIFTWARE) [cont.].

In 2009 only the Oh! Canada and Baby giftware sets were issued. The other twenty-five cent Occasions coins are now incorporated into cards, see page 24.

Designers:
Obv.: Susanna Blunt
Rev.: RCM Staff
Composition: Nickel plated steel
Weight: 4.40 g
Diameter: 23.88 mm
Finish: Circulation, Decal
Case of Issue: See Gift Sets, pages 266-268, 274-275

Engravers:
Obv.: Susan Taylor
Rev.: RCM Staff
Thickness: 1.58 mm
Edge: Reeded
Die Axis: ↑↑

OCCASIONS - 2009

**Common Obv.
With RCM Logo**

**Four Maple Leaves
Oh! Canada Set**

**Teddy Bear
Baby Set**

DATE	DESCRIPTION	SOURCE	QUANTITY SOLD	ISSUE PRICE	FINISH	MS-65 NC
2009	Four Maple Leaves, Oh! Canada Set	Occasions	14,451	N.I.I.	Circulation	15.
2009	Teddy Bear, Baby Set	Gift Sets	25,182	N.I.I.	Circulation	15.

OCCASIONS - 2010

For 2010, the Wedding Occasion twenty-five cent coin was moved back to the Wedding Gift Set series.

**Common Obv.
Without RCM Logo**

**Carriage
Baby Set**

**Heart and Roses
Wedding Set**

**Three Maple Leaves
Oh! Canada Set**

DATE	DESCRIPTION	SOURCE	QUANTITY SOLD	ISSUE PRICE	FINISH	MS-65 NC
2010	Carriage, Baby Set	Occasions	N/A	N.I.I.	Circulation	15.
2010	Heart and Rose, Wedding Set	Gift	N/A	N.I.I.	Circulation	15.
2010	Maple Leaves, Oh! Canada Set	Sets	N/A	N.I.I.	Circulation	15.

CARDS WITH COINS (OCCASIONS) 2009-2010

TWENTY-FIVE CENTS, CARDS WITH COINS, 2009-2010 (GIFTWARE).

In 2009 a series of four cards incorporating twenty-five cent Occasions coloured coins was released into the gift market.

Designers:
Obv.: Susanna Blunt
Rev.: RCM Staff
Composition: Nickel plated steel
Weight: 4.40 g
Diameter: 23.88 mm
Finish: Circulation, Decal
Case of Issue: Folder

Engravers:
Obv.: Susan Taylor
Rev.: RCM Staff
Thickness: 1.58 mm
Edge: Reeded
Die Axis: ↑↑

OCCASIONS - 2009

Common Obv. With RCM Logo

Balloons, Streamers Birthday Card

Doves and Rings Wedding Card

Fireworks Congratulation Card

Stylized Flower Thank You Card

DATE	DESCRIPTION	QUANTITY SOLD	ISSUE PRICE	FINISH	MS-65 NC
2009	Balloons and Streamers, Birthday Card	9,663	9.95	Circulation	15.
2009	Doves and Rings, Wedding Card	7,571	9.95	Circulation	15.
2009	Fireworks, Congratulations Card	4,126	9.95	Circulation	15.
2009	Stylised Flower, Thank You Card	4,415	9.95	Circulation	15.

OCCASIONS - 2010

Common Obv. Without RCM Logo

Flowers Thank You Card

Gift Box Birthday Card

Stars Congratulations Card

DATE	DESCRIPTION	QUANTITY SOLD	ISSUE PRICE	FINISH	MS-65 NC
2010	Flowers, Thank You Card	N/A	9.95	Circulation	10.
2010	Gift Box, Birthday Card	N/A	9.95	Circulation	10.
2010	Stars, Congratulations Card	N/A	9.95	Circulation	10.

ISSUES OF THE VANCOUVER 2010 OLYMPIC WINTER GAMES

TWENTY-FIVE CENTS, VANCOUVER 2010 WINTER OLYMPIC GAMES, 2007-2008.

The painted maple leaf outline twenty-five cent coins were co-issued with Petro Canada and encased in a collector card format. The coins are listed in issue date order. The Collector Cards though numbered 1 to 15 do not necessarily correspond to the issue date order. The Alpine Skiing painted reverse was issued with a 2007 and 2008 dated obverse.

2007 Obv.
Olympic Games

2010
Olympic
Logo

Designers and Engravers:
Obv.: Susanna Blunt, Susan Taylor
Rev.: Glen Green, RCM Staff
Composition: Nickel plated steel
Weight: 4.40 g
Diameter: 23.88 mm
Thickness: 1.58 mm
Edge: Reeded
Die Axis: ↑↑
Finish: Circulation, Painted

Curling

Ice Hockey

Biathlon

Alpine Skiing

Collector Card No. 4
2007 Alpine Skiing

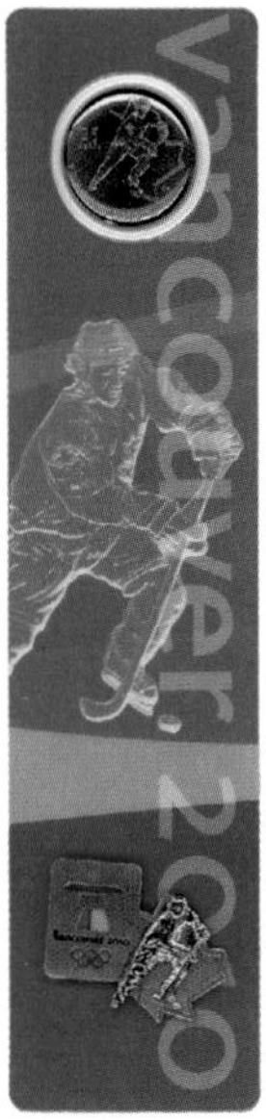

Ice Hockey
Bookmark and
Lapel Pin

DATE	DESCRIPTION	QUANTITY SOLD	ISSUE PRICE	FINISH	MARKET VALUE
2007	Curling, Sport Card (painted leaf)	90,756	7.95	Circulation	12.
2007	Curling, Bookmark and Lapel Pin	5,332	9.95	Circulation	10.
2007	Ice Hockey, Sport Card (painted leaf)	100,839	7.95	Circulation	12.
2007	Ice Hockey, Bookmark and Lapel Pin	9,062	9.95	Circulation	10.
2007	Biathlon, Sport Card (painted leaf)	30,279	7.95	Circulation	12.
2007	Biathlon, Bookmark and Lapel Pin	Not issued	—	—	—
2007	Alpine Skiing,, Sport Card (painted leaf) dated 2007	919	7.95	Circulation	40.
2007	Alpine Skiing, Bookmark and Lapel Pin	6,172	9.95	Circulation	10.
2008	Alpine Skiing,, Sport Card (painted leaf) dated 2008	40,470	7.95	Circulation	20.

ISSUES OF THE VANCOUVER 2010 OLYMPIC WINTER GAMES (cont.)

TWENTY-FIVE CENTS, VANCOUVER 2010 WINTER OLYMPIC GAMES, 2008-2009.

2008 Obv.
Olympic Games

Snowboarding

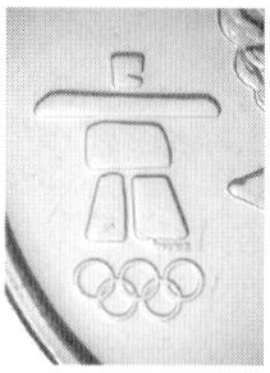

2010
Olympic
Logo

Designers and Engravers:
Obv.: Susanna Blunt, Susan Taylor
Rev.: Glen Green, RCM Staff
Composition: Nickel plated steel
Weight: 4.40 g
Diameter: 23.88 mm
Thickness: 1.58 mm
Edge: Reeded
Die Axis: ↑↑
Finish: Circulation, Painted

Freestyle Skiing

Figure Skating

Bobsleigh

Cross Country Skiing

Snowboarding
Bookmark and
Lapel Pin

Speed Skating

Collector Card No. 6
Snowboarding

DATE	DESCRIPTION	QUANTITY SOLD	ISSUE PRICE	FINISH	MARKET VALUE
2008	Snowboarding, Sport Card (painted leaf)	40,771	7.95	Circulation	12.
2008	Snowboarding, Bookmark and Lapel Pin	5,150	9.95	Circulation	10.
2008	Freestyle Skiing,, Sport Card (painted leaf)	35,447	7.95	Circulation	12.
2008	Freestyle Skiing,, Bookmark and Lapel Pin	Not Issued	—	—	—
2008	Figure Skating , Sport Card (painted leaf)	16,479	7.95	Circulation	12.
2008	Figure Skating., Bookmark and Lapel Pin	6,047	9.95	Circulation	10.
2008	Bobsleigh, Sport Card (painted leaf)	1,383	7.95	Circulation	12.
2008	Bobsleigh, Bookmark and Lapel Pin	Not Issued	—	—	—
2009	Cross Country Skiing, Sport Card (painted leaf)	261	7.95	Circulation	12.
2009	Cross Country Skiing, Bookmark and Lapel Pin	Not Issued	—	—	—
2009	Speed Skating, Sport Card (painted leaf)	309	7.95	Circulation	12.
2009	Speed Skating, Bookmark and Lapel Pin	3,529	9.95	Circulation	10.

ISSUES OF THE VANCOUVER 2010 OLYMPIC WINTER GAMES (cont.)

TWENTY-FIVE CENTS, GOLDEN MOMENTS OLYMPIC COMMEMORATIVES, 2009.

The Golden Moments twenty-five cent coins were issued to commemorate the gold medals won at the Salt Lake City Winter Olympic Games by the Canadian men's and women's hockey teams in 2002, and the gold medal won by Cindy Klassen at the 2006 Turin Winter Olympic Games.

While three different commemorative designs are present, there is also three different major finish varieties within each design, making a total of nine major varieties in this series. Adding to the complication are two minor varieties within the Men's Ice Hockey colourised coins, that of a raised and incused 2, making the grand total ten varieties.

Seven varieties are listed in Canadian Coins, Volume One, page 167, and six are listed here in Volume Two. The overlapping colourised varieties are duplicated in each volume.

The Men's Ice Hockey, colourised, raised 2 variety is NOT found in Petro Canada Sport Cards.

DESIGNS	FINISH VARIETIES	DIE VARIETIES
Men's Ice Hockey	Circulation	Raised 2
	Colourised	Incused 2
	Painted	
Women's Ice Hockey	Circulation	
	Colourised	
	Painted	
Cindy Klassen	Circulation	
	Colourised	
	Painted	

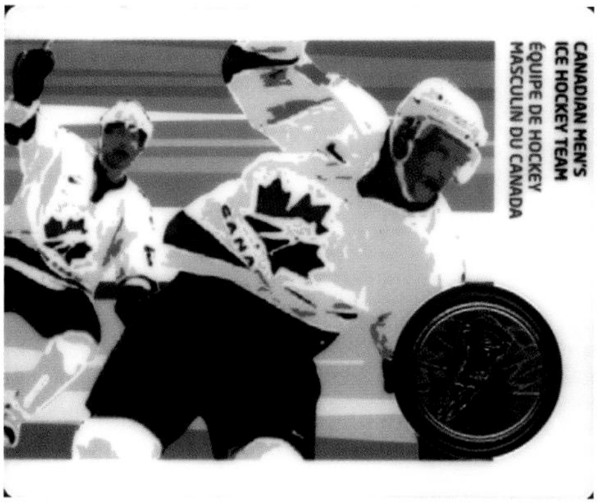

Collector Card No. 12
Canadian Men's Ice Hockey Team

Collector Card No. 13
Canadian Women's Ice Hockey Team

Collector Card No. 14
Cindy Klassen Speed Skating

ISSUES OF THE VANCOUVER 2010 OLYMPIC WINTER GAMES (cont.)

TWENTY-FIVE CENTS, GOLDEN MOMENTS OLYMPIC COMMEMORATIVES, 2009 (cont.).

Obverse
2009

Designers and Engravers:
Obv.: Susanna Blunt, Susan Taylor
Rev.: Jason Bouwman, RCM Staff
Composition: Nickel plated steel
Weight: 4.40 g **Edge:** Reeded
Diameter: 23.88 mm **Die Axis:** ↑↑
Thickness: 1.58 mm
Finish: 1. Circulation, Colourised
2. Brilliant Uncirculated, Painted

Men's Ice Hockey
Colourised Red

Colourised leaf
Incused 2

Men's Ice Hockey
Painted Red

Painted leaf
Incused 2

Women's Ice Hockey
Colourised Red

Colourised Leaf

Women's Ice Hockey
Painted Red

Painted leaf

Cindy Klassen
Speed Skating
Colourised Red

Colourised Leaf

Cindy Klassen
Speed Skating
Painted Red

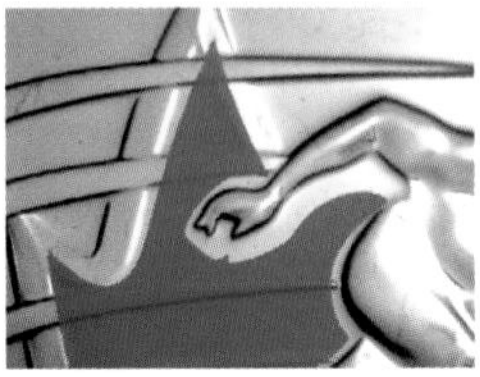

Painted leaf

DATE	DESCRIPTION	SOURCE	QUANTITY SOLD	ISSUE PRICE	FINISH	MS-65
2009	Men's Ice Hockey, Incused “2”, Colourised	Sport Card	N/A	7.95	Circulation	5.
2009	Men's Ice Hockey Incused “2”, Painted	Spec. Ed. Set	8,564	N.I.I.	BU	8.
2009	Women's Ice Hockey, Colourised	Sport Card	N/A	7.95	Circulation	5.
2009	Women's Ice Hockey, Painted	Sp. Ed. Set	8,564	N.I.I.	BU	8.
2009	Cindy Klassen, Speed Skating, Colourised	Sport Card	N/A	7.95	Circulation	5.
2009	Cindy Klassen, Speed Skating, Painted	Spec. Ed. Set	8,564	N.I.I.	BU	8.

ISSUES OF THE VANCOUVER 2010 PARALYMPIC WINTER GAMES

TWENTY-FIVE CENTS, VANCOUVER 2010 PARALYMPIC WINTER GAMES SPORT CARDS, 2007 and 2009.

2007 Obv.
Paralympic Games

2010
Paralympic
Logo

Designers and Engravers:
Obv.: Susanna Blunt, Susan Taylor
Rev.: Glen Green, RCM Staff
Composition: Nickel plated steel
Weight: 4.40 g
Edge: Reeded
Diameter: 23.88 mm
Die Axis: ↑↑
Thickness: 1.58 mm
Finish: Circulation, Painted

Wheelchair Curling
Painted Leaf

Ice Sledge Hockey
Painted Leaf

The Wheelchair Curling Mule

The Vancouver Olympic obverse was paired with the Paralympic Wheelchair Curling reverse to create a mule. This coin was not issued for circulation, but is found in the Vancouver 2010 Brilliant Uncirculated Sets of 2007, which were assembled in Ottawa. See page 262 for the set listing.

2007 Obverse with
Olympic Logo

Wheelchair Curling
Reverse

Collector Card No. 3
Wheelchair Curling

DATE	DESCRIPTION	QUANTITY SOLD	ISSUE PRICE	FINISH	MARKET VALUE
2007	Wheelchair Curling, Sport Card (painted leaf)	34,956	7.95	Circulation	12.
2007	Wheelchair Curling, Mule	N/A	N.I.I.	BU	225.
2009	Ice Sledge Hockey Sport Card (painted leaf)	N/A	7.95	Circulation	12.

NOTE ON TWENTY-FIVE CENT ISSUES

The Petro Canada sport card twenty-five cent issues of 2007, 2008 and 2009 have a painted outline of a maple leaf supporting a central design. There are twelve different designs. The painted coins were inserted into sport cards and bookmarks which were encased in a plastic film. This film is all but impossible to remove without removing the painted outline from the coin.

ISSUES OF THE VANCOUVER 2010 OLYMPIC AND PARALYMPIC WINTER GAMES

TWENTY-FIVE CENTS, VANCOUVER 2010 OLYMPIC AND PARALYMPIC WINTER GAMES, SILVER PROOF SET, 2007-2009.

The twenty-five cent silver proof coins were issued in a presentation case. The set contains twelve coins and a one ounce sterling silver bar. Single proof coins may only be obtained from a break-up of this set.

Designers:
Obv.: Susanna Blunt
Rev.: Glen Green

Engravers:
Obv.: Susan Taylor
Rev.: RCM Staff

Composition: 92.5% Ag, 7.5 Cu
Silver content: Single Coin: 5.365 g, 0.172 tr oz
Bar: 28.77 g, 0.925 tr oz
Set: 93.15 g, 3.00 tr oz
Weight: 5.80 g
Diameter: 23.6 mm
Thickness: 1.7 mm
Edge: Reeded
Die Axis: ↑↑
Finish: Proof
Case of Issue: Black leatherette clam case, 13-hole flocked insert, encapsulated coins, COA

DATE	DESCRIPTION	QUANTITY SOLD	ISSUE PRICE	FINISH	PR-67 UHC	PR-68 UHC
2007	Curling	N.I.I.	—	Proof	20.	25.
2007	Ice Hockey	N.I.I.	—	Proof	20.	25.
2007	Wheelchair Curling	N.I.I.	—	Proof	20.	25.
2007	Biathlon	N.I.I.	—	Proof	20.	25.
2007	Alpine Skiing,	N.I.I.	—	Proof	20.	25.
2008	Snowboarding	N.I.I.	—	Proof	20.	25.
2008	Free Style Skiing	N.I.I.	—	Proof	20.	25.
2008	Bobsleigh	N.I.I.	—	Proof	20.	25.
2008	Figure Skating	N.I.I.	—	Proof	20.	25.
2009	Cross Country Skiing	N.I.I.	—	Proof	20.	25.
2009	Speed Skating	N.I.I.	—	Proof	20.	25.
2009	Ice Sledge Hockey	N.I.I.	—	Proof	20.	25.
	Complete Set, 12 coins, 1 one ounce silver bar	3,172	199.95	—	200.	—

TWENTY-FIVE CENT DERIVATIVES VANCOUVER 2010 OLYMPIC AND PARALYMPIC WINTER GAMES

DATE	DESCRIPTION	QUANTITY SOLD	ISSUE PRICE	FINISH	MARKET VALUE
2007	**Vancouver 2010 Coin Collector Card** (card only)	104,400	4.95	—	5.
2007	**Magnetic lapel pin,** Curling	3,118	9.95	Circulation	10.
2007	**Magnetic lapel pin,** Ice Hockey	3,158	9.95	Circulation	10.
2007	**Magnetic lapel pin,** Alpine Skiing	3,013	9.95	Circulation	10.
2008	**Magnetic lapel pin,** Snowboarding	6,095	9.95	Circulation	10.
2008	**Alpine Skiing**, Twenty-five cents (painted) and lapel pin	3,350	9.95	Circulation	10.
2008	**Snowboarding**, Twenty-five cents (painted) and lapel pin	2,922	9.95	Circulation	10.
2007-2010	**Magnetic Lapel Pin** for interchangeable sport coin	RCM	9.95	Circulation	10.
2007-2010	**Green See Through Tin Can**, Magnetic lapel pin, 5 twenty-five cent coins of various sports	RCM	14.95	Circulation	15.
2007-2010	**Green Tin Can** to hold the 15 Petro Canada Collector Cards	RCM	5.95	—	6.

ISSUES OF THE VANCOUVER 2010 OLYMPIC AND PARALYMPIC WINTER GAMES

TWENTY-FIVE CENTS, VANCOUVER 2010 OLYMPIC WINTER GAMES MASCOTS, 2008, (GIFTWARE).

The three mascots, Miga and Quatchi for the Olympic Winter Games, and Sumi for the Paralympic Winter Games, appear on many souvenirs for the Vancouver Winter Games.

Designers:
Obv.: Susanna Blunt
Rev.: Design Team of the Vancouver Organising Committee for the 2010 Olympic and Paralympic Games

Engravers:
Rev.: Susan Taylor
Rev.: RCM Staff

Composition: Nickel plated steel
Weight: 4.40 g
Diameter: 23.88 mm
Finish: Circulation, Decal
Thickness: 1.6 mm
Edge: Reeded
Die Axis: ↑↑
Case of Issue: Introduction Folder "Meet The Vancouver 2010 Mascots!"

Common Obv.

Miga

Quatchi

Sumi

Sumi Introduction Folder
"Meet The Vancouver 2010 Mascots!"

DATE	DESCRIPTION	QUANTITY SOLD	ISSUE PRICE	FINISH	MARKET VALUE
2008	Miga	14,654	10.95	Circulation	15.
2008	Quatchi	15,310	10.95	Circulation	15.
2008	Sumi	15,333	10.95	Circulation	15.

BIRD SERIES

TWENTY-FIVE CENTS, COLOURISED BIRD SERIES, 2007-2010 (GIFTWARE).
This series features popular Canadian birds as depicted by artist Arnold Nogy.

Designers:
Obv.: Susanna Blunt
Rev.: Arnold Nogy
Composition: Nickel plated steel
Weight: 12.61 to 13.0 g
Diameter: 35.00 mm
Finish: Specimen, Decal

Engravers:
Obv.: Susan Taylor
Rev.: RCM Staff
Thickness: 2.0 mm
Edge: Plain
Die Axis: ↑↑

Case of Issue: Maroon leatherette clam style case, black flocked insert, encapsulated coin, COA

2007 Common Obv. With RCM Logo

Ruby-Throated Hummingbird

Red-Breasted Nuthatch

2008 Common Obv. With RCM Logo

Downy Woodpecker

Northern Cardinal

2010 Common Obv. Without RCM Logo

Goldfinch

Blue Jay

DATE	DESCRIPTION	QUANTITY SOLD	ISSUE PRICE	FINISH	MS-65 NC
2007	Ruby-Throated Hummingbird	17,174	24.95	Specimen	75.
2007	Red-Breasted Nuthatch	11,909	24.95	Specimen	150.
2008	Downy Woodpecker	14,282	24.95	Specimen	75.
2008	Northern Cardinal	11,604	24.95	Specimen	75.
2010	Goldfinch	14,000	24.95	Specimen	35.
2010	Blue Jay	14,000	24.95	Specimen	35.

TWENTY-FIVE CENTS, 90TH ANNIVERSARY OF THE END OF WORLD WAR I SET, 2008 (GIFTWARE).

These two twenty-five cent pieces were issued in a 2008 commemorative set to mark the ninetieth anniversary of the end of World War I. The 35 mm crown-size coin depicts the Tomb of the Unknown Soldier at the National War Memorial in Ottawa.

The standard 25-cent colourised Poppy coin was released into circulation during 2008. It was also incorporated into a bookmark that sold in the gift market. A donation of $1.00 per bookmark sold was given to the Legion's Dominion Command Fund .

2008 TOMB OF THE UNKNOWN SOLDIER

Designers and Engravers:
Obv.: Susanna Blunt, Susan Taylor
Rev.: David Craig, RCM Staff
Composition: Nickel plated steel
Weight: 12.61 g
Diameter: 35.00 mm
Thickness: 3.4 mm
Edge: Plain
Die Axis: ↑↑
Finish: Specimen

2008 COLOURISED POPPY

Specifications: See 2005 Colourised Poppy, page 18
Cases of Issue:
1. Illustrated folder: Two coins, Serialised
2. Bookmark: twenty-five cent coin only

DATE	DESCRIPTION	SOURCE	QUANTITY SOLD	ISSUE PRICE	FINISH	MS-65 NC
2008	Tomb of the Unknown Soldier and Poppy	Folder	Incl. below	N.I.I.	Specimen	25.
2008	Poppy "Remembrance"	Folder	Incl. below	N.I.I.	Circulation	5.
2008	Set of Two Coins	Folder	10,167	24.95	—	25.
2008	Poppy, Bookmark	Bookmark	489	12.95	Circulation	15.

Note: **1.** While the finish on the Tomb of the Unknown Soldier, large size twenty-five cent coin, is listed by the Royal Canadian Mint as specimen, it certainly is not a specimen finish when compared with coins of their specimen set issues of 1996 to 2009.

2. The "quantity sold" figure is understated. The 2008 RCM Report omitted the quantity sold number for that year. That number should been added to the 489 from the RCM Report for 2009.

NOTE ON GIFTWARE

Giftware is produced solely for the souvenir market. In most cases it is packaged in such a way that the coin is never meant to be removed from its package, let alone fill any legal tender status. Even though it is issued as Non Circulating legal tender, it is doubtful that anyone would accept it in exchange for goods or services, for it is not in a form recognisable by the general public as a medium of change.

TWENTY-FIVE CENTS, 100TH ANNIVERSARY OF ANNE OF GREEN GABLES©, 1908-2008 (GIFTWARE).

This coin was issued to commemorate the 100th anniversary *Anne of Green Gables*, which was first published in 1908.

Designers and Engravers:
Obv.: Susanna Blunt, Susan Taylor
Rev.: Ben Stahl
Composition: Nickel plated steel
Weight: 12.61 g
Diameter: 35.00 mm
Thickness: 2.00 mm
Edge: Plain
Die Axis: ↑↑
Finish: Specimen, Decal
Case of Issue: Illustrated folder, Serialised

DATE	DESCRIPTION	QUANTITY SOLD	ISSUE PRICE	FINISH	MS-65 NC
2008 (1908-)	Anne of Green Gables©	32,795	19.95	Specimen	25.

TWENTY-FIVE CENTS, NOTRE-DAME-DU-SAGUENAY, 2009 (GIFTWARE).

The Lady of the Saguenay Fjord sits high on Cape Trinité in the majestic Saguenay Fjord, three hundred metres above sea level. The solid wooden statue was designed by Louis Jobin in 1881.

Designers and Engravers:
Obv.: Susanna Blunt, Susan Taylor
Rev.: Promotion Saguenay, RCM Staff
Composition: Nickel plated steel
Weight: 11.7 g
Diameter: 35.0 mm
Thickness: 2.0 mm
Edge: Plain
Die Axis: ↑↑
Finish: Specimen, Ddecal

DATE	DESCRIPTION	QUANTITY SOLD	ISSUE PRICE	FINISH	MS-65 NC
2009	Notre-Dame-Du-Saguenay	16,653	14.95	Specimen	25.

TWENTY-FIVE CENTS, REMEMBRANCE DAY POPPIES, 2010, (GIFTWARE).

This twenty-five cent coin is included in the Remembrance Day Collector Card. This card also has two die-cut holes to house the 2004 and 2008 "Poppy" coins.

Designers and Engravers:
Obv.: Susanna Blunt, Susan Taylor
Rev.: Cosme Saffioti, Stan Witten
Composition: Nickel plated steel
Weight: 4.40 g
Diameter: 23.88 mm **Edge:** Reeded
Thickness: 1.58 mm **Die Axis:** ↑↑
Finish: Circulation, Colourised
Case of Issue: See Derivatives, page 36

DATE / COMP. MARK	DESCRIPTION	QUANTITY SOLD	ISSUE PRICE	FINISH	MS-65 NC	MS-66 NC	MS-67 NC
2010	Remembrance Day Poppies, colourised	N/A	9.95	Circulation	5.	10.	30.

TWENTY-FIVE CENT DERIVATIVES

DATE	DESCRIPTION	QUANTITY SOLD	ISSUE PRICE	ISSUER	FINISH	MARKET VALUE
1999	**MILLENNIUM SET OF 12 CARDS** each containing a 1999 millennium twenty-five cent coin in a credit card format	N/A	N/A	RCM	MS-65	30.
1999	**JANUARY** "A Country Unfolds"	N/A	N/A	RCM	MS-65	2.
1999	**FEBRUARY** "Etched in Stone"	N/A	N/A	RCM	MS-65	2.
1999	**MARCH** "The Log Drive"	N/A	N/A	RCM	MS-65	2.
1999	**APRIL** "Our Northern Heritage"	N/A	N/A	RCM	MS-65	2.
1999	**MAY** "The Voyageurs"	N/A	N/A	RCM	MS-65	2.
1999	**JUNE** "From Coast to Coast"	N/A	N/A	RCM	MS-65	2.
1999	**JULY** "A Nation of People"	N/A	N/A	RCM	MS-65	2.
1999	**AUGUST** "The Pioneer Spirit"	N/A	N/A	RCM	MS-65	2.
1999	**SEPTEMBER** "Canada Through a Child's Eye"	N/A	N/A	RCM	MS-65	2.
1999	**OCTOBER** "A Tribute to the First Nation"	N/A	N/A	RCM	MS-65	2.
1999	**NOVEMBER** "The Airplane Opens the North"	N/A	N/A	RCM	MS-65	2.
1999	**DECEMBER** "This is Canada"	N/A	N/A	RCM	MS-65	2.
2000	**MILLENNIUM SET OF 12 CARDS** each containing a 2000 millennium twenty-five cent coin in a credit card format	N/A	N/A	RCM	MS-65	30.
2000	**JANUARY** - Pride "Tomorrow Today"	N/A	N/A	RCM	MS-65	2.
2000	**FEBRUARY** - Ingenuity "Building for Tomorrow"	N/A	N/A	RCM	MS-65	2.
2000	**MARCH** - Achievement "The Power to Excel"	N/A	N/A	RCM	MS-65	2.
2000	**APRIL** - Health "Quest for a Cure"	N/A	N/A	RCM	MS-65	2.
2000	**MAY** - Natural Legacy "Our Natural Treasures"	N/A	N/A	RCM	MS-65	2.
2000	**JUNE** - Harmony "Hand in Hand"	N/A	N/A	RCM	MS-65	2.
2000	**JULY** - Celebration "Celebrating our Future"	N/A	N/A	RCM	MS-65	2.
2000	**AUGUST** - Family "The Ties That Bind"	N/A	N/A	RCM	MS-65	2.
2000	**SEPTEMBER** - Wisdom "The Legacy"	N/A	N/A	RCM	MS-65	2.
2000	**OCTOBER** - Creativity "Expression For All Time"	N/A	N/A	RCM	MS-65	2.
2000	**NOVEMBER** - Freedom "Strong and Free"	N/A	N/A	RCM	MS-65	2.
2000	**DECEMBER** - Community "Canada in the World"	N/A	N/A	RCM	MS-65	2.
2000	**APRIL**, CIBC "Run For The Cure" Credit Card	N/A	N/A	RCM, CIBC	MS-65	2.
2000	**THE ADVENTURES OF ZAC AND PENNY MONEY** Set of twelve 2000 Millennium twenty five cent coins in a display card; six booklets of stories and games	6,888	N/A	RCM	MS-65	25.
2004P	**WALKING BUNDLE** Twenty-five cent 'Moose' coin, T-shirt, Water bottle, Pouch	11,413	19.95	RCM	MS-65	50.
2004	**2004 ROYAL CANADIAN MINT ANNUAL REPORT** Twenty-five cent "Poppy" coin, sterling silver, selectively gold plated	12,677	24.95	RCM	PR-67	35.
2005P	**BOOKMARK** Twenty-five cent "Poppy" coin; Victory pin	29,951	12.95	RCM	MS-65	20.
2005	**60TH ANNIV. 1945-2005** Liberation Set, Netherlands	3,500	49.95	RCM	SP-66	110.
2006	**BOOKMARK** Twenty-five cent "Breast Cancer" coin; colourised; Lapel pin	40,911	13.95	RCM	MS-65	15.
2006	**CANADA DAY 2006**, Twenty-five cents, colourised; Four crayons and a colouring sheet	N/A	9.95	RCM	MS-65	25.
2007	**CANADA DAY**, Twenty-five cents, colourised coin, activity kit	N/A	9.95	RCM	MS-65	20.
2008	**CANADA DAY,** Twenty-five cents, colourised coin, activity kit	N/A	9.95	RCM	MS-65	20.
2009	**CANADA DAY** Twenty-five cents, colourised coin, activity kit	N/A	14.95	RCM	MS-65	25.
2010	**REMEMBRANCE DAY COLLECTOR CARD**, includes 2010 twenty-five cent Remembrance Day coin; two die-cut holes for 2004 and 2008 twenty-five cent Poppy coins; postcard	N/A	9.95	RCM	MS-65	10.

FIFTY CENTS

DISCOVERING NATURE SERIES, 1995-2000

FIFTY CENTS, BIRDS OF CANADA SERIES, 1995.

The first set in the Discovering Nature Series commemorates birds that are native to Canada. This is the first of six sets totalling 24 coins. They are the first sterling silver fifty cents to be issued since 1919.

Designers:
Obv.: Dora de Pédery-Hunt
Rev.: Coins 1-4 Jean-Luc Grondin
Coins 5-8 Dwayne Harty

Engravers:
Obv.: Dora de Pédery-Hunt
Rev.: See reverse illustration

Composition: 92.5% Ag, 7.5% Cu
Silver content: 8.603 g, 0.277 tr oz
Weight: 9.30 g
Diameter: 27.13 mm
Thickness: 2.08 mm
Edge: Reeded
Die Axis: ↑↑
Finish: Proof
Case of Issue: Coins 1 - 4 Encapsulated coin in presentation box with illustrated booklet.
Coins 5 to 6 (A) Two coin set; encapsulated coins
(B) Four coin set; encapsulated coins

Coin No. 1
Atlantic Puffins
Sheldon Beveridge

Coin No. 2
Whooping Crane
Stan Witten

Coin No. 3
Gray Jays
Sheldon Beveridge

Coin No. 4
White-tailed Ptarmigans
Cosme Saffioti

FIFTY CENTS, LITTLE WILD ONES SERIES, 1996.

The second set commemorates the young wildlife of Canada in their natural habitat.

Coin No. 5
Moose Calf
Ago Aarand

Coin No. 6
Wood Ducklings
Sheldon Beveridge

Coin No. 7
Cougar Kittens
Stan Witten

Coin No. 8
Black Bear Cubs
Sheldon Beveridge

DATE	COIN No.	DESCRIPTION	QUANTITY SOLD	ISSUE PRICE	FINISH	PR-67 UHC	PR-68 UHC
1995	1	Atlantic Puffins	Total	—	Proof	20.	30.
1995	2	Whooping Crane	mintage	29.95	Proof	20.	30.
1995	3	Gray Jays	all coins	—	Proof	20.	30.
1995	4	White-tailed Ptarmigans	172,377	29.95	Proof	20.	30.
1995	—	4 coin set	—	56.95	Proof	65.	—
1996	5	Moose Calf	Total	—	Proof	20.	30.
1996	6	Wood Ducklings	mintage	29.95	Proof	20.	30.
1996	7	Cougar Kittens	all coins	—	Proof	20.	30.
1996	8	Black Bear Cubs	206,552	29.95	Proof	20.	30.
1996	—	4 coin set	—	56.95	Proof	65.	—

Note: Coins 1-2, 3-4, 5-6 and 7-8 were issued in 2 coin sets, issue price $29.95.

DISCOVERING NATURE SERIES, 1995-2000 (cont.)

FIFTY CENTS, CANADA'S BEST FRIENDS SERIES, 1997.

The silver 50¢ set of 1997 honours the friendship and loyalty of four of Canada's favourite canine companions.

Designers:
Obv.: Dora de Pédery-Hunt
Rev.: Coins 9-12 Arnold A. Nogy
Coins 13-16 Pierre Leduc

Engravers:
Obv.: Dora de Pédery-Hunt
Rev.: See reverse illustration

Composition: 92.5% Ag, 7.5% Cu
Silver content: 8.603 g, 0.277 tr oz
Weight: 9.30 g
Diameter: 27.13 mm
Thickness: 2.08 mm
Edge: Reeded
Die Axis: ↑↑
Finish: Proof
Case of Issue: Encapsulated coin in presentation box, plus illustrated booklet.

Coin No. 9
Newfoundland
William Woodruff

Coin No. 10
Nova Scotia Duck Tolling Retriever
Stan Witten

Coin No. 11
Labrador Retriever
Sheldon Beveridge

Coin No. 12
Canadian Eskimo Dog
Cosme Saffioti

FIFTY CENTS, CANADA'S OCEAN GIANTS SERIES, 1998.

The silver 50¢ set of 1998 shows the grace and beauty of the whales that are seen off our coasts.

Coin No. 13
Killer Whale
William Woodruff

Coin No. 14
Humpback Whale
Sheldon Beveridge

Coin No. 15
Beluga Whale
Cosme Saffioti

Coin No. 16
Blue Whale
Stan Witten

DATE	COIN No.	DESCRIPTION	QUANTITY SOLD	ISSUE PRICE	FINISH	PR-67 UHC	PR-68 UHC
1997	9	Newfoundland	Total	19.95	Proof	20.	35.
1997	10	Nova Scotia Duck Tolling Retriever	mintage	19.95	Proof	20.	25.
1997	11	Labrador Retriever	all coins	19.95	Proof	20.	25.
1997	12	Canadian Eskimo Dog	184,536	19.95	Proof	20.	25.
1997	—	Set of 4 coins	—	59.95	Proof	65.	—
1998	13	Killer Whale	Total	19.95	Proof	20.	25.
1998	14	Humpback Whale	mintage	19.95	Proof	20.	25.
1998	15	Beluga Whale	all coins	19.95	Proof	20.	25.
1998	16	Blue Whale	133,310	19.95	Proof	20.	25.
1998	—	Set of 4 coins	—	59.95	Proof	65.	—

DISCOVERING NATURE SERIES, 1995-2000 (cont.)

FIFTY CENTS, CATS OF CANADA SERIES, 1999.

This set, issued in 1999, honours four species of domestic and wild felines found in Canada, a salute to our rich Canadian wildlife.

Designers:
Obv.: Dora de Pédery-Hunt
Rev.: Coins 17-20, John Crosby
Coin 21, 23, Jean-Luc Grondin
Coin 22, 24, Pierre Leduc

Engravers:
Obv.: Dora de Pédery-Hunt
Rev.: See reverse illustration

Composition: 92.5% Ag, 7.5% Cu
Silver content: 8.603 g, 0.277 tr oz
Weight: 9.30 g
Diameter: 27.13 mm
Thickness: 2.08 mm
Edge: Reeded
Die Axis: ↑↑
Finish: Proof
Case of Issue: Encapsulated coin in presentation box, plus illustrated booklet.

Coin No. 17
Tonkinese
Susan Taylor

Coin No. 18
Lynx
Susan Taylor

Coin No. 19
Cymric
Susan Taylor

Coin No. 20
Cougar
Susan Taylor

FIFTY CENTS, CANADIAN BIRDS OF PREY, SERIES, 2000.

The sixth and last set of the series features the hunting birds indigenous to Canada.

Coin No. 21
Bald Eagle
William Woodruff

Coin No. 22
Osprey
Susan Taylor

Coin No. 23
Great Horned Owl
Susan Taylor

Coin No. 24
Red-Tailed Hawk
Stan Witten

DATE	COIN No.	DESCRIPTION	QUANTITY SOLD	ISSUE PRICE	FINISH	PR-67 UHC	PR-68 UHC
1999	17	Tonkinese	Total	19.95	Proof	40.	60.
1999	18	Lynx	mintage	19.95	Proof	40.	60.
1999	19	Cymric	all coins	19.95	Proof	40.	60.
1999	20	Cougar	83,423	19.95	Proof	40.	60.
1999	—	Set of 4 coins	—	59.95	Proof	125.	—
2000	21	Bald Eagle	Total	19.95	Proof	25.	30.
2000	22	Osprey	mintage	19.95	Proof	25.	30.
2000	23	Great Horned Owl	all coins	19.95	Proof	25.	30.
2000	24	Red-Tailed Hawk	123,628	19.95	Proof	25.	30.
2000	—	Set of 4 coins	—	59.95	Proof	75.	—

CANADIAN SPORTS FIRSTS SERIES, 1998-2000

FIFTY CENTS, CANADIAN SPORTS FIRSTS SERIES, 1998.

A new sport series of sterling silver 50¢ coins began in 1998 with the issue of the following four coins. The series comprises a total of twelve coins, four issued each of the years 1998, 1999 and 2000.

Designers:
Obv.: Dora de Pédery-Hunt
Rev.: Coins 1 to 4: F. G. Peter
Coins 5 to 8: D. H. Curley

Engravers:
Obv.: Dora de Pédery-Hunt
Rev.: See reverse illustration

Composition: 92.5% Ag, 7.5% Cu
Silver content: 8.603 g, 0.277 tr oz
Weight: 9.30 g
Diameter: 27.13 mm
Thickness: 2.08 mm
Edge: Reeded
Die Axis: ↑↑
Finish: Proof
Case of Issue: Singles: Lithographed metal box, black flocked insert, encapsulated coin.
Set: Twelve coin metal container.

Coin No. 1
First Official Amateur Figure Skating Championships, 1888
Sheldon Beveridge

Coin No. 2
First Canadian Ski Running/Ski Jumping Championships, 1898
Ago Aarand

Coin No. 3
First Overseas Can. Soccer Tour, 1888
Stan Witten

Coin No. 4
Gilles Villeneuve Victory, Grand Prix of Canada for F1 Auto Racing, 1978
Cosme Saffioti

FIFTY CENTS, CANADIAN SPORTS FIRSTS SERIES, 1999.

The 1999 50¢ sterling silver coin set commemorates important dates in the history of Canadian sports. The designs reflect both the history of the sport and the growth and development into national pastimes.

Coin No. 5
1904-1999 First Canadian Open Golf Championship, 1904
William Woodruff

Coin No. 6
1874-1999 First Int'l Yacht Race Canada vs U.S.A. 1874
Stan Witten

Coin No. 7
1909-1999 First Grey Cup in Canadian Football, 1909
Cosme Saffioti

Coin No. 8
1891-1999 Invention of Basketball by Canadian James Naismith
Sheldon Beveridge

DATE	COIN No.	DESCRIPTION	QUANTITY SOLD	ISSUE PRICE	FINISH	PR-67 UHC	PR-68 UHC
1998	1	First Official Amateur Figure Skating Chmpshp, 1888	Total	19.95	Proof	20.	40.
1998	2	First Canadian Ski Running/Ski Jumping Chmpshp, 1898	mintage	19.95	Proof	20.	40.
1998	3	First Overseas Canadian Soccer Tour, 1888	all coins	19.95	Proof	20.	40.
1998	4	Gilles Villeneuve Victory, Grand Prix, F1 Auto Racing, 1978	56,428	19.95	Proof	20.	40.
1998	—	Set of 4 coins	—	59.95	Proof	60.	—
1999	5	First Canadian Open Golf Chmpshp, 1904	Total	19.95	Proof	20.	40.
1999	6	First Int'l Yacht Race between Canada and U.S.A., 1874	mintage	19.95	Proof	20.	40.
1999	7	First Grey Cup in Canadian Football, 1909	all coins	19.95	Proof	20.	40.
1999	8	Invention of Basketball by Canadian James Naismith, 1891	52,115	19.95	Proof	20.	40.
1999	—	Set of 4 coins	—	59.95	Proof	60.	—

CANADIAN SPORTS FIRSTS SERIES, 1998-2000 (cont.)

FIFTY CENTS, CANADIAN SPORTS FIRSTS SERIES, 2000.

The 2000 50¢ Sterling Silver coin set celebrates the first competitions in Hockey, Curling, Steeplechase and Five Pin Bowling held in Canada. This is the last set in the twelve coin series.

Designers:
Obv.: Dora de Pédery-Hunt
Rev.: Brian Hughes

Engravers:
Obv.: Dora de Pédery-Hunt
Rev.: See reverse illustration

Composition: 92.5% Ag, 7.5% Cu
Silver content: 8.603 g, 0.277 tr oz
Weight: 9.30 g
Diameter: 27.13 mm
Thickness: 2.08 mm
Edge: Reeded
Die Axis: ↑↑
Finish: Proof
Case of Issue: Singles: Lithographed metal box, black flocked insert, encapsulated coin.
Set: Twelve coin metal case.

Coin No. 9
1875-2000 First Recorded Hockey Game
Stan Witten

Coin No. 10
1760-2000 Introduction of Curling to North America
Cosme Saffioti

Coin No. 11
1840-2000 First Steeplechase Race in British North America
Susan Taylor

Coin No. 12
1910-2000 Birth of the First 5-Pin Bowling League
William Woodruff

DATE	COIN No.	DESCRIPTION	QUANTITY SOLD	ISSUE PRICE	FINISH	PR-67 UHC	PR-68 UHC
2000	9	First Recorded Hockey Game, 1875	Total	19.95	Proof	20.	40.
2000	10	Introduction of Curling to North America, 1760	mintage	19.95	Proof	20.	40.
2000	11	First Steeplechase Race in British North America, 1840	all coins	19.95	Proof	20.	40.
2000	12	Birth of the First 5-Pin Bowling League, 1910	50,091	19.95	Proof	20.	40.
2000	—	Set of 4 coins	—	59.95	Proof	75.	100.

FIFTY CENT HISTORICAL COMMEMORATIVE SERIES, 1998-2008

FIFTY CENTS, 90TH ANNIVERSARY OF THE ROYAL CANADIAN MINT, 1908-1998.

Issued to commemorate the opening of the Royal Canadian Mint, a five-coin set was struck featuring the same reverse designs as the original 1908 coins, except for the double date 1908-1998. The set was issued in two finishes, matte and mirror proof.

Designers and Engravers:
Obv.: Dora de Pédery-Hunt
Rev.: Ago Aarand, W. H. J. Blakemore
Composition: 92.5% Ag, 7.5% Cu
Silver content: 10.749 g, 0.346 tr oz
Weight: 11.62 g
Diameter: 29.72 mm
Thickness: 2.0 mm
Edge: Reeded
Die Axis: ↑↑
Finish: See below
Case of Issue: See Special Issue Proof Sets, page 285

DATE	DESCRIPTION	QUANTITY SOLD	ISSUE PRICE	FINISH	PR-67 UHC	PR-68 UHC
1998 (1908-)	90th Anniv. R.C. Mint	18,376	N.I.I.	Matte Proof	20.	40.
1998 (1908-)	90th Anniv. R.C. Mint	24,893	N.I.I.	Mirror Proof	20.	50.

FIFTY CENTS, 50TH ANNIVERSARY OF THE CORONATION OF QUEEN ELIZABETH II, 1953-2003.

This fifty cent coin is from the Special Edition Proof Set issued in 2003 to commemorate the 50th anniversary of the Coronation of Queen Elizabeth II.

Designers and Engravers:
Obv.: Mary Gillick
Rev.: Thomas Shingles
Composition: 92.5% Ag, 7.5% Cu
Silver content: 10.749 g, 0.346 tr oz
Weight: 11.62 g
Diameter: 29.72 mm
Thickness: 1.9 mm
Edge: Reeded
Die Axis: ↑↑
Finish: Proof
Case of Issue: See Special Issue Proof Sets, page 286

DATE	DESCRIPTION	QUANTITY SOLD	ISSUE PRICE	FINISH	PR-67 UHC	PR-68 UHC
2003 (1953-)	50th Anniv. Coronation Queen Elizabeth II	21,537	N.I.I.	Proof	50.	100.

FIFTY CENT HISTORICAL COMMEMORATIVE SERIES, 1998-2008 (cont.)

FIFTY CENTS, COAT OF ARMS OF CANADA, 2004.

The Coat of Arms of Canada, which graced the George VI fifty-cent coin in 1937, has evolved over the years. This four coin set, besides tracing that evolution, records the portrait changes of Elizabeth II.

Obverse Designers: Portraits

1953-1964 Mary Gillick
1965-1989 Arnold Machin
1990-2003 Dora de Pédery-Hunt
2003-2004 Susanna Blunt

Reverse Designers: Arms of Canada

1953 Small date: G. E. Kruger-Gray
Large date: Thomas Shingles
1954-1958 Thomas Shingles after G. E. Kruger-Gray
1959-1996 Thomas Shingles
1997-2004 C. Bursey-Sabourin

Composition: 92.5% Ag, 7.5% Cu
Silver content: 8.603 g, 0.277 tr oz
Weight: 9.30 g
Diameter: 27.13 mm
Thickness: 2.08 mm
Edge: Reeded
Die Axis: ↑↑
Finish: Proof
Case of Issue: Maroon leatherette case, black flocked interior, encapsulated coins, COA

1953-1964

1953

1965-1989

1954-1958

1990-2003

1959-1996

2003-2004

1997-2004

DATE	DESCRIPTION	QUANTITY SOLD	ISSUE PRICE	FINISH	PR-67 UHC	PR-68 UHC
2004	Laureate Portrait	—	—	Proof	20.	30.
2004	Tiara Portrait	—	—	Proof	20.	30.
2004	Royal Diademed Portrait	—	—	Proof	20.	30.
2004	Uncrowned Portrait	—	—	Proof	20.	30.
2004	Total coins	12,230	—	Proof	—	—
2004	Total Sets	3,057	79.95	Proof	65.	—

FIFTY CENT HISTORICAL COMMEMORATIVE SERIES, 1998-2008 (cont.)

FIFTY CENTS, ROYAL CANADIAN MINT ANNUAL REPORT, SELECTIVELY GOLD PLATED, 2006.

This sterling silver gold-plated 50¢ coin dated 2006 was issued in 2007 with the 2006 Royal Canadian Mint Annual Report. This was the last year a coin was combined with the Royal Canadian Mint Report.

Designers and Engravers:
Obv.: Susanna Blunt, Susan Taylor
Rev.: C. Bursey-Sabourin
Composition: 92.5% Ag, 7.5% Cu
Silver content: 8.603 g, 0.277 tr oz
Weight: 9.30 g
Diameter: 27.12 mm
Thickness: 1.85 mm
Edge: Reeded
Die Axis: ↑↑
Finish: Proof, Selectively gold plated
Case of Issue: 2006 Royal Canadian Mint Report

DATE	DESCRIPTION	QUANTITY SOLD	ISSUE PRICE	FINISH	PR-67 UHC	PR-68 UHC
2006	RCM Annual Report	4,162	25.95	Proof	40.	50.

FIFTY CENTS, 100TH ANNIVERSARY OF THE ROYAL CANADIAN MINT, 1908-2008.

This fifty cent coin is from the Coin and Stamp Set issued in 2008 to commemorate the 100th anniversary of the Royal Canadian Mint. It was also issued with the 2008 Royal Canadian Mint Centennial Book.

Designers and Engravers:
Obv.: Susanna Blunt, Susan Taylor
Rev.: RCM Staff
Composition: 92.5% Ag, 7.5% Cu
Silver content: 10.915 g, 0.351 tr oz
Weight: 11.8 g
Diameter: 29.72 mm
Thickness: 2.0 mm
Edge: Reeded
Die Axis: ↑↑
Finish: Proof
Case of Issue: Wooden case with plaque, flock insert, encapsulated coin, COA

DATE	DESCRIPTION	QUANTITY SOLD	ISSUE PRICE	FINISH	PR-67 UHC	PR-68 UHC
2008 (1908-)	100th Anniversary, Royal Canadian Mint	3,248	44.95	Proof	50.	65.

CANADIAN FESTIVALS SERIES, 2001-2003

FIFTY CENTS, CANADIAN FESTIVALS SERIES, 2001-2002.

The Royal Canadian Mint introduced a new series of sterling silver 50-cent coins in 2001 commemorating Canadian Festivals. Each coin represents a Canadian Province, Territory or Community, celebrating it's culture, history and traditions with colourful festivals. The 13-coin set was issued over three years, starting in 2001 and ending 2003. and was available by subscription in 2001 for $249.95 with coins being shipped as they became available.

Designers:
Obv.: Dora de Pédery-Hunt
Rev.: See below

Engravers:
Obv.: Dora de Pédery-Hunt
Rev.: See reverse illustration

Composition: 92.5% Ag, 7.5% Cu
Silver content: 8.603 g, 0.277 tr oz
Weight: 9.30 g
Diameter: 27.13 mm
Thickness: 2.08 mm
Edge: Reeded
Die Axis: ↑↑
Finish: Proof
Case of Issue: A: Singles; Multicoloured printed card folder with encapsulated coin.
B: Thirteen coin set; Canadian Festivals subscription coffee table book.

ISSUES OF 2001.

Common Obverse

**Coin No. 1
Quebec Winter Carnival
(Quebec)
S. Daigneault/S. Witten**

**Coin No. 2
Toonik Tyme
(Nunavut)
J. Mardon, J. Osio**

**Coin No. 3
Newfoundland and
Labrador Folk Festival
(Newfoundland)
D. Craig, C. Saffioti**

**Coin No. 4
Festival of Fathers
(Prince Edward Island)
B. Whiteway,
W. Woodruff**

ISSUES OF 2002.

**Coin No. 5
Annapolis Valley
Blossom Festival
(Nova Scotia)
B. Ross, J. Osio**

**Coin No. 6
Stratford Festival
of Canada
(Ontario)
L. McGaw, S. Taylor**

**Coin No. 7
Folklorama
(Manitoba)
William Woodruff**

**Coin No. 8
Calgary Stampede
(Alberta)
M. Grant, S. Witten**

**Coin No. 9
Squamish Days
Logger Sports
(British Columbia)
José Osio**

DATE	COIN No.	DESCRIPTION	QUANTITY SOLD	ISSUE PRICE	FINISH	PR-67 UHC	PR-68 UHC
2001	1	Quebec	1. Total	21.95	Proof	30.	40.
2001	2	Nunavut	mintage	21.95	Proof	30.	40.
2001	3	Newfoundland	all coins	21.95	Proof	30.	40.
2001	4	Prince Edward Island	58,123	21.95	Proof	30.	40.
2002	5	Nova Scotia	2. Total	21.95	Proof	30.	40.
2002	6	Ontario	mintage	21.95	Proof	30.	40.
2002	7	Manitoba	all	21.95	Proof	30.	40.
2002	8	Alberta	coins	21.95	Proof	30.	40.
2002	9	British Columbia	61,900	21.95	Proof	30.	40.

FIFTY CENTS, CANADIAN FESTIVALS SERIES, 2003.

The third issue in the 13-coin set commemorates festivals across Canada.

Designers:
Obv.: Dora de Pédery-Hunt
Rev.: See below

Engravers:
Obv.: Dora de Pédery-Hunt
Rev.: See reverse illustration

Composition: 92.5% Ag, 7.5% Cu
Silver content: 8.603 g, 0.277 tr oz
Weight: 9.30 g
Diameter: 27.13 mm
Thickness: 2.08 mm
Edge: Reeded
Die Axis: ↑↑
Finish: Proof
Case of Issue: A: Singles; Multicoloured printed card folder with encapsulated coin.
B: Thirteen coin set; Canadian Festivals subscription coffee table book.

ISSUES OF 2003.

Common obverse

Coin No. 10
Yukon Festival
(Yukon)
Ken Anderson
José Osio

Coin No. 11
Back to Batoche
(Saskatchewan)
David Hannan
Stan Witten

Coin No. 12
Great Northern
Arts Festival
(Inuvik)
Dawn Oman
Susan Taylor

Coin No. 13
Festival Acadien de
Caraquet
(New Brunswick)
Hudson Design Group
Susan Taylor

DATE	COIN No.	DESCRIPTION	QUANTITY SOLD	ISSUE PRICE	FINISH	PR-67 UHC	PR-68 UHC
2003	10	Yukon	Total	21.95	Proof	30.	40.
2003	11	Saskatchewan	mintage	21.95	Proof	30.	40.
2003	12	Inuvik	all coins	21.95	Proof	30.	40.
2003	13	New Brunswick	26,451	21.95	Proof	30.	40.
2001-2003	—	Set of 13 coins	—	249.95	Proof	200.	—

CANADA'S FOLKLORE AND LEGENDS SERIES

FIFTY CENTS, CANADA'S FOLKLORE AND LEGENDS SERIES, 2001-2002.

A new series of 50-cent sterling silver coins celebrates Canadian Folklore and Legends. Official release date was April 11, 2001.

Designers:
Obv.: Dora de Pédery-Hunt
Rev.: See below

Engravers:
Obv.: Dora de Pédery-Hunt
Rev.: See reverse illustration

Composition: 92.5% Ag, 7.5% Cu
Silver content: 8.603 g, 0.277 tr oz
Weight: 9.30 g
Diameter: 27.13 mm
Thickness: 2.08 mm
Edge: Reeded
Die Axis: ↑↑
Finish: Proof
Case of Issue: Multicoloured printed card folder with encapsulated coin.

ISSUES OF 2001

Common Obverse

Coin No. 1
The Sled
Valentina Hotz-Entin
Susan Taylor

Coin No. 2
The Maiden's Cave
Peter Kiss
Susan Taylor

Coin No. 3
Les Petits Sauteux
Miyuki Tanobe
José Osio

DATE	COIN No.	DESCRIPTION	QUANTITY SOLD	ISSUE PRICE	FINISH	PR-67 UHC	PR-68 UHC
2001	1	The Sled	Mintage	24.95	Proof	25.	40.
2001	2	The Maiden's Cave	2001 coins	24.95	Proof	25.	40.
2001	3	Les Petits Sauteux	28,979	24.95	Proof	25.	40.

ISSUES OF 2002

Common Obverse

Coin No. 4
The Pig That Wouldn't Get Over the Stile
Laura Jolicoeur
José Osio

Coin No. 5
Shoemaker in Heaven
Francine Gravel
Cosme Saffioti

Coin No. 6
Le Vaisseau Fantome
Colette Boivin
William Woodruff

DATE	COIN No.	DESCRIPTION	QUANTITY SOLD	ISSUE PRICE	FINISH	PR-67 UHC	PR-68 UHC
2002	4	The Pig That Wouldn't Get Over the Stile	Mintage	24.95	Proof	25.	40.
2002	5	Shoemaker in Heaven	2002 coins	24.95	Proof	25.	40.
2002	6	Le Vaisseau Fantome	19,789	24.95	Proof	25.	40.

CANADA'S GOLDEN FLOWER SERIES

FIFTY CENTS, CANADA'S GOLDEN FLOWER SERIES, 2002-2007.

Beginning in 2002 the Royal Canadian Mint issued a series of sterling silver, selectively gold plated proof fifty cent coins to commemorate different events which had a floral theme.

2002 and 2003
Common obverse

2002
50th Anniversary of the Canadian Tulip Festival
Anthony Testa
Stan Witten

2003
Golden Daffodil
Symbol of Hope
Christie Paquet
Stan Witten

Designers and Engravers:
2002-2003
Obv.: Dora de Pédery-Hunt
Rev.: See reverse illustration
2004-2007
Obv.: Susanna Blunt
Susan Taylor
Rev.: See reverse illustration

Composition: 92.5% Ag, 7.5% Cu, 22-karat gold plate on design
Silver content: 8.603 g, 0.277 tr oz
Weight: 9.30 g
Diameter: 27.13 mm
Thickness: 2.16 mm
Edge: Reeded
Die Axis: ↑↑
Finish: Proof, Selectively gold plated

2004 and 2007
Common obverse

2004
Golden Easter Lily
Christie Paquet
Stan Witten

2005
Golden Rose
Christie Paquet

2006
Golden Daisy
Christie Paquet

2007
Golden Forget-Me-Not
Christie Paquet

Cases of Issue: 2002-2004: Folders dated 2002, 2003 and 2004, encapsulated coin
2005-2006: Maroon plastic display case, black plastic insert, encapsulated coin, COA
2007: Maroon clam style case, black flocked insert, encapsulated coin, COA

DATE	DESCRIPTION	QUANTITY SOLD	ISSUE PRICE	FINISH	PR-67 UHC	PR-68 UHC
2002	Canadian Tulip Festival, 50th Anniversary	19,986	24.95	Proof	75.	100.
2003	Golden Daffodil, Symbol of Hope	36,293	34.95	Proof	40.	60.
2004	Golden Easter Lily	24,495	34.95	Proof	40.	60.
2005	Golden Rose	17,418	34.95	Proof	50.	70.
2006	Golden Daisy	18,190	36.95	Proof	45.	65.
2007	Golden Forget-Me-Mot	10,845	38.95	Proof	45.	65.

CANADIAN BUTTERFLY COLLECTION

FIFTY CENTS, CANADIAN BUTTERFLY COLLECTION, 2004-2006.

This series on Canada's butterflies contains the first hologram fifty cent coin.

Designers:
Obv.: Susanna Blunt
Rev.: See below

Engravers:
Obv.: Susan Taylor
Rev.: See reverse illustration

Composition: 92.5% Ag, 7.5% Cu
Silver content: 8.603 g, 0.277 tr oz
Weight: 9.30 g
Diameter: 27.13 mm
Thickness: 2.08 mm
Edge: Reeded
Die Axis: ↑↑
Finish: Proof, Decal, Hologram, Selectively gold plated
Cases of Issue: 2004: Red leatherette clam style case, black flocked insert, encapsulated coin, COA
2005-2006: Maroon plastic display case, black plastic insert, encapsulated coin, COA

Common Obverse

2004
Canadian Tiger Swallowtail Butterfly
Designer: Jianping Yan
Engraver: RCM Staff

2004
Canadian Clouded Sulphur Butterfly
Designer: Susan Taylor
Engraver: Susan Taylor

2005
Monarch Butterfly
Designer: Susan Taylor
Engraver: Susan Taylor

2005
Spangled Fritillary Butterfly
Designer: Jianping Yan
Engraver: Jianping Yan

2006
Short-tailed Swallowtail Butterfly
Designer: Susan Taylor
Engraver: Susan Taylor

2006
Silvery Blue Butterfly
Designer: Jianping Yan
Engraver: Jianping Yan

DATE	DESCRIPTION	QUANTITY SOLD	ISSUE PRICE	FINISH	PR-67 UHC	PR-68 UHC
2004	Canadian Tiger Swallowtail Butterfly, Hologram	20,462	39.95	Proof	45.	70.
2004	Canadian Clouded Sulphur Butterfly, Selectively gold plated	15,281	39.95	Proof	45.	70.
2005	Monarch Butterfly, Decal	35,950	39.95	Proof	45.	70.
2005	Spangled Fritillary Butterfly, Hologram	Incl. above	39.95	Proof	45.	70.
2006	Short-tailed Swallowtail Butterfly, Decal	24,568	39.95	Proof	45.	70.
2006	Silvery Blue Butterfly, Hologram	Incl. above	39.95	Proof	45.	70.

SECOND WORLD WAR SERIES

FIFTY CENTS, QUEST FOR PEACE AND FREEDOM DURING THE SECOND WORLD WAR, 2005.

The 60th anniversary of the end of World War II, 1945-2005, and the part Canada played, are commemorated in this six coin sterling silver set. The coins were issued one per month from May 2005 to October 2005.

Common Obverse

Designers:
Obv.: Susanna Blunt
Rev.: Peter Mossman
Composition: 92.5% Ag, 7.5% Cu
Silver content: 8.603 g, 0.277 tr oz
Weight: 9.30 g
Diameter: 27.13 mm
Thickness: 2.08 mm
Case of Issue: Red leatherette case, black flocked insert, encapsulated coin, COA

Engravers:
Obv.: Susan Taylor
Rev.: José Osio
Edge: Reeded
Die Axis: ↑↑
Finish: Specimen

Battle of Britain
October 1940

Liberation of the Netherlands
September 1944

Conquest of Sicily
August 1943

Battle of the Scheldt
November 1944

Raid on Dieppe
August 1942

Battle of the Atlantic
1939-1945

DATE	DESCRIPTION	ISSUE DATE	QUANTITY SOLD	ISSUE PRICE	FINISH	SP-66	SP-67
2005	Battle of Britain	May	20,000	—	Specimen	40.	50.
2005	Liberation of the Netherlands	June	20,000	—	Specimen	40.	50.
2005	Conquest of Sicily	July	20,000	—	Specimen	40.	50.
2005	Battle of the Scheldt	August	20,000	—	Specimen	40.	50.
2005	Raid on Dieppe	September	20,000	—	Specimen	40.	50.
2005	Battle of the Atlantic	October	20,000	—	Specimen	40.	50.
2005	Set of 6 coins and display case	—	20,000	149.95	Specimen	200.	—

NHL HOCKEY SERIES, 2005-2010

Over the years 2005-2010 the Royal Canadian Mint issued many coins, mostly giftware, commemorating the Canadian teams of the National Hockey League.

FIFTY CENTS, NHL HOCKEY LEGENDS, 2005.

Hockey greats are commemorated on this legends series, issued in sets of four coins each: Jean Beliveau, Guy Lafleur, Jacques Plante and Maurice Richard of the Montreal Canadiens, and Johnny Bower, Tim Horton, Darryl Sittler and Dave Keon of the Toronto Maple Leafs.

Common Obverse

Designers:
Obv.: Susanna Blunt
Rev.: RCM Staff

Engravers:
Obv.: Susan Taylor
Rev.: RCM Staff

Composition: 92.5% Ag, 7.5% Cu
Silver content: 8.603 g, 0.277 tr oz
Weight: 9.30 g
Diameter: 27.13 mm
Thickness: 2.08 mm
Edge: Reeded
Die Axis: ↑↑
Finish: Specimen, Painted
Case of Issue: Maroon plastic display case, black plastic insert, encapsulated coin, COA

2005 MONTREAL CANADIENS

Jean Beliveau

Guy Lafleur

Jacques Plante

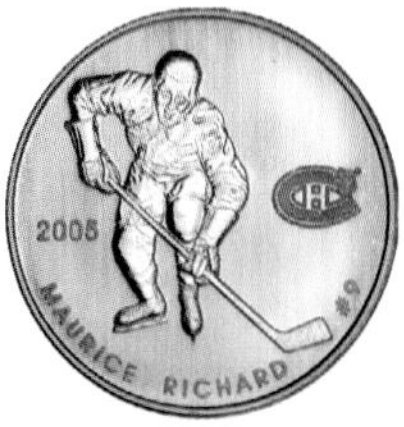

Maurice Richard

DATE	DESCRIPTION	QUANTITY SOLD	ISSUE PRICE	FINISH	SP-66	SP-67
2005	Jean Beliveau	N/A	N.I.I.	Specimen	35.	50.
2005	Guy Lafleur	N/A	N.I.I.	Specimen	35.	50.
2005	Jacques Plante	N/A	N.I.I.	Specimen	35.	50.
2005	Maurice Richard	N/A	N.I.I.	Specimen	35.	50.
2005	Set of 4 coins (Montreal)	N/A	99.95	Specimen	125.	—

2005 TORONTO MAPLE LEAFS

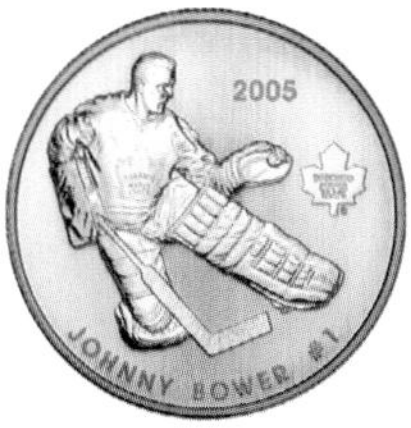

Johnny Bower

Tim Horton

Darryl Sittler

Dave Keon

DATE	DESCRIPTION	QUANTITY SOLD	ISSUE PRICE	FINISH	SP-66	SP-67
2005	Johnny Bower	N/A	N.I.I.	Specimen	35.	50.
2005	Tim Horton	N/A	N.I.I.	Specimen	35.	50.
2005	Darryl Sittler	N/A	N.I.I.	Specimen	35.	50.
2005	Dave Keon	N/A	N.I.I.	Specimen	35.	50.
2005	Set of 4 coins (Toronto)	N/A	99.95	Specimen	125.	—

Note: The Royal Canadian Mint Report of 2005 lists the quantity sold as 11,765 total sets.

NHL HOCKEY SERIES, 2005-2010 (cont.)

FIFTY CENTS, 2008-2009 NHL SEASON, 2009 (GIFTWARE).

The fifty cent issues for the 2008-2009 Hockey Season were embedded in an official NHL puck and then blister packed. Each coin has a lenticular (dual image) reverse which by rotating the coin transfers from the old to the new team logo.

Designers:
Obv.: Susanna Blunt
Rev.: Logos of the NHL
Composition: Nickel plated steel, Lenticular
Weight: 6.90 g
Diameter: 35.0 mm
Finish: Specimen, Lenticular
Case of Issue: Blister packaged

Engravers:
Obv.: Susan Taylor
Rev.: Logos of the NHL
Thickness: 2.0 mm
Edge: Plain
Die Axis: ↑↑

2009 HOCKEY PUCKS

Common Obverse

Calgary Flames

Edmonton Oilers

Montreal Canadiens

Ottawa Senators

Toronto Maple Leafs

Vancouver Canucks

DATE	DESCRIPTION	QUANTITY SOLD	ISSUE PRICE	FINISH	MS-65 NC
2009	Calgary Flames	270	24.95	Specimen	25.
2009	Edmonton Oilers	248	24.95	Specimen	25.
2009	Montreal Canadiens	1,266	24.95	Specimen	25.
2009	Ottawa Senators	310	24.95	Specimen	25.
2009	Toronto Maple Leafs	606	24.95	Specimen	25.
2009	Vancouver Canucks	318	24.95	Specimen	25.

NHL HOCKEY SERIES, 2005-2010 (cont.)

FIFTY CENTS, MONTREAL CANADIENS CENTENNIAL COIN SERIES, 1909-2009 (GIFTWARE).

In 2009 the 100th anniversary of the Montreal Canadiens hockey club was commemorated with six giftware fifty cent coins displaying the hockey jerseys worn by the Montreal players over the last 100 years. Each coin is sealed within a plastic sport card.

Designers:
Obv.: Susanna Blunt
Rev.: Logos of the NHL
Composition: Nickel plated steel, colourised
Weight: N/A
Diameter: 30.0 mm
Finish: Speciman, Decal

Engravers:
Obv.: Susan Taylor
Rev.: Logos of the NHL
Thickness: N/A
Edge: Plain
Die Axis: ↑↑
Case of Issue: Collector Card

2009 MONTREAL CANADIENS CENTENNIAL

Common Obverse

Coin No. 1
Montreal Canadiens
Home Jersey

Coin No. 2
1945-1946
Montreal Canadiens
Road Jersey

Coin No. 3
1915-1916
Le Club de
Hockey Canadiens

Coin No. 4
1912-1913
"CAC"

Coin No 5
1910-1911
Club Athletique
Canadien

Coin No 6
1909-1910
Club de Hockey
le Canadien

DATE	DESCRIPTION	QUANTITY SOLD	ISSUE PRICE	FINISH	MS-65 NC
2009 (1909-)	Montreal Canadiens Home Jersey	N/A	9.99	Specimen	15.
2009 (1909-)	Montreal Canadiens Road Jersey	N/A	9.99	Specimen	15.
2009 (1909-)	Le Club de Hockey Canadiens	N/A	9.99	Specimen	15.
2009 (1909-)	"CAC"	25,016	9.99	Specimen	15.
2009 (1909-)	Club Athletique Canadien	25,004	9.99	Specimen	15.
2009 (1909-)	Club de Hockey le Canadien	25,004	9.99	Specimen	15.
2009 (1909-)	Complete Set, 6 coins and an album	496	59.95	Specimen	60.

NOTE FOR COLLECTORS

1. Single Collector Cards were issued by Jean Coutu, while the Royal Canadian Mint issued only complete sets.
2. Quantity sold figures are incomplete due to year-end overruns.

NHL HOCKEY SERIES, 2005-2010 (cont.)

FIFTY CENTS, 2009-2010 NHL SEASON, 2009-2010 (GIFTWARE).

Designers:
Obv.: Susanna Blunt
Rev.: RCM Staff
Composition: Nickel plated steel, colourised
Weight: 12.90 g
Diameter: 35.0 mm
Finish: Specimen, Decal

Engravers:
Obv.: Susan Taylor
Rev.: RCM Staff
Thickness: 2.0 mm
Edge: Plain
Die Axis: ↑↑
Case of Issue: Tent Card

2009-2010 NHL SEASON

Common Obverse

Calgary Flames

Edmonton Oilers

Montreal Canadiens

Ottawa Senators

Toronto Maple Leafs

Vancouver Canucks

DATE	DESCRIPTION	QUANTITY SOLD	ISSUE PRICE	FINISH	MS-65 NC
2009-2010	Calgary Flames	3,518	14.95	Specimen	15.
2009-2010	Edmonton Oilers	3,562	14.95	Specimen	15.
2009-2010	Montreal Canadiens	9,865	14.95	Specimen	15.
2009-2010	Ottawa Senators	3,293	14.95	Specimen	15.
2009-2010	Toronto Maple Leafs	5,981	14.95	Specimen	15.
2009-2010	Vancouver Canucks	3,563	14.95	Specimen	15.

HOLIDAY LENTICULAR SERIES, 2007-2010

FIFTY CENTS, HOLIDAY LENTICULAR SERIES, 2007-2010 (GIFTWARE).

Beginning in 2007 a large size fifty-cent lenticular coin was issued for the Holiday Season gift market.

Designers:
Obv.: Susanna Blunt
Rev.: C. Bursey-Sabourin

Engravers:
Obv.: Susan Taylor
Rev.: RCM Staff

Composition: 2007-2009: Brass plated steel
2010: Copper plated steel

Weight: 12.61 g
Diameter: 35.00 mm
Thickness: 2.00 mm
Edge: Plain
Die Axis: ↑↑
Finish: Specimen, Lenticular

Case of Issue: 2007-2008, 2010: Maroon leatherette clam style case, black flocked insert, encapsulated coin, COA
2009: Black leatherette clam style case, black flocked insert, encapsulated coin, COA

2007-2008

Obverse with RCM Logo 2007-2008

2007 Holiday Ornaments

2008 Holiday Snowman

2009-2010

Obverse without RCM Logo 2009-2010

2009 Holiday Toy Train

2010 Santa Claus and the Red-nosed Reindeer

DATE	DESCRIPTION	QUANTITY SOLD	ISSUE PRICE	FINISH	MS-65 NC
2007	Holiday Ornaments	16,989	25.95	Specimen	40.
2008	Holiday Snowman	21,679	25.95	Specimen	50.
2009	Holiday Toy Train	19,103	25.95	Specimen	40.
2010	Santa Claus and the Red-Nosed Reindeer	N/A	26.95	Specimen	30.

TRIANGULAR COIN SERIES, 2008-2009

FIFTY CENTS (triangular), MILK DELIVERY, 2008.

From the late 19th century to the middle of the 20th century milk and other dairy products were delivered to the home by a milkman who was paid by a token previously purchased.

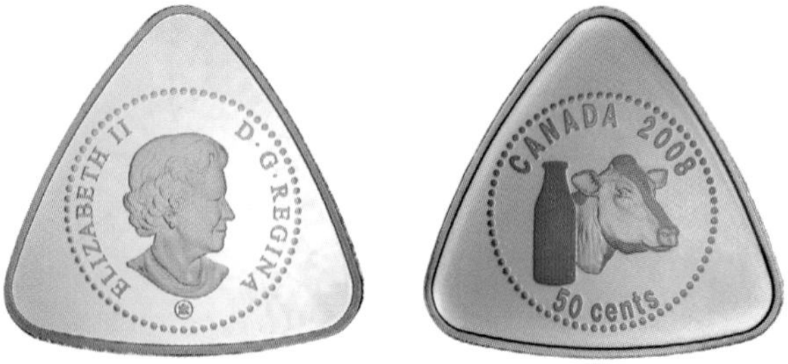

Designers and Engravers:
Obv.: Susanna Blunt, Susan Taylor
Rev.: RCM Staff
Composition: 92.5% Ag, 7.5% Cu
Silver content: 18.50 g, 0.595 tr oz
Weight: 20.00 g
Size: 36.0 x 34.06 mm
Thickness: 2.70 mm
Edge: Interrupted serrations
Die Axis: ↑↑
Finish: Proof, enamel effect on reverse
Case: Maroon leatherette clam style case, black flocked insert, encapsulated coin, COA

FIFTY CENTS (triangular), SIX STRING NATION GUITAR, 2009.

Jowi Taylor brought together the rich Canadian Heritage of materials to produce the Six String Nation Guitar. The guitar made its debut on Parliament Hill during the 2006 Canada Day celebrations.

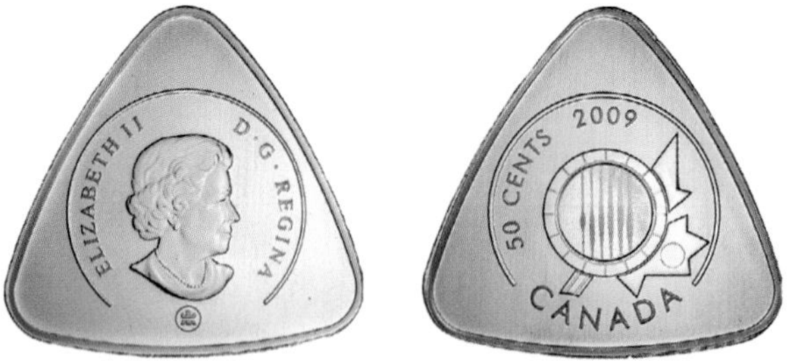

Designers and Engravers:
Obv.: Susanna Blunt, Susan Taylor
Rev.: RCM Staff
Composition: 75% Cu, 25% Ni
Weight: 19.1 g
Size: 36.0 x 34.06 mm
Thickness: 2.70 mm
Edge: Interrupted serration
Die Axis: ↑↑
Finish: Specimen, Selective hologram on reverse
Case: Folder

DATE	DESCRIPTION	QUANTITY SOLD	ISSUE PRICE	FINISH	SP-66	SP-67	PR-67 UHC	PR-68 UHC
2008	Milk Delivery	24,448	49.95	Proof	—	—	50.	60.
2009	Six String Nation Guitar	13,602	34.95	Specimen	50.	60.	—	—

SPECIAL NOTE ON FINISHES

It is very important to understand the different finishes the Royal Canadian Mint uses on their various issues. These finishes are altered from time-to-time as the Mint develops new products.

For example, the brilliant relief against a parallel lined background finish first used on bullion coins was carried forward in 1996 to be used on the coins contained in the specimen set.

In 2006 this finish was used on giftware coins such as the twenty-five cent coin issued to celebrate the 80th birthday of Queen Elizabeth II.

Now, in 2010, we have a new specimen finish (brilliant relief against a laser-lined background) which is used for the coins contained in the specimen set. There are now two different specimen finishes being utilised on Canadian coinage.

Circulation, uncirculated, and brilliant uncirculated (proof-like) finishes are another very confusing mixture of finishes, see page xxiv for a further explanation.

VANCOUVER 2010 OLYMPIC AND PARALYMPIC WINTER GAMES

FIFTY CENTS, MASCOT COLLECTOR CARDS, 2010 (GIFTWARE).

Three mascots were adopted for the Vancouver 2010 Winter Games, Miga and Quatchi for the Olympic Games and Sumi for the Paralympic Games.

These crown-size fifty-cent coins are embedded in plastic within a collector card format. As with all embedded Royal Canadian Mint giftware, the coins are very difficult to remove from their packaging without damaging the image on the coin.

Designers:
Obv.: Susanna Blunt
Rev.: RCM Staff

Engravers:
Obv.: Susan Taylor
Rev.: RCM Staff

Composition: Nickel plated steel
Weight: 12.61 g
Diameter: 35.00 mm
Finish: Specimen, Decal
Thickness: 2.00 mm
Edge: Plain
Die Axis: ↑↑
Case of Issue: Twelve collector cards were issued with the mascots in different sport poses. These coins are embedded in plastic.

Common Obverse

Coin No. 1
Miga Ice Hockey

Coin No. 2
Quatchi Ice Hockey

Coin No. 3
Sumi Paralympic
Ice Sledge Hockey

Coin No. 4
Quatchi and Miga
Figure Skating

Coin No. 5
Quatchi and Miga
Bobsleigh

Coin No. 6
Miga Ariels

Coin No. 7
Miga Skeleton

Coin No. 8
Quatchi Snowboard Cross

VANCOUVER 2010 OLYMPIC AND PARALYMPIC WINTER GAMES (cont.)

FIFTY CENTS, MASCOT COLLECTOR CARDS, 2010 (GIFTWARE) [CONT.].

Common Obverse

Coin No. 9
Miga Alpine Skiing

Coin No. 10
Sumi Paralympic Alpine Skiing

Coin No.11
Quatchi Parallel Giant Slalom

Coin No. 12
Miga Speed Skating

DATE	CARD No.	DESCRIPTION	QUANTITY SOLD	ISSUE PRICE	FINISH	MS-65 NC
2010	1	Miga Ice Hockey	3,096	9.95	Specimen	15.
2010	2	Quatchi Ice Hockey	3,010	9.95	Specimen	15.
2010	3	Sumi Paralympic Ice Sledge Hockey	2,137	9.95	Specimen	15.
2010	4	Quatchi and Miga Figure Skating	2,981	9.95	Specimen	15.
2010	5	Quatchi and Miga Bobsleigh	2,119	9.95	Specimen	15.
2010	6	Miga Ariels	2,114	9.95	Specimen	15.
2010	7	Miga Skeleton	1,672	9.95	Specimen	15.
2010	8	Quatchi Snowboard Cross	2,090	9.95	Specimen	15.
2010	9	Miga Alpine Skiing	2,309	9.95	Specimen	15.
2010	10	Sumi Paralympic Alpine Skiing	1,902	9.95	Specimen	15.
2010	11	Quatchi Parallel Giant Slalom	1,730	9.95	Specimen	15.
2010	12	Miga Speed Skating	1,825	9.95	Specimen	15.
—	—	Collector Card Album	—	12.95	—	15.

Image of Miga Speed Skating courtesy of the Royal Canadian Mint.

VANCOUVER 2010 OLYMPIC AND PARALYMPIC WINTER GAMES (cont.)

FIFTY CENTS, MASCOT HOCKEY PUCKS, 2010.

The Miga, Quatachi, and Sumi Ice Hockey coins also were issued embedded in NHL official hockey pucks.

Miga Ice Hockey

Quatche Ice Hockey

Sumi Ice Hockey

Designers:
Obv.: Susanna Blunt
Rev.: RCM Staff
Composition: Nickel plated steel
Weight: 12.61 g
Diameter: 35.00 mm
Finish: Specimen, Decal
Cases of Issue: Blister packaged

Engravers:
Obv.: Susan Taylor
Rev.: RCM Staff
Thickness: 2.00 mm
Edge: Plain
Die Axis: ↑↑

DATE	CARD No.	DESCRIPTION	QUANTITY SOLD	ISSUE PRICE	FINISH	MS-65 NC
2010	1	Miga Ice Hockey	2,179	25.95	Specimen	30.
2010	2	Quatchi Ice Hockey	2,524	25.95	Specimen	30.
2010	3	Sumi Paralympic Ice Sledge Hockey	1,570	25.95	Specimen	30.

VANCOUVER 2010 OLYMPIC AND PARALYMPIC WINTER GAMES (cont.)

FIFTY CENTS, VANCOUVER 2010 LENTICULAR, 2010 (GIFTWARE).

This fifty cent lenticular coin with images of the Vancouver skyline and Inukshuk is found in the Vancouver 2010 Gold Collector's Set which was issued in conjunction with Canada Post, see page 277.

Designers and Engravers:
Obv.: Susanna Blunt, Susan Taylor
Rev.: RCM Staff
Composition: Nickel plated steel
Weight: 13.0 g
Diameter: 35.0 mm
Thickness: 2.0 mm
Edge: Plain
Die Axis: ↑↑
Finish: Specimen, Lenticular
Case of Issue: See Collector Sets, page 277

DATE	DESCRIPTION	QUANTITY SOLD	ISSUE PRICE	FINISH	MS-65 NC
2010	Lenticular Images of Vancouver and Inukshuk	11,384	N.I.I.	Specimen	50.

DINOSAUR EXHIBIT SERIES

FIFTY CENTS, DINOSAUR EXHIBIT LENTICULAR SERIES, 2010 (GIFTWARE).

The Royal Canadian Mint in conjunction with various Canadian Museums created this new series of lenticular coins featuring prehistoric dinosaurs found in Canada.

Designers:
Obv.: Susanna Blunt
Rev.: RCM Staff
Composition: Brass plated steel
Weight: 12.9 g
Diameter: 35.0 mm
Finish: Specimen, Lenticular
Case of Issue: Folded panel containing six collector trading cards

Engravers:
Obv.: Susan Taylor
Rev.: RCM Staff
Thickness: 2.0 mm
Edge: Plain
Die Axis: ↑↑

Common Obverse

Daspletosaurus Torosus

Albertosaurus

Sinosauropteryx

DATE	DESCRIPTION	QUANTITY SOLD	ISSUE PRICE	FINISH	MS-65 NC
2010	Daspletosaurus Torosus	N/A	24.95	Specimen	25.
2010	Albertosaurus	N/A	24.95	Specimen	25.
2010	Sinosauropteryx	N/A	24.95	Specimen	25.

FIFTY CENT DERIVATIVES

DATE	DESCRIPTION	QUANTITY SOLD	ISSUE PRICE	ISSUER	FINISH	MARKET VALUE
2001	**CANADA PROVINCIAL CREST** Credit Card Type	N/A	N/A	RCM	MS-65	5.
2003	**CORONATION COIN AND STAMP SET** Two one cent coins, 1953 and 2003; Two fifty cent coins, 2002 Jubilee, 2003 Uncrowned Portrait; Two mint and two cancelled stamps of Her Majesty's Jubilee and Coronation; Presentation case	14,743	N/A	RCM	MS-65	50.
2008	**100TH ANNIVERSARY COIN AND STAMP SET** Fifty cent coin, double-dated 1908-2008, fifty-two cent postage stamp, wooden presentation case, booklet	16,000	44.95	RCM/PO	PR-67	50.
2008	**ROYAL CANADIAN MINT CENTENNIAL BOOK** Fifty cent coin, double-dated 1908-2008, postage stamp, 200-page book					
	English	136	99.95	RCM	PR-67	100.
	French	46	99.95	RCM	PR-67	100.
2010	**DASPLETOSAURUS TOROSUS** fifty cent coin, six trading cards, folder	N/A	24.95	RCM	MS-65	25.
2010	**ALBERTOSAURUS**. fifty cent coin, six trading cards, folder	N/A	24.95	RCM	MS-65	25.
2010	**SINOSAUROPTERYX**, fifty cent coin, six trading cards, folder	N/A	24.95	RCM	MS-65	25.

ONE DOLLAR ISSUES

SILVER DOLLAR ISSUES, 1971-2010

ONE DOLLAR, BRITISH COLUMBIA CENTENNIAL, 1871-1971.

The first non-circulating silver dollar was issued to the public in 1971. It commemorates the entry of British Columbia into Confederation in 1871, with the design based upon the provincial arms. The obverse features a modification of the Machin portrait in which the portrait of the Queen was reduced slightly and her hair extensively redone.

Designers and Engravers:
Obv.: Arnold Machin, Patrick Brindley
Rev.: Patrick Brindley
Composition: 50% Ag, 50% Cu
Silver content: 11.65 g, 0.375 tr oz
Weight: 23.30 g **Thickness:** 2.95 mm
Diameter: 36.07 mm **Die Axis:** ↑↑
Edge: Reeded **Finish:** Specimen
Case A: Black leatherette clam style case, Coat of Arms, maroon and black insert
Case B: Black leatherette clam case, Coat of Arms, white and black insert

DATE	DESCRIPTION	QUANTITY SOLD	ISSUE PRICE	FINISH	SP-66	SP-67
1971 (1871-)	British Columbia Centennial	585,217	3.00	Specimen	15.	17.

ONE DOLLAR, VOYAGEUR DESIGN, 1972.

The reverse of the 1972 silver dollar is the voyageur design somewhat modified from its last use on the 1966 silver dollar. One of the most noticeable differences is the substitution of beads for denticles at the rim.

Designers and Engravers:
Obv.: Arnold Machin, Patrick Brindley
Rev.: Emanuel Hahn, Terry Smith
Composition: 50% Ag, 50% Cu
Silver content: 11.65 g, 0.375 tr oz
Weight: 23.30 g **Thickness:** 2.95 mm
Diameter: 36.07 mm **Die Axis:** ↑↑
Edge: Reeded **Finish:** Specimen
Case: Black leatherette clam style case, Coat of Arms, maroon and black insert

DATE	DESCRIPTION	QUANTITY SOLD	ISSUE PRICE	FINISH	SP-66	SP-67
1972	Voyageur	341,581	3.00	Specimen	15.	17.

ONE DOLLAR, ROYAL CANADIAN MOUNTED POLICE CENTENNIAL, 1973.

The reverse of the 1973 silver dollar recognizes the founding of the North West Mounted Police which later became the Royal Canadian Mounted Police.

Designers and Engravers:
Obv.: Arnold Machin, Patrick Brindley
Rev.: Paul Cedarberg, Patrick Brindley
Composition: 50% Ag, 50% Cu
Silver content: 11.65 g, 0.375 tr oz
Weight: 23.30 g **Thickness:** 2.95 mm
Diameter: 36.07 mm **Die Axis:** ↑↑
Edge: Reeded **Finish:** Specimen
Case A: Black leatherette clam style case, Coat of Arms, maroon and black insert
Case B: Blue leatherette clam style case, gilt RCMP crest, maroon and black insert

DATE	DESCRIPTION	QUANTITY SOLD	ISSUE PRICE	FINISH	SP-66	SP-67
1973 (1873-)	R.C.M.P., Case A	904,723	3.00	Specimen	15.	17.
1973 (1873-)	R.C.M.P., Case B	Included	3.00	Specimen	30.	35.

ONE DOLLAR, WINNIPEG CENTENNIAL, 1974.

The 100th anniversary of the establishment of Winnipeg, Manitoba, as a city is marked by the reverse of the 1974 silver dollar. The design is identical to that of the nickel dollar, see page 88.

Designers and Engravers:
Obv.: Arnold Machin, Patrick Brindley
Rev.: Paul Pederson, Patrick Brindley
Composition: 50% Ag, 50% Cu
Silver content: 11.65 g, 0.375 tr oz
Weight: 23.30 g **Thickness:** 2.95 mm
Diameter: 36.07 mm **Die Axis:** ↑↑
Edge: Reeded **Finish:** Specimen
Case: Black leatherette clam style case, Coat of Arms, maroon and black plastic insert, encapsulated coin

DATE	DESCRIPTION	QUANTITY SOLD	ISSUE PRICE	FINISH	SP-66	SP-67
1974 (1874-)	Winnipeg Centennial	628,183	3.50	Specimen	15.	17.

ONE DOLLAR, CALGARY CENTENNIAL, 1975.

For the centenary of the founding of Calgary, Alberta, the silver dollar of 1975 bears a special reverse showing a cowboy atop a bucking bronco. Oil wells and the modern city skyline appear in the background.

Designers and Engravers:
Obv.: Arnold Machin, Patrick Brindley
Rev.: D. D. Paterson, Patrick Brindley
Composition: 50% Ag, 50% Cu
Silver content: 11.65 g, 0.375 tr oz
Weight: 23.30 g **Thickness:** 2.95 mm
Diameter: 36.07 mm **Die Axis:** ↑↑, ↑↓
Edge: Reeded **Finish:** Specimen
Case: Black leatherette clam style case, Coat of Arms maroon and black plastic insert, encapsulated coin

DATE	DESCRIPTION	QUANTITY SOLD	ISSUE PRICE	FINISH	SP-66	SP-67
1975 (1875-)	Calgary Centennial, ↑↑, Medal Axis	833,095	3.50	Specimen	15.	17.
1975 (1875-)	Calgary Centennial, ↑↓, Coinage Axis	Included	3.50	Specimen	Only One	Known

ONE DOLLAR, LIBRARY OF PARLIAMENT, 1976.

The reverse of the 1976 silver dollar commemorates the 100th anniversary of the completion of the Library of Parliament. This attractive building was the only part of the original centre block of the Parliament Buildings that was saved during the disastrous fire of 1916. It is still in use and is a popular tourist attraction in Ottawa.

Designers and Engravers:
Obv.: Arnold Machin, Patrick Brindley
Rev.: Walter Ott
Composition: 50% Ag, 50% Cu
Silver content: 11.65 g, 0.375 tr oz
Weight: 23.30 g **Thickness:** 2.95 mm
Diameter: 36.07 mm **Die Axis:** ↑↑
Edge: Reeded **Finish:** Specimen
Case A: Black leatherette clam style case, Coat of Arms, maroon and black insert, encapsulated coin
Case B: Blue leatherette clam style case, Coat of Arms, light blue insert with purple satin cloth printed "Library of Parliament - Bibliothèque du Parlément 1876-1976"

DATE	DESCRIPTION	QUANTITY SOLD	ISSUE PRICE	FINISH	SP-66	SP-67
1976 (1876-)	Library of Parliament, Case A	483,722	4.00	Specimen	15.	17.
1976 (1876-)	Library of Parliament, Case B	Included	4.00	Specimen	17.	20.

ONE DOLLAR, SILVER JUBILEE ELIZABETH II, 1977.

During 1977 Queen Elizabeth II celebrated the 25th anniversary of her accession to the throne. Many countries, including Canada, recognized the event with a special commemorative coin. The design on the reverse depicts the throne of the Senate of Canada, which is used by the Queen or the Governor General for ceremonial occasions. The obverse was specifically designed for this coin and bears a special legend and the dates 1952-1977.

Designers and Engravers:
Obv.: Arnold Machin, RCM Staff
Rev.: Raymond Lee, Ago Aarand
Composition: 50% Ag, 50% Cu
Silver content: 11.65 g, 0.375 tr oz
Weight: 23.30 g **Thickness:** 2.95 mm
Diameter: 36.07 mm **Die Axis:** ↑↑
Edge: Reeded **Finish:** Specimen
Case A: Black leatherette case, Coat of Arms, maroon and black plastic insert, encapsulated coin
Case B: Maroon leatherette case, Coat of Arms, maroon and black plastic insert, encapsulated coin
Case C: Maroon velveteen case, Coat of Arms, maroon velveteen insert, encapsulated coin

DATE	DESCRIPTION	QUANTITY SOLD	ISSUE PRICE	FINISH	SP-66	SP-67
1977 (1952-)	Elizabeth II Silver Jubilee, Case A	744,848	4.25	Specimen	15.	17.
1977 (1952-)	Elizabeth II Silver Jubilee, Case B	Incl. above	—	Specimen	17.	20.
1977 (1952-)	Elizabeth II Silver Jubilee, Case C	Incl. above	—	Specimen	17.	20.

ONE DOLLAR, 11TH COMMONWEALTH GAMES, EDMONTON, 1978.

The 1978 silver dollar commemorates the 11th Commonwealth Games, held in Edmonton, Alberta, August 3-12 of that year. The reverse design features the symbol of the Games in the centre, and the official symbols of the ten sports which comprise the Games along the perimeter. The obverse was modified specifically for this issue.

Designers and Engravers:
Obv.: Arnold Machin, RCM Staff
Rev.: Raymond Taylor, Victor Coté
Composition: 50% Ag, 50% Cu
Silver content: 11.65 g, 0.375 tr oz
Weight: 23.30 g **Thickness:** 2.95 mm
Diameter: 36.07 mm **Die Axis:** ↑↑
Edge: Reeded **Finish:** Specimen
Case: Black leatherette square case, Coat of Arms, maroon and black plastic insert, encapsulated coin, COA

DATE	DESCRIPTION	QUANTITY SOLD	ISSUE PRICE	FINISH	SP-66	SP-67
1978	Commonwealth Games	640,000	4.50	Specimen	15.	17.

ONE DOLLAR, GRIFFON TRICENTENNIAL, 1679-1979.

The 300th anniversary of the first voyage by a commercial ship on the Great Lakes is commemorated on the reverse of the 1979 silver dollar.

Designers and Engravers:
Obv.: Arnold Machin, Patrick Brindley
Rev.: Walter Schluep, Terry Smith
Composition: 50% Ag, 50% Cu
Silver content: 11.65 g, 0.375 tr oz
Weight: 23.30 g **Thickness:** 2.95 mm
Diameter: 36.07 mm **Die Axis:** ↑↑
Edge: Reeded **Finish:** Specimen
Case: Black leatherette square case, maroon insert, encapsulated coin, COA

DATE	DESCRIPTION	QUANTITY SOLD	ISSUE PRICE	FINISH	SP-66	SP-67
1979 (1679-)	Griffon Tricentennial	688,671	5.50	Specimen	15.	17.

ONE DOLLAR, ARCTIC TERRITORIES CENTENNIAL, 1980.

The 1980 commemorative silver dollar marks the centenary of the transfer of the Arctic islands from the British Government to the Government of the Dominion of Canada.

Designers and Engravers:
Obv.: Arnold Machin, Patrick Brindley
Rev.: D. D. Paterson, Walter Ott
Composition: 50% Ag, 50% Cu
Silver content: 11.65 g, 0.375 tr oz
Weight: 23.30 g **Thickness:** 2.95 mm
Diameter: 36.07 mm **Die Axis:** ↑↑
Edge: Reeded **Finish:** Specimen
Case: Black leatherette square case, maroon insert, encapsulated coin, COA

DATE	DESCRIPTION	QUANTITY SOLD	ISSUE PRICE	FINISH	SP-66	SP-67
1980	Arctic Territories Centennial	389,564	22.00	Specimen	20.	25.

ONE DOLLAR, TRANS-CANADA RAILWAY CENTENNIAL, 1981.

The 1981 silver dollar commemorates the 100th anniversary of the approval by the Canadian government to build the Trans-Canada Railway. This is the first year of issue by the Mint of two different qualities of silver dollars.

Designers and Engravers:
Obv.: Arnold Machin, Patrick Brindley
Rev.: Christopher Gorey, Walter Ott
Composition: 50% Ag, 50% Cu
Silver content: 11.65 g, 0.375 tr oz
Weight: 23.30 g
Diameter: 36.07 mm **Thickness:** 2.95 mm
Edge: Reeded, **Die Axis:** ↑↑
Finish: Proof or Brilliant Uncirculated
Proof: Black leatherette square case, maroon insert, encapsulated coin, COA
BU: Clear plastic outer case, black plastic insert, silver sleeve, encapsulated coin

DATE	DESCRIPTION	QUANTITY SOLD	ISSUE PRICE	FINISH	65	66	67	68
1981	Trans-Canada Railway Centennial	353,742	18.00	Proof	—	—	20.	25.
1981	Trans-Canada Railway Centennial	148,647	14.00	BU	15.	17.	—	—

ONE DOLLAR, REGINA CENTENNIAL, 1982.

This silver dollar commemorates the centennial of the founding of Regina 1882.

Designers and Engravers:
Obv.: Arnold Machin, RCM Staff
Rev.: Huntley Brown, Walter Ott
Composition: 50% Ag, 50% Cu
Silver content: 11.65 g, 0.375 tr oz
Weight: 23.30 g
Diameter: 36.07 mm **Thickness:** 2.95 mm
Edge: Reeded **Die Axis:** ↑↑
Finish: Proof or Brilliant Uncirculated
Proof: Black leatherette square case, maroon insert, encapsulated coin, COA
BU: Clear plastic outer case, black plastic insert, silver sleeve, encapsulated coin

DATE	DESCRIPTION	QUANTITY SOLD	ISSUE PRICE	FINISH	65	66	67	68
1982 (1882-)	Regina Centennial	577,959	15.25	Proof	—	—	15.	17.
1982 (1882-)	Regina Centennial	144,989	10.95	BU	15.	17.	—	—

ONE DOLLAR, WORLD UNIVERSITY GAMES, 1983.

The coin commemorates the World University Games held in Edmonton, Alberta, during July of that year.

Designers and Engravers:
Obv.: Arnold Machin, Patrick Brindley
Rev.: Carola Tietz, Walter Ott
Composition: 50% Ag, 50% Cu
Silver content: 11.65 g, 0.375 tr oz
Weight: 23.30 g
Diameter: 36.07 mm **Thickness:** 2.95 mm
Edge: Reeded **Die Axis:** ↑↑
Finish: Proof or Brilliant Uncirculated
Proof: Black leatherette square case, maroon insert, encapsulated coin, COA
BU: Clear plastic outer case, black plastic insert, silver sleeve, encapsulated coin

DATE	DESCRIPTION	QUANTITY SOLD	ISSUE PRICE	FINISH	65	66	67	68
1983	World University Games	340,068	16.15	Proof	—	—	15.	17.
1983	World University Games	159,450	10.95	BU	15.	17.	—	—

ONE DOLLAR, TORONTO SESQUICENTENNIAL, 1984.

The 1984 silver dollar commemorates the 150th anniversary of the incorporation of the City of Toronto in 1834.

Designers and Engravers:
Obv.: Arnold Machin, Patrick Brindley
Rev.: D. J. Craig, Walter Ott
Composition: 50% Ag, 50% Cu
Silver content: 11.65 g, 0.375 tr oz
Weight: 23.30 g
Diameter: 36.07 mm **Thickness:** 2.95 mm
Edge: Reeded **Die Axis:** ↑↑
Finish: Proof or Brilliant Uncirculated
Proof: Black leatherette square case, maroon insert, encapsulated coin, COA
BU: Clear plastic outer case, black plastic insert, silver sleeve, encapsulated coin

DATE	DESCRIPTION	QUANTITY SOLD	ISSUE PRICE	FINISH	65	66	67	68
1984 (1834-)	Toronto Sesquicentennial	571,563	17.50	Proof	—	—	15.	17.
1984 (1834-)	Toronto Sesquicentennial	133,563	11.40	BU	15.	17.	—	—

ONE DOLLAR, NATIONAL PARKS CENTENNIAL, 1985.

The 1985 silver dollar commemorates the 100th anniversary of an important part of Canada's heritage, the National Parks.

Designers and Engravers:
Obv.: Arnold Machin, Patrick Brindley
Rev.: Karel Rohlicek, Walter Ott
Composition: 50% Ag, 50% Cu
Silver content: 11.65 g, 0.375 tr oz
Weight: 23.30 g
Diameter: 36.07 mm **Thickness:** 2.95 mm
Edge: Reeded **Die Axis:** ↑↑
Finish: Proof or Brilliant Uncirculated
Proof: Black leatherette square case, maroon insert, encapsulated coin, COA
BU: Clear plastic outer case, black plastic insert, silver sleeve, encapsulated coin

DATE	DESCRIPTION	QUANTITY SOLD	ISSUE PRICE	FINISH	65	66	67	68
1985 (1885-)	National Parks Centennial	537,297	17.50	Proof	—	—	15.	17.
1985 (1885-)	National Parks Centennial	162,873	12.00	BU	15.	17.	—	—

ONE DOLLAR, VANCOUVER CENTENNIAL, 1986.

This coin commemorates the 100th anniversary of the founding of Vancouver and the arrival of the first trans-Canada train in Vancouver. Canadian Pacific Engine No. 371 was the first to arrive, in 1886.

Designers and Engravers:
Obv.: Arnold Machin, Patrick Brindley
Rev.: E. J. Morrison, Victor Coté, Walter Ott
Composition: 50% Ag, 50% Cu
Silver content: 11.65 g, 0.375 tr oz
Weight: 23.30 g
Diameter: 36.07 mm **Thickness:** 2.95 mm
Edge: Reeded **Die Axis:** ↑↑
Finish: Proof or Brilliant Uncirculated
Proof: Black leatherette square case, maroon insert, encapsulated coin, COA
BU: Clear plastic outer case, black plastic insert, silver sleeve, encapsulated coin

DATE	DESCRIPTION	QUANTITY SOLD	ISSUE PRICE	FINISH	65	66	67	68
1986 (1886-)	Vancouver Centennial	496,418	18.00	Proof	—	—	15.	17.
1986 (1886-)	Vancouver Centennial	124,574	12.25	BU	15.	17.	—	—

ONE DOLLAR, JOHN DAVIS, 1987.

This coin commemorates the 400th anniversary of John Davis' historic expedition in search of the North West Passage.

Designers and Engravers:
Obv.: Arnold Machin, Patrick Brindley
Rev.: Christopher Gorey, Victor Coté
Composition: 50% Ag, 50% Cu
Silver content: 11.65 g, 0.375 tr oz
Weight: 23.30 g
Diameter: 36.07 mm **Thickness:** 2.95 mm
Edge: Reeded **Die Axis:** ↑↑
Finish: Proof or Brilliant Uncirculated
Proof: Black leatherette square case, maroon insert, encapsulated coin, COA
BU: Clear plastic outer case, black plastic insert, silver sleeve, encapsulated coin

DATE	DESCRIPTION	QUANTITY SOLD	ISSUE PRICE	FINISH	65	66	67	68
1987 (1587-)	John Davis	405,688	19.00	Proof	—	—	15.	17.
1987 (1587-)	John Davis	118,722	14.00	BU	15.	17.	—	—

ONE DOLLAR, SAINT-MAURICE IRONWORKS, 1988.

This coin commemorates the 250th anniversary of the Saint-Maurice Ironworks, Canada's first heavy industry.

Designers and Engravers:
Obv.: Arnold Machin, Patrick Brindley
Rev.: R. R. Carmichael, Sheldon Beveridge
Composition: 50% Ag, 50% Cu
Silver content: 11.65 g, 0.375 tr oz
Weight: 23.30 g
Diameter: 36.07 mm **Thickness:** 2.95 mm
Edge: Reeded **Die Axis:** ↑↑
Finish: Proof or Brilliant Uncirculated
Proof: Black leatherette square case, maroon insert, encapsulated coin, COA
BU: Clear plastic outer case, black plastic insert, silver sleeve, encapsulated coin

DATE	DESCRIPTION	QUANTITY SOLD	ISSUE PRICE	FINISH	65	66	67	68
1988	Saint-Maurice Ironworks	259,230	20.00	Proof	—	—	15.	17.
1988	Saint-Maurice Ironworks	106,702	15.00	BU	15.	17.	—	—

ONE DOLLAR, MACKENZIE RIVER BICENTENNIAL, 1989.

The bicentennial of the first full length voyage of the Mackenzie River by Alexander Mackenzie and his European crew, all the way to the Arctic Ocean, is commemorated on the 1989 silver dollar.

Designers and Engravers:
Obv.: Arnold Machin, Patrick Brindley
Rev.: John Mardon, Sheldon Beveridge
Composition: 50% Ag, 50% Cu
Silver content: 11.65 g, 0.375 tr oz
Weight: 23.30 g
Diameter: 36.07 mm **Thickness:** 2.95 mm
Edge: Reeded **Die Axis:** ↑↑
Finish: Proof or Brilliant Uncirculated
Proof: Black leatherette square case, maroon insert, encapsulated coin, COA
BU: Clear plastic outer case, black plastic insert, silver sleeve, encapsulated coin

DATE	DESCRIPTION	QUANTITY SOLD	ISSUE PRICE	FINISH	65	66	67	68
1989	Mackenzie River Bicentennial	272,319	21.75	Proof	—	—	25.	30.
1989	Mackenzie River Bicentennial	110,650	16.25	BU	15.	17.	—	—

ONE DOLLAR, HENRY KELSEY TRICENTENNIAL, 1990.

The 300th anniversary of Henry Kelsey's ventures into the Canadian West is commemorated on the 1990 silver dollar.

Designers and Engravers:
Obv.: Dora de Pédery-Hunt
Rev.: D. J. Craig, Ago Aarand
Composition: 50% Ag, 50% Cu
Silver content: 11.65 g, 0.375 tr oz
Weight: 23.30 g
Diameter: 36.07 mm **Thickness:** 2.95 mm
Edge: Reeded **Die Axis:** ↑↑
Finish: Proof or Brilliant Uncirculated
Proof: Black leatherette square case, maroon insert, encapsulated coin, COA
BU: Clear plastic outer case, black plastic insert, silver sleeve, encapsulated coin

DATE	DESCRIPTION	QUANTITY SOLD	ISSUE PRICE	FINISH	65	66	67	68
1990 (1690-)	Henry Kelsey Tricentennial	222,983	22.95	Proof	—	—	25.	30.
1990 (1690-)	Henry Kelsey Tricentennial	85,763	16.75	BU	15.	17.	—	—

ONE DOLLAR, 175TH ANNIVERSARY OF THE FRONTENAC, 1991.

The 1991 silver dollar commemorates the 175th anniversary of the first steamship to sail on the Great Lakes. Built by a partnership of Kingston merchants in 1816, the Frontenac established a regular passenger and freight route between Prescott and Burlington by 1817, thus becoming the first Canadian steamship to operate on Lake Ontario.

Designers and Engravers:
Obv.: Dora de Pédery-Hunt
Rev.: D. J. Craig, Sheldon Beveridge
Composition: 50% Ag, 50% Cu
Silver content: 11.65 g, 0.375 tr oz
Weight: 23.30 g
Diameter: 36.07 mm **Thickness:** 2.95 mm
Edge: Reeded **Die Axis:** ↑↑
Finish: Proof or Brilliant Uncirculated
Proof: Black leatherette square case, maroon insert, encapsulated coin, COA
BU: Clear plastic outer case, black plastic insert, silver sleeve, encapsulated coin

DATE	DESCRIPTION	QUANTITY SOLD	ISSUE PRICE	FINISH	65	66	67	68
1991 (1816-)	175th Anniversary of the Frontenac	222,892	22.95	Proof	—	—	25.	30.
1991 (1816-)	175th Anniversary of the Frontenac	82,642	16.75	BU	15.	17.	—	—

ONE DOLLAR, KINGSTON TO YORK STAGECOACH, 1992.

The coin commemorates the 175th anniversary of the first stage coach service between Kingston and York in January 1817. Samuel Purdy was only able to maintain regular service during the winter months, hence the sleigh with runners. This is the first issue of a dollar coin in sterling silver since the pattern dollar was struck in London by the Royal Mint in 1911.

Designers and Engravers:
Obv.: Dora de Pédery-Hunt
Rev.: Karsten Smith, Susan Taylor
Composition: 92.5 Ag, 7.5% Cu
Silver content: 23.29 g, 0.75 tr oz
Weight: 25.175 g
Diameter: 36.07 mm **Thickness:** 2.95 mm
Edge: Reeded **Die Axis:** ↑↑
Finish: Proof or Brilliant Uncirculated
Proof: Black leatherette square case, maroon insert, encapsulated coin, COA
BU: Clear plastic outer case, black plastic insert, silver sleeve, encapsulated coin

DATE	DESCRIPTION	QUANTITY SOLD	ISSUE PRICE	FINISH	65	66	67	68
1992	Kingston to York Stagecoach	187,612	23.95	Proof	—	—	35.	40.
1992	Kingston to York Stagecoach	78,160	17.50	BU	30.	32.	—	—

ONE DOLLAR, 100TH ANNIVERSARY OF THE STANLEY CUP, 1893-1993.

The 1993 silver dollar commemorates the 100th anniversary of the Stanley Cup, first presented during the 1892 - 1893 season to the Montreal Amateur Athletic Association team by Lord Stanley.

Designers and Engravers:
Obv.: Dora de Pédery-Hunt
Rev.: Stewart Sherwood, Sheldon Beveridge
Composition: 92.5 Ag, 7.5% Cu
Silver content: 23.29 g, 0.75 tr oz
Weight: 25.175 g
Diameter: 36.07 mm **Thickness:** 2.95 mm
Edge: Reeded **Die Axis:** ↑↑
Finish: Proof or Brilliant Uncirculated
Proof: Black leatherette square case, maroon insert, encapsulated coin, COA
BU: Clear plastic outer case, black plastic insert, silver sleeve, encapsulated coin

DATE	DESCRIPTION	QUANTITY SOLD	ISSUE PRICE	FINISH	65	66	67	68
1993 (1893-)	100th Anniv. of the Stanley Cup	294,314	23.95	Proof	—	—	40.	45.
1993 (1893-)	100th Anniv. of the Stanley Cup	88,150	17.50	BU	35.	40.	—	—

ONE DOLLAR, R.C.M.P. NORTHERN DOG TEAM PATROL, 1994.

The 1994 silver dollar commemorates the 25th anniversary of the last RCMP Northern Dog Team Patrol.

Designers and Engravers:
Obv.: Dora de Pédery-Hunt
Rev.: Ian Sparkes, Ago Aarand
Composition: 92.5 Ag, 7.5% Cu
Silver content: 23.29 g, 0.75 tr oz
Weight: 25.175 g
Diameter: 36.07 mm **Thickness:** 2.95 mm
Edge: Reeded **Die Axis:** ↑↑
Finish: Proof or Brilliant Uncirculated
Proof: Black leatherette square case, maroon insert, encapsulated coin, COA
BU: Clear plastic outer case, black plastic insert, silver sleeve, encapsulated coin

DATE	DESCRIPTION	QUANTITY SOLD	ISSUE PRICE	FINISH	65	66	67	68
1994 (1969-)	R.C.M.P. Northern Dog Team Patrol	178,485	24.50	Proof	—	—	40.	45.
1994 (1969-)	R.C.M.P. Northern Dog Team Patrol	65,295	17.95	BU	30.	32.	—	—

ONE DOLLAR, 325TH ANNIVERSARY OF THE HUDSON'S BAY COMPANY, 1995.

From 1670 to the current day the history of the Hudson's Bay Company has been intertwined with that of Canada.

Designers and Engravers:
Obv.: Dora de Pédery-Hunt
Rev.: Vincent McIndoe, Susan Taylor
Composition: 92.5 Ag, 7.5% Cu
Silver content: 23.29 g, 0.75 tr oz
Weight: 25.175 g
Diameter: 36.07 mm **Thickness:** 2.95 mm
Edge: Reeded **Die Axis:** ↑↑
Finish: Proof or Brilliant Uncirculated
Proof: Black leatherette square case, maroon insert, encapsulated coin, COA
BU: Clear plastic outer case, black plastic insert, silver sleeve, encapsulated coin

DATE	DESCRIPTION	QUANTITY SOLD	ISSUE PRICE	FINISH	65	66	67	68
1995	325th Anniv. Hudson's Bay Co.	166,259	24.50	Proof	—	—	35.	40.
1995	325th Anniv. Hudson's Bay Co.	61,819	17.95	BU	30.	32.	—	—

ONE DOLLAR, 200TH ANNIVERSARY JOHN MCINTOSH, 1996.

John McIntosh arrived in Canada in 1796 and settled in Ontario. The 1996 silver dollar pays tribute to the originator of Canada's most important commercial apple.

Designers and Engravers:
Obv.: Dora de Pédery-Hunt
Rev.: Roger Hill, Sheldon Beveridge
Composition: 92.5 Ag, 7.5% Cu
Silver content: 23.29 g, 0.75 tr oz
Weight: 25.175 g
Diameter: 36.07 mm **Thickness:** 2.95 mm
Edge: Reeded **Die Axis:** ↑↑
Finish: Proof or Brilliant Uncirculated
Proof: Black leatherette square case, maroon insert, encapsulated coin, COA
BU: Clear plastic outer case, black plastic insert, silver sleeve, encapsulated coin

DATE	DESCRIPTION	QUANTITY SOLD	ISSUE PRICE	FINISH	65	66	67	68
1996 (1796-)	200th Anniversary John McIntosh	133,779	29.95	Proof	—	—	45.	50.
1996 (1796-)	200th Anniversary John McIntosh	58,834	19.95	BU	30.	32.	—	—

ONE DOLLAR, 25TH ANNIVERSARY 1972 CANADA/RUSSIA HOCKEY SERIES, 1997.

Paul Henderson's winning goal won the 1972 series for Canada. In 1997 three gift packages were offered: (1) A sterling silver pin / uncirculated dollar, (2) A numbered colour reproduction print / uncirculated dollar. (3) Phone card / stamp set / uncirculated dollar.

Designers and Engravers:
Obv.: Dora de Pédery-Hunt
Rev.: Walter Burden, Stan Witten
Composition: 92.5 Ag, 7.5% Cu
Silver content: 23.29 g, 0.75 tr oz
Weight: 25.175 g
Diameter: 36.07 mm **Thickness:** 2.95 mm
Edge: Reeded **Die Axis:** ↑↑
Finish: Proof or Brilliant Uncirculated
Proof: Black leatherette square case, maroon insert, encapsulated coin, COA
BU: Clear plastic outer case, black plastic insert, silver sleeve, encapsulated coin

DATE	DESCRIPTION	QUANTITY SOLD	ISSUE PRICE	FINISH	65	66	67	68
1997 (1972-)	25th Anniv. Canada/Russia Hockey Series	184,965	29.95	Proof	—	—	40.	45.
1997 (1972-)	25th Anniv. Canada/Russia Hockey Series	155,252	19.95	BU	30.	32.	—	—

ONE DOLLAR, 10TH ANNIVERSARY OF THE ONE DOLLAR LOON, 1997.

The sterling silver Flying Loon was issued singly. All were sold by the Numismatic Department of the Royal Canadian Mint as limited editions during 1997.

Designers and Engravers:
Obv.: Dora de Pédery-Hunt
Rev.: Jean-Luc Grondin, Sheldon Beveridge
Composition: 92.5 Ag, 7.5% Cu
Silver content: 23.29 g, 0.75 tr oz
Weight: 25.175 g
Diameter: 36.07 mm **Thickness:** 2.95 mm
Edge: Reeded **Die Axis:** ↑↑
Finish: Proof
Case: Black leatherette clam case, maroon flocked insert, encapsulated coin, COA

DATE	DESCRIPTION	QUANTITY SOLD	ISSUE PRICE	FINISH	PR-67 UHC	PR-68 UHC
1997 (1987-)	10th Anniv. of the One Dollar Loon	24,995	49.95	Proof	130.	140.

ONE DOLLAR, 125TH ANNIVERSARY ROYAL CANADIAN MOUNTED POLICE, 1998.

The design for the 1998 silver dollar by Adeline Halvorson features a mounted police officer in a 1900s uniform.

Designers and Engravers:
Obv.: Dora de Pédery-Hunt
Rev.: Adeline Halvorson, Sheldon Beveridge
Composition: 92.5 Ag, 7.5% Cu
Silver content: 23.29 g, 0.75 tr oz
Weight: 25.175 g
Diameter: 36.07 mm **Thickness:** 2.95 mm
Edge: Reeded **Die Axis:** ↑↑
Finish: Proof or Brilliant Uncirculated
Proof: Dark green clam display case, green insert, encapsulated coin, COA
BU: Multicoloured plastic slide case, encapsulated coin

DATE	DESCRIPTION	QUANTITY SOLD	ISSUE PRICE	FINISH	65	66	67	68
1998 (1873-)	125th Anniversary R.C.M.P.	130,795	29.95	Proof	—	—	35.	40.
1998 (1873-)	125th Anniversary R.C.M.P.	81,376	19.95	BU	30.	32.	—	—

ONE DOLLAR, 225TH ANNIVERSARY OF THE VOYAGE OF JUAN PEREZ, 1774-1999.

In 1774 Juan Perez led an expedition which made the first documented sighting of the Queen Charlotte Islands. The reverse of this coin illustrates the 225-ton frigate *The Santiago*, one of the Queen Charlotte Islands and the Haida canoes approaching the ship.

Designers and Engravers:
Obv.: Dora de Pédery-Hunt
Rev.: D. J. Craig, Stan Witten
Composition: 92.5 Ag, 7.5% Cu
Silver content: 23.29 g, 0.75 tr oz
Weight: 25.175 g
Diameter: 36.07 mm **Thickness:** 2.95 mm
Edge: Reeded **Die Axis:** ↑↑
Finish: Proof or Brilliant Uncirculated
Proof: Dark green clam display case, green flocked insert, encapsulated coin, COA
BU: Multicoloured plastic slide case, encapsulated coin

DATE	DESCRIPTION	QUANTITY SOLD	ISSUE PRICE	FINISH	65	66	67	68
1999 (1774-)	225th Anniv. Voyage Juan Perez	126,435	29.95	Proof	—	—	35.	40.
1999 (1774-)	225th Anniv. Voyage Juan Perez	67,655	19.95	BU	30.	32.	—	—

ONE DOLLAR, INTERNATIONAL YEAR OF OLDER PERSONS, 1999.

The United Nations, in October 1999, declared 1999 as the International Year of Older Persons. The 1999 silver dollar supports Canada's concept of "A Society for All Ages.

Designers and Engravers:
Obv.: Dora de Pédery-Hunt
Rev.: S. Armstrong-Hodgson, William Woodruff
Composition: 92.5 Ag, 7.5% Cu
Silver content: 23.29 g, 0.75 tr oz
Weight: 25.175 g
Diameter: 36.07 mm
Thickness: 2.95 mm
Edge: Reeded
Die Axis: ↑↑
Finish: Proof
Case: Multicoloured case, black insert, encapsulated coin, COA

DATE	DESCRIPTION	QUANTITY SOLD	ISSUE PRICE	FINISH	PR-67 UHC	PR-68 UHC
1999	Int'l Year of Older Persons	24, 976	49.95	Proof	45.	55.

ONE DOLLAR, VOYAGE OF DISCOVERY, 2000.

Poised on the launch pad to the next millennium, Canada's voyage of discovery promises to be one of energy, ability and achievement.

Designers and Engravers:
Obv.: Dora de Pédery-Hunt
Rev.: D. F. Warkentin, Cosme Saffioti
Composition: 92.5 Ag, 7.5% Cu
Silver content: 23.29 g, 0.75 tr oz
Weight: 25.175 g
Diameter: 36.07 mm **Thickness:** 2.95 mm
Edge: Reeded **Die Axis:** ↑↑
Finish: Proof or Brilliant Uncirculated
Proof: Dark green clam case, green insert, encapsulated coin, COA
BU: Multicoloured plastic slide case, encapsulated coin

DATE	DESCRIPTION	QUANTITY SOLD	ISSUE PRICE	FINISH	65	66	67	68
2000	Voyage of Discovery	121,575	29.95	Proof	—	—	35.	40.
2000	Voyage of Discovery	62,975	19.95	BU	30.	32.	—	—

ONE DOLLAR, 50TH ANNIVERSARY OF THE NATIONAL BALLET OF CANADA, 1951-2001.

The National Ballet of Canada is Canada's premier dance company, which ranks as one of the world's top international companies. Founded in 1951 by English dancer Celia Franca, the classical company is the only Canadian company to present a full range of traditional full evening ballet classics.

Designers and Engravers:
Obv.: Dora de Pédery-Hunt
Rev.: Scott McKowen, Susan Taylor
Composition: 92.5 Ag, 7.5% Cu
Silver content: 23.29 g, 0.75 tr oz
Weight: 25.175 g
Diameter: 36.07 mm **Thickness:** 2.95 mm
Edge: Reeded **Die Axis:** ↑↑
Finish: Proof or Brilliant Uncirculated
Proof: Dark green clam case, green insert, encapsulated coin, COA
BU: Multicoloured plastic slide case, encapsulated coin

DATE	DESCRIPTION	QUANTITY SOLD	ISSUE PRICE	FINISH	65	66	67	68
2001 (1951-)	50th Anniv. National Ballet of Canada	89,390	30.95	Proof	—	—	35.	40.
2001 (1951-)	50th Anniv. National Ballet of Canada	53,668	20.95	BU	30.	32.	—	—

ONE DOLLAR, 90TH ANNIVERSARY OF THE STRIKING OF CANADA'S 1911 SILVER DOLLAR, 2001.

The 1911 Canadian silver dollar is the most valuable Canadian coin. Only three examples exist, two sterling silver trial strikes and one lead trial strike. The 2001 dollar commemorates its ninetieth anniversary.

Designers and Engravers:
Obv.: Dora de Pédery-Hunt
Rev.: RCM Staff, Cosmi Saffioti
Composition: 92.5 Ag, 7.5% Cu
Silver content: 23.29 g, 0.75 tr oz
Weight: 25.175 g
Diameter: 36.07 mm **Thickness:** 2.95 mm
Edge: Reeded **Die Axis:** ↑↑
Finish: Proof
Case: Dark green clam case, green insert, encapsulated coin, COA

DATE	DESCRIPTION	QUANTITY SOLD	ISSUE PRICE	FINISH	PR-67 UHC	PR-68 UHC
2001 (1911-)	90th Anniv. Canada's 1911 Silver Dollar	24,996	49.95	Proof	65.	75.

ONE DOLLAR, 50TH ANNIVERSARY QUEEN ELIZABETH II'S ACCESSION TO THE THRONE, 2002.

For the first time a silver dollar carries a double date (1952-2002) on the obverse.

Designers and Engravers:
Obv.: Dora de Pédery-Hunt
Rev.: RCM Staff, Susan Taylor
Composition: 92.5 Ag, 7.5% Cu
Silver content: 23.29 g, 0.75 tr oz
Weight: 25.175 g
Diameter: 36.07 mm **Thickness:** 2.95 mm
Edge: Reeded **Die Axis:** ↑↑
Finish: Proof or Brilliant Uncirculated
Proof: Dark green clam case, green insert, encapsulated coin, COA
BU: Multicoloured plastic slide case, encapsulated coin

DATE	DESCRIPTION	QUANTITY SOLD	ISSUE PRICE	FINISH	65	66	67	68
2002 (1952-)	50th Anniv. Elizabeth II's Accession, Silver	29,688	33.95	Proof	—	—	35.	40.
2002 (1952-)	50th Anniv. Elizabeth II's Accession, Gold-plated	65,315	N.I.I.	Proof	—	—	60.	65.
2002 (1952-)	50th Anniv. Elizabeth II's Accession, Silver	65,410	24.95	BU	30.	32.	—	—

ONE DOLLAR, QUEEN ELIZABETH THE QUEEN MOTHER, 2002.

Available only in proof finish, this silver dollar honours the life of Queen Elizabeth the Queen Mother.

Designers and Engravers:
Obv.: Dora de Pédery-Hunt
Rev.: RCM Staff, Susan Taylor
Composition: 92.5 Ag, 7.5% Cu
Silver content: 23.29 g, 0.75 tr oz
Weight: 25.175 g
Diameter: 36.07 mm **Thickness:** 2.95 mm
Edge: Reeded **Die Axis:** ↑↑
Finish: Proof
Case: Dark green clam case, green insert, encapsulated coin, COA

DATE	DESCRIPTION	QUANTITY SOLD	ISSUE PRICE	FINISH	PR-67 UHC	PR-68 UHC
2002 (1900-)	Queen Elizabeth, the Queen Mother	9,994	49.95	Proof	400.	450.

ONE DOLLAR, 100TH ANNIVERSARY OF THE COBALT DISCOVERY, 1903-2003.

This coin marks 100 years since Fred LaRose, a blacksmith, threw his hammer at a fox, of course missing the fox, but striking a rock revealing a gleaming vein of silver. This is the first issue of a pure silver (.9999 fine) dollar by the Royal Canadian Mint.

Designers and Engravers:
Obv.: Dora de Pédery-Hunt
Rev.: John Mardon, William Woodruff
Composition: 99.99% Ag
Silver content: 25.172 g, 0.809 tr oz
Weight: 25.175 g
Diameter: 36.07 mm **Thickness:** 3.02 mm
Edge: Reeded **Die Axis:** ↑↑
Finish: Proof or Brilliant Uncirculated
Proof: Dark green clam case, green insert, encapsulated coin, COA
BU: Multicoloured plastic slide case, encapsulated coin

DATE	DESCRIPTION	QUANTITY SOLD	ISSUE PRICE	FINISH	65	66	67	68
2003 (1903-)	100th Anniv. Cobalt Silver Discovery	88,536	36.95	Proof	—	—	40.	45.
2003 (1903-)	100th Anniv. Cobalt Silver Discovery	51,130	28.95	BU	30.	32.	—	—

GOLD ONE DOLLAR, 50TH ANNIVERSARY QUEEN ELIZABETH II'S ACCESSION TO THE THRONE, 2003.

This undated gold issue is based on the 2002 reverse Accession design, and the new uncrowned obverse design for 2003. This gold dollar was sold on eBay, September 25th, 2003, with 100% of the proceeds being donated to charities.

Designers and Engravers:
Obv.: Dora de Pédery-Hunt
Rev.: RCM Staff, Susan Taylor
Composition: 99.99% Ag
Gold content: 25.172 g, 0.809 tr oz
Weight: 25.175 g
Diameter: 36.07 mm
Thickness: 2.66 mm
Edge: Reeded
Die Axis: ↑↑
Finish: Proof
Case: Not known

DATE	DESCRIPTION	QUANTITY SOLD	ISSUE PRICE	FINISH	65	66	67	68
2003	50th Anniv. Accession and Coronation of Elizabeth II, Gold	One	—	Proof	UNIQUE			

ONE DOLLAR, 50TH ANNIVERSARY OF THE CORONATION OF QUEEN ELIZABETH II, 1953-2003.

This silver dollar is a reissue of the dollar first struck during the coronation year, 1953. The design is differentiated by the double dates 1953-2003 on the obverse, as opposed to the single date on the reverse of the 1953 dollar.

Designers and Engravers:
Obv.: Mary Gillick, Thomas Shingles
Rev.: Emanuel Hahn
Composition: 99.99% Ag
Silver content: 25.172 g, 0.809 tr oz
Weight: 25.175 g
Diameter: 36.07 mm
Thickness: 3.02 mm
Edge: Reeded
Die Axis: ↑↑
Finish: Proof
Case: See Special Issue Proof Sets, page 286

DATE	DESCRIPTION	QUANTITY SOLD	ISSUE PRICE	FINISH	PR-67 UHC	PR-68 UHC
2003 (1953-)	50th Anniv. Coronation Elizabeth II	21,537	N.I.I.	Proof	50.	60.

ONE DOLLAR, UNCROWNED PORTRAIT OF QUEEN ELIZABETH II, 2003.

This was a special edition dollar with the new obverse design for 2003, and the reverse honouring the "Voyageurs" design of Canada's first circulating silver dollar. A fine gold (.9999) example of this design was struck by the Royal Canadian Mint and sold on eBay with the proceeds going to charities.

Designers and Engravers:
Obv.: Susanna Blunt, Susan Taylor
Rev.: Emanuel Hahn, RCM Staff
Composition: Gold: 99.99% Au
Silver: 99.99% Ag
Bullion content: Gold: 25.172 g, 0.801 tr oz
Silver: 25.172 g, 0.801 tr oz
Weight: Gold: 25.175 g, Silver: 25.175 g
Diameter: 36.07 mm
Thickness: Gold: 2.66 mm
Silver: 3.02 mm
Edge: Reeded **Die Axis:** ↑↑
Finish: Proof

Case: Gold: Unknown
Silver: Black leatherette clam case, maroon insert, encapsulated coin, COA

DATE	DESCRIPTION	QUANTITY SOLD	ISSUE PRICE	FINISH	65	66	67	68
2003	Uncrowned Portrait Queen Elizabeth II, Silver	29,586	51.95	Proof	—	—	50.	60.
2003	Uncrowned Portrait Queen Elizabeth II, Gold	One	—	Proof	UNIQUE			

ONE DOLLAR, 400TH ANNIVERSARY OF THE FIRST FRENCH SETTLEMENT IN NORTH AMERICA, 1604-2004.

In 1604 a tiny island, in what was to be called the St. Croix River, became the first French settlement in North America.

A 2004 Ile Sainte-Croix stamp and coin set was issued containing this silver dollar counterstamped with a fleur-de-lis privy mark.

Proof

BU, Privy Mark Reverse

Designers:
Obv.: Susanna Blunt
Rev.: R. R. Carmichael

Engravers:
Rev.: Susan Taylor
Rev.: Stan Witten

Composition: 99.99% Ag
Silver content: 25.172 g, 0.809 tr oz
Weight: 25.175 g
Diameter: 36.07 mm
Thickness: 3.02 mm
Edge: Reeded
Die Axis: ↑↑
Finish: Proof or Brilliant Uncirculated
Case of Issue A: Dark green leatherette clam case, green insert, encapsulated coin, COA
B: Multicoloured plastic slide case, encapsulated coin
C: Privy Mark Dollar, see Derivatives, page 106

DATE	DESCRIPTION	QUANTITY SOLD	ISSUE PRICE	FINISH	65	66	67	68
2004 (1604-)	First French Settlement	106,974	36.95	Proof	—	—	40.	45.
2004 (1604-)	First French Settlement	42,582	28.95	BU	30.	32.	—	—
2004 (1604-)	First French Settlement, Privy Mark	8,315	N.I.I.	BU	150.	160.	—	—

ONE DOLLAR, "THE POPPY" ARMISTICE DAY COMMEMORATIVE, 2004.

Throughout the world the poppy has become one of the most powerful symbols that honours the men and women who gave their lives for freedom. For the circulation "Poppy" twenty-five cents coin see *Canadian Coins: Volume One Numismatic Issues*:

Designers and Engravers:
Obv.: Susanna Blunt, Susan Taylor
Rev.: Stan Witten, Cosmi Saffioti
Composition: 99.99% Ag
Silver content: 25.172 g, 0.801 tr oz
Weight: 25.175 g
Diameter: 36.07 mm **Thickness:** 2.95 mm
Edge: Reeded **Die Axis:** ↑↑
Finish: Proof
Case: Maroon leatherette clam style case, black flock insert, encapsulated coin, COA

DATE	DESCRIPTION	QUANTITY SOLD	ISSUE PRICE	FINISH	PR-67 UHC	PR-68 UHC
2004	"The Poppy" Armistice Day	24,527	49.95	Proof	85.	95.

ONE DOLLAR, 40TH ANNIVERSARY OF CANADA'S NATIONAL FLAG, 1965-2005.

The Canadian flag, which is composed of the symbolic maple leaf and the national colours first proclaimed in 1921, was raised for the first time February 15th, 1965, on Parliament Hill

The 2005 brilliant uncirculated silver dollar was also issued in a gift set which included and interactive CD Rom (see Derivatives, page 106).

Proof

Proof, Selectively gold plated

Proof, Red enamel

Designers:
Obv.: Susanna Blunt
Rev.: William Woodruff
Composition: 99.99% Ag
Silver content: 25.172 g, 0.801 tr oz
Weight: 25.175 g
Diameter: 36.07 mm
Finish:
1. Proof
2. Proof, Selectively gold plated
3. Proof, Red enamel
4. Brilliant Uncirculated

Case of Issue: Maroon plastic slide case, black plastic insert, encapsulated coin, COA

Engravers:
Rev.: Susan Taylor
Rev.: William Woodruff

Thickness: 3.02 mm
Die Axis: ↑↑
Edge: Reeded

DATE	DESCRIPTION	SOURCE	QUANTITY SOLD	ISSUE PRICE	FINISH	65	66	67	68
2005 (1965-)	Proof	Pr. Single	95,431	34.95	Proof	—	—	40.	45.
2005 (1965-)	Proof, Selectively Gold plated	Pr. Set	63,562	N.I.I.	Proof	—	—	75.	85.
2005 (1965-)	Proof, Red enamel	Pr. Single	4,898	99.95	Proof	—	—	450.	500.
2005 (1965-)	Brilliant Uncirculated	BU Single	50,948	24.95	BU	30.	32.	—	—

ONE DOLLAR, 150TH ANNIVERSARY OF THE VICTORIA CROSS, 2006.

Instituted by Queen Victoria in 1856, a total of 1,351 Victoria Cross medals have been awarded, with 94 being awarded to Canadians.

Proof

Proof, Selectively gold plated

Designers:
Obv.: Susanna Blunt
Rev.: RCM Staff
Composition: 99.99% Ag
Silver content: 25.172 g, 0.801 tr oz
Weight: 25.175 g
Diameter: 36.07 mm

Engravers:
Rev.: Susan Taylor
Rev.: RCM Staff
Thickness: 3.02 mm
Edge: Reeded
Die Axis: ↑↑

Finish: **1.** Proof **2.** Proof, Selectively gold plated **3.** Brilliant Uncirculated
Case of Issue: Maroon plastic slide case, black plastic insert, encapsulated coin, COA

DATE	DESCRIPTION	SOURCE	QUANTITY SOLD	ISSUE PRICE	FINISH	65	66	67	68
2006	Victoria Cross, Proof	Pr. Single	55,599	34.95	Proof	—	—	50.	60.
2006	Victoria Cross, Proof, Selectively gold plated	Pr. Set	53,822	N.I.I.	Proof	—	—	125.	135.
2006	Victoria Cross, Brilliant Uncirculated	BU Single	27,254	24.95	BU	40.	45.	—	—

ONE DOLLAR, MEDAL OF BRAVERY, 2006.

The Canadian Medal of Bravery was established in 1972 and is awarded by the Governor General of Canada in recognition of "Acts of Bravery in hazardous circumstances".

Proof

Proof, Red enamel

Designers:
Obv.: Susanna Blunt
Rev.: RCM Staff
Composition: 99.99% Ag
Silver content: 25.172 g, 0.801 tr oz
Weight: 25.175 g
Diameter: 36.07 mm

Engravers:
Rev.: Susan Taylor
Rev.: RCM Staff
Thickness: 3.02 mm
Edge: Reeded
Die Axis: ↑↑

Finish: **1.** Proof **2.** Proof, Red enamel
Case of Issue: Maroon plastic slide case, black plastic insert, encapsulated coin, COA

DATE	DESCRIPTION	SOURCE	QUANTITY SOLD	ISSUE PRICE	FINISH	PR-67 UHC	PR-68 UHC
2006	Medal of Bravery	Pr. Single	8,343	54.95	Proof	55.	60.
2006	Medal of Bravery, Red enamel	Pr. Single	4,999	99.95	Proof	175.	185.

ONE DOLLAR, THAYENDANEGEA, 2007.

Born in 1743, Thayendanegea (Joseph Brant) was a Mohawk Chief who fought along side the British during the American Revolution. Brant died in Canada, November 24th, 1807.

Proof

Proof, Selectively gold plated

Proof, Enamelled

Designers:
Obv.: Susanna Blunt
Rev.: Laurie McGaw

Engravers:
Rev.: Susan Taylor
Rev.: RCM Staff

Composition: 92.5% Ag, 7.5% Cu
Silver content: 23.29 g, 0.749 tr oz
Weight: 25.175 g
Diameter: 36.07 mm
Thickness: 3.02 mm
Edge: Reeded
Die Axis: ↑↑
Finish: **1.** Proof
2. Proof, Selectively gold plated
3. Proof, Enamelled
4. Brilliant Uncirculated
Case of Issue: Maroon plastic slide case, black plastic insert, encapsulated coin, COA

DATE	DESCRIPTION	SOURCE	QUANTITY SOLD	ISSUE PRICE	FINISH	65	66	67	68
2007	Thayendanegea, Proof	Pr. Single	32,837	42.95	Proof	—	—	40.	45.
2007	Thayendanegea, Proof, Selectively gold plated	Pr. Set	37,413	N.I.I.	Proof	—	—	120.	125.
2007	Thayendanegea, Proof, Enamelled	Pr. Single	5,181	129.95	Proof	—	—	120.	125.
2007	Thayendanegea, Brilliant Uncirculated	BU Single	16,378	34.95	BU	30.	35.	—	—

ONE DOLLAR, CELEBRATION OF THE ARTS, 2007.

This coin was issued to commemorate the 50th anniversary of the founding of the Canada Council of the Arts.

Designers and Engravers:
Obv.: Susanna Blunt, Susan Taylor
Rev.: Friedrich Peter, RCM Staff
Composition: 92.5% Ag, 7.5% Cu
Silver content: 23.29 g, 0.749 tr oz
Weight: 25.175 g
Diameter: 36.07 mm **Thickness:** 2.95 mm
Edge: Reeded **Die Axis:** ↑↑
Finish: Proof
Case: Maroon plastic slide case, black plastic insert, encapsulated coin, COA

DATE	DESCRIPTION	SOURCE	QUANTITY SOLD	ISSUE PRICE	FINISH	PR-67 UHC	PR-68 UHC
2007	Celebration of the Arts	Pr. Single	6,704	54.95	Proof	65.	70.

ONE DOLLAR, 400TH ANNIVERSARY OF QUEBEC CITY, 1608-2008.

Founded in 1608 by Samuel de Champlain, Quebec City is one of the oldest cities in North America, and the only one north of Mexico with its ramparts surrounding the Old City still intact.

Proof

Proof, Selectively gold plated

Designers:
Obv.: Susanna Blunt
Rev.: Suzanne Duranceau

Engravers:
Rev.: Susan Taylor
Rev.: RCM Staff

Composition: 92.5% Ag, 7.5% Cu
Silver Content: 23.29 g, 0.749 tr oz
Weight: 25.175 g
Diameter: 36.07 mm
Thickness: 3.02 mm
Edge: Reeded
Die Axis: ↑↑
Finish:
1. Proof
2. Proof, Selectively gold plated
3. Brilliant Uncirculated

Case of Issue: Maroon leatherette clam style case, black flocked insert, encapsulated coin, COA

DATE	DESCRIPTION	SOURCE	QUANTITY SOLD	ISSUE PRICE	FINISH	65	66	67	68
2008 (1608-)	Quebec City, Proof	Pr. Single	65,000	42.95	Proof	—	—	45.	50.
2008 (1608-)	Quebec City, Proof, Selectively gold plated	Pr. Set	38,630	N.I.I.	Proof	—	—	100.	110.
2008 (1608-)	Quebec City, Brilliant Uncirculated	BU Single	35,000	34.95	BU	30.	35.	—	—

ONE DOLLAR, CELEBRATING THE ROYAL CANADIAN MINT CENTENNIAL, 1908-2008.

The Ottawa Branch of the Royal Mint, London, struck their first coins on January 2nd, 1908. In 1931 control of the Ottawa Mint passed to Canada and it was renamed the Royal Canadian Mint.

Designers and Engravers:
Obv.: Susanna Blunt, Susan Taylor
Rev.: Jason Bouwman, RCM Staff
Composition: 92.5% Ag, 7.5% Cu
Silver content: 23.29 g, 0.749 tr oz
Weight: 25.175 g
Diameter: 36.07 mm **Thickness:** 3.1 mm
Edge: Reeded **Die Axis:** ↑↑
Finish: Proof, Selectively gold plated
Case : Maroon leatherette clam style case, black flocked insert, encapsulated coin, COA

DATE	DESCRIPTION	SOURCE	QUANTITY SOLD	ISSUE PRICE	FINISH	PR-67 UHC	PR-68 UHC
2008 (1908-)	Royal Canadian Mint Centennial	Pr. Single	15,000	59.95	Proof	90.	100.

ONE DOLLAR, "THE POPPY" ARMISTICE, 1918-2008.

A red poppy is worn every November 11th, in memory of our war veterans.

Designers and Engravers:
Obv.: Susanna Blunt, Susan Taylor
Rev.: Cosme Saffioti, RCM Staff
Composition: 92.5% Ag, 7.5% Cu
Silver content: 27.75 g, 0.892 tr oz
Weight: 30.0 g
Diameter: 36.2 mm **Thickness:** 3.3 mm
Edge: Reeded **Die Axis:** ↑↑
Finish: Proof
Case: Maroon leatherette clam style case, black flocked insert, encapsulated coin, COA

DATE	DESCRIPTION	SOURCE	QUANTITY SOLD	ISSUE PRICE	FINISH	PR-67 UHC	PR-68 UHC
2008 (1918-)	"The Poppy" Armistice	Pr. Single	4,994	139.95	Proof	225.	250.

Note: There is slight confusion in the Royal Canadian Mint's press release in which the finish on this coin is stated as "proof" in one section and "proof-like" in another. It is listed in this table as proof as that is the finish carried on the certificate of authenticity which accompanies with the coins.

ONE DOLLAR, 100TH ANNIVERSARY OF FLIGHT IN CANADA, 1909-2009.

J. A. Douglas McCurdy, a native of Baddeck, flew the Aerial Experiment Association's Silver Dart on February 23rd, 1909 over the frozen Bras d'Or Lakes, in Nova Scotia. This was the first controlled flight in Canada and the British Empire.

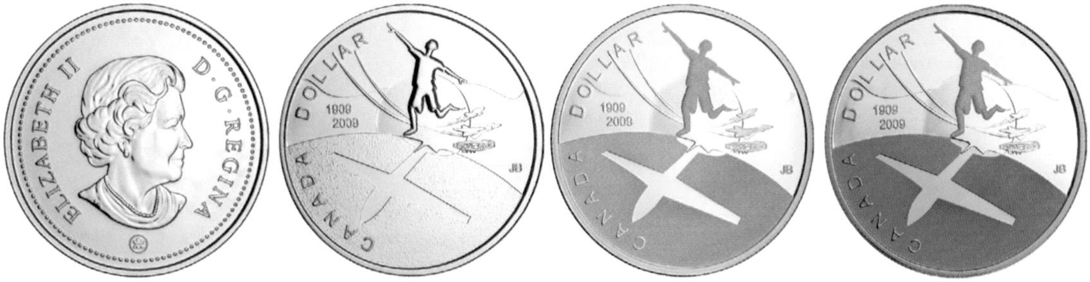

Brilliant Uncirculated — Proof — Proof, Selectively gold plated

Designers:
Obv.: Susanna Blunt
Rev.: Jason Bouwman

Engravers:
Obv.: Susan Taylor
Rev.: RCM Staff

Composition: 92.5% Ag, 7.5% Cu
Silver content: 23.29 g, 0.749 tr oz
Weight: 25.175 g
Diameter: 36.07 mm
Thickness: 3.1 mm
Edge: Reeded
Die Axis: ↑↑
Finish: Proof or Brilliant Uncirculated
Case of Issue: Maroon leatherette clam style case, black flocked insert, encapsulated coin, COA

DATE	DESCRIPTION	SOURCE	QUANTITY SOLD	ISSUE PRICE	FINISH	65	66	67	68
2009 (1909-)	Flight, Proof	Pr. Single	25,000	47.95	Proof	—	—	50.	55.
2009 (1909-)	Flight, Proof, Selectively gold plated	Pr. Set	27,549	N.I.I.	Proof	—	—	85.	95.
2009 (1909-)	Flight, Brilliant Uncirculated	BU Single	13,074	39.95	BU	40.	45.	—	—

ONE DOLLAR, 100TH ANNIVERSARY MONTREAL CANADIENS, 1909-2009.

The Montreal Canadiens, Montreal's hockey team, celebrated their 100th anniversary in 2009.

Designers:
Obv.: Susanna Blunt
Rev.: Jason Bouwman

Engravers:
Obv.: Susan Taylor
Rev.: RCM Staff

Composition: 92.5% Ag, 7.5% Cu
Silver content: 23.29 g, 0.749 tr oz
Weight: 25.175 g
Diameter: 36.07 mm
Thickness: 3.1 mm
Edge: Reeded
Die Axis: ↑↑
Finish: Proof, Selectively gold plated
Case of Issue: 1. Black leatherette clam style case, black flocked insert, encapsulated coin, COA
2. Acrylic stand

DATE	DESCRIPTION	SOURCE	QUANTITY SOLD	ISSUE PRICE	FINISH	PR-67 UHC	PR-68 UHC
2009 (1909-)	Montreal Canadiens	Pr. Single	10,093	69.95	Proof	200.	225.
2009 (1909-)	Montreal Canadiens	Stand	4,907	74.95	Proof	200.	225.

ONE DOLLAR, VANCOUVER 2010, THE SUN, 2010.

The Sun, representing life, abundance, healing and peace, has been the cornerstone in the cultures of Canada's many First Nation communities.

Designers and Engravers:
Obv.: Susanna Blunt, Susan Taylor
Rev.: Xwa lack tun (Ricky Harry)
Composition: 92.5% Ag, 7.5% Cu
Silver content: 27.75 g, 0.892 tr oz
Weight: 30.0 g
Diameter: 36.2 mm
Thickness: 3.3 mm
Edge: Plain
Die Axis: ↑↑
Finish: Proof
Case: Black leatherette clam style case, black flocked insert, encapsulated coin, COA, Vancouver 2010 Olympic Winter Games theme sleeve

DATE	DESCRIPTION	SOURCE	QUANTITY SOLD	ISSUE PRICE	FINISH	PR-67 UHC	PR-68 UHC
2010	The Sun	Pr. Single	1,278	139.95	Proof	200.	225.

ONE DOLLAR, 100TH ANNIVERSARY OF THE ROYAL CANADIAN NAVY, 1910-2010.

Founded in 1910 by the passage of the Naval Service Act, the Royal Canadian Navy served in three wars and many conflicts during the last 100 years. *HMCS Sackville,* one of the original Flower Class Corvettes is portrayed on this commemorative silver dollar,

Designers and Engravers:
Obv.: Susanna Blunt, Susan Taylor
Rev.: Yves Bérubé, RCM Staff
Composition: 92.5% Ag, 7.5% Cu
Silver content: 23.29 g, 0.749 tr oz
Weight: 25.175 g
Diameter: 36.07 mm **Thickness:** 3.0 mm
Edge: Reeded **Die Axis:** ↑↑
Finish: Proof
Case: Maroon leatherette clam style case, black flocked insert, encapsulated coin

DATE	DESCRIPTION	SOURCE	QUANTITY SOLD	ISSUE PRICE	FINISH	65	66	67	68
2010	Proof	Pr. Single	50,000	52.95	Proof	—	—	55.	60.
2010	Proof, Selectively gold plated	Pr. Set	55,000	N.I.I.	Proof	—	—	85.	95.
2010	Brilliant Uncirculated	BU	30,000	46.95	BU	50.	55.	—	—

ONE DOLLAR, 75TH ANNIVERSARY OF CANADA'S VOYAGEUR SILVER DOLLAR, 1935-2010.

The first circulating silver dollar was released in 1935. Emanuel Hahn's Voyageur design has become the classic symbol of Canada's silver dollars. This coin was also included in the 75th Anniversary of Canada's First Silver Dollar set, see page 287.

Designers and Engravers:
Obv.: Emanuel Hahn
Rev.: Percy Metcalfe
Composition: 92.5% Ag, 7.5% Cu
Silver content: 23.29 g, 0.749 tr oz
Weight: 25.175 g
Diameter: 36.07 mm **Thickness:** 3.0 mm
Edge: Reeded **Die Axis:** ↑↑
Finish: Proof
Case: Maroon leatherette clam style case, black flocked insert, encapsulated coin

DATE	DESCRIPTION	SOURCE	QUANTITY SOLD	ISSUE PRICE	FINISH	PR-67 UHC	PR-68 UHC
2010 (-1935)	75th Anniv. First Canadian Silver Dollar	Pr. Single	7,500	69.95	Proof	100.	125.

ONE DOLLAR, ENAMELLED POPPY, 2010.

"In Flander's Field where poppies grow," the poppy has become the flower of remembrance for Allied Service Personnel lost in the wars.

Designers and Engravers:
Obv.: Susanna Blunt, Susan Taylor
Rev.: Christie Paquet, RCM Staff
Composition: 92.5% Ag, 7.5% Cu
Silver content: 23.29 g, 0.749 tr oz
Weight: 25.175 g
Diameter: 36.07 mm **Thickness:** 3.1 mm
Edge: Reeded **Die Axis:** ↑↑
Finish: Proof, Red enamel
Case: Maroon leatherette clam style case, black flocked insert, encapsulated coin, COA

DATE	DESCRIPTION	SOURCE	QUANTITY SOLD	ISSUE PRICE	FINISH	PR-67 UHC	PR-68 UHC
2010	Poppy, Enamelled	Pr. Single	5,000	139.95	Proof	200.	225.

CASED NICKEL DOLLAR ISSUES, 1968-1984

At the start of 1968 the Royal Canadian Mint began the conversion from silver to nickel coinage. The first to participate was the Numismatic Department, which was based in Hull, Quebec. The Hull Mint was opened circa 1965 to carry the increased demand for numismatic products which was overwhelming the Ottawa facilities.

The first full set of nickel coinage, the five, ten and fifty cents, and one dollar coins are found in the Royal Canadian Mint's uncirculated set of 1968.

Nickel coinage is more difficult to strike than silver coinage, and the Mint needed to adjust their process. One of these adjustments was to reduce the size of the fifty cents and one dollar coins.

The finish on the coin was also a problem, the proof-like finish of silver was not as easily duplicated on nickel. Thus, the quality of finish varied from 1968 to 1976 when new presses for the Olympic Coin Program were put into use. The Mint did produce proof-like nickel coinage for their uncirculated sets, but not consistently, for at times the standard of finish dropped to circulation. It is best to treat the finish for this period as "brilliant uncirculated" not proof-like, for even the experts have difficulty determining the quality of the finish during this time period.

ONE DOLLAR, VOYAGEUR DESIGN, 1968 and 1969.

A cased 1968 and 1969 nickel dollar was available from the Numismatic Department of the Mint during 1968-69, but the department did not aggressively market this product until 1970. Thus the years 1968 and 1969 saw the development of the "cased dollar" line with the evolution of a "clam" style case.

Designers and Engravers:
Obv.: Arnold Machin, Patrick Brindley
Rev.: Raymond Taylor, Walter Ott
Composition: Nickel
Weight: 15.62 g
Diameter: 32.13 mm **Thickness:** 2.3 mm
Edge: Reeded **Die Axis:** ↑↑
Finish: Brilliant Uncirculated
Case: Black leatherette, gold side trim, gilt Royal Canadian Mint Building crest, blue interior, black insert, gilt Coat of Arms of Canada

DATE	DESCRIPTION	QUANTITY SOLD	ISSUE PRICE	FINISH	MS-65 NC	MS-66 NC	MS-67 NC
1968	Voyageur	N/A	N/A	BU	5.	8.	40.
1969	Voyageur	N/A	N/A	BU	5.	8.	40.

ONE DOLLAR, MANITOBA CENTENNIAL, 1870-1970.

Canada's first commemorative nickel dollar has a special reverse featuring a prairie crocus in recognition of the centenary of Manitoba's entry into Confederation. The finish on the cased dollar is brilliant uncirculated.

Designers and Engravers:
Obv.: Arnold Machin, Patrick Brindley
Rev.: Raymond Taylor, Walter Ott
Composition: Nickel
Weight: 15.62 g
Diameter: 32.13 mm **Thickness:** 2.3 mm
Edge: Reeded **Die Axis:** ↑↑
Finish: Brilliant Uncirculated

Case of Issue: **A:** Black leatherette square case, gilt RCM crest, blue insert
B: Maroon leatherette rectangular case, gold stamped crest of Canada, red interior, black insert
C: Black leatherette rectangular case, gold stamped Japanese characters, Maple Leaf, Canada, red interior, black insert. Card insert. (Sold at the Canada pavilion in Japan, during 1970.)

DATE	DESCRIPTION	QUANTITY SOLD	ISSUE PRICE	FINISH	MS-65 NC	MS-66 NC	MS-67 NC
1970 (1870-)	Manitoba, Case A	349,120	2.00	BU	5.	8.	35.
1970 (1870-)	Manitoba, Case B	Included	N/A	BU	5.	8.	35.
1970 (1870-)	Manitoba, Case C	Included	N/A	BU	5.	8.	35.

ONE DOLLAR, BRITISH COLUMBIA CENTENNIAL, 1871-1971.

The nickel dollar for 1971 commemorates the entry in 1871 of British Columbia into Confederation. Its design is based on the arms of the province, with a shield at the bottom and dogwood blossoms at the top. The design of the brilliant uncirculated nickel dollar is identical to that of the circulating issue.

Designers and Engravers:
Obv.: Arnold Machin, Patrick Brindley
Rev.: Thomas Shingles
Composition: Nickel
Weight: 15.62 g
Diameter: 32.13 mm **Thickness:** 2.3 mm
Edge: Reeded **Die Axis:** ↑↑
Finish: Brilliant Uncirculated
Case: Blue leatherette clam case, Coat of Arms of Canada, blue and black insert

DATE	DESCRIPTION	QUANTITY SOLD	ISSUE PRICE	FINISH	MS-65 NC	MS-66 NC	MS-67 NC
1971 (1871-)	British Columbia Centennial	181,091	2.00	BU	5.	8.	30.

ONE DOLLAR, VOYAGEUR DESIGN, 1972.

The cased brilliant uncirculated nickel dollar issued by the numismatic department of the Royal Canadian Mint has the same design as the circulating dollar.

Designers and Engravers:
Obv.: Arnold Machin, Patrick Brindley
Rev.: Emanuel Hahn, Terry Smith
Composition: Nickel
Weight: 15.62 g
Diameter: 32.13 mm **Thickness:** 2.3 mm
Edge: Reeded **Die Axis:** ↑↑
Finish: Brilliant Uncirculated
Case: Blue leatherette clam case, Coat of Arms of Canada, blue and black insert

DATE	DESCRIPTION	QUANTITY SOLD	ISSUE PRICE	FINISH	MS-65 NC	MS-66 NC	MS-67 NC
1972	Voyageur	143,392	2.00	BU	5.	8.	30.

ONE DOLLAR, PRINCE EDWARD ISLAND CENTENNIAL, 1873- 1973.

The 100th anniversary of the entry of Prince Edward Island into Confederation is commemorated with the reverse design depicting the provincial legislature building in Charlottetown.

Designers and Engravers:
Obv.: Arnold Machin, Patrick Brindley
Rev.: Terry Manning, Walter Ott
Composition: Nickel
Weight: 15.62 g
Diameter: 32.13 mm **Thickness:** 2.3 mm
Edge: Reeded **Die Axis:** ↑↑
Finish: Brilliant Uncirculated
Case: Blue leatherette clam case, Coat of Arms of Canada, blue and black insert

DATE	DESCRIPTION	QUANTITY SOLD	ISSUE PRICE	FINISH	MS-65 NC	MS-66 NC	MS-67 NC
1973 (1873-)	Prince Edward Island Centennial	466,881	2.00	BU	5.	8.	200.

ONE DOLLAR, WINNIPEG CENTENNIAL, 1974.

The 100th anniversary of the establishment of Winnipeg, Manitoba, as a city is marked by the reverse of the 1974 dollar. The 1974 cased specimen silver dollar carries the same design, see page 64.

Designers and Engravers:
Obv.: Arnold Machin, Patrick Brindley
Rev.: Paul Pederson, Patrick Brindley
Composition: Nickel
Weight: 15.62 g
Diameter: 32.13 mm **Thickness:** 2.3 mm
Edge: Reeded **Die Axis:** ↑↑
Finish: Brilliant Uncirculated
Case: Blue leatherette clam case, Coat of Arms of Canada, blue and black insert

DATE	DESCRIPTION	QUANTITY SOLD	ISSUE PRICE	FINISH	MS-65 NC	MS-66 NC	MS-67 NC
1974 (1874-)	Winnipeg Centennial	363,786	2.00	BU	5.	8.	60.

ONE DOLLAR, VOYAGEUR DESIGN, 1975-1976.

With falling popularity, the cased nickel dollars were discontinued in 1976.

Designers and Engravers:
Obv.: Arnold Machin, Patrick Brindley
Rev.: Emanuel Hahn, Terry Smith
Composition: Nickel
Weight: 15.62 g
Diameter: 32.13 mm **Thickness:** 2.3 mm
Edge: Reeded **Die Axis:** ↑↑
Finish: Specimen
Case: Blue leatherette clam case, Coat of Arms of Canada, blue and black insert

DATE	DESCRIPTION	QUANTITY SOLD	ISSUE PRICE	FINISH	MS-65 NC	MS-66 NC	MS-67 NC
1975	Voyageur	88,102	2.50	BU	5.	8.	100.
1976	Voyageur	74,209	2.50	BU	5.	8.	125.

NOTES ON NICKEL AND BRONZE DOLLARS

It is important to remember the nickel dollar series 1968 to 1987 was issued, in most instances, for circulation (business strikes), however, they were also issued as collector items either singly or in sets. This section, pages 86 to 89, lists only the single pliofilm pouched or cased nickel dollars for the period 1968 to 1984.

The term "proof-like" which applied to the silver dollars and sets of the period 1953-1967, was not carried forward to the nickel dollar coinage of 1968-1987. Coin of the period 1968 to 1984 have a brilliant uncirculated finish.

Pricing is based on third party, professionally graded coins. It is difficult for the average collector to determine the niceties between MS-65 (NC) and MS-67 (NC). NC is non-circulating.

ONE DOLLAR, CONSTITUTION, 1982

The reverse of the 1982 nickel dollar, which commemorates the Constitution, features a faithful reproduction of the celebrated painting of the Fathers of Confederation, with the inscription "1867 CONFEDERATION" above the painting and "CONSTITUTION 1982" beneath it.

Designers and Engravers:
Obv.: Arnold Machin, RCM Staff
Rev.: Ago Aarand, RCM Staff
Composition: Nickel
Weight: 15.62 g
Diameter: 32.13 mm **Thickness:** 2.3 mm
Edge: Reeded **Die Axis:** ↑↑
Finish: Proof
Case: Maroon square case with maple leaf logo, maroon insert, encapsulated coin

DATE	DESCRIPTION	QUANTITY SOLD	ISSUE PRICE	FINISH	PR-67 UHC	PR-68 UHC
1982 (1867-)	Constitution	107,353	9.75	Proof	10.	15.

ONE DOLLAR, 450TH ANNIVERSARY OF JACQUES CARTIER LANDING, 1534-1984.

The 450th year of Jacques Cartier's landing at Gaspé, Quebec, was honoured on July 24, 1984, by the issuing of a commemorative nickel dollar.

Designers and Engravers:
Obv.: Arnold Machin, RCM Staff
Rev.: Hector Greville, Victor Coté
Composition: Nickel
Weight: 15.62 g
Diameter: 32.13 mm **Thickness:** 2.3 mm
Edge: Reeded **Die Axis:** ↑↑
Finish: Proof
Case: Green velvet square case, green insert, encapsulated coin

DATE	DESCRIPTION	QUANTITY SOLD	ISSUE PRICE	FINISH	PR-67 UHC	PR-68 UHC
1984 (1534-)	450th Anniv. of Jacques Cartier Landing	87,776	9.75	Proof	10.	15.

NICKEL-BRONZE DOLLAR ISSUES, 1987-1995

ONE DOLLAR, LOON, 1987.

A proof striking of the loon dollar was issued by the numismatic department of the Royal Canadian Mint in 1987 commemorating the introduction of the nickel-bronze dollar.

Designers and Engravers:
Obv.: Arnold Machin, Patrick Brindley,
Rev.: R. R. Carmichael, Terry Smith
Composition: 91.5% Ni, 8.5 Bronze
Weight: 7.0 g
Diameter: 26.50 mm **Thickness:** 1.9 mm
Edge: Plain **Die Axis:** ↑↑
Finish: Proof
Case: Royal blue velvet square case, blue insert, encapsulated coin

DATE	DESCRIPTION	QUANTITY SOLD	ISSUE PRICE	FINISH	PR-67 UHC	PR-68 UHC
1987	Loon, Nickel-Bronze	178,120	13.50	Proof	15.	20.

ONE DOLLAR, 125TH ANNIVERSARY OF CANADA, 1867-1992.

This coin is part of the "125" coin program by the numismatic department of the Royal Canadian Mint. This proof coin is the companion piece to the circulating issue of the same design.

Designers and Engravers:
Obv.: Dora de Pédery-Hunt
Rev.: Rita Swanson, Ago Aarand
Composition: 91.5% Ni, 8.5% Bronze
Weight: 7.0 g
Diameter: 26.50 mm **Thickness:** 1.9 mm
Edge: Plain **Die Axis:** ↑↑
Finish: Proof
Case: Royal blue velvet square case, blue insert, encapsulated coin

DATE	DESCRIPTION	QUANTITY SOLD	ISSUE PRICE	FINISH	PR-67 UHC	PR-68 UHC
1992 (1867-)	125th Anniversary of Canada	24,227	19.95	Proof	15.	20.

ONE DOLLAR, REMEMBRANCE, 1994.

The 1994 nickel Loon dollar depicts the War Memorial, built to commemorate the participation of all Canadians in the First World War. The memorial was rededicated in 1982 to include veterans of the Second World War and the Korean War.

Designers and Engravers:
Obv.: Dora de Pédery-Hunt
Rev.: Terry Smith, Ago Aarand
Composition: 91.5% Ni, 8.5% Bronze
Weight: 7.0 g
Diameter: 26.50 mm **Thickness:** 1.9 mm
Edge: Plain **Die Axis:** ↑↑
Finish: Proof
Case: Royal blue velvet square case, blue insert, encapsulated coin, COA

DATE	DESCRIPTION	QUANTITY SOLD	ISSUE PRICE	FINISH	PR-67 UHC	PR-68 UHC
1994	Remembrance	54,524	19.95	Proof	15.	20.

ONE DOLLAR, PEACEKEEPING, 1995.

This coin commemorates Canada's role in the United Nations peacekeeping forces. For the circulating issues see the 65th edition, Volume One, 2011.

Designers and Engravers:
Obv.: Dora de Pédery-Hunt
Rev.: J.K. Harman, R.G. Henriguez
C. H. Oberlander, Susan Taylor,
Ago Aarand
Composition: 91.5% Ni, 8.5% Bronze
Weight: 7.0 g
Diameter: 26.50 mm **Thickness:** 1.9 mm
Edge: Plain **Die Axis:** ↑↑
Finish: Proof
Case: Royal blue velvet square case, blue insert, encapsulated coin, COA

DATE	DESCRIPTION	QUANTITY SOLD	ISSUE PRICE	FINISH	PR-67 UHC	PR-68 UHC
1995	Peacekeeping	43,293	17.95	Proof	15.	20.

NICKEL-BRONZE DOLLARS
"SPECIMEN" FINISH
BIRD SERIES, 1997-2010

ONE DOLLAR, 10TH ANNIVERSARY OF THE ONE DOLLAR LOON, 1987-1997.

The Flying Loon one dollar coin was issued only in "Oh! Canada!" and Specimen Sets of 1997 (see pages 272 and 279). Single coins have been removed from sets.

Designers and Engravers:
Obv.: Dora de Pédery-Hunt
Rev.: Jean-Luc Grondin, Sheldon Beveridge
Composition: 91.5% Ni, 8.5% Bronze
Weight: 7.0 g
Diameter: 26.50 mm **Thickness:** 1.9 mm
Edge: Plain **Die Axis:** ↑↑
Finish: Specimen
Case: See Sets, pages 272 and 279

DATE	DESCRIPTION	QUANTITY SOLD	ISSUE PRICE	FINISH	SP-66	SP-67
1997 (1987-)	Flying Loon	181,719	N.I.I.	Specimen	30.	35.

ONE DOLLAR, 15TH ANNIVERSARY OF THE LOON DOLLAR, 1987-2002.

First struck in 1987, the one dollar coin with the image of a solitary Common Loon soon became Canada's most popular coin, affectionately called the "Loonie." The 2002 commemorative dollar, depicting a loon family, with the male loon doing his "dance" was issued only in special edition specimen sets for 2002. Single coins have been removed from sets.

Designers and Engravers:
Obv.: Dora de Pédery-Hunt
Rev.: Cosme Saffioti
Composition: 91.5% Ni, 8.5% Bronze
Weight: 7.0 g
Diameter: 26.50 mm **Thickness:** 1.9 mm
Edge: Plain **Die Axis:** ↑↑
Finish: Specimen
Case: See Specimen Sets, page 280

DATE	DESCRIPTION	QUANTITY SOLD	ISSUE PRICE	FINISH	SP-66	SP-67
2002 (1987-)	15th Anniversary of the Loon Dollar	67,672	N.I.I.	Specimen	45.	50.

ONE DOLLAR, CANADA GOOSE, 2004.

This bronze dollar was issued only in the 2004 specimen set as a tribute to Jack Miner, one of the world's most influential conservationists. Miner founded a bird sanctuary near Kingsville, Ontario, in 2004. These coins were issued only in specimen sets.

Designers and Engravers:
Obv.: Susanna Blunt, Susan Taylor
Rev.: Susan Taylor
Composition: 91.5% Ni, 8.5% Bronze
Weight: 7.0 g
Diameter: 26.50 mm **Thickness:** 1.9 mm
Edge: Plain **Die Axis:** ↑↑
Finish: Specimen
Case: See Specimen Sets, page 280

DATE	DESCRIPTION	QUANTITY SOLD	ISSUE PRICE	FINISH	SP-66	SP-67
2004	Canada Goose	46,493	N.I.I.	Specimen	55.	65.

ONE DOLLAR, ELUSIVE LOON, 2004.

This dollar coin was issued only as part of the Elusive Loon "$1 Limited Edition Stamp and Coin Set", a joint venture between the Royal Canadian Mint and Canada Post. The Elusive Loon coin, which carries a maple leaf privy mark, was issued in a wooden presentation case along with mint and cancelled $1.00 Loon stamps.

Designers and Engravers:
Obv.: Susanna Blunt, Susan Taylor
Rev.: Christie Paquet
Composition: 91.5% Ni, 8.5% Bronze
Weight: 7.0 g
Diameter: 26.50 mm **Thickness:** 1.9 mm
Edge: Plain **Die Axis:** ↑↑
Finish: Specimen
Case: Wooden case, flocked insert, COA

DATE	DESCRIPTION	QUANTITY SOLD	ISSUE PRICE	FINISH	SP-66	SP-67
2004	Elusive Loon	25,105	N.I.I.	Specimen	60.	70.

ONE DOLLAR, TUFTED PUFFIN, 2005.

Issued only in the 2005 specimen set, the limited edition one dollar coin features one of British Columbia's most captivating sea birds. Coins sold singly have been removed from specimen sets. (See page 280).

Designers and Engravers:
Obv.: Susanna Blunt, Susan Taylor
Rev.: Christie Paquet
Composition: 91.5% Ni, 8.5% Bronze
Weight: 7.0 g
Diameter: 26.50 mm **Thickness:** 1.9 mm
Edge: Plain **Die Axis:** ↑↑
Finish: Specimen
Case: See Specimen Sets, page 280

DATE	DESCRIPTION	QUANTITY SOLD	ISSUE PRICE	FINISH	SP-66	SP-67
2005	Tufted Puffin	39,818	N.I.I.	Specimen	65.	75.

ONE DOLLAR, SNOWY OWL, 2006.

Issued only in the 2006 Specimen Set, the limited edition one dollar coin features the official bird of Quebec.

Designers and Engravers:
Obv.: Susanna Blunt, Susan Taylor
Rev.: Glen Loates, RCM Staff
Composition: 91.5% Ni, 8.5% Bronze
Weight: 7.0 g
Diameter: 26.50 mm **Thickness:** 1.9 mm
Edge: Plain **Die Axis:** ↑↑
Finish: Specimen
Case: See Specimen Sets, page 280

DATE	DESCRIPTION	QUANTITY SOLD	ISSUE PRICE	FINISH	SP-66	SP-67
2006	Snowy Owl	39,935	N.I.I.	Specimen	65.	75.

ONE DOLLAR, TRUMPETER SWAN, 2007.

This coin was available only in the limited edition Specimen Sets of 2007. The Trumpeter Swan has a wing span of over two metres.

Designers and Engravers:
Obv.: Susanna Blunt, Susan Taylor
Rev.: Kerri Burnett, RCM Staff
Composition: 91.5% Ni, 8.5% Bronze
Weight: 7.0 g
Diameter: 26.50 mm **Thickness:** 1.9 mm
Edge: Plain **Die Axis:** ↑↑
Finish: Specimen
Case: See Specimen Sets, page 280

DATE	DESCRIPTION	QUANTITY SOLD	ISSUE PRICE	FINISH	SP-66	SP-67
2007	Trumpeter Swan	27,056	N.I.I.	Specimen	65.	75.

ONE DOLLAR, COMMON EIDER, 2008.

Issued only in the limited edition Specimen Set of 2008 the Common Eider is found along the coast of North America.

Designers and Engravers:
Obv.: Susanna Blunt, Susan Taylor
Rev.: M. Dobson, RCM Staff
Composition: 91.5% Ni, 8.5% Bronze
Weight: 7.0 g
Diameter: 26.50 mm **Thickness:** 1.9 mm
Edge: Plain **Die Axis:** ↑↑
Finish: Specimen
Case: See Specimen Sets, page 280

DATE	DESCRIPTION	QUANTITY SOLD	ISSUE PRICE	FINISH	SP-66	SP-67
2008	Common Eider	21,227	N.I.I.	Specimen	50.	60.

ONE DOLLAR, GREAT BLUE HERON, 2009.

The Great Blue Heron is a large wading bird found near the shores of open water, and in the wet lands of North America.

Designers and Engravers:
Obv.: Susanna Blunt, Susan Taylor
Rev.: Chris Jordison, RCM Staff
Composition: 91.5% Ni, 8.5% Bronze
Weight: 7.0 g
Diameter: 26.50 mm **Thickness:** 1.9 mm
Edge: Plain **Die Axis:** ↑↑
Finish: Specimen
Case: See Specimen Sets, page 280

DATE	DESCRIPTION	QUANTITY SOLD	ISSUE PRICE	FINISH	SP-66	SP-67
2009	Great Blue Heron	21,677	N.I.I.	Specimen	55.	65.

ONE DOLLAR, NORTHERN HARRIER, 2010.

The Northern Harrier is a bird of prey found throughout the northern hemisphere of Canada.

Designers and Engravers:
Obv.: Susanna Blunt, Susan Taylor
Rev.: Arnold Nogy, RCM Staff
Composition: 91.5% Ni, 8.5% Bronze
Weight: 7.0 g
Diameter: 26.50 mm **Thickness:** 1.9 mm
Edge: Plain **Die Axis:** ↑↑
Finish: Specimen
Case: See Specimen Sets, page 280

DATE	DESCRIPTION	QUANTITY SOLD	ISSUE PRICE	FINISH	SP-66	SP-67
2010	Northern Harrier	35,000	N.I.I.	Specimen	55.	65.

NICKEL-BRONZE DOLLAR ISSUES, 2002-2010

ONE DOLLAR, CENTRE ICE LOON, 1987-2002.

A "Centre Ice" 22-karat gold-plated loon dollar coin was issued as part of a souvenir album, entitled "Going For Gold." It was jointly offered by the Royal Canadian Mint, Canada Post, and Maclean's Magazine to commemorate the Olympic gold medals for hockey won by the Canadian Mens' and Women's teams in the Salt Lake City Winter Olympic Games in 2002.

Designers and Engravers:
Obv.: Dora de Pédery-Hunt
Rev.: R. R. Carmichael, Cosme Saffioti
Composition: 91.5% Ni, 8.5% Bronze
Weight: 7.0 g
Diameter: 26.50 mm **Thickness:** 1.9 mm
Edge: Plain **Die Axis:** ↑↑
Finish: Proof, gold plated
Case: See Derivatives, page 106

DATE	DESCRIPTION	QUANTITY SOLD	ISSUE PRICE	FINISH	PR-67 UHC	PR-68 UHC
2002 (1987-)	Centre Ice Loon, Gold-plated bronze	25,000	N.I.I.	Proof	50.	60.

MONTREAL CANADIENS, 100TH ANNIVERSARY DOLLAR, 1909-2009.

Canada Post and the Royal Canadian Mint offered two different sets in 2009 for the 100th anniversary of the Montreal Canadiens:

1. Montreal Canadiens 100th Anniversary Pack which included a lacquered anniversary dollar and a lenticular souvenir sheet
2. Montreal Canadiens 100th Anniversary Set which included three different dollars coins (lacquered, painted Canadiens crest, and gold plated) plus a lenticular souvenir sheet.

Common obverse

Lacquered

Painted Crest

Gold plated

Designers:
Obv.: Susanna Blunt
Rev.: RCM Staff
Composition: 91.5% Ni, 8.5% Bronze
Weight: 7.0 g
Diameter: 26.50 mm
Finish: 1. Uncirculated, Lacquered
2. Uncirculated, Painted crest
3. Uncirculated, Gold plated
Case of Issue: See Derivatives, page 106

Engravers:
Obv.: Susan Taylor
Rev.: RCM Staff
Thickness: 2.0 mm
Die Axis: ↑↑
Edge: Plain

DATE	DESCRIPTION	SOURCE	QUANTITY SOLD	ISSUE PRICE	FINISH	MS-65 NC	MS-66 NC
2009 (1909-)	Montreal Canadiens, Lacquered	Collector Set / Pack	N/A	N.I.I.	Lacquered	10.	15.
2009 (1909-)	Montreal Canadiens, Painted crest	Collector Set	526	N.I.I.	Coloured	25.	35.
2009 (1909-)	Montreal Canadiens, Gold plated	Collector Set	9,500	N.I.I.	Gold plated	30.	40.

ONE DOLLAR, 100TH ANNIVERSARY OF THE CANADIAN NAVY, 1910-2010.

An enlisted seaman of 1910 and a female officer of 2010 in front of *HMCS Halifax*, the lead ship in the Navy's current fleet are depicted on this commemorative coin.

Designers and Engravers:
Obv.: Susanna Blunt, Susan Taylor
Rev.: Bonnie Ross, RCM Staff
Composition: 1. Nickel bronze
2. Nickel bronze, gold plated
Weight: 7.0 g
Diameter: 26.50 mm **Thickness:** 1.9 mm
Edge: Plain **Die Axis:** ↑↑
Finish: Uncirculated, Gold plated
Case: See Derivatives, page 106,
Special Edition Uncirculated Sets, page 263

DATE	DESCRIPTION	QUANTITY SOLD	ISSUE PRICE	FINISH	MS-65 NC	MS-66 NC
2010 (1910-)	Canadian Navy Centennial	N/A	N.I.I.	Uncirculated	5.	10.
2010 (1910-)	Canadian Navy Centennial, Gold plated	20,000	19.95	Uncirculated	25.	35.

ONE DOLLAR, 100TH ANNIVERSARY OF THE SASKATCHEWAN ROUGHRIDERS, 1910-2010.

Designers and Engravers:
Obv.: Susanna Blunt, Susan Taylor
Rev.: Saskatchewan Roughriders Football Club, RCM Staff
Composition: 1. Nickel bronze
2. Nickel bronze, gold plated
Weight: 7.0 g
Diameter: 26.50 mm **Thickness:** 1.9 mm
Edge: Reeded **Die Axis:** ↑↑
Finish: 1. Uncirculated
2. Gold plated
Case: 1. Uncirculated, See Special Edition Uncirculated Sets, page 263
2. Gold plated, See Derivatives, page 106

DATE	DESCRIPTION	QUANTITY SOLD	ISSUE PRICE	FINISH	MS-65 NC	MS-66 NC
2010 (1910-)	Saskatchewan Roughriders	N/A	N.I.I.	Uncirculated	5.	10.
2010 (1910-)	Saskatchewan Roughriders, Gold plated	N/A	19.95	Uncirculated	20.	30.

NOTE TO COLLECTORS

The Canadian Navy and Saskatchewan Roughriders uncirculated nickel-bronze dollars are also found in the 2010 Special Edition Uncirculated Set, see page 263.

LOON STYLE NICKEL DOLLAR ISSUES, 2008-2010

ONE DOLLAR, 2007-2008 NHL HOCKEY SEASON, 2008 (GIFTWARE). ROAD JERSEY CRESTS.

This series of dollars is found in the NHL Teams Sets, see page 270.

Designers:
Obv.: Susanna Blunt
Rev.: RCM Staff
Composition: Nickel
Weight: 7.0 g
Diameter: 26.50 mm
Case of Issue: Road Jersey Crests: Uncirculated set folder

Engravers:
Obv.: Susan Taylor
Rev.: RCM Staff
Thickness: 1.9 mm
Edge: Plain
Finish: Uncirculated, Decal

Common obverse

Calgary Flames

Edmonton Oilers

Montreal Canadiens

Ottawa Senators

Toronto Maple Leafs

Vancouver Canucks

DATE	DESCRIPTION	SOURCE	QUANTITY SOLD	ISSUE PRICE	FINISH	MS-65 NC	MS-66 NC
2008	Calgary Flames, Road Jersey	NHL Set	N/A	N.I.I.	Uncirculated	20.	25.
2008	Edmonton Oilers, Road Jersey	NHL Set	1,584	N.I.I.	Uncirculated	20.	25.
2008	Montreal Canadiens, Road Jersey	NHL Set	2,659	N.I.I.	Uncirculated	20.	25.
2008	Ottawa Senators, Road Jersey	NHL Set	1,633	N.I.I.	Uncirculated	20.	25.
2008	Toronto Maple Leafs, Road Jersey	NHL Set	N/A	N.I.I.	Uncirculated	20.	25.
2008	Vancouver Canucks, Road Jersey	NHL Set	1,302	N.I.I.	Uncirculated	20.	25.

ONE DOLLAR, 2007-2008 NHL HOCKEY SEASON, 2008 CONTINUED (GIFTWARE).
HOME JERSEY CRESTS

This series of dollars is found embedded in official NHL hockey pucks which are blister packaged.

Designers:
Obv.: Susanna Blunt
Rev.: RCM Staff
Composition: Nickel
Weight: 7.0 g
Diameter: 26.50 mm

Engravers:
Obv.: Susan Taylor
Rev.: RCM Staff
Thickness: 1.9 mm
Edge: Plain
Finish: Uncirculated, Decal

Case of Issue: Home Jersey Crests: Embedded in an official NHL puck, blister packaged

2008
Common Obverse

Calgary Flames

Edmonton Oilers

Montreal Canadiens

Ottawa Senators

Toronto Maple Leafs

Vancouver Canucks

DATE	DESCRIPTION	SOURCE	QUANTITY SOLD	ISSUE PRICE	FINISH	MS-65 NC	MS-66 NC
2008	Calgary Flames, Home Jersey	NHL Pucks	1,304	15.95	Uncirculated	20.	25.
2008	Edmonton Oilers, Home Jersey	NHL Pucks	484	15.95	Uncirculated	20.	25.
2008	Montreal Canadiens. Home Jersey	NHL Pucks	62	15.95	Uncirculated	20.	25.
2008	Ottawa Senators, Home Jersey	NHL Pucks	775	15.95	Uncirculated	20.	25.
2008	Toronto Maple Leafs, Home Jersey	NHL Pucks	2,605	15.95	Uncirculated	20.	25.
2008	Vancouver Canucks, Home Jersey	NHL Pucks	1,160	15.95	Uncirculated	20.	25.

ONE DOLLAR, 2008-2009 NHL HOCKEY SEASON, 2009 (GIFTWARE).

These nickel coloured dollar coins which feature the team logos are each embedded in a mini-puck attached to a key chain. The key chain along with a mini hockey stick and an informative insert card are enclosed in a blister pack.

Designers:
Obv.: Susanna Blunt
Rev.: RCM Staff
Composition: Nickel
Weight: 6.50 g
Diameter: 26.50 mm
Case of Issue: Blister packaged

Engravers:
Obv.: Susan Taylor
Rev.: RCM Staff
Thickness: 1.7 mm
Edge: Plain
Finish: Uncirculated, Decal

Common obverse

Calgary Flames

Edmonton Oilers

Montreal Canadiens

Ottawa Senators

Toronto Maple Leafs

Vancouver Canucks

DATE	DESCRIPTION	SOURCE	QUANTITY SOLD	ISSUE PRICE	FINISH	MS-65 NC	MS-66 NC
2009	Calgary Flames, Home Jersey	Mini Puck	73	24.95	Uncirculated	20.	25.
2009	Edmonton Oilers, Home Jersey	Mini Puck	49	24.95	Uncirculated	20.	25.
2009	Montreal Canadiens, Home Jersey	Mini Puck	326	24.95	Uncirculated	20.	25.
2009	Ottawa Senators, Home Jersey	Mini Puck	95	24.95	Uncirculated	20.	25.
2009	Toronto Maple Leafs, Home Jersey	Mini Puck	199	24.95	Uncirculated	20.	25.
2009	Vancouver Canucks, Home Jersey	Mini Puck	101	24.95	Uncirculated	20.	25.

ONE DOLLAR, 2008-2009 NHL HOCKEY SEASON, 2009 CONTINUED (GIFTWARE).

Road hockey jerseys folded in the shape of a heart are the central device on these nickel dollars. The coloured dollars are included in NHL Team Uncirculated Sets for the 2008-2009 season.

Designers:
Obv.: Susanna Blunt
Rev.: RCM Staff
Composition: Nickel
Weight: 7.0 g
Diameter: 26.50 mm
Cases of Issue: Blister packaged

Engravers:
Obv.: Susan Taylor
Rev.: RCM Staff
Thickness: 1.9 mm
Edge: Plain
Finish: Uncirculated, Decal

Common Obv.

Calgary Flames

Edmonton Oilers

Montreal Canadiens

Ottawa Senators

Toronto Maple Leafs

Vancouver Canucks

DATE	DESCRIPTION	SOURCE	QUANTITY SOLD	ISSUE PRICE	FINISH	MS-65 NC	MS-66 NC
2009	Calgary Flames, Road Jersey	NHL Sets	382	24.95	Uncirculated	20.	25.
2009	Edmonton Oilers, Road Jersey	NHL Sets	472	24.95	Uncirculated	20.	25.
2009	Montreal Canadiens, Road Jersey	NHL Sets	4,857	24.95	Uncirculated	20.	25.
2009	Ottawa Senators, Road Jersey	NHL Sets	387	24.95	Uncirculated	20.	25.
2009	Toronto Maple Leafs, Road Jersey	NHL Sets	1,328	24.95	Uncirculated	20.	25.
2009	Vancouver Canucks, Road Jersey	NHL Sets	794	24.95	Uncirculated	20.	25.

ONE DOLLAR, VANCOUVER 2010 LUCKY LOONIE, 2010.

This painted nickel dollar bearing the official emblem of the Vancouver 2010 Olympic Winter Games was used extensively in many giftware products. See Derivatives, page 106.

Designers and Engravers:
Obv.: Susanna Blunt, Susan Taylor
Rev.: RCM Staff
Composition: Nickel
Weight: 7.0 g
Diameter: 26.50 mm **Thickness:** 1.9 mm
Edge: Plain **Die Axis:** ↑↑
Finish: Uncirculated, Painted
Case: See Derivatives, page 106

DATE	DESCRIPTION	QUANTITY SOLD	ISSUE PRICE	FINISH	MS-65 NC	MS-66 NC
2010	Inukshuk, Vancouver 2010 Lucky Loonie, Painted	N/A	N.I.I.	Uncirculated	30.	35.

LOON STYLE STERLING SILVER DOLLAR ISSUES, 2004-2010

ONE DOLLAR, STERLING SILVER, LUCKY LOONIE, OLYMPIC LOGO, 2004.

This coin was issued as a Lucky Loonie for the Athens 2004 Olympic Summer Games.

Designers and Engravers:
Obv.: Susanna Blunt, Susan Taylor
Rev.: R. R. Carmichael, RCM Staff
Composition: 92.5% Ag, 7.5% Cu
Silver content: 6.475 g, 0.208 tr oz
Weight: 7.0 g
Diameter: 26.50 mm **Thickness:** 1.9 mm
Edge: Plain **Die Axis:** ↑↑
Finish: Proof, Painted
Case: Maroon leatherette square case, black flocked insert, encapsulated coin, COA

DATE	DESCRIPTION	SOURCE	QUANTITY SOLD	ISSUE PRICE	FINISH	PR-67 UHC	PR-68 UHC
2004	"Lucky Loonie"	Pr. Single	19,994	39.95	Proof	65.	75.

ONE DOLLAR, STERLING SILVER, SNOWFLAKE, 2006.

This Snowflake loon style silver dollar was issued in a blue Holiday folder with a Christmas carol CD and a picture frame.

Designers and Engravers:
Obv.: Susanna Blunt, Susan Taylor
Rev.: RCM Staff
Composition: 92.5% Ag, 7.5% Cu
Silver content: 6.475 g, 0.208 tr oz
Weight: 7.0 g
Diameter: 26.50 mm **Thickness:** 1.9 mm
Edge: Plain **Die Axis:** ↑↑
Finish: Proof, Painted
Case: Blue Holiday Folder

DATE	DESCRIPTION	SOURCE	QUANTITY SOLD	ISSUE PRICE	FINISH	PR-67 UHC	PR-68 UHC
2006	Snowflake, Painted	Holiday Set	34,014	34.95	Proof	65.	75.

ONE DOLLAR, STERLING SILVER, LOON SETTLING LUCKY LOONIE, OLYMPIC LOGO, 2006.

This coin was issued as a Lucky Loonie for the Turin 2006 Olympic Winter Games.

Designers and Engravers:
Obv.: Susanna Blunt, Susan Taylor
Rev.: RCM Staff
Composition: 92.5% Ag, 7.5% Cu
Silver content: 6.475 g, 0.208 tr oz
Weight: 7.0 g
Diameter: 26.50 mm **Thickness:** 1.7 mm
Edge: Plain **Die Axis:** ↑↑
Finish: Proof, Painted
Case: Maroon leatherette square case, black flocked insert, encapsulated coin, COA

DATE	DESCRIPTION	SOURCE	QUANTITY SOLD	ISSUE PRICE	FINISH	PR-67 UHC	PR-68 UHC
2006	Loon Settling, Lucky Loonie	Pr. Single	19,973	39.95	Proof	45.	55.

ONE DOLLAR, STERLING SILVER, LULLABY LOONIE, 2006.

The sterling silver Lullaby Loonie silver dollar was issued in the following packaging: 1) a presentation folder containing a baby's lullabies CD and a sterling silver Lullaby Loonie one dollar coin; 2). a box containing two baby keepsake tins (one for baby's first tooth and the other for a lock of hair) and a sterling silver Lullaby Loonie one dollar coin, and 3). a presentation folder containing a baby's lullabies CD, a sterling silver Lullaby Loonie one dollar coin, and a silver plated picture frame.

Designers and Engravers:
Obv.: Susanna Blunt, Susan Taylor
Rev.: RCM Staff
Composition: 92.5% Ag, 7.5% Cu
Silver content: 6.475 g, 0.208 tr oz
Weight: 7.0 g **Thickness:** 1.9 mm
Diameter: 26.50 mm **Die Axis:** ↑↑
Edge: Plain **Finish:** Proof
Case: See description

DATE	DESCRIPTION	SOURCE	QUANTITY SOLD	ISSUE PRICE	FINISH	PR-67 UHC	PR-68 UHC
2006	Lullaby Loonie	Folder and CD	18,225	29.95	Proof	30.	40.
2006	Lullaby Loonie	Keepsake Box	Included	34.95	Proof	30.	40.
2006	Lullaby Loonie	CD and Picture Frame	Included	34.95	Proof	30.	40.
2006	Lullaby Loonie	Premium Baby Gift Set	Included	N.I.I.	Proof	30.	40.

ONE DOLLAR, STERLING SILVER, BABY RATTLE, 2007.

The sterling silver Baby Rattle one dollar coin was issued along with a CD of lullabies in a colourful folder. A gold plated Baby Rattle one dollar coin was included in the Premium Gift Baby Set, see page 286.

Designers and Engravers:
Obv.: Susanna Blunt, Susan Taylor
Rev.: RCM Staff
Composition: 92.5% Ag, 7.5% Cu
Silver content: 6.475 g, 0.208 tr oz
Weight: 7.0 g
Diameter: 26.50 mm **Thickness:** 1.9 mm
Edge: Plain **Die Axis:** ↑↑
Finish: **1.** Proof
2. Proof gold plated
Case: See description

DATE	DESCRIPTION	SOURCE	QUANTITY SOLD	ISSUE PRICE	FINISH	PR-67 UHC	PR-68 UHC
2007	Baby Rattle, Silver	Folder and CD	3,207	34.95	Proof	50.	60.
2007	Baby Rattle, Gold plated	Premium Baby Gift Set	1,911	N.I.I.	Proof	100.	110.

ONE DOLLAR, STERLING SILVER, "ABC" BUILDING BLOCKS, 2007.

The "ABC" Building Blocks sterling silver one dollar coin was issued in a "Baby Keepsake Box" which also contained two small tins, one for baby's first tooth and the other for a lock of hair.

Designers and Engravers:
Obv.: Susanna Blunt, Susan Taylor
Rev.: RCM Staff
Composition: 92.5% Ag, 7.5% Cu
Silver content: 6.475 g, 0.208 tr oz
Weight: 7.0 g **Thickness:** 1.9 mm
Diameter: 26.50 mm **Die Axis:** ↑↑
Edge: Plain **Finish:** Proof
Case: See description

DATE	DESCRIPTION	SOURCE	QUANTITY SOLD	ISSUE PRICE	FINISH	PR-67 UHC	PR-68 UHC
2007	"ABC" Building Blocks	Keepsake Box	3,229	34.95	Proof	50.	60.

ONE DOLLAR, STERLING SILVER LOON, 2007-2008.

The sterling silver one dollar loon was issued in 2007 and 2008 for use in baby and wedding giftware sets. It was incorporated into: For 2007: Premium sterling silver wedding proof set with medallion, see page 286

For 2008:
1. Premium sterling silver wedding proof set with medallion, see page 286
2. Premium sterling silver baby proof set
3. Baby keepsake tins, sterling silver loon dollar
4. CD and picture frame, sterling silver loon dollar

Designers and Engravers:
Obv.: Susanna Blunt, Susan Taylor
Rev.: R. R. Carmichael, Terry Smith
Composition: 92.5% Ag, 7.5% Cu
Silver content: 6.475 g, 0.208 tr oz
Weight: 7.0 g
Diameter: 26.50 mm **Thickness:** 1.9 mm
Edge: Plain **Die Axis:** ↑↑
Finish: Proof **Case:** See above

DATE	DESCRIPTION	SOURCE	QUANTITY SOLD	ISSUE PRICE	FINISH	PR-67 UHC	PR-68 UHC
2007	Sterling Silver Loon	Premium Wedding Gift Set	849	N.I.I.	Proof	50.	60.
2008	Sterling Silver Loon	Premium Wedding Gift Set	N/A	N.I.I.	Proof	50.	60.
2008	Sterling Silver Loon	Premium Baby Gift Set	N/A	N.I.I.	Proof	50.	60.
2008	Sterling Silver Loon	Keepsake Box	N/A	N.I.I.	Proof	50.	60.
2008	Sterling Silver Loon	CD and Picture Frame Holder	N/A	N.I.I.	Proof	50.	60.

ONE DOLLAR, STERLING SILVER, OLYMPIC LOON DANCE, LUCKY LOONIE, OLYMPIC LOGO, 2008.

This coin was issued as a Lucky Loonie for the Beijing 2008 Olympic Summer Games.

Designers and Engravers:
Obv.: Susanna Blunt, Susan Taylor
Rev.: RCM Staff
Composition: 92.5% Ag, 7.5% Cu
Silver content: 6.475 g, 0.208 tr oz
Weight: 7.0 g **Thickness:** 1.9 mm
Diameter: 26.50 mm **Die Axis:** ↑↑
Edge: Plain **Finish:** Proof, Painted
Case: Maroon leatherette clam style case, black flocked insert, encapsulated coin, COA Olympic theme outer sleeve

DATE	DESCRIPTION	SOURCE	QUANTITY SOLD	ISSUE PRICE	FINISH	PR-67 UHC	PR-68 UHC
2008	Olympic Loon Dance, Lucky Loonie	Pr. Single	52,987	49.95	Proof	50.	60.

ONE DOLLAR, STERLING SILVER, VANCOUVER 2010 LUCKY LOONIE, ANTICIPATING THE GAMES, 2010.

This is the third coin in the Lucky Loonie Inukshuk series issued for the Vancouver 2010 Winter Olympic Games. This coin is a sterling silver painted proof.

Designers and Engravers:
Obv.: Susanna Blunt, Susan Taylor
Rev.: RCM Staff
Composition: 92.5% Ag, 7.5% Cu
Silver content: 6.475 g, 0.208 tr oz
Weight: 7.0 g **Thickness:** 1.70 mm
Diameter: 26.50 mm **Die Axis:** ↑↑
Edge: Plain **Finish:** Proof, Painted
Case: Black leatherette case, black flocked insert, encapsulated coin, COA, Olympic theme sleeve

DATE	DESCRIPTION	SOURCE	QUANTITY SOLD	ISSUE PRICE	FINISH	PR-67 UHC	PR-68 UHC
2010	Anticipating the Games	Pr. Single	13,285	54.95	Proof	55.	65.

ONE DOLLAR DERIVATIVES

DATE	DESCRIPTION	QUANTITY SOLD	ISSUE PRICE	ISSUER	FINISH	MARKET VALUE
1997	**Silver Dollar, Canada/Russia Hockey;** Two 45¢ mint stamps; $5 phone card; Multicoloured folder	N/A	29.95	RCM, CP	MS-65	25.
1997	**Silver Dollar, Canada/Russia Hockey;** Sterling silver pin	N/A	29.95	RCM	MS-65	25.
1997	**Silver Dollar, Canada/Russia Hockey;** Print	N/A	24.95	RCM	MS-65	25.
1997	**Silver Dollar, Canada/Russia Hockey;** Phone card/stamp set	N/A	N/A	RCM	MS-65	30.
1998	**Loon Dollar;** Mint and cancelled one dollar stamps; Blue presentation case	N/A	17.99	RCM, CP	MS-65	10.
1998	**Silver Dollar, 125th Anniv. R.C.M.P.;** Pin	N/A	29.95	RCM	MS-65	22.
1999	**Silver Dollar, 225th Anniv. Juan Perez;** Journal Gift Set; Multicoloured folder	N/A	N/A	RCM, CP	MS-65	22.
2000	**Loon Dollar**, Mint and cancelled one dollar stamps; Blue presentation case	N/A	17.99	RCM, CP	MS-65	10.
2000	**Loon Dollar**, Encapsulated in a credit card	N/A	N/A	RCM	MS-65	5.
2001	**Loon Dollar**, Encapsulated in a credit card	N/A	N/A	RCM	MS-65	5.
2001	**Loon /Sacagawea Dollars**, Folder	N/A	N/A	RCM, USM	MS-65	10.
2002	**Centre Ice Loon**, 22kt gold-plated bronze; block of four 48¢ stamps, Two Olympic Edition Macleans' magazines (one English, one French); "Going For Gold" Souvenir album, COA	25,000	54.95	RCM, CP, MM	PR-67	50.
2004	**Silver Dollar, 2004 French Settlement with privy mark;** 2004 silver ¼ Euro; Canada 49¢ stamps, mint/cancelled; France .90 Euro stamps, mint/cancelled; Wooden presentation case, blue insert, encapsulated coins, COA	8,273	99.95	RCM, CP	MS-65	325.
2004	**Elusive Loon with Privy Mark**, Mint and cancelled one dollar stamps; Wooden presentation case	12,550	25.22	RCM, CP	PR-67	60.
2005	**Silver Dollar, 40th Anniversary of Canada's National Flag**, CD-Rom; Presentation folder	N/A	34.95	RCM	MS-65	35.
2006	**Lucky Loonie Bookmark** "Celebrate the Legend"	10,095	N/A	RCM	MS-65	15.
2008	**Nickel Bronze Lucky Loonie** embedded in Lucite	N/A	N/A	RCM	MS-65	15.
2009	**Montreal Canadiens 100th Anniversary Pack**, 100th anniv. dollar coin and a lenticular souvenir sheet	15,473	19.95	RCM	MS-65	20.
2009	**Montreal Canadiens 100th Anniversary Collector Set**, three one dollar coins (lacquered, coloured crest, gold plated), a sheet of three stamps, a lenticular souvenir sheet, 15 named retired jersey plaquettes, souvenir booklet	526	149.95	RCM	MS-65	150.
2010	**Vancouver 2010 Colourised Nickel Bronze Lucky Loonie,** encapsulated and embedded in NHL puck; Blister packaged	30,396	19.95	RCM	MS-65	25.
2010	**Sport Bag Tag**, colourised Vancouver 2010 Lucky Loonie dollar and lapel pin, green "See In Tin" container.	N/A	14.95	RCM	MS-65	25.
2010	**Lanyard**, colourised Vancouver 2010 Lucky Loonie dollar	N/A	14.95	RCM	MS-65	25.
2010	**Hockey Player Lapel Pin Set**, colourised 2010 Lucky Loonie dollar and six "hockey player" lapel pins.	N/A	N/A	RCM	MS-65	75.
2010	**100th Anniversary Canadian Navy Coin and Stamp Set**, Gold plated nickel-bronze dollar; souvenir stamp sheet; 40-page booklet; square aluminum tin	20,000	39.95	RCM, CP	MS-65	40.
2010	**100th Anniversary Saskatchewan Roughriders,** Gold plated nickel-bronze dollar; pop-up helmet packaging	N/A	19.95	RCM	MS-65	20.

Note: CP = Canada Post; MM = Maclean's Magazine; RCM = Royal Canadian Mint; USM = United States Mint

TWO DOLLARS

The first Canadian two dollar coin was issued in 1996 to replace the two dollar bank note which was then withdrawn from circulation. To mark this event the Numismatic Department of the Royal Canadian Mint issued four different planchet varieties in two different finishes.

TWO DOLLARS, POLAR BEAR, 1996.

The 1996 two dollar Piedfort was not issued singly, but as part of a set. See the Two Dollar Derivatives, page 113.

Obv.: Nickel / Bronze

Obv.: Nickel / Bronze

Obv.: Gold / Gold

Rev.: Gold / Gold

Designers:
Obv.: Dora de Pédery-Hunt
Rev.: Brent Townsend

Engravers:
Rev.: Dora de Pédery-Hunt
Rev.: Ago Aarand

Composition:	**Nickel Ring** 99.0% Ni	**Silver Ring** 92.5% Ag 07.5% Cu	**White Gold Ring** 17.2% Au 77.6% Ag, 5.2% Cu
	Bronze Core 92.0 % Cu 6.0% Al, 2.0% Ni	**Silver Gilt Core** 92.5% Ag 07.5% Cu	**Yellow Gold Core** 91.7% Au 04.1% Ag, 4.2% Cu

	Standard	**Standard**	**Piedford**	**Standard**
Weight (g):	Ring 4.84 Core 2.46 Total 7.30	Ring 5.86 Core 2.97 Total 8.83	Ring 11.72 Core 5.94 Total 17.66	Ring 6.31 Core 5.09 Total 11.40
Content: Gold	—	—	—	0.185 tr oz
Silver	—	0.263 tr oz	0.525 tr oz	0.164 tr oz
Diameter (mm):	Ring 28.00 Core 16.80	Ring 28.07 Core 16.80	Ring 28.07 Core 16.80	Ring 28.00 Core 16.80
Thickness (mm):	1.80	1.90	3.60	1.80
Edge:	Interrupted Serration	Interrupted Serration	Interrupted Serration	Interrupted Serration
Die Axis:	↑↑	↑↑	↑↑	↑↑
Finish:	Specimen, Proof	Proof	Proof	Proof

Case of Issue: Nickel / Bronze, Specimen: Blue presentation folder
Nickel / Bronze, Proof: Black leatherette case, blue insert, encapsulated coin, COA
Silver / Gilt, Proof: Black suede case, blue insert, encapsulated coin, COA
Gold / Gold, Proof: Blue suede case, blue insert, encapsulated coin, COA

DATE	DESCRIPTION	QUANTITY SOLD	ISSUE PRICE	FINISH	65	66	67	68
1996	Nickel / Bronze, Blue folder	74,669	10.95	Specimen	—	10.	15.	—
1996	Nickel / Bronze, Black leatherette case	66,843	24.95	Proof	—	—	15.	20.
1996	Silver / Gilt, Black suede case	N/A	N/A	Proof	—	—	20.	25.
1996	Silver / Gilt, Piedfort, See Derivatives	11,526	N.I.I.	Proof	—	—	150.	175.
1996	Gold / Gold, Blue case	5,000	299.95	Proof	—	—	400.	450.

NOTE ON TWO DOLLAR ISSUES

1. The blue presentation folder was printed "uncirculated" but the $2 coin it held was of specimen quality.
2. Piedfort is a term used to describe a double thickness or essaie coin, usually struck for approval, see Derivatives page 113.

TWO DOLLARS, NUNAVUT, PROOF COMMEMORATIVE, 1999.

This coin commemorates the formation of Nunavut, Canada's third territory, in 1999. The design honours the native drum dance.

Obv.: Nickel / Bronze

Rev.: Nickel / Bronze

Obv.: Gold / Gold

Rev.: Gold / Gold

Designers:
Obv.: Dora de Pédery-Hunt
Rev.: G. Arnaktauyok

Engravers:
Obv.: Dora de Pédery-Hunt
Rev.: Ago Aarand, José Osio

Composition:	**Nickel Ring** 99.0% Ni	**Silver Ring** 92.5% Ag 07.5% Cu	**White Gold Ring** 17.2% Au 77.6% Ag, 5.2% Cu
	Bronze Core 92.0 % Cu 6.0% Al, 2.0% Ni	**Silver Gilt Core** 92.5% Ag 07.5% Cu	**Yellow Gold Core** 91.7% Au 04.1% Ag, 4.2% Cu
	Standard	**Standard**	**Standard**
Weight (g):	Ring 4.84 Core 2.46 Total 7.30	Ring 5.86 Core 2.97 Total 8.83	Ring 6.31 Core 5.09 Total 11.40
Content: Gold	—	—	0.185 tr oz
Silver	—	0.263 tr oz	0.164 tr oz
Diameter (mm):	Ring 28.00 Core 16.80	Ring 28.07 Core 16.80	Ring 28.00 Core 16.80
Thickness (mm):	1.80	1.90	1.80
Edge:	Interrupted Serration	Interrupted Serration	Interrupted Serration
Die Axis:	↑↑	↑↑	↑↑
Finish:	Brilliant Uncirculated, Specimen	Proof	Proof

Case of Issue:
Nickel / Bronze, Brilliant Uncirculated: Blue presentation folder
Nickel / Bronze, Specimen: Maple wood case, encapsulated coin, window box
Silver / Gilt, Proof: Green leatherette case, black insert, encapsulated coin, COA
Gold / Gold, Proof: Antique case, black insert, encapsulated coin, COA

DATE	DESCRIPTION	SOURCE	QUANTITY SOLD	ISSUE PRICE	FINISH	65	66	67	68
1999	Nickel / Bronze	BU Set	N/A	N/A	BU	10.	15.	—	—
1999	Nickel / Bronze	Specimen Set, Maple wood case	20,000	N/A	Specimen	—	20.	25.	—
1999	Silver / Gilt	Proof Set, Single	39,873	24.95	Proof	—	—	20.	25.
1999	Gold / Gold	Single Case	4,298	299.95	Proof	—	—	350.	375.

VARIETIES OF 1999.

Three different reverse dies were used to produce the three different finishes on the 1999 Nunavut commemorative two dollar coins.

1. Reverse Circulation Die: Incused narrow ring encircling the join between the ring and the core.
2. Reverse Specimen Die: Incused wide ring encircling the join between the ring and the core.
3. Reverse Proof Die: No encircling ring between the ring and the core.

Reverse
Narrow Ring
Brilliant Uncirculated
Dies

Reverse
Wide Ring
Specimen Dies

Reverse:
No Ring
Proof Dies

Two varieties of brilliant uncirculated sets were produced in 1999. The standard set, where the $2 coin was produced with a pair of brilliant uncirculated dies, and the Mule variety where the $2 coin was produced with an obverse brilliant uncirculated die and a reverse proof die. See page 257 for the listings of the 1999 brilliant uncirculated sets.

Nickel bronze, no ring reverse mule

DATE	DESCRIPTION	QUANTITY SOLD	ISSUE PRICE	FINISH	65	66	67	68
1999	Mule from Brilliant Uncirculated Sets	Unknown	N.I.I.	BU	300.	350.	—	—

TWO DOLLARS, PATH OF KNOWLEDGE COMMEMORATIVE, 2000.

The mother polar bear passes to her cubs the lessons of survival on the Arctic ice floes.

Obverse
Nickel / Bronze

Reverse
Nickel / Bronze

Obverse
Gold / Gold

Reverse
Gold / Gold

Designers:
Obv.: Dora de Pédery-Hunt
Rev.: Tony Bianco

Engravers:
Obv.: Dora de Pédery-Hunt
Rev.: Cosme Saffioti

Composition:	**Nickel Ring** 99.0% Ni	**Silver Ring** 92.5% Ag 07.5% Cu	**White Gold Ring** 17.2% Au 77.6% Ag, 5.2% Cu
	Bronze Core 92.0 % Cu 6.0% Al, 2.0% Ni	**Silver Gilt Core** 92.5% Ag 07.5% Cu	**Yellow Gold Core** 91.7% Au 04.1% Ag, 4.2% Cu
	Standard	**Standard**	**Standard**
Weight (g):	Ring 4.84 Core 2.46 Total 7.30	Ring 5.86 Core 2.97 Total 8.83	Ring 6.31 Core 5.09 Total 11.40
Content: Gold	—	—	0.185 tr oz
Silver	—	0.263 tr oz	0.164 tr oz
Diameter (mm):	Ring 28.00 Core 16.80	Ring 28.07 Core 16.80	Ring 28.00 Core 16.80
Thickness (mm):	1.80	1.90	1.80
Edge:	Interrupted Serration	Interrupted Serration	Interrupted Serration
Die Axis:	↑↑	↑↑	↑↑
Finish:	Brilliant Uncirculated, Specimen	Proof	Proof

Case of Issue: Nickel / Bronze, Specimen: Maple wood case, encapsulated coin, sleeve
Silver / Gilt, Proof: Green leatherette case, black insert, encapsulated coin, COA
Gold / Gold, Proof: Antique case, black insert, encapsulated coin, COA

DATE	DESCRIPTION	SOURCE	QUANTITY SOLD	ISSUE PRICE	FINISH	65	66	67	68
2000	Nickel / Bronze, wood case	BU Set	186,985	15.95	BU	10.	15.	—	—
2000	Nickel / Bronze	Specimen Single	1,500	N/A	Specimen	—	25.	30.	—
2000	Nickel / Bronze	Specimen Set	N/A	34.95	Specimen	—	20.	30.	—
2000	Silver / Gilt Silver	Proof Single	39,768	24.95	Proof	—	—	20.	25.
2000	Gold / Gold	Proof Single	5,881	299.95	Proof	—	—	350.	375.

TWO DOLLARS, POLAR BEAR, 2000-2001.

Designers and Engravers:
Obv.: Dora de Pédery-Hunt
Rev.: Brent Townsend, Ago Aarand
Composition: Bronze
Ring: 99.0% Nickel
Core: 92.0% Cu, 6.0% Al, 2.0% Ni
Weight: Ring: 4.84 g, Core: 2.46 g
Total weight: 7.3 g
Diameter: Ring: 28.50 mm, Core: 16.80 mm
Thickness: 1.80 mm
Edge: Interrupted Serration
Die Axis: ↑↑ **Finish:** Specimen
Case: Maple wood case, encapsulated coin, sleeve

DATE	DESCRIPTION	QUANTITY SOLD	ISSUE PRICE	FINISH	SP-66	SP-67
2000	Nickel / Bronze, wood case	20,000	N/A	Specimen	25.	30.
2001	Nickel / Bronze, wood case	20,000	N/A	Specimen	25.	30.

TWO DOLLARS, PROUD POLAR BEAR, STERLING SILVER, 2004.

Issued jointly by the Royal Canadian Mint and Canada Post, the $2 Proud Polar Bear Stamp and Coin Set contains the first single metal two dollar Canadian coin. The set comprises mint and cancelled $2.00 stamps, along with the $2.00 sterling silver coin. The two dollar coin is unusual in that it carries two maple leaf privy marks.

Designer and Engravers:
Obv.: Susanna Blunt, Susan Taylor
Rev.: Stan Witten
Composition: 92.5% Ag, 7.5% Cu
Silver content: 8.14 g, 0.262 tr oz
Weight: 8.8 g **Edge:** Reeded
Diameter: 27.95 mm **Die Axis:** ↑↑
Thickness: 1.70 mm **Finish:** Proof
Case: See Derivatives, page 113

DATE	DESCRIPTION	QUANTITY SOLD	ISSUE PRICE	FINISH	PR-67 UHC	PR-68 UHC
2004	Proud Polar Bear, Sterling silver	12,607	N.I.I.	Proof	65.	75.

TWO DOLLARS, 10TH ANNIVERSARY, GOLD, 1996-2006.

This gold $2 coin does not carry the karat marks similar to the previous gold issues of 1996, 1999 and 2000.

Designers and Engravers:
Obv.: Susanna Blunt, Susan Taylor
Rev.: Brent Townsend, Ago Aarand
Composition:
Yellow Gold Ring: 91.7% Au, 4.1% Ag, 4.2% Cu
White Gold Core: 17.5% Au, 77.6 Ag, 5.2% Cu
Gold content: Gold: 10.352 g, 0.333 tr oz
Silver: 3.151 g, 0.101 tr oz
Weight: Ring: 10.62 g, Core: 3.60 g
Total: 14.22 g
Diameter: Ring: 28.00 mm, Core: 16.80 mm
Thickness: 1.80 mm
Edge: Interrupted Serration
Die Axis: ↑↑ **Finish:** Proof
Case: Maroon clam style case, black insert, encapsulated coin, COA

DATE	DESCRIPTION	QUANTITY SOLD	ISSUE PRICE	FINISH	PR-67 UHC	PR-68 UHC
2006 (1996-)	Yellow gold ring / White gold core	2,068	399.95	Proof	650.	700.

TWO DOLLARS, CHURCHILL REVERSE, RCM LOGO, 1996-2006.

In 2006 a contest was held to name a new polar bear design to appear of the 10th anniversary two dollar coin. The name "Churchill" was the winner. The 10th anniversary coin has the double dates above the Queen's portrait and the Royal Mint logo below.

Designers and Engravers:
Obv.: Susanna Blunt, Susan Taylor
Rev.: Tony Bianco, Stan Witten
Composition:
Ring: 99.9% Ni
Core: 92.0% Cu, 6.0% Al, 2.0% Ni
Weight: 7.3 g
Diameter: Ring: 28.00 mm, Core: 16.80 mm
Thickness: 1.80 mm
Edge: Interrupted Serration
Die Axis: ↑↑
Finish: Brilliant Uncirculated
Case: See Special Uncirculated Sets, page 261

DATE	DESCRIPTION	QUANTITY SOLD	ISSUE PRICE	FINISH	MS-65 NC	MS-66 NC
2006 (1996-)	Churchill Reverse	31,636	N.I.I.	BU	15.	20.

TWO DOLLARS, TWO LYNX KITTENS, YOUNG WILDLIFE SERIES, 2010.

The reclusive Lynx is commemorated on the two dollar coin found in the 2010 Special Edition Specimen Set, page 281.

Designers and Engravers:
Obv.: Susanna Blunt, Susan Taylor
Rev.: Christie Paquet, RCM Staff
Composition:
Ring: 99.9% Ni
Core: 92.0% Cu, 6.0% Al, 2.0% Cu
Weight: 7.5 g
Diameter: Ring: 28.00 mm, Core: 16.80 mm
Thickness: 1.90 mm
Edge: Interrupted Serration
Die Axis: ↑↑
Finish: Specimen; Brilliant portrait, frosted relief lined background
Case: See Special Edition Specimen Sets, page 281

DATE	DESCRIPTION	QUANTITY SOLD	ISSUE PRICE	FINISH	SP-66	SP-67
2010	Two Lynx Kittens	15,000	N.I.I.	Specimen	45.	50.

TWO DOLLAR DERIVATIVES

The following single coins, coin and note sets, or coin and stamp sets are based on the numismatic two dollar coin.

DATE	DESCRIPTION	QUANTITY SOLD	ISSUE PRICE	ISSUER	FINISH	MARKET VALUE
1996	**Two Dollar Coin, Specimen;** $2 Regular bank note; Blue folder	91,427	29.95	RCM	SP-66	25.
1996	**Encapsulated Two Dollar Coin, Proof**; Encapsulated $2 BRX Replacement note; Blue presentation case	27,103	79.95	RCM	PR-67	40.
1996	**Encapsulated Two Dollar Coin, Piedfort**; Encapsulated pair of uncut $2 BRX replacement notes; Blue/green presentation case	11,526	179.95	RCM	PR-67	175.
1996	**Two Dollar Coin, Brilliant Uncirculated**; $2 regular issue note; 45¢ mint stamp; Blue/green presentation case	N/A	N/A	RCM, CP	MS-65	20.
1998W	**Two Dollar Coin**; Mint and cancelled $2 stamps; Blue presentation case	N/A	N/A	RCM, CP	MS-65	20.
1999	**Two Dollar Nunavut Coin**; Mint and cancelled 46¢ stamps; Blue presentation case	N/A	17.95	RCM, CP	MS-65	20.
2000W	**Two Dollar Coin**; Mint and cancelled $2 stamps; Blue presentation case	20,000	19.99	RCM, CP	MS-65	20.
2000	**Two Dollar Coin, "Path of Knowledge" (Three Bears);** Credit card-like holder	N/A	N/A	RCM	MS-65	10.
2001	**Two Dollar Coin;** Credit card-like holder	N/A	N/A	RCM	MS-65	10.
2004	**Two Dollar Proud Polar Bear Coin;** Mint and cancelled $2 stamps; Wooden presentation case	12,607	29.95	RCM, CP	PR-67	70.

ROYAL CANADIAN MINT MARKS ON COINS

"P" is a composition mark for coins struck on multi-ply plated (nickel or copper on steel) planchets

"W" is the mint mark for coins struck at the Winnipeg Mint.

The "Circle M" is the Royal Canadian Mint logo

THREE DOLLARS

THREE DOLLARS, THE BEAVER, SQUARE, 2006.

Designers and Engravers:
Obv.: Susanna Blunt, Susan Taylor
Rev.: Cosme Saffioti, RCM Staff
Composition: 92.50% Ag, 7.50 %Cu plated in 24kt gold
Silver content: 10.84 g, 0.349 tr oz
Weight: 11.72 g
Size: 27.0 x 27.0 mm **Edge:** Plain
Thickness: 1.8 mm **Die Axis:** ↑↑
Finish: Specimen
Case: Maroon plastic slide case; black plastic insert; encapsulated coin, COA

DATE	DESCRIPTION	QUANTITY SOLD	ISSUE PRICE	FINISH	SP-66	SP-67
2006	The Beaver	20,000	45.95	Specimen	250.	275.

THREE DOLLARS, RETURN OF THE TYEE, 2010.

Salmon has long been the essential food source of the Northwest Coast people. The largest species of Pacific salmon is the Chinook, or black salmon, called the Tyee (King) by the First Nation People. Two tyee are arranged in a circle, representing the "Circle of Life."

Designers and Engravers:
Obv.: Susanna Blunt, Susan Taylor
Rev.: Jody Broomfield, RCM Staff
Composition: 99.99% Ag
Silver content: 7.96 g, 0.256 tr oz
Weight: 7.96 g
Diameter: 27.0 mm **Edge:** Reeded
Thickness: 1.9 mm **Die Axis:** ↑↑
Finish: Proof, Selectively plated in pink and yellow gold
Case: Maroon clam style case; black flocked insert; encapsulated coin, COA

DATE	DESCRIPTION	QUANTITY SOLD	ISSUE PRICE	FINISH	PR-67 UHC	PR-68 UHC
2010	Return of the Tyee	15,000	54.95	Proof	60.	70.

WILDLIFE CONSERVATION SERIES

THREE DOLLARS, CONSERVATION WILDLIFE SERIES, SQUARE, 2010.

Designers:
Obv.: Susanna Blunt
Rev.: Jason Bouwman

Engravers:
Obv.: Susan Taylor
Rev.: RCM Staff

Composition: 92.50% Ag; 7.50% Cu, gold plated
Silver content: 11.1 g, 0.357 tr oz
Weight: 12.0 g
Size: 27.1 x 27.1 mm
Thickness: 2.0 mm
Edge: Plain
Die Axis: ↑↑
Finish: Specimen, gold plated
Case: Maroon leatherette clam style case; black flocked insert; encapsulated coin, COA

Common Obverse

Barn Owl

Polar Bear

DATE	DESCRIPTION	QUANTITY SOLD	ISSUE PRICE	FINISH	SP-66	SP-67
2010	Barn Owl	15,000	59.95	Specimen	65.	75.
2010	Polar Bear	15,000	59.95	Specimen	65.	75.

FOUR DOLLARS

FOUR DOLLARS, DINOSAUR COLLECTION, 2007-2010.

Over 65 million years ago Alberta and Saskatchewan were covered by a great sub-tropical inland sea, home to more than thirty five dinosaur species. Currently there are five coins in this series.

Obverse
With RCM Logo

Designers and Engravers:
Obv.: Susanna Blunt, Susan Taylor
Rev.: Kerri Burnett, RCM Staff
Composition: 99.99% Ag
Silver content: 15.87 g, 0.510 tr oz
Weight: 15.87 g
Edge: Reeded
Diameter: 34.0 mm
Die Axis: ↑↑
Thickness: 2.10 mm
Finish: Proof, Selective aging effect
Case: Maroon clam style case, black flocked insert, encapsulated coin, COA

2007
Parasaurolophus

2008
Triceratops

2009
Tyrannosaurus Rex

2010
Dromaeosaurus

Obverse
Without RCM Logo

2010
Euoplocephalus Tutus

DATE	DESCRIPTION	QUANTITY SOLD	ISSUE PRICE	FINISH	PR-67 UHC	PR-68 UHC
2007	Parasaurolophus	14,946	39.95	Proof	300.	350.
2008	Triceratops	13,046	39.95	Proof	125.	150.
2009	Tyrannosaurus Rex	13,572	39.95	Proof	100.	125.
2010	Dromaeosaurus	8,982	42.95	Proof	55.	65.
2010	Euoplocephalus Tutus	13,000	49.95	Proof	50.	60.

FOUR DOLLARS, HANGING THE STOCKINGS, 2009.

The link between stockings and Christmas began to emerge with the legend of Saint Nicholas, when he dropped three small bags of gold down the chimney and into the stockings of the three daughters of a poor man, to help with their dowries.

Designers and Engravers:
Obv.: Susanna Blunt, Susan Taylor
Rev.: Tony Bianco, RCM Staff
Composition: 99.99% Ag
Silver content: 15.87 oz, .510 tr oz
Weight: 15.87 g
Size: 34.0 mm
Thickness: 2.0 mm
Edge: Reeded
Die Axis: ↑↑
Finish: Proof
Case: Maroon clam style case; black flocked insert; encapsulated coin, COA

DATE	DESCRIPTION	QUANTITY SOLD	ISSUE PRICE	FINISH	PR-67 UHC	PR-68 UHC
2009	Hanging The Stockings	6,011	42.95	Proof	55.	65.

FIVE DOLLARS

FIVE DOLLARS, NORMAN BETHUNE COMMEMORATIVE, 1998.

In 1998 the Royal Canadian Mint produced a $5 silver coin to commemorate the 60th anniversary of Dr. Norman Bethune's arrival in China. The coin was issued as part of a two coin set, in conjunction with China Gold Coin Incorporation (CGCI).

Designers:
Obv.: Dora de Pédery-Hunt
Rev.: Harry Chan

Engravers:
Obv.: Dora de Pédery-Hunt
Rev.: Ago Aarand, Stan Witten

Case of Issue: Brown plastic two-hole red insert, encapsulated coin, COA, box cover in Chinese brocade

MINT	COMPOSITION	WEIGHT (G)	SILVER CONTENT	DIAMETER	EDGE	THICKNESS
CGCI	99.99% silver	31.10	31.10 g, 1.00 tr oz	40.0	Reeded	3.2 mm
RCM	99.99% silver	31.39	31.39 g, 1.01 tr oz	38.0	Reeded	3.3 mm

DATE	DESCRIPTION	QUANTITY SOLD	ISSUE PRICE	FINISH	PR-67 UHC	PR-68 UHC
1998	Bethune - CGCI	N.I.I.	—	Proof	70.	80.
1998	Bethune - RCM	N.I.I.	—	Proof	70.	80.
1998	Set of 2 coins	65,831	98.00	Proof	125.	—

FIVE DOLLARS, THE VIKING SETTLEMENT, 1999.

This coin commemorates the Viking landing at L'Anse-aux-Meadows, Newfoundland, circa 1000 A.D. Norway issued a 20 Kroner coin in 1999 also commemorating the same Viking Landing. These two coins were offered as a set.

1999 Obverse
Designer and Engraver:
Dora de Pédery-Hunt

Canada $5
Designer: D. Curley
Engraver: S. Witten

1999 Obverse
Designer and Engraver:
Unknown

Norway 20 Kroner
Designer and Engraver:
Unknown

Composition: 81.0% Cu, 9.0% Ni, 10.0 Zi
Weight: 9.9 g
Edge: Plain
Thickness: 2.5 mm
Diameter: 27.0 mm
Finish: Proof
Case: Oval imitation resin stone case, two-holes; brown insert, encapsulated coins, printed cardboard outer sleeve.

DATE	DESCRIPTION	QUANTITY SOLD	ISSUE PRICE	FINISH	PR-67 UHC	PR-68 UHC
1999	Canada $5	—	—	Proof	30.	40.
1999	Norway 20 Kroner	—	—	Proof	30.	40.
1999	Set of 2 coins	28,450	N/A	Proof	50.	55.

FIVE DOLLARS, 100TH ANNIVERSARY OF THE FIRST WIRELESS TRANSMISSION, 2001.

On December 12th, 1901, Gugliemo Marconi (1874-1937) successfully transmitted the first wireless message across the Atlantic from Poldhu in Cornwall, England, to Signal Hill in St. John's, Newfoundland. To commemorate this anniversary the Royal Canadian Mint, in conjunction with the Royal Mint, issued this two-coin set.

2001 Obverse
Designer and Engraver:
Dora de Pédery-Hunt

Canada $5
Designer and Engraver:
Cosme Saffioti

2001 Obverse
Des.: I. Rank-Bradley
Engraver: Robert Evans

British £2
Des.: Royal Mint Staff
Engraver: Robert Evans

	Canada $5	British £2
Composition:	Coin: 92.5% Ag, 7.5% Cu Cameo: 24-karat gold plate	Coin: 92.5% Ag, 7.5% Cu Outer circle: Plated 22kt gold Inner disc: 92.5% Ag, 7.5% Cu
Silver Content:	15.69 g, 0.504 tr oz	22.20 g, 0.714 tr oz
Weight:	16.96 g	24.0 g
Diameter:	28.40 mm	28.40 mm
Thickness:	N/A	N/A
Edge:	Reeded	Lettering
Die Axis:	↑↑	↑↓

Finish: Proof
Case of Issue: Brown resin oval case with a Marconi stamp on upper lid, brown flocked insert, encapsulated coin, COA, brown printed cardboard box.

DATE	DESCRIPTION	QUANTITY SOLD	ISSUE PRICE	FINISH	PR-67 UHC	PR-68 UHC
2001	Canada $5	—	—	Proof	50.	60.
2001	U.K. £2	—	—	Proof	50.	60.
2001	Set of 2 coins	15,011	99.95	Proof	90.	—

FIVE DOLLARS, 2006 F.I.F.A. WORLD CUP, 2003.

The Canadian Soccer Association, founded in 1912, has been affiliated with the Federation International de Football Association since 1913. The 2006 World Cup championship was held in Germany.

Designers and Engravers:
Obv.: Susanna Blunt, Susan Taylor
Rev.: Urszula Walerzak, José Osio
Composition: 99.99% Ag
Silver content: 31.30 g, 1.01 tr oz
Weight: 31.3 g
Diameter: 38.0 mm
Thickness: 3.1 mm
Edge: Reeded
Die Axis: ↑↑
Finish: Proof
Case: Black case, black flocked insert, encapsulated coin, COA, multicoloured sleeve

DATE	DESCRIPTION	QUANTITY SOLD	ISSUE PRICE	FINISH	PR-67 UHC	PR-68 UHC
2003	2006 F.I.F.A. World Cup	21,542	39.95	Proof	50.	60.

FIVE DOLLARS, 100TH ANNIVERSARY OF THE CANADIAN OPEN CHAMPIONSHIP, 2004

Issued jointly by the Royal Canadian Mint and Canada Post to celebrate the 100th Anniversary of the tournament, this limited edition framed set contains both a five dollar and ten cent coin. These coins were issued in various combinations.

Designers and Engravers:
Obv.: Susanna Blunt, Susan Taylor
Rev.: Cosme Saffioti
Composition: 99.99% Ag
Silver content: 27.90 g, 0.90 tr oz
Weight: 27.9 g
Diameter: 38.0 mm
Thickness: 3.0 mm
Edge: Reeded
Die Axis: ↑↑
Finish: Proof
Case: See Derivatives, page 124

DATE	DESCRIPTION	QUANTITY SOLD	ISSUE PRICE	FINISH	PR-67 UHC	PR-68 UHC
2004	100th Anniv. Canadian Open Championship	18,750	N.I.I.	Proof	45.	55.

Note: N.I.I. denotes Not Issued Individually.

FIVE DOLLARS, CANADIAN WILDLIFE SERIES, 2004-2006.

These five dollar coins were part of a coin and stamp set series which was issued jointly by the Royal Canadian Mint and Canada Post to pay homage to Canada's diverse wildlife. See derivatives, page 124.

2004
The Majestic Moose
Obv. Des.: Susanna Blunt
Obv. Engr.: Susan Taylor
Rev. Des.: D. Preston-Smith
Rev. Engr.: Stan Witten

2005 Common Obverse
Designer: Susanna Blunt
Engraver: Susan Taylor

White-tailed Deer and Fawn
Designer: Xerxes Irani
Engraver: José Osio

The Atlantic Walrus and Calf
Designer: Pierre Leduc
Engraver: José Osio

2006 Common Obverse
Designer: Susanna Blunt
Engraver: Susan Taylor

Peregrine Falcon and Nestlings
Designer: Dwayne Harty
Engraver: José Osio

Sable Island Horse and Foal
Designer: Christie Paquet
Engraver: José Osio

Composition: 99.99% Ag
Silver content: 28.00 g, 0.90 tr oz
Weight: 28.00 g
Diameter: 38.0 mm
Case of Issue: See Derivatives, page 124

Thickness: 3.0 mm
Die Axis: ↑↑
Edge: Reeded
Finish: Proof

DATE	DESCRIPTION	QUANTITY SOLD	ISSUE PRICE	FINISH	PR-67 UHC	PR-68 UHC
2004	The Majestic Moose	12,822	N.I.I.	Proof	200.	225.
2005	White-tailed Deer and Fawn	6,439	N.I.I.	Proof	55.	65.
2005	The Atlantic Walrus and Calf	5,519	N.I.I.	Proof	55.	65.
2006	Peregrine Falcon and Nestlings	7,226	N.I.I.	Proof	65.	85.
2006	Sable Island Horse and Foal	10,108	N.I.I.	Proof	70.	90.

FIVE DOLLARS, 60TH ANNIVERSARY OF THE END OF THE SECOND WORLD WAR, 2005.

In the six years of conflict Canada had enlisted more than one million men and women in His Majesty's Armed Forces. Of these, more than 45,000 gave their lives in the cause of peace.

Obverse

Reverse

Reverse with Maple Leaf Privy Mark

Designers:
Obv.: Susanna Blunt
Rev.: Peter Mossman

Engravers:
Obv.: Susan Taylor
Rev.: Christie Paquet

Composition: 99.99% Ag
Silver content: 31.50 g, 1.01 tr oz
Weight: 31.5 g
Diameter: 38.0 mm
Edge: Reeded
Thickness: 3.2 mm
Die Axis: ↑↑
Finish: See below
Case of Issue: Maroon plastic display case, black plastic insert, encapsulated coin, COA

DATE	DESCRIPTION	QUANTITY SOLD	ISSUE PRICE	FINISH	66	67	68
2005	60th Anniv. WWII	25,000	39.95	Specimen	50.	60.	—
2005	60th Anniv. WWII with Privy Maple Leaf Mark	10,000	N.I.I.	Proof	—	125.	150.

FIVE DOLLARS, COMMEMORATING THE CENTENNIAL OF THE PROVINCES OF ALBERTA AND SASKATCHEWAN, 2005.

Common obverse
Designer: Susanna Blunt
Engraver: Susan Taylor

Alberta Centennial
Designer: Michelle Grant
Engraver: Stan Witten

Saskatchewan Centennial
Designer: Paulett Sapergia
Engraver: José Osio

Composition: 99.99% Ag
Silver content: 25.20 g, 0.81 tr oz
Weight: 25.2 g
Diameter: 36.0 mm
Edge: Reeded
Thickness: 3.1 mm
Die Axis: ↑↑
Finish: Proof
Case of Issue: Maroon plastic display case, black plastic insert, encapsulated coin, COA

DATE	DESCRIPTION	QUANTITY SOLD	ISSUE PRICE	FINISH	PR-67 UHC	PR-68 UHC
2005	Alberta Centennial	20,000	49.95	Proof	45.	50.
2005	Saskatchewan Centennial	20,000	49.95	Proof	40.	50.

FIVE DOLLARS, BREAST CANCER AWARENESS, 2006.

Designers and Engravers:
Obv.: Susanna Blunt, Susan Taylor
Rev.: Christie Paquet, RCM Staff
Composition: 99.99% Ag
Silver content: 25.17 g, 0.81 tr oz
Weight: 25.175 g
Diameter: 36.07 mm
Thickness: 3.1 mm
Die Axis: ↑↑
Edge: Reeded
Finish: Proof, Painted
Case: Maroon plastic display case, black plastic insert, encapsulated coin, COA

DATE	DESCRIPTION	QUANTITY SOLD	ISSUE PRICE	FINISH	PR-67 UHC	PR-68 UHC
2006	Breast Cancer Awareness, Painted	11,048	59.95	Proof	65.	75.

FIVE DOLLARS, CANADIAN FORCES SNOWBIRDS, 2006.

Designers and Engravers:
Obv.: Susanna Blunt, Susan Taylor
Rev.: Jianping Yan, RCM Staff
Composition: 99.99% Ag
Silver content: 25.17 g, 0.81 tr oz
Weight: 25.175 g
Diameter: 36.07 mm
Thickness: 3.1 mm
Die Axis: ↑↑
Edge: Reeded
Finish: Proof, Double hologram
Case of Issue: See Derivatives, page 124

DATE	DESCRIPTION	QUANTITY SOLD	ISSUE PRICE	FINISH	PR-67 UHC	PR-68 UHC
2006	Canadian Forces Snowbirds; Double hologram	10,034	N.I.I.	Proof	65.	75.

FIVE DOLLARS, 80TH ANNIVERSARY OF CANADA IN JAPAN, 2009.

The legation of Japan opened in Ottawa in 1928, and in 1929 Canada established its mission in Tokyo. With a mintage of 40,000 worldwide, only 5,000 coins were for sale in Canada.

Designers and Engravers:
Obv.: Susanna Blunt, Susan Taylor
Rev.: RCM Staff
Composition: 92.5% Ag, 7.5% Cu
Silver content: 23.29 g, 0.75 tr oz
Weight: 25.175 g
Diameter: 36.07 mm
Thickness: 3.1 mm
Die Axis: ↑↑
Edge: Reeded
Finish: Proof
Case: Maroon leatherette clam style case, black flocked insert, encapsulated coin, COA

DATE	DESCRIPTION	QUANTITY SOLD	ISSUE PRICE	FINISH	PR-67 UHC	PR-68 UHC
2009 (1929-)	80th Anniversary of Canada in Japan	27,872	N/A	Proof	80.	90.

FIVE DOLLAR DERIVATIVES

DATE	DESCRIPTION	QUANTITY SOLD	ISSUE PRICE	ISSUER	FINISH	MARKET VALUE
2004	**Five Dollar Coin,** Majestic Moose. Two $5 stamps (one mint, one cancelled); COA; Wooden presentation case	12,822	39.95	RCM, CP	PR-67	250.
2004	**Five Dollar and Ten Cent Coins**, Canadian Open Chmpshp.; two commemorative stamps (one mint, one cancelled); two golf tees; RCM medallion; Framed; COA	18,750	49.99	RCM, CP	PR-67	75.
2005	**Allied Forces Silver Proof Set**, six coins: Australia, Canada, Russia, U.S.A. and U.K.	10,000	£245.	RCM, BRM	PR-67	500.
2005	**Five Dollar Coin**, White-tailed Deer and Fawn. Two $1 stamps (one mint, one cancelled); COA; Wooden presentation case.	6,439	49.55	RCM, CP	PR-67	65.
2005	**Five Dollar Coin**, Atlantic Walrus and Calf; Two $1 stamps (one mint, one cancelled); COA; Wooden presentation case.	5,519	49.55	RCM, CP	PR-67	65.
2006	**Five Dollar Coin**, Peregrine Falcon and Nestlings. Two $2 stamps (one mint, one cancelled). COA. Wooded presentation case.	7,226	49.55	RCM, CP	PR-67	85.
2006	**Five Dollar Coin**, Sable Island Horse and Foal. Two $2 stamps (one mint, one cancelled). COA. Wooded presentation case.	10,108	49.55	RCM, CP	PR-67	90.
2006	**Five Dollar Coin**, Snowbirds; Four 51¢ stamps (two mint, two on a "uniquely cancelled" souvenir sheet; Booklet; Numbered plaque; Metallic box	10,034	59.95	RCM, CP	PR-67	75.

FIVE AND TEN DOLLARS

MONTREAL SUMMER OLYMPIC GAMES, SILVER ISSUES, 1973-1976.

In 1976, Montreal, Quebec, hosted the XXI Olympiad. To commemorate and help finance Canada's first Olympics, the federal government agreed to produce a series of twenty-eight silver and two gold coins (see section following for the $100 gold coins). There are seven series of silver coins. Each series has two $5 and two $10 coins, making a total of fourteen coins of each denomination. Each series depicts different Olympic themes on the reverse and has a common design (except for the date) on the obverse. The date on the coins is usually the year of minting. Orders for the Olympic coins were accepted up to the end of December 1976, so a small unit continued to function into 1977 on the Olympic Coin Program. Mintage by series was never recorded, but the annual reports of the Royal Canadian Mint give the following figures by year: 1973 - 537,898 $10, 543,098 $5; 1974 - 3,949,878 $10, 3,981,140 $5; 1975 - 4,952,433 $10, 3,970,000 $5; 1976 - 3,970,514 $10, 3,775,259 $5. These figures do not necessarily coincide with the actual post office sales figures for the coins.

The Olympic coins were offered to the collector in two finishes, brilliant uncirculated and proof. The uncirculated issues were packaged and offered for sale in four different formats: (1) encapsulated (single coins only in styrene crystal capsules); (2) one-coin "standard" case (single coins in black case with red interior); (3) four-coin "custom" set (two $5 and two $10 coins by series in black case with gold trim and red insert); and (4) four-coin "prestige" set (two $5 and two $10 coins by series in matte black leatherette case with blue insert).

The proof coins were only offered in sets, and the "deluxe" case of issue was made of Canadian white birch with a specially tanned steer hide cover with a black insert.

Because of the fluctuating price of silver during the years of the program (1973 to 1976), the original issue prices varied somewhat from series to series.

SERIES I TO VII

The following information is common to all twenty-eight $5.00 and $10.00 silver coins. Naturally, the date changes with the year of issue.

SPECIFICATIONS

FIVE DOLLARS
Composition: 92.5% Ag, 7.5% Cu
Silver content: 22.48 g, 0.72 tr oz
Weight: 24.30 g
Diameter: 38.00 mm
Thickness: 2.35 mm
Edge: Reeded
Die Axis: ↑↑
Finish: Proof and Uncirculated
Case of Issue: See above

TEN DOLLARS
Composition: 92.5% Ag, 7.5% Cu
Silver content: 44.95 g, 1.44 tr oz
Weight: 48.60 g
Diameter: 45.00 mm
Thickness: 3.15 mm
Edge: Reeded
Die Axis: ↑↑
Finish: Proof and Uncirculated
Case of Issue: See above

Original Issue Prices

PACKAGE TYPE	SERIES I	SERIES II	SERIES III-VII
$5 Encapsulated	6.00	7.50	8.00
$10 Encapsulated	12.00	15.00	15.75
Set of 4 Encapsulated	36.00	45.00	47.50
$5 in Standard Case	7.50	9.00	9.00
$10 in Standard Case	14.00	17.00	17.00
Set of 4 in Standard Case	43.00	52.00	52.00
Custom Set	45.00	55.00	55.00
Prestige Set	50.00	60.00	60.00
Deluxe Proof Set	72.50	82.50	82.50

MONTREAL SUMMER OLYMPIC GAMES — SERIES I

1973 $10 Obverse
Designer: Arnold Machin
Engraver: Patrick Brindley

Coin No. 1
Map of the World
Reverse design was photochemically etched

Coin No. 3
Montreal Skyline
Ago Aarand

1973 $5 Obverse
Designer: Arnold Machin
Engraver: Patrick Brindley

Coin No. 2
Map of North America
Reverse design was photochemically etched

Coin No. 4
Kingston and Sailboats
Terrence Smith

Theme: Geographic
Official Release Date: December 13, 1973. The Series I issuing period began in late 1973 and was carried over into 1974.
Designer of Reverse: Georges Huel, worked by invitation.
Reverse Engravers: See above
Issue Price: See page 125
Finish: Proof and circulation

DATE	DESCRIPTION	QUANTITY SOLD	FINISH	65	66	67	68
1973	$5 Map of North America	537,898	Circulation	25.	30.	60.	—
1973	$5 Map of North America	Included	Proof	—	—	25.	30.
1973	$5 Kingston and Sailboats	Included	Circulation	25.	30.	60.	—
1973	$5 Kingston and Sailboats	Included	Proof	—	—	25.	30.
1973	$10 Map of the World	543,098	Circulation	50.	55.	85.	—
1973	$10 Map of the World	Included	Proof	—	—	50.	55.
1973	$10 Montreal Skyline	Included	Circulation	50.	55.	85.	—
1973	$10 Montreal Skyline	Included	Proof	—	—	50.	55.

Note: Mintage numbers are simply estimates based on the 1974-1976 Royal Canadian Mint reports.

MONTREAL SUMMER OLYMPIC GAMES —1973-1974 Mule

During the latter half of 1974, a dated obverse die - possibly made in advance for the Series II coins - was paired inadvertently with a Series I reverse die of the Map of the World resulting in the production and release of a Series I-Series II mule dated 1974. The 1973-1974 Mule was found in the 1973 four-coin custom sets, and mostly those with a European release location.

DATE	DESCRIPTION	QUANTITY SOLD	FINISH	MS-65	MS-66	MS-67
1973-74	$10 1974 Obverse - 1973 Map Reverse	Unknown	Circulation	350.	450.	—

NOTE TO COLLECTORS

The 1976 Montreal Summer Olympic Games were financed by the sale of five and ten dollar sterling silver coins issued over a four year period (1973-1976). The volume of coins soon overcame any collector demand. Their value is based on face, or intrinsic value, whichever is greater. Currently, the intrinsic value is the driving force, and this will vary day-to-day with the silver market.

INTRINSIC VALUE OF MONTREAL OLYMPIC COINS

PRICE OF SILVER	$5	$10	FOUR COIN SET
$20.00	$14.40	$28.80	$84.40
$25.00	$18.00	$36.00	$108.00
$30.00	$21.60	$43.20	$129.60
$35.00	$25.20	$50.40	$151.10
$40.00	$28.80	$57.60	$172.80
$45.00	$32.40	$64.80	$194.40
$50.00	$36.00	$72.00	$216.00
$55.00	$39.60	$79.20	$237.60
$60.00	$43.20	$86.40	$259.20

MONTREAL SUMMER OLYMPIC GAMES — SERIES II

1974 $10 Obverse
Designer: Arnold Machin
Engraver: Patrick Brindley

Coin No. 5
Head of Zeus
Patrick Brindley

Coin No. 7
Temple of Zeus
Walter Ott

1974 $5 Obverse
Designer: Arnold Machin
Engraver: Patrick Brindley

Coin No. 6
Athlete with Torch
Patrick Brindley

Coin No. 8
Olympic Rings
and Wreath
Walter Ott

Theme: Olympic Motifs
Official Release Date: September 16, 1974
Designer of Reverse: Anthony Mann, winner of an invitational competition.
Reverse Engravers: See above
Issue Price: See page 125
Finish: Proof and circulation

DATE	DESCRIPTION	QUANTITY SOLD	FINISH	65	66	67	68
1974	$5 Athlete with Torch	1,990,570	Circulation	25.	30.	60.	—
1974	$5 Athlete with Torch	Included	Proof	—	—	25.	30.
1974	$5 Olympic Rings and Wreath	Included	Circulation	25.	30.	60.	—
1974	$5 Olympic Rings and Wreath	Included	Proof	—	—	25.	30.
1974	$10 Head of Zeus	1,974,939	Circulation	50.	55.	85.	—
1974	$10 Head of Zeus	Included	Proof	—	—	50.	55.
1974	$10 Temple of Zeus	Included	Circulation	50.	55.	85.	—
1974	$10 Temple of Zeus	Included	Proof	—	—	50.	55.

MONTREAL SUMMER OLYMPIC GAMES — SERIES III

1974 $10 Obverse
Designer: Arnold Machin
Engraver: Patrick Brindley

Coin No. 9
Lacrosse
Walter Ott

Coin No. 11
Cycling
Ago Aarand

1974 $5 Obverse
Designer: Arnold Machin
Engraver: Patrick Brindley

Coin No. 10
Canoeing
Patrick Brindley

Coin No. 12
Rowing
Terrence Smith

Theme: Early Canadian Sports
Official Release Date: April 16, 1975
Designer of Reverse: Ken Danby, winner of an invitational competition.
Engravers: See above
Issue Price: See page 125
Finish: Proof and circulation

DATE	DESCRIPTION	QUANTITY SOLD	FINISH	65	66	67	68
1974	$5 Canoeing	1,990,570	Circulation	25.	30.	60.	—
1974	$5 Canoeing	Included	Proof	—	—	25.	30.
1974	$5 Rowing	Included	Circulation	25.	30.	60.	—
1974	$5 Rowing	Included	Proof	—	—	25.	30.
1974	$10 Lacrosse	1,974,939	Circulation	50.	55.	85.	—
1974	$10 Lacrosse	Included	Proof	—	—	50.	55.
1974	$10 Cycling	Included	Circulation	50.	55.	85.	—
1974	$10 Cycling	Included	Proof	—	—	50.	55.

MONTREAL SUMMER OLYMPIC GAMES — SERIES IV

1975 $10 Obverse
Designer: Arnold Machin
Engraver: Patrick Brindley

Coin No. 13
Men's Hurdles
Patrick Brindley

Coin No. 15
Women's Shot Put
Patrick Brindley

1975 $5 Obverse
Designer: Arnold Machin
Engraver: Patrick Brindley

Coin No. 14
Marathon
Walter Ott

Coin No. 16
Women's Javelin
Walter Ott

Theme: Olympic Track and Field Sports
Official Release Date: August 12, 1975
Designer of Reverse: Leo Yerxa, winner of an invitational competition.
Engravers: See above
Issue Price: See page 125
Finish: Proof and circulation

DATE	DESCRIPTION	QUANTITY SOLD	FINISH	65	66	67	68
1975	$5 Marathon	1,985,000	Circulation	25.	30.	60.	—
1975	$5 Marathon	Included	Proof	—	—	25.	30.
1975	$5 Women's Javelin	Included	Circulation	25.	30.	60.	—
1975	$5 Women's Javelin	Included	Proof	—	—	25.	30.
1975	$10 Men's Hurdles	2,476,217	Circulation	50.	55.	85.	—
1975	$10 Men's Hurdles	Included	Proof	—	—	50.	55.
1975	$10 Women's Shot Put	Included	Circulation	50.	55.	85.	—
1975	$10 Women's Shot Put	Included	Proof	—	—	50.	55.

MONTREAL SUMMER OLYMPIC GAMES — SERIES V

1975 $10 Obverse
Designer: Arnold Machin
Engraver: Patrick Brindley

Coin No. 17
Paddling
Reverse design was photochemically etched

Coin No. 19
Sailing
Reverse design was photochemically etched

1975 $5 Obverse
Designer: Arnold Machin
Engraver: Patrick Brindley

Coin No. 18
Diving
Reverse design was photochemically etched

Coin No. 20
Swimming
Reverse design was photochemically etched

Theme: Olympic Summer Sports
Official Release Date: December 1, 1975
Designer of Reverse: Lynda Cooper, winner of an open national competition.
Engravers: See above
Issue Price: See page 125
Finish: Proof and circulation

DATE	DESCRIPTION	QUANTITY SOLD	FINISH	65	66	67	68
1975	$5 Diving	1,985,000	Circulation	25.	30.	60.	—
1975	$5 Diving	Included	Proof	—	—	25.	30.
1975	$5 Swimming	Included	Circulation	25.	30.	60.	—
1975	$5 Swimming	Included	Proof	—	—	25.	30.
1975	$10 Paddling	2,476,216	Circulation	50.	55.	85.	—
1975	$10 Paddling	Included	Proof	—	—	50.	55.
1975	$10 Sailing	Included	Circulation	50.	55.	85.	—
1975	$10 Sailing	Included	Proof	—	—	50.	55.

MONTREAL SUMMER OLYMPIC GAMES — SERIES VI

1976 $10 Obverse
Designer: Arnold Machin
Engraver: Patrick Brindley

Coin No. 21
Field Hockey
Reverse design was photochemically etched

Coin No. 23
Soccer
Reverse design was photochemically etched

1976 $5 Obverse
Designer: Arnold Machin
Engraver: Patrick Brindley

Coin No. 22
Fencing
Reverse design was photochemically etched

Coin No. 24
Boxing
Reverse design was photochemically etched

Theme: Olympic Team and Body Contact Sports
Official Release Date: March 1, 1976
Designer of Reverse: Shigeo Fukada, winner of an open international competition.
Engravers: See above
Issue Price: See page 125
Finish: Proof and circulation

DATE	DESCRIPTION	QUANTITY SOLD	FINISH	65	66	67	68
1976	$5 Fencing	1,887,630	Circulation	25.	30.	60.	—
1976	$5 Fencing	Included	Proof	—	—	25.	30.
1976	$5 Boxing	Included	Circulation	25.	30.	60.	—
1976	$5 Boxing	Included	Proof	—	—	25.	30.
1976	$10 Field Hockey	1,985.257	Circulation	50.	55.	85.	—
1976	$10 Field Hockey	Included	Proof	—	—	50.	55.
1976	$10 Soccer	Included	Circulation	50.	55.	85.	—
1976	$10 Soccer	Included	Proof	—	—	50.	55.

MONTREAL SUMMER OLYMPIC GAMES — SERIES VII

1976 $10 Obverse
Designer: Arnold Machin
Engraver: Patrick Brindley

Coin No. 25
Olympic Stadium
Ago Aarand

Coin No. 27
Olympic Velodrome
Terrence Smith

1976 $5 Obverse
Designer: Arnold Machin
Engraver: Patrick Brindley

Coin No. 26
Olympic Village
Sheldon Beveridge

Coin No. 28
Olympic Flame
Walter Ott

Theme: Olympic Games Souvenir Designs
Official Release Date: June 1, 1976
Designer of Reverse: Elliott John Morrison, winner of an invitational competition.
Engravers: See above
Issue Price: See page 125
Finish: Proof and circulation

DATE	DESCRIPTION	QUANTITY SOLD	FINISH	65	66	67	68
1976	$5 Olympic Village	1,887,629	Circulation	25.	30.	60.	—
1976	$5 Olympic Village	Included	Proof	—	—	30.	30.
1976	$5 Olympic Flame	Included	Circulation	25.	30.	60.	—
1976	$5 Olympic Flame	Included	Proof	—	—	30.	30.
1976	$10 Olympic Stadium	1,985,257	Circulation	50.	55.	85.	—
1976	$10 Olympic Stadium	Included	Proof	—	—	50.	55.
1976	$10 Olympic Velodrome	Included	Circulation	50.	55.	85.	—
1976	$10 Olympic Velodrome	Included	Proof	—	—	50.	55.

EIGHT DOLLARS

EIGHT DOLLARS, GREAT GRIZZLY, 2004.

Designers and Engravers:
Obv.: Susanna Blunt, Susan Taylor
Rev.: Unknown, Susan Taylor
Composition: 92.5% Ag, 7.5% Cu
Silver content: 26.64 g, 0.856 tr oz
Weight: 28.8 g
Diameter: 39.0 mm
Thickness: 2.75 mm
Edge: Reeded
Die Axis: ↑↑
Finish: Proof
Case: See Derivatives, page 136

DATE	DESCRIPTION	QUANTITY SOLD	ISSUE PRICE	FINISH	PR-67 UHC	PR-68 UHC
2004	Great Grizzly	12,942	N.I.I.	Proof	90.	100.

EIGHT DOLLARS, 120TH ANNIVERSARY OF THE CANADIAN PACIFIC RAILWAY, 2005.

A set of two eight dollar coins was issued in 2005. One honours the Chinese workers in Canada for their enormous contributions; the other commemorates the opening of the Transcontinental Railway in 1885.

Designers:
Obv.: Susanna Blunt
Rev.: RCM Staff
Composition: 99.99% Ag with gold plated inner core
Silver content: 32.15 g, 1.03 tr oz
Weight: 32.15 g
Diameter: 40.0 mm
Thickness: N/A
Case of Issue: Not known

Engravers:
Obv.: Susan Taylor
Rev.: RCM Staff

Edge: Reeded
Die Axis: ↑↑
Finish: Proof

DATE	DESCRIPTION	QUANTITY SOLD	ISSUE PRICE	FINISH	PR-67 UHC	PR-68 UHC
2005	Railway Bridge	—	N.I.I.	Proof	65.	75.
2005	Chinese Memorial	—	N.I.I.	Proof	65.	75.
2005	Set of 2 coins	9,892	120.00	Proof	100.	—

EIGHT DOLLARS, THE SHAPE OF TRADE IN ANCIENT CHINA, 2007.

Designers and Engravers:
Obv.: Susanna Blunt, Susan Taylor
Rev.: Harvey Chan, RCM Staff
Composition: 99.99% Ag
Silver content: 25.18 g, 0.81 tr oz
Weight: 25.18 g
Diameter: 36.1 mm
Thickness: 2.90 mm
Edge: Reeded
Die Axis: ↑↑
Finish: Proof
Case: Maroon clam style case, black flock insert, encapsulated coin, COA

DATE	DESCRIPTION	QUANTITY SOLD	ISSUE PRICE	FINISH	PR-67 UHC	PR-68 UHC
2007	Ancient China	19,996	49.95	Proof	60.	70.

EIGHT DOLLARS, MAPLE OF LONG LIFE, 2007.

Designers and Engravers:
Obv.: Susanna Blunt, Susan Taylor
Rev.: Jianping Yan, RCM Staff
Composition: 99.99% Ag
Silver content: 25.18 g, 0.81 tr oz
Weight: 25.18 g
Diameter: 36.07 mm
Thickness: 2.85 mm
Edge: Reeded
Die Axis: ↑↑
Finish: Proof, Hologram
Case: Maroon clam style case, black flock insert, encapsulated coin, COA

DATE	DESCRIPTION	QUANTITY SOLD	ISSUE PRICE	FINISH	PR-67 UHC	PR-68 UHC
2007	Maple of Long Life	12,427	45.95	Proof	60.	70.

EIGHT DOLLARS, MAPLE OF WISDOM, 2009.

Designers and Engravers:
Obv.: Susanna Blunt, Susan Taylor
Rev.: Simon Ng, RCM Staff
Composition: 92.5% Ag, 7.5% Cu
Silver content: 23.40 g, 0.752 tr oz
Weight: 25.3 g
Diameter: 36.07 mm
Thickness: 3.00 mm
Edge: Reeded
Die Axis: ↑↑
Finish: Proof, Hologram and crystal
Case: Maroon clam style case, black flock insert, encapsulated coin, COA

DATE	DESCRIPTION	QUANTITY SOLD	ISSUE PRICE	FINISH	PR-67 UHC	PR-68 UHC
2009	Maple of Wisdom	7,273	88.88	Proof	100.	110.

EIGHT DOLLARS, MAPLE OF STRENGTH, 2010.

Designers and Engravers:
Obv.: Susanna Blunt, Susan Taylor
Rev.: Simon Ng, RCM Staff
Composition: 92.5% Ag, 7.5% Cu
Silver content: 23.40 g, 0.752 tr oz
Weight: 25.3 g
Diameter: 36.07 mm
Thickness: 3.00 mm
Edge: Reeded
Die Axis: ↑↑
Finish: Proof, Hologram
Case: Maroon clam style case, black flock insert, encapsulated coin, COA

DATE	DESCRIPTION	QUANTITY SOLD	ISSUE PRICE	FINISH	PR-67 UHC	PR-68 UHC
2010	Maple of Strength	8,888	88.88	Proof	90.	100.

EIGHT DOLLAR DERIVATIVES

DATE	DESCRIPTION	QUANTITY SOLD	ISSUE PRICE	ISSUER	FINISH	MARKET VALUE
2004	**Eight Dollar Great Grizzly;** Two postage stamps; Wooden presentation case	12,942	48.88	RCM, CP	PR-67	95.

TEN DOLLARS

TEN DOLLARS, YEAR OF THE VETERAN, 2005.

Designers and Engravers:
Obv.: Susanna Blunt, Susan Taylor
Rev.: Elaine Goble, Susan Taylor
Composition: 99.99% Ag
Silver content: 25.175 g, 0.81 tr oz
Weight: 25.175 g
Diameter: 36.07 mm
Thickness: 3.1 mm
Edge: Reeded
Die Axis: ↑↑
Finish: Proof
Case: Maroon plastic case, black plastic insert, encapsulated coin, COA.

DATE	DESCRIPTION	QUANTITY SOLD	ISSUE PRICE	FINISH	PR-67 UHC	PR-68 UHC
2005	Year of the Veteran	6,549	49.95	Proof	75.	85.

TEN DOLLARS, COMMEMORATING THE VISIT OF POPE JOHN PAUL II TO CANADA, 2005.

Designers and Engravers:
Obv.: Susanna Blunt, Susan Taylor
Rev.: Susan Taylor
Composition: 99.99% Ag
Silver content: 25.175 g, 0.81 tr oz
Weight: 25.175 g
Diameter: 36.07 mm
Thickness: 3.1 mm
Edge: Reeded
Die Axis: ↑↑
Finish: Proof
Case: Maroon plastic case, black plastic insert, encapsulated coin, COA.

DATE	DESCRIPTION	QUANTITY SOLD	ISSUE PRICE	FINISH	PR-67 UHC	PR-68 UHC
2005	Pope John Paul II	24,716	49.95	Proof	50.	60.

TEN DOLLARS, FORTRESS OF LOUISBOURG, NATIONAL HISTORIC SERIES, 2006.

Designers and Engravers:
Obv.: Susanna Blunt, Susan Taylor
Rev.: Marcos Hallam, RCM Staff
Composition: 99.99% Ag
Silver content: 25.175 g, 0.81 tr oz
Weight: 25.175 g
Diameter: 36.07 mm
Thickness: 3.1 mm
Edge: Reeded
Die Axis: ↑↑
Finish: Proof
Case: Maroon plastic case, black plastic insert, encapsulated coin, COA.

DATE	DESCRIPTION	QUANTITY SOLD	ISSUE PRICE	FINISH	PR-67 UHC	PR-68 UHC
2006	Fortress of Louisbourg	5,544	49.95	Proof	65.	75.

TEN DOLLARS, BLUE WHALE, 2010.

This is the last coin and stamp set in the Canadian Wildlife Series which was co-produced by the Royal Canadian Mint and Canada Post.

Designers and Engravers:
Obv.: Susanna Blunt, Susan Taylor
Rev.: Pierre Leduc, RCM Staff
Composition: 92.50% Ag, 7.50% Cu
Silver content: 25.70 g, 0.826 tr oz
Weight: 27.78 g
Diameter: 40.0 mm
Thickness: 2.7 mm
Edge: Reeded
Die Axis: ↑↑
Finish: Proof
Case: See Derivatives below

DATE	DESCRIPTION	QUANTITY SOLD	ISSUE PRICE	FINISH	PR-67 UHC	PR-68 UHC
2010	Blue Whale	10,000	N.I.I.	Proof	65.	75.

Image of the Blue Whale coin courtesy of the Royal Canadian Mint.

TEN DOLLARS, 75TH ANNIVERSARY OF THE FIRST BANK NOTES ISSUED BY THE BANK OF CANADA, 2010.

The design on this coin is a reproduction of the allegory that appeared on the original 1935 $10 bank note; a seated woman surrounded by a variety of farm produce to symbolise the harvest.

Designers and Engravers:
Obv.: Susanna Blunt, Susan Taylor
Rev.: RCM Staff
Composition: 99.99% Ag
Silver content: 15.90 g, 0.511 tr oz
Weight: 15.90 g
Diameter: 34.0 mm
Thickness: 2.2 mm
Edge: Reeded
Die Axis: ↑↑
Finish: Proof
Case: Maroon leatherette clam style case; black flock insert, encapsulated coin, COA.

DATE	DESCRIPTION	QUANTITY SOLD	ISSUE PRICE	FINISH	PR-67 UHC	PR-68 UHC
2010 (1935-)	75th Anniv. of First Notes Issued by Bank of Canada	7,500	54.95	Proof	55.	65.

TEN DOLLAR DERIVATIVES

DATE	DESCRIPTION	QUANTITY SOLD	ISSUE PRICE	ISSUER	FINISH	MARKET VALUE
2010	**Ten Dollar Blue Whale;** Souvenir sheet of two $10 Blue Whale postage stamps; Booklet; Maple wood case	10,000	79.95	RCM, CP	PR-67	80.

FIFTEEN DOLLARS

FIFTEEN DOLLARS, 100TH ANNIVERSARY OF THE OLYMPIC MOVEMENT, 1992-1996.

The International Olympic Committee initiated a commemorative coin programme to mark the centennial of the modern Olympic movement in 1996. Five mints, those of Canada, Australia, France, Austria and Greece, participated by each issuing one gold and two silver coins over a five year period. The total collection comprises five gold and ten silver coins.

The Royal Canadian Mint issued the first three coins in 1992. The silver fifteen dollar coins are listed here, the 1992 $175 gold coin on page 210.

The Standard Catalogue lists only the coins issued by Royal Canadian Mint.

Common Obverse
Designer and Engraver:
Dora de Pédery-Hunt

Coin No. 1
Speed Skater,
Pole Vaulter, Gymnast
Designer: David Craig
Engraver: Sheldon Beveridge

Coin No. 2
The Spirit Of the Generations
Designer: Stewart Sherwood
Engraver: Terry Smith

Composition: 92.5% Ag, 7.5% Cu
Silver content: 31.108 g, 1.00 tr oz
Weight: 33.63 g
Diameter: 40.0 mm
Edge: Lettering: Citius, Altius, Fortius
Cases of Issue: Singly: Burgundy leatherette case
Set: Wooden display case
Thickness: 3.1 mm
Die Axis: ↑↑
Finish: Proof

DATE	DESCRIPTION	QUANTITY SOLD	ISSUE PRICE	FINISH	PR-67 UHC	PR-68 UHC
1992	Speed Skater	105,645	46.95	Proof	45.	50.
1992	Speed Skater, No edge lettering	Included	46.95	Proof	500.	600.
1992	Spirit of the Generations	Included	46.95	Proof	45.	50.
1992	Spirit of the Generations, No edge lettering	Included	46.95	Proof	500.	600.

CHINESE LUNAR CALENDAR SERIES

FIFTEEN DOLLARS, CHINESE LUNAR CALENDAR STERLING SILVER COIN SERIES, 1998-2009.

Starting in 1998 with the year of the Tiger, the mint embarked on a twelve year series of Chinese Lunar calendar coins which ended in 2009. The twelve sterling silver coins were issued one per year to commemorate the start of each new year of the twelve year cycle. The coins were available singly or by subscription. The subscription was for a five year period beginning in 1999 and ending in 2003. The five coins, shipped one per year, were offered at a fixed price of $428.28 including a sterling silver medallion housed in a 13-hole presentation box made of embossed red velvet and gold moiré. The single presentation box is a smaller version of the larger one, red and gold moiré.

Obverse 1998
Designer and Engraver:
Dora de Pédery-Hunt

Year of the Tiger 1998
Designer: Harvey Chan
Engraver: Stan Witten

Obverse 1999
Designer and Engraver:
Dora de Pédery-Hunt

Year of the Rabbit 1999
Designer: Harvey Chan
Engraver: José Osio

Obverse 2000
Designer and Engraver:
Dora de Pédery-Hunt

Year of the Dragon 2000
Designer: Harvey Chan
Engraver: José Osio

Obverse 2001
Designer and Engraver:
Dora de Pédery-Hunt

Year of the Snake 2001
Designer: Harvey Chan
Engraver: José Osio

Obverse 2002
Designer and Engraver:
Dora de Pédery-Hunt

Year of the Horse 2002
Designer: Harvey Chan
Engraver: José Osio

Obverse 2003
Designer and Engraver:
Dora de Pédery-Hunt

Year of the Ram 2003
Designer: Harvey Chan
Engraver: José Osio

Note: Coins illustrated smaller than actual size.

FIFTEEN DOLLARS, CHINESE LUNAR CALENDAR STERLING SILVER COIN SERIES, 1998-2009 (cont.).

Obverse 2004
Designer and Engraver:
Dora de Pédery-Hunt

Year of the Monkey 2004
Designer: Harvey Chan
Engraver: Stan Witten

Obverse 2005
Designer and Engraver:
Dora de Pédery-Hunt

Year of the Rooster 2005
Designer: Harvey Chan
Engraver: José Osio

Obverse 2006
Designer and Engraver:
Dora de Pédery-Hunt

Year of the Dog 2006
Designer: Harvey Chan
Engraver: José Osio

Obverse 2007
Designer and Engraver:
Dora de Pédery-Hunt

Year of the Pig 2007
Designer: Harvey Chan
Engraver: José Osio

Obverse 2008
Designer and Engraver:
Dora de Pédery-Hunt

Year of the Rat 2008
Designer: Harvey Chan
Engraver: José Osio

Obverse 2009
Designer and Engraver:
Dora de Pédery-Hunt

Year of the Ox 2009
Designer: Harvey Chan
Engraver: José Osio

Designers:
Obv.: See coin
Rev.: See coin

Engravers:
Obv.: See coin
Rev.: See coin

Composition: 92.5% Ag, 7.5% Cu,
24-karat gold plated cameo
Silver content: 30.71 to 31.45 g, 0.987 to 1.011 tr oz
Weight: 33.2 to 34.00 g
Diameter: 40.0 mm
Thickness: 3.0 to 3.35 mm

Edge: Reeded
Die Axis: ↑↑
Finish: Proof, gold-plated cameo

Cases of Issue: Set: A thirteen-hole embossed red velvet presentation box with gold moiré sides. Included is a sterling silver medallion carrying the twelve signs of the zodiac.
Singly: Embossed red velvet presentation box as above, encapsulated, COA

FIFTEEN DOLLARS, CHINESE LUNAR CALENDAR PRICING.

DATE	DESCRIPTION	QUANTITY SOLD	ISSUE PRICE	FINISH	PR-67 UHC	PR-68 UHC
1998	Empty case to hold 12 sterling silver coins and a sterling silver medallion	—	—	—	250.	—
1998	Year of the Tiger	68,888	68.88	Proof	450.	500.
1999	Year of the Rabbit	77,791	72.88	Proof	95.	105.
2000	Year of the Dragon	88,634	72.88	Proof	150.	175.
2001	Year of the Snake	60,754	94.88	Proof	100.	110.
2002	Year of the Horse	59,395	94.88	Proof	125.	135.
2003	Year of the Ram	53,714	94.88	Proof	95.	105.
2004	Year of the Monkey	46,175	105.88	Proof	150.	160.
2005	Year of the Rooster	44,690	105.88	Proof	135.	145.
2006	Year of the Dog	41,634	112.88	Proof	110.	120.
2007	Year of the Pig	10,752	88.88	Proof	100.	110.
2008	Year of the Rat	9,209	88.88	Proof	115.	125.
2009	Year of the Ox	7,096	88.88	Proof	100.	120.

FIFTEEN DOLLARS, CHINESE LUNAR CALENDAR DERIVATIVES

2003 Year of the Ram

DATE	DESCRIPTION	QUANTITY SOLD	ISSUE PRICE	ISSUER	FINISH	MARKET VALUE
1998	**Year of the Tiger**, Fifteen dollar coin; Souvenir stamp sheet; Presentation album	8,000	88.88	RCM, CP	PR-67	525.
1999	**Year of the Rabbit,** as 1998	8,000	88.88	RCM, CP	PR-67	125.
2000	**Year of the Dragon**, as 1998	10,000	88.88	RCM, CP	PR-67	175.
2000	**Year of the Dragon**, 18kt gold stamp, Mint stamp, Presentation case	N/A	N/A	RCM, CP	PR-67	800.
2001	**Year of the Snake**, as 1998	8,000	94.88	RCM, CP	PR-67	160.
2002	**Year of the Horse**, as 1998	8,000	98.88	RCM, CP	PR-67	135.
2003	**Year of the Ram**, as 1998	8,000	98.88	RCM, CP	PR-67	125.
2004	**Year of the Monkey**, as 1998	8,000	105.88	RCM, CP	PR-67	175.
2005	**Year of the Rooster**, as 1998	8,000	105.88	RCM, CP	PR-67	175.
2006	**Year of the Dog,** as 1998	8,000	112.88	RCM, CP	PR-67	145.
2007	**Year of the Pig**, as 1998	8,000	112.88	RCM, CP	PR-67	135.
2008	**Year of the Rat**, as 1998	8,000	112.88	RCM, CP	PR-67	140.
2009	**Year of the Ox**, as 1998	8,000	112.88	RCM, CP	PR-67	135.

VIGNETTES OF ROYALTY SERIES

FIFTEEN DOLLARS, VIGNETTES OF ROYALTY SERIES, 2008-2009.

Common Obverse

Victoria
Designer: Leonard C. Wyon
Engraver: RCM Staff

Edward VII
Designer: G. W. De Saulles
Engraver: RCM Staff

George V
Designer: E. B. MacKennal
Engraver: RCM Staff

George VI
Designer: T. H. Paget
Engraver: RCM Staff

Elizabeth II
Designer: Mary Gillick
Engraver: RCM Staff

Designers:
Obv.: Susanna Blunt
Rev.: Susan Taylor

Engravers:
Obv.: See coin
Rev.: See coin

Composition: 92.5% Ag, 7.5% Cu
Silver content: 27.75 g, 0.89 tr oz
Weight: 30.00 g
Diameter: 36.15 mm
Thickness: 3.20 mm
Edge: Plain
Die Axis: ↑↑
Finish: Proof-like
Cases of Issue: Singly: Maroon clam style case, black flocked insert, encapsulated coin, COA
Set: Five-hole maroon clam style case to hold the series of coins.

DATE	DESCRIPTION	ISSUE DATE	QUANTITY SOLD	ISSUE PRICE	FINISH	PL-67	PL-68
2008	Victoria	Oct. 31, 2007	3,442	99.95	Proof-like	100.	110.
2008	Edward VII	July 23, 2008	6,261	99.95	Proof-like	115.	125.
2008	George V	Oct. 1, 2008	—	99.95	Proof-like	100.	110.
2009	George VI	Apr. 15, 2009	10,045	99.95	Proof-like	100.	110.
2009	Elizabeth II	Oct. 1, 2009	2,643	99.95	Proof-like	100.	110.
—	Vignettes of Royalty Set, 5 coins	—	N/A	499.95	Proof-like	575.	—

NOTES FOR COLLECTORS

1. The RCM Report of 2009 does not breakdown the “quantity sold” figures for the George V and George VI coins, but group list all under George VI.
2. It is interesting to note that after 55 years the Royal Canadian Mint recognises a proof-like finish. The vignettes are struck in ultra high relief on a proof-like background.

PLAYING CARD MONEY SERIES

FIFTEEN DOLLARS, PLAYING CARD MONEY SERIES, 2008-2009.

This series was issued to commemorate the issue of playing cards used as money during times of chronic shortages in the 17th and 18th centuries in New France.

2008 Obverse

Jack of Hearts

Queen of Spades

2009 Obverse

King of Hearts

Ten of Spades

Designers:
Obv.: Susanna Blunt
Rev.: Original artwork by Henry Beau
Public Archives of Canada

Engravers:
Rev.: Susan Taylor
Rev.: RCM Staff

Composition: 92.5% Ag, 7.5% Cu
Silver content: 29.193 g, 0.938 tr oz
Weight: 31.56 g
Size: 49.8 x 28.6 mm
Die Axis: ↑↑
Thickness: 2.40 to 2.7 mm
Edge: Plain
Finish: Proof, Painted; Gold plate on edge
Cases of Issue: Singly: Maroon clam style case, black flocked insert, encapsulated coin, COA
Set: Four-hole maroon clam style case, black flocked insert, encapsulated coins

DATE	DESCRIPTION	ISSUE DATE	QUANTITY SOLD	ISSUE PRICE	FINISH	PR-67 UHC	PR-68 UHC
2008	Jack of Hearts	July 23, 2008	11,362	89.95	Proof	100.	110.
2008	Queen of Spades	Oct. 1, 2008	8,714	89.95	Proof	100.	110.
2009	King of Hearts	Apr. 15, 2009	5,798	89.95	Proof	100.	110.
2009	Ten of Spades	July 22, 2009	5,921	89.95	Proof	100.	110.
—	Playing Card Money Set	—	278	359.80	Proof	375.	—

LUNAR LOTUS SERIES

FIFTEEN DOLLARS, SILVER LUNAR LOTUS SERIES, 2010-2021.

A new Lunar Calendar series was introduced in 2010. The new series, beginning with the 2010 Year of the Tiger, will run for twelve years. The scalloped coin is reminiscent of a lotus flower.

2010 Obverse

Year of the Tiger 2010

2011 Obverse

Year of the Rabbit 2011

Designers and Engravers:
Obv.: Susanna Blunt, Susan Taylor
Rev.: Three Degrees Creative Group Inc., RCM Staff
Composition: 92.5% Ag, 7.5% Cu
Silver content: 24.327 g, 0.782 tr oz
Weight: 26.3 g
Diameter (scalloped): 38.00 mm
Thickness: 2.85 mm
Edge: Plain
Die Axis: ↑↑
Finish: Proof

Cases of Issue: Singly: Silver satin-like covered case, black flocked insert, encapsulated coin, COA.
Set: Hardwood exterior with high-gloss finish and silk-screened paper. Interior has high-gloss finish in Chinese red with a silver design. Wooden insert accommodates 12 coins.

DATE	DESCRIPTION	QUANTITY SOLD	ISSUE PRICE	FINISH	PR-67 UHC	PR-68 UHC
2010	Year of the Tiger	10,268	88.88	Proof	90.	100.
2011	Year of the Rabbit	19,888	88.88	Proof	90.	100.

CLASSIC CHINESE ZODIAC SERIES

FIFTEEN DOLLARS, CLASSIC CHINESE ZODIAC SERIES, 2010-2021.

A second Lunar Calendar series was introduced in 2010. This new series is distributed by the Asian Business Centre and the Royal Canadian Mint. The proposed quantity was 9,999 units.

Common Obverse

Year of the Tiger 2010

Year of the Rabbit 2011

Designers:
Obv.: Susanna Blunt
Rev.: Aries Cheung

Engravers:
Obv.: Susan Taylor
Rev.: RCM Staff

Composition: 99.99% Ag
Silver content: 31.39 g, 1.01 tr oz
Weight: 31.39 g
Diameter: 38.00 mm
Thickness: 3.2 mm

Edge: Reeded
Die Axis: ↑↑
Finish: Proof

Cases of Issue: Singly: Silver satin-like covered case, black flocked insert, encapsulated coin, COA.
Set: Hardwood exterior with high-gloss finish and silk-screened paper. Interior has high-gloss finish in Chinese red with a silver design. Wooden insert accommodates 12 coins.

DATE	DESCRIPTION	QUANTITY SOLD	ISSUE PRICE	FINISH	PR-67 UHC	PR-68 UHC
2010	Year of the Tiger	9,999	88.88	Proof	90.	100.
2011	Year of the Rabbit	9,999	98.88	Proof	90.	100.

TWENTY DOLLARS

CALGARY OLYMPIC WINTER GAMES

TWENTY DOLLARS, CALGARY OLYMPIC WINTER GAMES, 1985-1988.

In 1988, Calgary, Alberta, hosted the XV Olympic Winter Games. To commemorate the event, and assist in the financing, the Federal Government, through the Royal Canadian Mint, agreed to produce a series of ten sterling silver coins and one gold coin. The silver coins were issued in sets of two $20.00 coins over the period September 1985 through September 1987. Unlike the 1976 Olympic coins, the Calgary Winter Olympic coins were issued in proof quality only.

The date on the coins (obverse) is the year of minting while the reverse carries the date 1988, the year of the games. Mintage was limited to a total of 5,000,000 coins, resulting if minted in equal numbers, in 500,000 complete sets of the ten coins. The first offering of the coins for sale by the Royal Canadian Mint was based on 350,000 complete sets at $370.00 per set. By the fifth series the complete set was being offered at $420.00.

Edge lettering was used for the first time on Canadian silver coins. "XV OLYMPIC WINTER GAMES - JEUX OLYMPIQUES D'HIVER" appeared on all ten silver coins. There are existing varieties that have missed the edge lettering process.

Designers: See each coin
Composition: 92.5% Ag, 7.5% Cu
Silver content: 31.51 g, 1.01 tr oz
Weight: 34.07 g
Diameter: 40 mm
Case: Green velvet, Olympic Logo, one or two coin display.

Engravers: See each coin
Thickness: 3.0 mm
Edge: Lettered
Die Axis: ↑↑
Finish: Proof

SERIES ONE

1985 Reverse
Arnold Machin

Coin No. 1 Downhill Skiing
Ian Stewart, Terrence Smith

Coin No. 2 Speed Skating
Friedrich Peter, Ago Aarand

SERIES TWO

1986 Obverse
Arnold Machin

Coin No. 3 Hockey
Ian Stewart, Victor Coté

Coin No. 4 Biathlon
John Mardon, Sheldon Beveridge

DATE	DESCRIPTION	ISSUE DATE	QUANTITY SOLD	ISSUE PRICE	FINISH	PR-67 UHC	PR-68 UHC
1985	Downhill Skiing	Sept. 15, 1985	406,360	37.00	Proof	35.	40.
1985	Speed Skating	Sept. 15, 1985	354,222	37.00	Proof	35.	40.
1985	Speed Skating, no edge lettering	Sept. 15, 1985	Included	37.00	Proof	200.	250.
1985	Set of 2 Series One coins	Sept. 15, 1985	Included	74.00	Proof	70.	—
1986	Hockey	Feb. 25, 1986	396,602	37.00	Proof	35.	40.
1986	Hockey, no edge lettering	Feb. 25, 1986	Included	37.00	Proof	200.	250.
1986	Biathlon	Feb. 25, 1986	308,086	37.00	Proof	35.	40.
1986	Biathlon, no edge lettering	Feb. 25, 1986	Included	37.00	Proof	200.	250.
1986	Set of 2 Series Two coins		Included	79.00	Proof	70.	—

CALGARY OLYMPIC WINTER GAMES (cont.)

SERIES THREE

1986 Obverse
Arnold Machin

Coin No. 5 Cross-Country Skiing
Ian Stewart, Terrence Smith

Coin No. 6 Free-Style Skiing
Walter Ott, Walter Ott

SERIES FOUR

1987 Obverse
Arnold Machin

Coin No. 7 Figure Skating
Raymond Taylor, Walter Ott

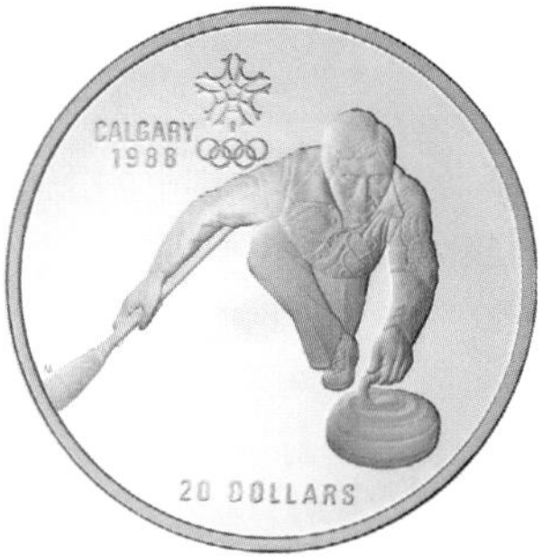

Coin No. 8 Curling
Walter Ott, Sheldon Beveridge

SERIES FIVE

1987 Obverse
Arnold Machin

Coin No. 9 Ski-Jumping
Raymond Taylor, David Kierans

Coin No. 10 Bobsleigh
John Mardon, Victor Coté

DATE	DESCRIPTION	ISSUE DATE	QUANTITY SOLD	ISSUE PRICE	FINISH	PR-67 UHC	PR-68 UHC
1986	Cross-Country Skiing	Aug. 18, 1986	303,199	39.50	Proof	35.	40.
1986	Free-Style Skiing	Aug. 18, 1986	294,322	39.50	Proof	35.	40.
1986	Free-Style Skiing, no edge lettering	Aug. 18, 1986	Included	39.50	Proof	200.	250.
1986	Set of 2 Series Three coins	Aug. 18, 1986	Included	79.00	Proof	70.	—
1987	Figure Skating	Mar. 14, 1987	334,875	39.50	Proof	35.	40.
1987	Curling	Mar. 14, 1987	286,457	39.50	Proof	35.	40.
1987	Set of 2 Series Four coins	Mar. 14, 1987	Included	79.00	Proof	70.	—
1987	Ski-Jumping	Aug. 11, 1987	290,954	42.00	Proof	35.	40.
1987	Bobsleigh	Aug. 11, 1987	274,326	42.00	Proof	35.	40.
1987	Set of 2 Series Five coins	Aug. 11, 1987	Included	84.00	Proof	70.	—

AVIATION COMMEMORATIVES

TWENTY DOLLARS, AVIATION COMMEMORATIVES, SERIES ONE, 1990-1994.

Canada's aviation heroes and achievements are commemorated on this series of twenty dollar sterling silver coins. The series consists of ten coins issued two per year over five years. For the first time each coin design contains a 24 karat gold covered oval cameo portrait of the aviation hero commemorated. All coins were issued in proof quality and a maximum of 50,000 of each coin was offered for sale during the program. The issue price of the ten coin case was $37.00.

Designers:
Obv. and Rev.: See each coin

Engravers:
Obv. and Rev.: See each coin

Composition: 92.5% Ag, 7.5% Cu, 24kt gold cameo
Silver content: 28.77 g, 0.925 tr oz
Weight: 31.103 g
Diameter: 38.0 mm
Thickness: 3.5 mm
Edge: Interrupted serration
Die Axis: ↑↑
Finish: Proof; 24-karat gold-covered cameo
Cases: Aluminum case in the shape of a wing. Two and ten coin display cases.

1990 Obverse
Designer and Engraver:
Dora de Pédery-Hunt

Coin No. 1
Avro Anson and the North American Harvard
Robert Leckie
Rev. Designer: Geoff Bennett
Rev. Engraver: S. Beveridge
Portrait Engr.: Terrence Smith

Coin No. 2
Avro Lancaster
J. E. Fauquier
Rev. Designer: R.R. Carmichael
Rev. Engraver: Ago Aarand
Portrait Engr.: S. Beveridge

1991 Obverse
Designer and Engraver:
Dora de Pédery-Hunt

Coin No. 3
A.E.A. Silver Dart
F.W. Baldwin / J.A.D. McCurdy
Rev. Designer: George Velinger
Rev. Engraver: S. Beveridge
Portrait Engr.: Terrence Smith

Coin No. 4
de Havilland Beaver
Phillip C. Garratt
Rev. Designer: Peter Mossman
Rev. Engraver: Ago Aarand
Portrait Engr.: William Woodruff

DATE	DESCRIPTION	SERIES	ISSUE DATE	QUANTITY SOLD	ISSUE PRICE	FINISH	PR-67 UHC	PR-68 UHC
1990	Avro Anson/N.A. Harvard	One	Sept. 15/90	41,844	55.50	Proof	60.	70.
1990	Avro Lancaster	One	Sept. 15/90	43,596	55.50	Proof	110.	125.
1991	A.E.A. Silver Dart	One	May 16/91	35,202	55.50	Proof	60.	70.
1991	de Havilland Beaver	One	May 16/91	36,197	55.50	Proof	60.	70.

1992 Obverse
Designer and Engraver:
Dora de Pédery-Hunt

Coin No. 5
Curtiss JN-4 (Canuck)
Sir Frank Wilton Baillie
Rev. Designer: George Velinger
Rev. Engr.: Sheldon Beveridge
Portrait Engr.: Terrence Smith

Coin No. 6
de Havilland Gipsy Moth
Murton A. Seymour
Rev. Designer: John Mardon
Rev. Engraver: Ago Aarand
Portrait Engr.: Susan Taylor

1993 Obverse
Designer and Engraver:
Dora de Pédery-Hunt

Coin No. 7
Fairchild 71c
James A. Richardson
Rev. Designer: R. R. Carmichael
Rev. Engraver: Susan Taylor
Portrait Engr.: Susan Taylor

Coin No. 8
Lockheed 14 Super Electra
Zebulon Lewis Leigh
Rev. Designer: R. R. Carmichael
Rev. Engraver: S. Beveridge
Portrait Engr.: S. Beveridge

1994 Obverse
Designer and Engraver:
Dora de Pédery-Hunt

Coin No. 9
Curtiss HS-2L
Stuart Graham
Rev. Designer: John Mardon
Rev. Engraver: S.Beveridge
Portrait Engr.: Susan Taylor

Coin No. 10
Canadian Vickers Vedette
Wilfred T. Reid
Rev. Designer: R. R. Carmichael
Rev. Engraver: S. Beveridge
Portrait Engr.: S. Beveridge

DATE	DESCRIPTION	SERIES	ISSUE DATE	QUANTITY SOLD	ISSUE PRICE	FINISH	PR-67 UHC	PR-68 UHC
1992	Curtiss JN-4 (Canuck)	One	Aug. 13/92	33,105	55.50	Proof	60.	70.
1992	de Havilland Gipsy Moth	One	Aug. 13/92	32,537	55.50	Proof	65.	75.
1993	Fairchild 71c	One	May 3/93	32,199	55.50	Proof	70.	80.
1993	Lockheed 14 Super Electra	One	May 3/93	32,550	55.50	Proof	70.	80.
1994	Curtiss HS-2L	One	Mar. 24/94	31,242	55.50	Proof	70.	80.
1994	Canadian Vickers Vedette	One	Mar. 24/94	30,880	55.50	Proof	70.	80.
1990-94	Set of 10 Series One coins	One	—	—	—	Proof	650.	—

TWENTY DOLLARS, AVIATION COMMEMORATIVES, SERIES TWO, 1995-1999.

This is the second series of the aviation cameo coins of Canada. The theme of this series is "Powered Flight in Canada — Beyond World War II." The obverses, physical and chemical specifications are the same as the first series.

SERIES TWO

1995 Obverse
Designer and Engraver:
Dora de Pédery-Hunt

Coin No. 1
Fleet 80 Canuck
J. Omer (Bob) Noury
Rev. Designer: Robert Bradford
Rev. Engraver: Cosme Saffioti
Portrait Engr.: Cosme Saffioti

Coin No. 2
DHC-1 Chipmunk
W. C. Russell Bannock
Rev. Designer: Robert Bradford
Rev. Engraver: William Woodruff
Portrait Engr.: Ago Aarand

1996 Obverse
Designer and Engraver:
Dora de Pédery-Hunt

Coin No. 3
Avro Canada CF-100 Canuck
Janus Zurakowski
Rev. Designer: Jim Bruce
Rev. Engraver: Stan Witten
Portrait Engr.: Cosme Saffioti

Coin No. 4
Avro Canada CF-105 Arrow
James A. Chamberlin
Rev. Designer: Jim Bruce
Rev. Engraver: William Woodruff
Portrait Engr.: S. Beveridge

1997 Obverse
Designer and Engraver:
Dora de Pédery-Hunt

Coin No. 5
Canadair F-86 Sabre
Fern Villeneuve
Rev. Designer: Ross Buckland
Rev. Engraver: William Woodruff
Portrait Engr.: Cosme Saffioti

Coin No. 6
Canadair CT-114 Tutor Jet
Edward Higgins
Rev. Designer: Ross Buckland
Rev. Engraver: Stan Witten
Portrait Engr.: Ago Aarand

1998 Obverse
Designer and Engraver:
Dora de Pédery-Hunt

Coin No. 7
Canadair CP-107 Argus
William S. Longhurst
Rev. Designer: Peter Mossman
Rev. Engraver: Sheldon Beveridge

Coin No. 8
Canadair CL-215 Waterbomber
Paul Gagnon
Rev. Designer: Peter Mossman
Rev. Engraver: Stan Witten
Portrait Engr.: William Woodruff

1999 Obverse
Designer and Engraver:
Dora de Pédery-Hunt

Coin No. 9
de Havilland DHC-6 Twin Otter
George A. Neal
Rev. Designer: Neil Aird
Rev. Engraver: Cosme Saffioti
Portrait Engr.: Cosme Saffioti

Coin No. 10
de Havilland DHC-8 Dash 8
Robert H. (Bob) Fowler
Rev. Designer: Neil Aird
Rev. Engraver: William Woodruff
Portrait Engr.: Cosme Saffioti

DATE	DESCRIPTION	SERIES	ISSUE DATE	ISSUE PRICE	QUANTITY SOLD	FINISH	PR-67 UHC	PR-68 UHC
1995	Fleet 80 Canuck	Two	Sept. 16/95	57.95	17,438	Proof	70.	80.
1995	DHC-1 Chipmunk	Two	Sept. 16/95	57.95	17,722	Proof	70.	80.
1996	CF-100 Canuck	Two	July 25/96	57.95	18,508	Proof	85.	95.
1996	CF-105 Arrow	Two	July 25/96	57.95	27,163	Proof	175.	185.
1997	F86 Sabre	Two	Aug. 15/97	57.95	16,440	Proof	80.	90.
1997	Tutor Jet	Two	Aug. 15/97	57.95	18,414	Proof	145.	160.
1998	Argus	Two	June 5/98	57.95	14,711	Proof	110.	120.
1998	Waterbomber	Two	June 5/98	57.95	15,237	Proof	125.	135.
1999	Twin Otter	Two	April 15/99	57.95	14,173	Proof	165.	175.
1999	Dash 8	Two	April 15/99	57.95	14,138	Proof	125.	135.
1995-99	Set of 10 Series Two coins	Two	—	—	—	Proof	1,000.	—

Note: In 1998 a special issue two-coin set (coins 7 and 8) boxed with a cardboard model was offered to collectors. See Derivatives, page 169.

TRANSPORTATION ON LAND, SEA AND RAIL SERIES

TWENTY DOLLARS, TRANSPORTATION ON LAND, SEA AND RAIL, 2000-2003.

Canada's first sterling silver hologram cameo twenty dollar coins were issued in 2000. This new series of twelve coins commemorates Canadian achievements in transportation. Each coin bears a holographic cameo of famous Canadian methods of transportation.

Designers:
Obv. and Rev.: See each coin

Engravers:
Obv. and Rev.: See each coin

Composition: 92.5% Ag, 7.5% Cu
Silver content: 28.77 g, 0.925 tr oz
Weight: 31.103 g
Thickness: 3.5 mm
Diameter: 38.0 mm
Die Axis: ↑↑
Edge: Interrupted serration
Finish: Proof, Holographic cameo
Case of Issue: Charcoal coloured anodized aluminum case with RCM logo, black flocked insert, COA.

TRANSPORTATION ON LAND, SEA AND RAIL, 2000.

2000 Obverse
Designer and Engraver
Dora de Pédery-Hunt

Coin No. 1
H.S. Taylor Steam Buggy
John Mardon
Cosme Saffioti

Coin No. 2
The Bluenose
J. Franklin Wright
Stan Witten

Coin No. 3
The Toronto
J. Mardon, Stan Witten
Cosme Saffioti

DATE	DESCRIPTION	ISSUE DATE	QUANTITY SOLD	ISSUE PRICE	FINISH	PR-67 UHC	PR-68 UHC
2000	H.S. Taylor Steam Buggy	Apr.18/2000	Total	59.95	Proof	65.	75.
2000	The Bluenose	Apr.18/2000	mintage	59.95	Proof	155.	175.
2000	The Toronto	Apr.18/2000	all coins	59.95	Proof	67.	75.
2000	Set of 3 coins	—	44,367	179.85	Proof	275.	—

TRANSPORTATION ON LAND, SEA AND RAIL, 2001.

2001 Obverse
Designer and Engraver
Dora de Pédery-Hunt

Coin No. 4
The Russell "Light Four"
Model L Touring Car
John Mardon, José Osio

Coin No. 5
The Marco Polo
J. Franklin Wright
Stan Witten

Coin No. 6
The Scotia
Don Curley
William Woodruff

DATE	DESCRIPTION	ISSUE DATE	QUANTITY SOLD	ISSUE PRICE	FINISH	PR-67 UHC	PR-68 UHC
2001	The Russell "Light Four"	Apr.17/2001	Total	59.95	Proof	70.	80.
2001	The Marco Polo	Apr.17/2001	mintage	59.95	Proof	85.	95.
2001	The Scotia	Apr.17/2001	all coins	59.95	Proof	60.	70.
2001	Set of 3 coins	—	41,828	179.85	Proof	200.	—

TRANSPORTATION ON LAND, SEA AND RAIL SERIES (cont.)

TWENTY DOLLARS, TRANSPORTATION ON LAND, SEA AND RAIL, 2002.

2002 Obverse
Designer and Engraver
Dora de Pédery-Hunt

Coin No. 7
The Gray-Dort
John Mardon
Cosme Saffioti

Coin No. 8
The William Lawrence
Bonnie Ross
William Woodruff

Coin No. 9
D-10 Locomotive
Dan Fell
William Woodruff

DATE	DESCRIPTION	ISSUE DATE	QUANTITY SOLD	ISSUE PRICE	FINISH	PR-67 UHC	PR-68 UHC
2002	The Gray-Dort	Apr.17/2002	Total	59.95	Proof	65.	75.
2002	The William Lawrence	Apr.17/2002	mintage	59.95	Proof	95.	105.
2002	D-10 Locomotive	Apr.17/2002	all coins	59.95	Proof	105.	115.
2002	Set of 3 coins	—	35,944	195.00	Proof	250.	—

TWENTY DOLLARS, TRANSPORTATION ON LAND, SEA AND RAIL, 2003.

2003 Obverse
Designer and Engraver
Dora de Pédery-Hunt

Coin No. 10
HMCS Bras d'Or
Hydrofoil designed by
DeHavilland in 1967
Donald Curley, Stan Witten

Coin No. 11
C.N.R. FA-1 Diesel Electric
Locomotive - No. 9400
John Mardon
William Woodruff

Coin No. 12
Bricklin SV-1 (Land)
designed by Malcolm in 1974
Brian Hughes
José Osio

DATE	DESCRIPTION	ISSUE DATE	QUANTITY SOLD	ISSUE PRICE	FINISH	PR-67 UHC	PR-68 UHC
2003	HMCS Bras d'Or	Apr.7/2003	Total	59.95	Proof	75.	85.
2003	C.N.R. FA-1 Diesel Electric Locomotive	Apr.7/2003	mintage	59.95	Proof	120.	130.
2003	Bricklin SV-1	Apr.7/2003	all coins	59.95	Proof	100.	125.
2003	Set of 3 coins	—	31,997	195.00	Proof	250.	—

Note: 1. The 2002 Land, Sea and Rail collection was offered with matching COA in a limited edition of 2,500.
2. Coins illustrated smaller than actual size.

NATURAL WONDERS COLLECTION

TWENTY DOLLARS, NATURAL WONDERS COLLECTION, 2003-2005.

The Royal Canadian Mint, in 2003, introduced a new series of twenty-dollar commemorative coins. Each coin will carry a holographic, decal, or selective gold plating image of one of Canada's natural wonders.

Designers: See coin
Engravers: See coin
Composition: 99.99% Ag
Silver content: 31.39 g, 1.01 tr oz
Weight: 31.39 g
Edge: Reeded
Diameter: 38.0 mm
Die Axis: ↑↑
Thickness: 3.5 mm
Finish: Proof, see below
Cases of Issue: (A) Veneer, wooden clam style case, light brown flocked interior, encapsulated coin, COA
(B) Red leatherette clam style case, flocked black insert, encapsulated coin, COA

2003 Obverse
Designer and Engraver:
Dora de Pédery-Hunt

Niagara Falls
Designer and Engraver:
Gary Corcoran

Rocky Mountains
Designer and Engraver:
José Osio

2004 Obverse
Designer: Susanna Blunt
Engraver: Susan Taylor

Icebergs
Designer: RCM Staff
Engraver: RCM Staff

Northern Lights
Designer: Gary Corcoran
Engraver: Stan Witten

DATE	DESCRIPTION	QUANTITY SOLD	ISSUE PRICE	FINISH	PR-67 UHC	PR-68 UHC
2003	Niagara Falls, Hologram	29,967	79.95	Proof	90.	100.
2003	Rocky Mountains, Decal	28,793	69.95	Proof	70.	80.
2004	Icebergs, Hologram	24,879	69.95	Proof	80.	90.
2004	Northern Lights, Double Image Hologram	34,135	79.95	Proof	95.	105.

TWENTY DOLLARS, NATURAL WONDERS COLLECTION, 2003-2005 (cont.).

2004 Obverse
Designer: Susanna Blunt
Engraver: Susan Taylor

Hopewell Rocks
Designer: Stan Witten
Engraver: Stan Witten

2005 Obverse
Designer: Susanna Blunt
Engraver: Susan Taylor

Diamonds
Designer: José Osio
Engraver: José Osio

DATE	DESCRIPTION	QUANTITY SOLD	ISSUE PRICE	FINISH	PR-67 UHC	PR-68 UHC
2004	Hopewell Rocks, Selectively gold plated	16,918	69.95	Proof	85.	95.
2005	Diamonds, Double Image Hologram	35,000	69.95	Proof	70.	80.

TALL SHIPS COLLECTION

TWENTY DOLLARS, TALL SHIPS COLLECTION, 2005-2007.

2005 Obverse

Three-Masted Ship
Designer: Bonnie Ross
Engraver: William Woodruff

Designers and Engravers:
Obv.: Susanna Blunt, Susan Taylor
Rev.: See coin
Composition: 99.99% Ag
Silver content: 31.39 g, 1.01 tr oz
Weight: 31.39 g
Diameter: 38.0 mm
Thickness: 3.0 mm
Edge: Reeded
Die Axis: ↑↑
Finish: Proof, Hologram
Case of Issue: Maroon plastic slide case, black plastic insert, encapsulated coin, COA

2006 Obverse

Ketch
Designer: John M. Horton
Engraver: Susan Taylor

2007 Obverse

Brigantine
Designer: Bonnie Ross
Engraver: William Woodruff

DATE	DESCRIPTION	QUANTITY SOLD	ISSUE PRICE	FINISH	PR-67 UHC	PR-68 UHC
2005	Three-Masted Ship, Hologram	18,276	69.95	Proof	80.	90.
2006	Ketch, Hologram	10,299	69.95	Proof	80.	90.
2007	Brigantine, Hologram	7,935	74.95	Proof	80.	90.

NATIONAL PARKS SERIES

TWENTY DOLLARS, NATIONAL PARKS SERIES, 2005-2006.

Designers: See coin
Engravers: See coin
Composition: 99.99% Ag
Silver content: 31.39 g, 1.01 tr oz
Weight: 31.39 g
Edge: Reeded
Diameter: 38.0 mm
Die Axis: ↑↑
Thickness: 3.0 mm
Finish: Proof
Case of Issue: Maroon plastic slide case, black plastic insert, encapsulated coin, COA

2005 Obverse
Designer: Susanna Blunt
Engraver: Susan Taylor

North Pacific Rim National Park Reserve of Canada (QU)
Designer: Susanna Blunt
Engraver: Stan Witten

Mingan Archipelago National Park Reserve of Canada
Designer: Pierre Leduc
Engraver: José Osio

2006 Obverse
Designer: Susanna Blunt
Engraver: Susan Taylor

Georgian Bay Islands National Park (ON)
Designer: Tony Bianco
Engraver: William Woodruff

Nahanni National Park Reserve of Canada (NWT)
Designer: Virginia Boulay
Engraver: William Woodruff

Jasper National Park of Canada (AL)
Designer: Michelle Grant
Engraver: William Woodruff

DATE	DESCRIPTION	QUANTITY SOLD	ISSUE PRICE	FINISH	PR-67 UHC	PR-68 UHC
2005	North Pacific Rim National Park Reserve of Canada (QU)	21,695	69.95	Proof	50.	60.
2005	Mingan Archipelago National Park Reserve of Canada	Included	69.95	Proof	65.	75.
2006	Georgian Bay Islands National Park (ON)	20,218	69.95	Proof	65.	75.
2006	Nahanni National Park Reserve of Canada (NWT)	Included	69.95	Proof	75.	85.
2006	Jasper National Park of Canada (AL)	Included	69.95	Proof	75.	85.

Note: 1. National Parks single quantities were not recorded in the RCM Reports of 2005 and 2006 as individual entries, but only as totals sold for those years. There will be a difference between the projected issue as noted on the certificate of authenticity and the actual number sold.

2. Coins illustrated smaller than actual size.

CANADIAN ARCHITECTURAL SERIES

TWENTY DOLLARS, CANADIAN ARCHITECTURAL SERIES, 2006.

Designers:
Obv.: Susanna Blunt
Rev.: Jianping Yan

Engravers:
Rev.: Susan Taylor
Rev.: RCM Staff

Composition: 99.99% Ag
Silver content: 31.10 g, 1.00 tr oz.
Weight: 31.10 g
Diameter: 38.0 mm
Thickness: 3.0 mm
Edge: Reeded
Die Axis: ↑↑
Finish: Proof, Photographic hologram
Case of Issue: Maroon plastic slide case, black plastic insert, encapsulated coin, COA

Obverse

Notre Dame Basilica

30th Anniversary CN Tower

Pengrowth Saddledome

DATE	DESCRIPTION	QUANTITY SOLD	ISSUE PRICE	FINISH	PR-67 UHC	PR-68 UHC
2006	Notre Dame Basilica, Photographic Hologram	30,906	69.95	Proof	75.	85.
2006	30th Anniv. CN Tower, Photographic Hologram	Included	69.95	Proof	75.	85.
2006	Pengrowth Saddledome, Photographic Hologram	Included	69.95	Proof	75.	85.

Note: Canadian Architectural Series quantities were not recorded individually in the RCM Report of 2006, but only as the total number of coins sold for the year. While the certificate of authenticity may show a mintage of 15,000 for each coin, it is apparent from the RCM Annual Report that this was not the case.

TWENTY DOLLARS, 125TH ANNIVERSARY OF THE FIRST INTERNATIONAL POLAR YEAR, 2007.

Designers:
Obv.: Susanna Blunt
Rev.: Laurie McGaw

Engravers:
Rev.: Susan Taylor
Rev.: RCM Staff

Composition: 92.5% Ag, 7.5% Cu
Silver content: 25.70 g, 0.826 tr oz
Weight: 27.78 g
Diameter: 40.0 mm
Thickness: 2.5 mm
Edge: Reeded
Die Axis: ↑↑
Finish: Proof and Proof Plasma
Case of Issue: Maroon clam style case, black flocked insert, encapsulated coin, COA

Common Obverse

Silver

Blue Plasma

DATE	DESCRIPTION	QUANTITY SOLD	ISSUE PRICE	FINISH	PR-67 UHC	PR-68 UHC
2007	125th Anniv. First Int'l Polar Year, Silver	9,164	64.95	Proof	65.	75.
2007	125th Anniv. First Int'l Polar Year, Blue Plasma	3,005	249.95	Proof	200.	225.

CRYSTAL SNOWFLAKE SERIES, 2007-2010

TWENTY DOLLARS, CRYSTAL SNOWFLAKE, 2007.

Designers and Engravers:
Obv.: Susanna Blunt, Susan Taylor
Rev.: Konrad Wachelko, RCM Staff
Composition: 92.5% Ag, 7.5% Cu
Silver content: 46.34 g, 1.490 tr oz
Weight: 50.1 g
Diameter: 38.0 mm
Thickness: 4.8 mm
Edge: Reeded
Die Axis: ↑↑
Finish: Proof, with crystallised Swarovski elements
Case: Maroon clam style case, black flocked insert, encapsulated coin, COA

DATE	DESCRIPTION	QUANTITY SOLD	ISSUE PRICE	FINISH	PR-67 UHC	PR-68 UHC
2007	Crystal Snowflake, Aquamarine	4,989	94.95	Proof	125.	135.
2007	Crystal Snowflake, Iridescent	4,980	94.95	Proof	500.	550.

TWENTY DOLLARS, CRYSTAL SNOWFLAKE, 2008.

Obverse with RCM Logo

2008 Amethyst Snowflake

2008 Sapphire Snowflake

Designers:
Obv.: Susanna Blunt
Rev.: Konrad Wachelko

Engravers:
Obv.: Susan Taylor
Rev.: RCM Staff

Composition: 99.99% Ag
Silver content: 31.39 g, 1.01 tr oz
Weight: 31.39 g
Diameter: 38.0 mm
Thickness: 3.2 mm
Edge: Reeded
Die Axis: ↑↑
Finish: Proof, with crystallised Swarovski elements
Case: Maroon clam style case, black flocked insert, encapsulated coin, COA

DATE	DESCRIPTION	QUANTITY SOLD	ISSUE PRICE	FINISH	PR-67 UHC	PR-68 UHC
2008	Crystal Snowflake, Amethyst	7,172	94.95	Proof	160.	175.
2008	Crystal Snowflake, Sapphire	7,765	94.95	Proof	350.	400.

CRYSTAL SNOWFLAKE SERIES, 2007-2010 (cont.)

Designers:
Obv.: Susanna Blunt
Rev.: Konrad Wachelko

Engravers:
Obv.: Susan Taylor
Rev.: RCM Staff

Composition: 99.99% Ag
Silver content: 31.39 g, 1.01 tr oz
Weight: 31.39 g
Diameter: 38.0 mm
Thickness: 3.2 mm
Edge: Reeded
Die Axis: ↑↑
Finish: Proof, with crystallised Swarovski elements
Case: Maroon clam style case, black flocked insert, encapsulated coin, COA

TWENTY DOLLARS, CRYSTAL SNOWFLAKE, 2009.

2009 Obverse

2009 Blue Snowflake

2009 Rose Snowflake

TWENTY DOLLARS, CRYSTAL SNOWFLAKE, 2010.

2010 Obverse

2010 Blue Snowflake

2010 Tanzanite Snowflake

DATE	DESCRIPTION	QUANTITY SOLD	ISSUE PRICE	FINISH	PR-67 UHC	PR-68 UHC
2009	Crystal Snowflake, Blue	7,477	94.95	Proof	135.	145.
2009	Crystal Snowflake, Rose	7,004	94.95	Proof	150.	160.
2010	Crystal Snowflake, Blue	7,500	99.95	Proof	100.	110.
2010	Crystal Snowflake, Tanzanite	7,500	99.95	Proof	100.	110.

HOLIDAY SERIES, 2007-2010

TWENTY DOLLARS, HOLIDAY SLEIGH RIDE, 2007.

Designers and Engravers:
Obv.: Susanna Blunt, Susan Taylor
Rev.: Tony Bianco, RCM Staff
Composition: 99.99% Ag
Silver content: 31.39 g, 1.01 tr oz
Weight: 31.39 g
Diameter: 38.0 mm
Thickness: 3.1 mm
Edge: Reeded
Die Axis: ↑↑
Finish: Proof
Case: Maroon clam style case, black flocked insert, encapsulated coin, COA

DATE	DESCRIPTION	QUANTITY SOLD	ISSUE PRICE	FINISH	PR-67 UHC	PR-68 UHC
2007	Holiday Sleigh Ride	6,804	69.95	Proof	70.	80.

TWENTY DOLLARS, HOLIDAY CAROLS, 2008.

Designers and Engravers:
Obv.: Susanna Blunt, Susan Taylor
Rev.: Tony Bianco, RCM Staff
Composition: 99.99% Ag
Silver content: 31.39 g, 1.01 tr oz
Weight: 31.39 g
Diameter: 38.0 mm
Thickness: 3.3 mm
Edge: Reeded
Die Axis: ↑↑
Finish: Proof
Case: Maroon clam style case, black flocked insert, encapsulated coin, COA

DATE	DESCRIPTION	QUANTITY SOLD	ISSUE PRICE	FINISH	PR-67 UHC	PR-68 UHC
2008	Holiday Carols	5,224	69.95	Proof	70.	80.

TWENTY DOLLARS, HOLIDAY PINE CONES, 2010.

Designers and Engravers:
Obv.: Susanna Blunt, Susan Taylor
Rev.: Susan Taylor, RCM Staff
Composition: 99.99% Ag
Silver content: 31.39 g,, 1.01 tr oz
Weight: 31.39 g
Diameter: 38.00 mm
Thickness: 3.2 mm
Edge: Reeded
Die Axis: ↑↑
Finish: Proof, with crystallised Swarovski elements
Case: Maroon clam style case, black flocked insert, encapsulated coin, COA

DATE	DESCRIPTION	QUANTITY SOLD	ISSUE PRICE	FINISH	PR-67 UHC	PR-68 UHC
2010	Holiday Pine Cones, Moonlight	5,000	99.95	Proof	100.	110.
2010	Holiday Pine Cones, Ruby	5,000	99.95	Proof	125.	135.

CRYSTAL RAINDROP SERIES, 2008-2010

TWENTY DOLLARS, CRYSTAL RAINDROP SERIES, 2008-2010.

Designers:
Obv.: Susanna Blunt
Rev.: Celia Godkin

Engravers:
Obv.: Susan Taylor
Rev.: RCM Staff

Composition: 99.99% Ag
Silver content: 31.39 g, 1.01 tr oz
Weight: 31.39 g
Diameter: 38.0 mm
Thickness: 3.1 mm
Edge: Reeded
Die Axis: ↑↑
Finish: Proof, colourised with crystallised Swarovski element
Case of Issue: Maroon clam style case, black flocked insert, encapsulated coin, COA

2008 Obverse
With RCM Logo

2008
Crystal Raindrop

2009-2010 Obverse
Without RCM Logo

2009
Autumn Crystal Raindrop

2010
Maple Leaf with Crystal Raindrop

DATE	DESCRIPTION	QUANTITY SOLD	ISSUE PRICE	FINISH	PR-67 UHC	PR-68 UHC
2008	Crystal Raindrop	13,122	89.95	Proof	150.	175.
2009	Autumn Crystal Raindrop	9,998	94.95	Proof	150.	175.
2010	Maple Leaf with Crystal Raindrop	10,000	104.95	Proof	105.	115.

TWENTY DOLLARS, GREAT CANADIAN LOCOMOTIVES SERIES, 2008-2010

Designers:
Obv.: Susanna Blunt
Rev.: RCM Engravers (from Canadian Canadian Pacific Railway Archives)

Engravers:
Obv.: Susan Taylor
Rev.: RCM Staff

Composition: 99.99% Ag
Silver content: 31.39 g, 1.01 tr oz
Weight: 31.39 g
Diameter: 38.0 mm
Thickness: 3.2 mm
Edge: Plain, edge lettering "ROYAL HUDSON", "JUBILEE" or "SELKIRK"
Die Axis: ↑↑
Finish: Proof
Case of Issue: Maroon leatherette clam style case, black flocked insert, encapsulated coin, COA

TWENTY DOLLARS, THE ROYAL HUDSON, 2008.

The Hudson, Locomotive 2850 was chosen to transport King George VI and Queen Elizabeth from Quebec City to Vancouver, during their royal visit of 1939. The royal crest was mounted on the engine and tender, and remained after the visit, thus *The Royal Hudson.*

TWENTY DOLLARS, THE JUBILEE, 2009.

The Jubilee was introduced in 1936 for the CPR's 50th anniversary of the completion of the Transcontinental Railway in 1886.

TWENTY DOLLARS, THE SELKIRK, 2010.

Classed as a 2-10-4 engine, *The Selkirk* engines were built by Montreal Locomotive Works for Canadian Pacific Railway to handle the steep grades of the Selkirk Mountains in British Columbia

DATE	DESCRIPTION	QUANTITY SOLD	ISSUE PRICE	FINISH	PR-67 UHC	PR-68 UHC
2008	The Royal Hudson	8,345	69.95	Proof	70.	80.
2009	The Jubilee	6,036	69.95	Proof	70.	80.
2010	The Selkirk	10,000	79.95	Proof	80.	90.

CANADIAN INDUSTRY SERIES, 2008-2009

TWENTY DOLLARS, AGRICULTURE TRADE, 2008.

Designers and Engravers:
Obv.: Susanna Blunt, Susan Taylor
Rev.: John Mardon, RCM Staff
Composition: 99.99% Ag
Silver content: 31.39 g, 1.01 tr oz
Weight: 31.39 g
Diameter: 38.0 mm
Thickness: 3.1 mm
Edge: Reeded
Die Axis: ↑↑
Finish: Proof
Case: Maroon clam style case, black flocked insert, encapsulated coin, COA

DATE	DESCRIPTION	QUANTITY SOLD	ISSUE PRICE	FINISH	PR-67 UHC	PR-68 UHC
2008	Agriculture Trade	5,802	69.95	Proof	70.	80.

TWENTY DOLLARS, COAL MINING TRADE, 2009.

Designers and Engravers:
Obv.: Susanna Blunt, Susan Taylor
Rev.: John Mardon, RCM Staff
Composition: 99.99% Ag
Silver content: 3.39 g, 1.01 tr oz
Weight: 31.39 g
Diameter: 38.0 mm
Thickness: 3.1 mm
Edge: Reeded
Die Axis: ↑↑
Finish: Proof
Case: Maroon clam style case, black flocked insert, encapsulated coin, COA

DATE	DESCRIPTION	QUANTITY SOLD	ISSUE PRICE	FINISH	PR-67 UHC	PR-68 UHC
2009	Coal Mining Trade	3,349	74.95	Proof	75.	85.

NHL SEASON, 2008-2009

TWENTY DOLLARS, 2008-2009 NHL TEAM GOALIE MASKS, 2009

The goalie mask, first introduced by all-star Montreal goalie Jacques Plante on November 1st, 1959, has become a necessary part of the goal tender's equipment.

Common Obverse

Designers and Engravers:
Obv.: Susanna Blunt, Susan Taylor
Rev.: Marcos Hallam, RCM Staff
Composition: 92.5% Ag, 7.5% Cu
Silver content: 25.70 g, 0.826 tr oz
Weight: 27.78 g
Diameter: 40.0 mm
Thickness: 2.6 mm
Edge: Reeded
Die Axis: ↑↑
Finish: Proof, Painted
Case of Issue: Lucite stand, encapsulated coin, COA, cardboard outer box

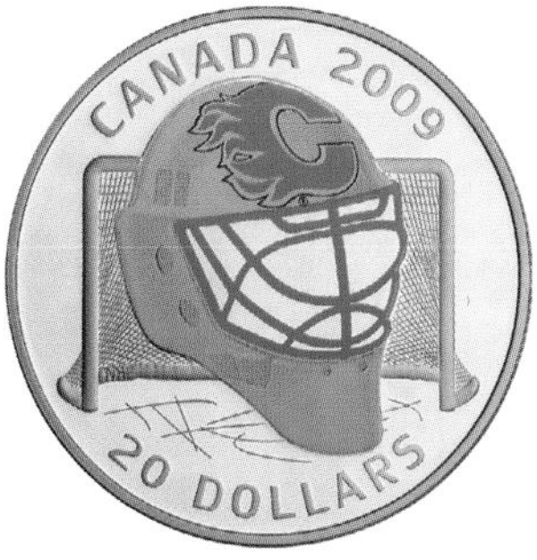

Calgary Flames

Edmonton Oilers

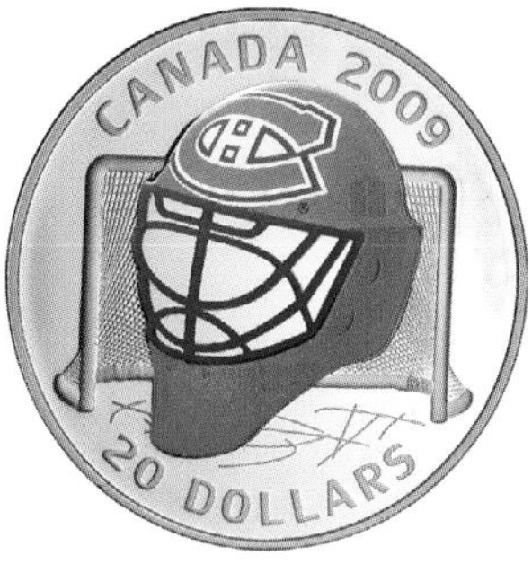

Montreal Canadiens

Ottawa Senators

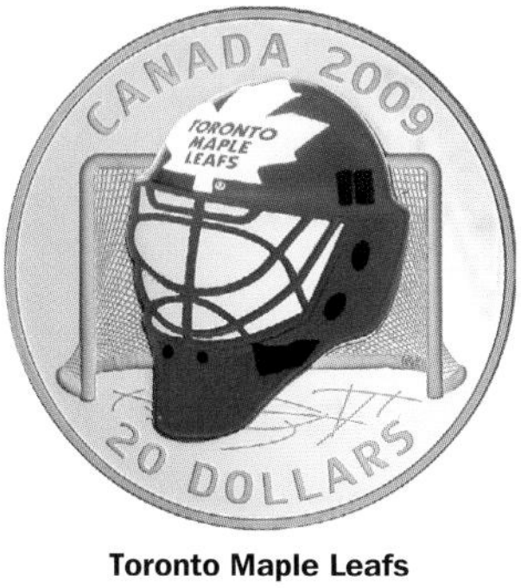

Toronto Maple Leafs

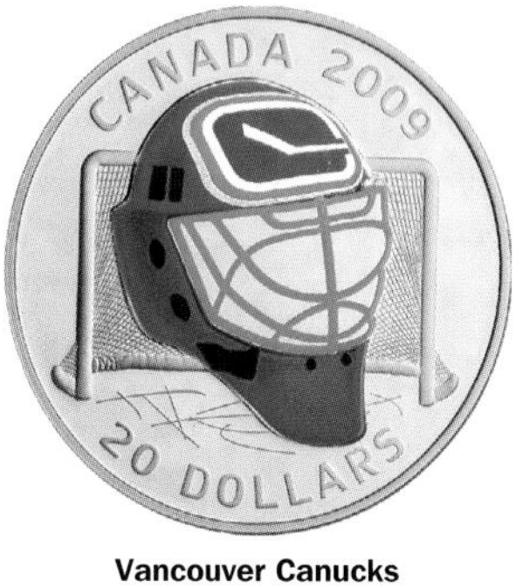

Vancouver Canucks

DATE	DESCRIPTION	QUANTITY SOLD	ISSUE PRICE	FINISH	PR-67 UHC	PR-68 UHC
2009	Calgary Flames	125	74.95	Proof	70.	80.
2009	Edmonton Oilers	147	74.95	Proof	70.	80.
2009	Montreal Canadiens	748	74.95	Proof	70.	80.
2009	Ottawa Senators	95	74.95	Proof	70.	80.
2009	Toronto Maple Leafs	244	74.95	Proof	70.	80.
2009	Vancouver Canucks	129	74.95	Proof	70.	80.

Note: Quantity sold numbers are those for 2009. The Royal Mint Annual Report for 2010 will report additional units sold.

TWENTY DOLLARS, SUMMER MOON MASK, 2009.

Designers and Engravers:
Obv.: Susanna Blunt, Susan Taylor
Rev.: Jody Broomfield
Composition: 99.99% Ag
Silver content: 31.39 g, 1.01 tr oz
Weight: 31.39 g
Diameter: 38.0 mm
Thickness: 3.2 mm
Edge: Reeded
Die Axis: ↑↑ **Finish:** Proof
Case: Maroon leatherette clam style case, black flocked insert, encapsulated coin, COA

DATE	DESCRIPTION	QUANTITY SOLD	ISSUE PRICE	FINISH	PR-67 UHC	PR-68 UHC
2009	Summer Moon Mask	2,834	69.95	Proof	95.	105.

TWENTY DOLLARS, 475TH ANNIVERSARY JACQUES CARTIER'S ARRIVAL AT GASPÉ, 1534-2009.

Designers and Engravers:
Obv.: Susanna Blunt, Susan Taylor
Rev.: John Mardon, RCM Staff
Composition: 99.99% Ag
Silver content: 31.39 g, 1.01 tr oz
Weight: 31.39 g
Diameter: 38.0 mm
Thickness: 3.2 mm
Edge: Reeded
Die Axis: ↑↑ **Finish:** Proof
Case: Maroon leatherette clam style case, black flocked insert, encapsulated coin, COA

DATE	DESCRIPTION	QUANTITY SOLD	ISSUE PRICE	FINISH	PR-67 UHC	PR-68 UHC
2009 (1534-)	475th Anniversary of Jacques Cartier's Arrival at Gaspé	1516	169.95	Proof	325.	350.

TWENTY DOLLARS, WATER LILY, 2010.

Designers and Engravers:
Obv.: Susanna Blunt, Susan Taylor
Rev.: Claudio D'Angelo, RCM Staff
Composition: 99.99% Ag
Silver content: 31.39 g, 1.01 tr oz
Weight: 31.39 g
Diameter: 38.0 mm
Thickness: 3.1 mm
Edge: Reeded
Die Axis: ↑↑
Finish: Proof, Painted, crystallised Swarovski element
Case of Issue: Maroon clam style case, black flocked insert, encapsulated coin, COA

DATE	DESCRIPTION	QUANTITY SOLD	ISSUE PRICE	FINISH	PR-67 UHC	PR-68 UHC
2010	Water Lily	10,000	104.95	Proof	105.	115.

TWENTY DOLLARS, 75TH ANNIVERSARY OF THE FIRST BANK NOTES ISSUED BY BANK OF CANADA, 2010.

The design on this coin is a reproduction of the allegory that appeared on the original 1935 $20 bank note; a woman symbolising agriculture admiring fruits of the field presented to her by a kneeling man.

Designers and Engravers:
Obv.: Susanna Blunt, Susan Taylor
Rev.: RCM Staff
Composition: 99.99% Ag
Silver content: 31.39 g, 1.01 tr oz
Weight: 31.39 g
Diameter: 38.0 mm
Thickness: 3.2 mm
Edge: Reeded
Die Axis: ↑↑ **Finish:** Proof
Case: Maroon leatherette clam style case, black flocked insert, encapsulated coin, COA

DATE	DESCRIPTION	QUANTITY SOLD	ISSUE PRICE	FINISH	PR-67 UHC	PR-68 UHC
2010 (1935-)	75th Anniversary of First Notes Issued by Bank of Canada	7,500	79.95	Proof	80.	90.

TWENTY DOLLAR DERIVATIVES

DATE	DESCRIPTION	QUANTITY SOLD	ISSUE PRICE	ISSUER	FINISH	MARKET VALUE
1998	**Twenty Dollars** Argus and Waterbomber boxed with cardboard model	N/A	N/A	RCM	PR-67	275.
2004	**Twenty Dollars** Northern Lights twenty dollar coin mounted in a frame with a large image of the Northern Lights	N/A	399.00	RCM	PR-67	200.

NOTE FOR COLLECTORS

The Bullion Department of the Royal Canadian Mint issued twenty dollar bullion coins in 2004 and 2005, see page 323.

TWENTY FIVE DOLLARS

TWENTY FIVE DOLLARS, VANCOUVER 2010 OLYMPIC WINTER GAMES, 2007.

Designers:
Obv.: Susanna Blunt
Rev.: See coin

Engravers:
Obv.: Susan Taylor
Rev.: William Woodruff

Composition: 92.5% Ag, 7.5% Cu
Silver content: 25.70 g, 0.826 tr oz
Weight: 27.78 g
Diameter: 40.0 mm
Die Axis: ↑↑
Thickness: 2.5 mm
Edge: Reeded
Finish: Proof, Selective hologram
Case of Issue: Singly: Black leatherette clam case; black flocked insert, encapsulated coin, COA, Olympic theme sleeve
Set: Black leatherette, 15-hole, square clam style case; two black flocked inserts (one with seven indentations, the other with eight; encapsulated coins; COA for each coin; Olympic theme sleeve

2007 Obverse

Curling
Designer: Steve Hepburn
Engraver: William Woodruff

Ice Hockey
Designer: Steve Hepburn
Engraver: William Woodruff

Athletes' Pride
Designer: Shelagh Armstrong
Engraver: William Woodruff

Biathlon
Designer: Bonnie Ross
Engraver: William Woodruff

Alpine Skiing
Designer: Brian Hughes
Engraver: William Woodruff

DATE	DESCRIPTION	DATE OF ISSUE	QUANTITY SOLD	ISSUE PRICE	FINISH	PR-67 UHC	PR-68 UHC
2007	Curling	Feb. 23, 2007	19,531	69.95	Proof	75.	85.
2007	Ice Hockey	April 14, 2007	22,512	69.95	Proof	75.	85.
2007	Athletes' Pride	July 11, 2007	21,886	69.95	Proof	75.	85.
2007	Biathlon	Sept. 12, 2007	16,003	69.95	Proof	75.	85.
2007	Alpine Skiing	Oct. 24, 2007	13,500	69.95	Proof	75.	85.

TWENTY FIVE DOLLARS, VANCOUVER 2010 OLYMPIC WINTER GAMES, 2008.

2008 Obverse

Snowboarding
Designer: Steve Hepburn
Engraver: William Woodruff

Freestyle Skiing
Designer: John Mardon
Engraver: William Woodruff

Home of the
2010 Olympic Winter Games
Designer: Shelagh Armstrong
Engraver: William Woodruff

Figure Skating
Designer: Steve Hepburn
Engraver: William Woodruff

Bobsleigh
Designer: Bonnie Ross
Engraver: William Woodruff

DATE	DESCRIPTION	DATE OF ISSUE	QUANTITY SOLD	ISSUE PRICE	FINISH	PR-67 UHC	PR-68 UHC
2008	Snowboarding	Feb. 20, 2008	6,377	71.95	Proof	75.	85.
2008	Freestyle Skiing	April 16, 2008	12,428	71.95	Proof	75.	85.
2008	Home of the 2010 Olympic Winter Games	July 23, 2008	12,606	71.95	Proof	75.	85.
2008	Figure Skating	Sept. 10, 2008	18,930	71.95	Proof	75.	85.
2008	Bobsleigh	Oct. 29, 2008	8,800	71.95	Proof	75.	85.

TWENTY FIVE DOLLARS, VANCOUVER 2010 OLYMPIC WINTER GAMES, 2009.

2009 Obverse

Speed Skating
Designer: Tony Bianco
Engraver: William Woodruff

Cross Country Skiing
Designer: Brian Hughes
Engraver: William Woodruff

Olympic Spirit
Designer: Shelagh Armstrong
Engraver: William Woodruff

Skeleton
Designer: Tony Bianco
Engraver: William Woodruff

Ski Jumping
Designer: John Mardon
Engraver: William Woodruff

DATE	DESCRIPTION	DATE OF ISSUE	QUANTITY SOLD	ISSUE PRICE	FINISH	PR-67 UHC	PR-68 UHC
2009	Speed Skating	Feb. 18, 2009	27,827	71.95	Proof	75.	85.
2009	Cross Country Skiing	April 15, 2009	14,292	71.95	Proof	75.	85.
2009	Olympic Spirit	June 17, 2009	10,224	71.95	Proof	75.	85.
2009	Skeleton	Aug.. 5, 2009	10,582	71.95	Proof	75.	85.
2009	Ski Jumping	Oct. 7, 2009	11,365	71.95	Proof	75.	85.
2007-2010	Set of 15 coins	—	4,764	—	Proof	1,000.	—

THIRTY DOLLARS

THIRTY DOLLARS, WELCOME FIGURE (DZUNUK'WA) TOTEM POLE, 2005.

Dzunuk'wa is a giant, hairy, black-bodied, big-breasted, wide-eyed female monster. She is physically strong enough to tear down large trees, spiritually powerful enough to resurrect the dead and possesses magical treasures and great wealth.

Designers and Engravers:
Obv.: Susanna Blunt, Susan Taylor
Rev.: Richard Hunt, RCM Staff
Composition: 92.5% Ag, 7.5% Cu
Silver content: 29.137 g, 0.937 tr oz
Weight: 31.50 g
Diameter: 40.0 mm
Edge: Reeded
Thickness: 3.0 mm
Die Axis: ↑↑
Finish: Proof
Case of Issue: Maroon plastic slide case, black plastic insert, encapsulated coin, COA

DATE	DESCRIPTION	QUANTITY SOLD	ISSUE PRICE	FINISH	PR-67 UHC	PR-68 UHC
2005	Welcome Figure Totem Pole	9,904	79.95	Proof	75.	85.

Note: An identical design is utilized on the $300 gold coin for 2005, see page 230.

THIRTY DOLLARS, DOG SLED TEAM, 2006.

Designers and Engravers:
Obv.: Susanna Blunt, Susan Taylor
Rev.: Arnold Nogy, José Osio
Composition: 92.5% Ag, 7.5% Cu
Silver content: 29.137 g, 0.937 tr oz
Weight: 31.50 g
Diameter: 40.0 mm
Edge: Reeded
Thickness: 3.0 mm
Die Axis: ↑↑
Finish: Proof, Painted
Case of Issue: Maroon plastic slide case, black plastic insert, encapsulated coin, COA

DATE	DESCRIPTION	QUANTITY SOLD	ISSUE PRICE	FINISH	PR-67 UHC	PR-68 UHC
2006	Dog Sled Team	7,384	89.95	Proof	110.	120.

Note: An identical design is utilized on the $250 gold coin for 2006, see page 219.

THIRTY DOLLARS, NATIONAL WAR MEMORIALS SERIES, 2006-2007.

Designers:
Obv.: Susanna Blunt
Rev.: See coin

Engravers:
Obv.: Susan Taylor
Rev.: See coin

Composition: 92.5% Ag, 7.5% Cu
Silver content: 29.137 g, 0.937 tr oz
Weight: 31.50 g
Diameter: 40.0 mm
Thickness: 3.0 mm
Edge: Reeded
Die Axis: ↑↑
Finish: Proof
Case of Issue: Maroon plastic slide case, black plastic insert, encapsulated coin, COA

2006 Obverse
Date on Obverse

2006 National War Memorial
Designer: Vernon March
Engraver: José Osio

2006 Beaumont-Hamel
Newfoundland Memorial
Designer: RCM Staff
Engraver: Susan Taylor

2007 Obverse
Date on Reverse

2007
Canadian National Vimy Memorial
Designer: RCM Staff
Engraver: José Osio

DATE	DESCRIPTION	QUANTITY SOLD	ISSUE PRICE	FINISH	PR-67 UHC	PR-68 UHC
2006	National War Memorial	8,876	79.95	Proof	100.	110.
2006	Beaumont-Hamel Newfoundland Memorial	15,325	79.95	Proof	100.	110.
2007	Canadian National Vimy Memorial	5,335	79.95	Proof	100.	110.

CANADIAN ACHIEVEMENT SERIES, 2006-2008

THIRTY DOLLARS, 5TH ANNIVERSARY OF CANADARM, 2006.

Designers and Engravers:
Obv.: Susanna Blunt, Susan Taylor
Rev.: Cecily Mok, RCM Staff
Composition: 92.5% Ag, 7.5% Cu
Silver content: 29.137 g, 0.937 tr oz
Weight: 31.50 g
Diameter: 40.0 mm
Edge: Reeded
Thickness: 3.0 mm
Die Axis: ↑↑
Finish: Proof, Decal
Case: Maroon plastic slide case, black plastic insert, encapsulated coin, COA

DATE	DESCRIPTION	QUANTITY SOLD	ISSUE PRICE	FINISH	PR-67 UHC	PR-68 UHC
2006	5th Anniversary of Canadarm	9,357	79.95	Proof	125.	135.

Note: An identical design is utilized on the $300 gold coin for 2006, see page 232.

THIRTY DOLLARS, PANORAMIC PHOTOGRAPHY IN CANADA, NIAGARA FALLS, 2007.

Designers and Engravers:
Obv.: Susanna Blunt, Susan Taylor
Rev.: Chris Jordison, RCM Staff
Composition: 92.5% Ag, 7.5% Cu
Silver content: 29.137 g, 0.937 tr oz
Weight: 31.50 g
Diameter: 40.0 mm
Edge: Reeded
Thickness: 2.8 mm
Die Axis: ↑↑
Finish: Proof, Hologram
Case: Maroon leatherette clam style case, black flocked insert, encapsulated coin, COA

DATE	DESCRIPTION	QUANTITY SOLD	ISSUE PRICE	FINISH	PR-67 UHC	PR-68 UHC
2007	Panoramic Photography in Canada, Niagara Falls	5,702	84.95	Proof	95.	105.

Note: An identical design is utilized on the $300 gold coin for 2007, see page 232.

THIRTY DOLLARS, IMAX®, 2008.

Designers and Engravers:
Obv.: Susanna Blunt, Susan Taylor
Rev.: IMAX® Corporation, RCM Staff
Composition: 92.5% Ag, 7.5% Cu
Silver content: 29.137 g, 0.937 tr oz
Weight: 31.50 g
Diameter: 40.0 mm
Edge: Reeded
Thickness: 2.8 mm
Die Axis: ↑↑
Finish: Proof, Hologram
Case: Maroon leatherette clam style case, black flocked insert, encapsulated coin, COA

DATE	DESCRIPTION	QUANTITY SOLD	ISSUE PRICE	FINISH	PR-67 UHC	PR-68 UHC
2008	IMAX®	3,861	84.95	Proof	80.	90.

Note: An identical design is utilized on the $300 gold coin for 2008, see page 232.

INTERNATIONAL YEAR OF ASTRONOMY

THIRTY DOLLARS, INTERNATIONAL YEAR OF ASTRONOMY, 2009.

Designers and Engravers:
Obv.: Susanna Blunt, Susan Taylor
Rev.: Colin Mayne, RCM Staff
Composition: 92.5% Ag, 7.5% Cu
Silver content: 31.22 g, 1.00 tr oz
Weight: 33.75 g
Diameter: 40.0 mm
Edge: Reeded
Thickness: 2.9 mm
Die Axis: ↑↑
Finish: Proof, Painted
Case: Maroon leatherette clam style case, black flocked insert, encapsulated coin, COA

DATE	DESCRIPTION	QUANTITY SOLD	ISSUE PRICE	FINISH	PR-67 UHC	PR-68 UHC
2009	International Year of Astronomy	7,174	89.95	Proof	95.	105.

FIFTY DOLLARS

FIFTY DOLLARS, THE FOUR SEASONS, 2006.

This fifty dollar coin, with a guaranteed weight of five ounces, depicts the maple tree during its stages of the four seasons.

Designers and Engravers:
Obv.: S. Blunt, S. Taylor
Rev..: T. Bianco, RCM Staff
Composition: 99.99% Ag
Silver content:
156.34 g, 5.026 tr oz
Weight: 156.36 g
Diameter: 64.8 mm
Thickness: 5.0
Edge: Reeded
Die Axis: ↑↑
Finish: Proof
Case: Black case, black flocked insert, encapsulated coin, COA

DATE	DESCRIPTION	QUANTITY SOLD	ISSUE PRICE	FINISH	PR-67 UHC	PR-68 UHC
2006	The Four Seasons	1,999	299.95	Proof	600.	650.

FIFTY DOLLARS, 60TH WEDDING ANNIVERSARY OF QUEEN ELIZABETH AND PRINCE PHILIP, 2007.

Designers and Engravers:
Obv.: S. Blunt, S. Taylor
Rev.: S. Hepburn, RCM Staff
Composition: 99.99% Ag
Silver content:
156.34 g, 5.026 tr oz
Weight: 156.36 g
Diameter: 65.0 mm
Thickness: 5.0
Edge: Reeded
Die Axis: ↑↑
Finish: Proof
Case: Maroon leatherette clam style case, black flocked insert; encapsulated coin, COA

DATE	DESCRIPTION	QUANTITY SOLD	ISSUE PRICE	FINISH	PR-67 UHC	PR-68 UHC
2007	60th Wedding Anniv. Queen Elizabeth / Prince Philip	1,957	299.95	Proof	350.	375.

Note: 1. An identical design is utilized on the $500 gold coin for 2007, see page 237.
2. Coins illustrated smaller than actual size.

FIFTY DOLLARS, 100TH ANNIVERSARY OF THE ROYAL CANADIAN MINT, 1908-2008.

Designers and Engravers:
Obv.: S. Blunt, S. Taylor
Rev.: RCM Staff
Composition: 99.99% Ag
Silver content:
157.65 g, 5.069 tr oz
Weight: 157.67 g
Diameter: 65.0 mm
Thickness: 5.15 mm
Edge: Reeded
Die Axis: ↑↑
Finish: Proof
Case: Maroon leatherette clam style case, black flocked insert, encapsulated coin, COA

DATE	DESCRIPTION	QUANTITY SOLD	ISSUE PRICE	FINISH	PR-67 UHC	PR-68 UHC
2008 (1908-)	100th Anniversary of the Royal Canadian Mint	2,078	369.95	Proof	375.	400.

FIFTY DOLLARS, 150TH ANNIVERSARY OF THE START OF THE CONSTRUCTION OF THE PARLIAMENT BUILDINGS, 1859-2009.

Designers and Engravers:
Obv.: S. Blunt, S. Taylor
Obv.: RCM Staff
Composition: 99.99% Ag
Silver content:
157.65 g, 5.069 tr oz
Weight: 157.67 g
Diameter: 65.00 mm
Thickness: 5.0 mm
Edge: Reeded
Die Axis: ↑↑
Finish: Proof
Case: Maroon leatherette clam style case, black flocked insert, encapsulated coin, COA

DATE	DESCRIPTION	QUANTITY SOLD	ISSUE PRICE	FINISH	PR-67 UHC	PR-68 UHC
2009 (1859-)	150th Anniv. Construction Parliament Buildings	910	459.95	Proof	475.	500.

Note: 1. Identical designs are utilized on the $300 gold coins for 2008 and 2009, see page 238.
2. Coins illustrated smaller than actual size.

FIFTY DOLLARS, 75TH ANNIVERSARY OF THE FIRST BANK NOTES ISSUED BY THE BANK OF CANADA, 2010.

The design on this coin is a reproduction of the allegory tht appeared on the original 1935 $50 bank note; a seated woman with elements of radio broadcasting to symbolise modern inventions.

Designers and Engravers:
Obv.: S. Blunt, S. Taylor
Obv.: RCM Staff
Composition: 99.99% Ag
Silver content:
157.65 g, 5.069 tr oz
Weight: 157.67 g
Diameter: 65.25 mm
Thickness: 5.0 mm
Edge: Reeded
Die Axis: ↑↑
Finish: Proof
Case: Maroon leatherette clam style case, black flocked insert, encapsulated coin, COA

DATE	DESCRIPTION	QUANTITY SOLD	ISSUE PRICE	FINISH	PR-67 UHC	PR-68 UHC
2010 (1935-)	75th Anniv. Bank of Canada Notes	2,000	389.95	Proof	450.	500.

Note: 1. An identical design is utilized on the $500 gold coin for 2010, see page 239.
2. Coin illustrated smaller than actual size.

TWO HUNDRED FIFTY DOLLARS

VANCOUVER 2010 OLYMPIC WINTER GAMES, 2007-2010

These are the first coins produced in pure silver by the Royal Canadian Mint with a guaranteed weight of one kilo.

Designers:
Obv.: Susanna Blunt
Rev.: See coin

Engravers:
Obv.: Susan Taylor
Rev.: See coin

Composition: 99.99% Ag
Silver content: 1,000.00 g, 32.151 tr oz
Weight: 1,000 g (1 kilo)
Diameter: 101.6 mm
Thickness: 12.5 mm
Edge: Plain
Die Axis: ↑↑
Finish: Proof, Ultra high relief
Case of Issue: Black display case, black flocked insert, encapsulated coin, COA; Vancouver 2010 Olympic Winter Games theme sleeve

TWO HUNDRED FIFTY DOLLARS, EARLY CANADA, 2007.

2007 Obverse

Designer: Stan Witten
Engraver: Stan Witten

TWO HUNDRED FIFTY DOLLARS, TOWARDS CONFEDERATION, 2008.

2008 Obverse

Designer: Susan Taylor
Engraver: Susan Taylor

DATE	DESCRIPTION	DATE OF ISSUE	QUANTITY SOLD	ISSUE PRICE	FINISH	PR-67 UHC	PR-68 UHC
2007	Early Canada	Feb. 23, 2007	2,500	1,299.95	Proof	1,650.	1,750.
2008	Towards Confederation	Feb. 20, 2008	2,500	1,599.95	Proof	1,650.	1,750.

VANCOUVER 2010 OLYMPIC WINTER GAMES, 2007-2010 (cont.)

TWO HUNDRED FIFTY DOLLARS, THE CANADA OF TODAY, 2009.

2009 Obverse

Designer: Design Team of the Vancouver Organising Committee for the 2010 Olympic and Paralympic Winter Games
Engraver: RCM Staff

TWO HUNDRED FIFTY DOLLARS, SURVIVING THE FLOOD, 2009.

2009 Obverse

Designer: Xwa lac tun (Ricky Harry)
Engraver: RCM Staff

DATE	DESCRIPTION	DATE OF ISSUE	QUANTITY SOLD	ISSUE PRICE	FINISH	PR-67 UHC	PR-68 UHC
2009	The Canada of Today	April 15, 2009	905	1,599.95	Proof	1,650.	1,750.
2009	Surviving the Flood	Nov. 17, 2009	815	1,599.95	Proof	1,650.	1,750.

Note: 1. Identical designs are utilized on the $300 gold coins for 2007, 2008 and 2009, see pages 240-241.
2. Coins illustrated smaller than actual size.

VANCOUVER 2010 OLYMPIC WINTER GAMES, 2007-2010 (cont.)

TWO HUNDRED FIFTY DOLLARS, THE EAGLE, 2010.

The eagle, an important First Nations symbol, represents power, peace and prestige. This is the first time a coin is offered in three different finishes.

Designers:
Obv.: Susanna Blunt
Rev.: Xwa lac tun (Ricky Harry)
Composition: 99.99% Ag
Silver content: 1,000.00 g, 32.151 tr oz
Weight: 1,000 g (1 kilo)
Die Axis: ↑↑

Engravers:
Obv.: Susan Taylor
Rev.: RCM Staff
Thickness: 12.5 mm
Edge: Plain
Diameter: 101.6 mm
Finish: Proof, Proof Enamel, and Proof Antique

Case of Issue: Black display case, black flocked insert, encapsulated coin, COA; Vancouver 2010 Olympic Winter Games theme sleeve

Obverse

The Eagle, Proof Enamel

DATE	DESCRIPTION	DATE OF ISSUE	QUANTITY SOLD	ISSUE PRICE	FINISH	PR-67 UHC	PR-68 UHC
2010	The Eagle, Proof	Nov. 19, 2009	500	1,649.95	Proof	1,650.	1,850.
2010	The Eagle, Proof Enamel	Nov. 19, 2009	500	1,649.95	Enamel	1,650.	1,850.
2010	The Eagle, Proof Antique	Nov. 19, 2009	500	1,649.95	Antique	1,650.	1,850.

Note: 1. An identical design is utilized on the $500 gold coin for 2010, see page 242.
2. Coin illustrated smaller than actual size.

125 TH ANNIVERSARY OF BANFF NATIONAL PARK

TWO HUNDRED FIFTY DOLLARS, 125TH ANNIVERSARY OF BANFF NATIONAL PARK, 2010.

Banff National Park was Canada's first national park, and the world's third, spanning 6,641 square kilometres of valleys, mountains, glaciers, forests, meadows, and rivers.

Designers:
Obv.: Susanna Blunt
Rev.: Tony Bianco

Composition: 99.99% Ag
Silver content: 1,000.00 g, 32.151 tr oz
Weight: 1,000 g (1 kilo)
Diameter: 101.8 mm

Engravers:
Obv.: Susan Taylor
Rev.: RCM Staff

Thickness: N/A
Edge: Plain
Die Axis: ↑↑
Finish: Proof

Case of Issue: Black display case, black flocked insert, encapsulated coin, COA

DATE	DESCRIPTION	QUANTITY SOLD	ISSUE PRICE	FINISH	PR-67 UHC	PR-68 UHC
2010	100th Anniversary of Banff	750	1,904.95	Proof	1,925.	1,950.

Note: 1. An identical design is utilized on the $500 gold coin for 2010, see page 243.
2. Coin illustrated smaller than actual size.

GOLD COINS

TWENTY-FIVE CENT GOLD COINS

CARIBOU, 2010.

Canada's smallest gold coin features the Caribou design by Emanuel Hahn first used on the 1937 twenty-five cent silver coin.

Actual Size

Designers and Engravers:
Obv.: Susanna Blunt, Susan Taylor
Rev.: Emanuel Hahn, RCM Staff
Composition: 99.99% Au
Gold content: 0.50 g, 0.016 tr oz
Weight: 0.50 g
Diameter: 11.0 mm
Edge: Reeded
Thickness: 0.6 mm
Die Axis: ↑↑
Finish: Proof
Case: Maroon leatherette clam style case, black flock insert, encapsulated coin,COA

DATE	DESCRIPTION	QUANTITY SOLD	ISSUE PRICE	FINISH	PR-67 UHC	PR-68 UHC
2010	Caribou	15,000	74.95	Proof	75.	85.

Note: Images shown larger than actual size.

ONE DOLLAR GOLD COINS

Designers:
Obv.: Susanna Blunt
Rev.: RCM Staff

Engravers:
Obv.: Susan Taylor
Rev.: RCM Staff

Composition: 99.99% Au
Gold content: 1.555 g, 0.050 tr oz
Weight: 1.555 g
Diameter: 14.10 mm
Thickness: 0.80 mm
Edge: Reeded
Die Axis: ↑↑
Finish: Proof
Case of Issue: Maroon plastic slide case, black plastic insert, encapsulated coin, COA

2006 GOLD LOUIS (1723 LOUIS D'OR MIRLITON)

Actual size

2007 GOLD LOUIS (1726 LOUIS D'OR AUX LUNETTES)

Actual size

2008 GOLD LOUIS (1720-1723 LOUIS D'OR AUX DEUX L)

Actual size

DATE	DESCRIPTION	QUANTITY SOLD	ISSUE PRICE	FINISH	PR-67 UHC	PR-68 UHC
2006	1723 Louis d'or Mirliton	5,648	102.95	Proof	115.	125.
2007	1726 Louis d'or Aux Lunettes	4,023	104.95	Proof	115.	125.
2008	1720 to 1723 Louis d'or aux deux L	3,793	124.95	Proof	115.	125.

Note: Images shown larger than actual size.

FIVE AND TEN DOLLAR GOLD COMMEMORATIVE COINS

FIVE AND TEN DOLLAR GOLD COMMEMORATIVES 1912-2002.

Issued to mark the 90th anniversary of Canada's first five and ten dollar gold coins in 1912, these double-dated 1912-2002 coins continue a commemorative series which began in 1998, with the issue recalling the first set of coins struck at the Ottawa Mint. Basing the overall design on the 1912 specimen coins from the Bank of Canada collection, the 1912-2002 gold coins differ only in the date and, of course, the obverse effigy.

$5 Obverse

$5 Reverse

$10 Obverse

$10 Reverse

Designers:
Obv.: Dora de Pédery-Hunt
Rev.: W. H. J. Blakemore

Engravers:
Obv.: Dora de Pédery-Hunt
Rev.: Cosme Saffioti

Denominations:	**$5**	**$10**
Composition:	90.0% Au, 10.0 Cu	90.0% Au, 10.0% Cu
Gold content:	7.52 g, 0.242 tr oz	15.05 g, 0.484 tr oz
Weight (grams):	8.36	16.72
Diameter (mm):	21.59	26.92
Thickness (mm):	N/A	N/A
Edge:	Reeded	Reeded
Finish:	Proof	Proof

Case of Issue: Two-coin clam style case

DATE	DESCRIPTION	QUANTITY SOLD	ISSUE PRICE	FINISH	PR-67 UHC	PR-68 UHC
2002 (1912-)	$5	—	N.I.I.	Proof	500.	550.
2002 (1912-)	$10	—	N.I.I.	Proof	1,000.	1,100.
2002 (1912-)	Set of 2 coins	1998	749.95	Proof	1,350.	—

TWENTY DOLLAR GOLD COIN

CENTENNIAL OF CONFEDERATION COMMEMORATIVE, 1967.

The highlight of the coins issued in 1967 to mark the centenary of Canadian Confederation was a $20 gold coin. It was issued only as part of a $40.00 specimen set (see page 281 for the set listing), but many were later removed from the sets for separate trading. The reverse design is an adaption of the Canadian coat of arms which appears on the 50-cent piece of 1960-1966. It is the only coin in the Centennial set that bears the single date 1967 instead of 1867-1967.

Designers and Engravers:
Obv.: Arnold Machin, Myron Cook
Rev.: Thomas Shingles, Myron Cook
Composition: 90.0% Au, 10.0% Cu
Gold content: 16.443 g, 0.529 tr oz
Weight: 18.27 g
Diameter: 27.05 mm
Edge: Reeded
Thickness: 2.30 mm
Die Axis: ↑↑
Finish: Specimen
Case: Black leather case, black flocked insert

DATE	DESCRIPTION	QUANTITY SOLD	ISSUE PRICE	FINISH	SP-66	SP-67
1967	Centennial of Confederation	334,288	N.I.I.	Specimen	825.	850.

FIFTY DOLLAR GOLD COIN

60TH ANNIVERSARY OF THE END OF THE SECOND WORLD WAR, 1945-2005.

World War II was a global conflict which began September 1st, 1939 when Germany invaded Poland. By September 3rd, 1939 Britain and France declared war on Germany.

There are several ending dates: VE (Victory in Europe) Day May 8th, 1945, and VJ Day (Victory in Japan) August 14th, 1945.

Designers and Engravers:
Obv.: Susanna Blunt, Susan Taylor
Rev.: Peter Mossman, Christie Paquet
Composition: 58.33% Au, 41.67% Ag
Gold content: 7.00 g, 0.225 tr oz
Silver content: 5.00 g, 0.161 tr oz
Weight: 12.00 g
Diameter: 27.00 mm
Thickness: 2.00 mm
Edge: Reeded
Die Axis: ↑↑
Finish: Specimen
Case: Maroon plastic slide case, black plastic insert, encapsulated coin, COA

DATE	DESCRIPTION	QUANTITY SOLD	ISSUE PRICE	FINISH	SP-66	SP-67
2005 (1945-)	60th Anniv. End of the Second World War	4,000	379.95	Specimen	350.	400.

Note: While the $50 gold coin is listed as proof quality on the certificate of authenticity, the finish on the coins examined is specimen.

SEVENTY-FIVE DOLLAR GOLD COINS

COMMEMORATING THE VISIT OF POPE JOHN PAUL II TO CANADA, 2005.

During a 12-day tour in April 2005, Pope John Paul II visited many cities in Canada, drawing over two million people to the Papal events. This was his third trip to Canada.

Designers and Engravers:
Obv.: Susanna Blunt, Susan Taylor
Rev.: Susan Taylor, Susan Taylor
Composition: 41.66% Au, 58.34 Ag
Gold content: 13.10 g, 0.421 tr oz
Silver content: 18.34 g, 0.590 tr oz
Weight: 31.44 g
Diameter: 36.07 mm
Thickness: 3.00 mm
Edge: Reeded
Die Axis: ↑↑
Finish: Proof
Case: Maroon plastic slide case, black plastic insert, encapsulated coin, COA

DATE	DESCRIPTION	QUANTITY SOLD	ISSUE PRICE	FINISH	PR-67 UHC	PR-68 UHC
2005	Commemorating the Visit of Pope John Paul II to Canada	1,870	544.95	Proof	650.	675.

NOTE ON POPE JOHN PAUL II COINS

In 2005 a set containing the $10 (silver) and $75 (gold) coins was issued to commemorate the visit to Canada of Pope John Paul II. This may have been a special presentation set as only nine were issued.

VANCOUVER 2010 OLYMPIC WINTER GAMES

COMMEMORATING THE VANCOUVER 2010 OLYMPIC WINTER GAMES, 2007-2009.

The Vancouver 2010 Olympic Winter Games $75 gold coins were sold singly or in three-coin sets. The three different sets offered were Canadian Wildlife, Canadian Icons and Vancouver 2010 Winter Games.

Designers:
Obv.: Susanna Blunt
Rev.: See coin

Engravers:
Obv.: Susan Taylor
Rev.: RCM Staff

Composition: 58.33% Au, 41.67% Ag
Gold content: 7.00 g, 0.225 tr oz
Silver content: 5.0 g, 0.161 tr oz
Weight: 12.00 g
Diameter: 27.00 mm
Thickness: 2.00 to 2.20 mm
Edge: Reeded
Die Axis: ↑↑
Finish: Proof, Colour on reverse
Case of Issue: Singly: Black display case, black flocked insert, encapsulated coin, COA; Vancouver 2010 Olympic Winter Games theme sleeve.
Sets: See page 191.

2007

Obverse

R.C.M.P.
Designer: Cecily Mok

Athletes' Pride
Designer: S. Armstrong

Canada Geese
Designer: Cecily Mok

2008

Obverse

Four Host First Nations
Des.: Kerri Burnett

Home of the 2010
Olympic Winter Games
Des.: Sheila Armstrong

Inukshuk
Des.: Sheila Armstrong

2009

Obverse

Wolf
Des.: Arnold Nogy

Olympic Spirit
Des.: Sheila Armstrong

Moose
Des.: Kerri Burnett

COMMEMORATING THE VANCOUVER 2010 OLYMPIC WINTER GAMES, 2007-2009, PRICING TABLE.

DATE	DESCRIPTION	DATE OF ISSUE	QUANTITY SOLD	ISSUE PRICE	FINISH	PR-67 UHC	PR-68 UHC
2007	Royal Canadian Mounted Police	Feb. 23, 2007	6,687	389.95	Proof	400.	425.
2007	Athletes' Pride	July 11, 2007	4,524	389.95	Proof	400.	425.
2007	Canada Geese	Oct. 24, 2007	4,418	409.95	Proof	425.	450.
2008	Four Host First Nations	Feb. 20, 2008	4,897	409.95	Proof	425.	450.
2008	Home of the Winter Games	July 23, 2008	4,581	433.95	Proof	450.	475.
2008	Inukshuk	Oct. 29, 2008	4,907	499.95	Proof	500.	525.
2009	Wolf	Feb. 18, 2009	4,161	499.95	Proof	500.	525.
2009	Olympic Spirit	June 17, 2009	4,479	499.95	Proof	500.	525.
2009	Moose	Sept. 9, 2009	4,075	499.95	Proof	500.	525.

SEVENTY-FIVE DOLLAR VANCOUVER WINTER OLYMPIC GAMES COIN SETS

Sets of the three $75 gold coins were offered for sale in acrylic holders. They were assembled in three themes: Wildlife, Icons and the Vancouver 2010 Olympic Winter Games.

DATE	DESCRIPTION	QUANTITY SOLD	ISSUE PRICE	ISSUER	FINISH	MARKET VALUE
2007-2009	**Canada Wildlife:** 2007 Canada Geese, 2009 Wolf, 2009 Moose; Acrylic holder	25	1,424.95	RCM	PR-67	1,325.
2007-2008	**Canadian Icons:** 2007 R.C.M.P., 2008 Four Host First Nations, 2008 Inukshuk; Acrylic holder	18	1,424.95	RCM	PR-67	1,325.
2007-2009	**Vancouver 2010 Winter Games:** 2007 Athletes' Pride, 2008 Home of the 2010 Olympic Winter Games, 2009 Olympic Spirit; Acrylic holder	32	1,424.95	RCM	PR-67	1,350.

FOUR SEASONS MAPLE LEAVES

FOUR SEASONS MAPLE LEAVES, 2010.

The four seasons, spring, summer, autumn, and winter bring an ever changing landscape to Canada. The evolving maple leaves best mirror this yearly cycle.

Obverse

Designers:
Obv.: Susanna Blunt
Rev.: See coin

Composition: 58.33% Au, 41.67% Ag
Gold content: 7.00 g, 0.225 tr oz
Silver content: 5.0 g, 0.161 tr oz
Weight: 12.00 g
Diameter: 27.00 mm

Engravers:
Obv.: Susan Taylor
Rev.: RCM Staff

Thickness: 2.00 mm
Edge: Reeded
Die Axis: ↑↑
Finish: Proof, Painted

Case: Singly: Maroon leatherette clam style case, black flock insert, encapsulated coin, COA
Sets: Maple wood display case, 4-hole black flock insert, encapsulated coins, serialised certificate, black sleeve

Spring
Designer: A. Nogy

Summer
Designer: M. Grant

Fall
Designer: C. D'Angelo

Winter
Designer: C. Godkin

DATE	DESCRIPTION	QUANTITY SOLD	ISSUE PRICE	FINISH	PR-67 UHC	PR-68 UHC
2010	Spring Maple Leaves	1,000	589.95	Proof	600.	625.
2010	Summer Maple Leaves	1,000	589.95	Proof	600.	625.
2010	Fall Maple Leaves	1,000	589.95	Proof	600.	625.
2010	Winter Maple Leaves	1,000	589.95	Proof	600.	625.
2010	Set of Four Coins	—	2,358.95	Proof	2,375.	—

ONE HUNDRED DOLLAR GOLD COINS

MONTREAL OLYMPIC COMMEMORATIVES, 1976.

As part of the series of collectors' coins struck to commemorate and help finance the XXI Olympiad, two separate $100 gold coins were issued in 1976. The reverse design for each shows an ancient Grecian athlete being crowned with laurel by the goddess Pallas Athena. The uncirculated issue is 14k gold and has beads around the rim. The proof issue is 22k gold, slightly smaller, and lacks rim beads.

1976 Obverse
14 kt Gold

1976 Reverse
14 kt Gold

Designers and Engravers:
Obv.: Arnold Machin, Walter Ott
Rev.: Dora de Pédery-Hunt, Walter Ott
Composition: 58.33% Au, 41.67% Au
Gold content: 7.78 g, 0.250 tr oz
Silver content: 5.56 g, 0.179 tr oz
Weight: 13.338 g **Edge:** Reeded
Diameter: 27.00 mm **Die Axis:** ↑↑
Thickness: 2.20 mm **Finish:** Circulation
Case: Plastic flip in a cardboard sleeve

1976 Obverse
22kt Gold

1976 Reverse
22kt Gold

Designers and Engravers:
Obv.: Arnold Machin, Walter Ott
Rev.: Dora de Pédery-Hunt, Walter Ott
Composition: 91.67% Au, 8.33% Ag
Gold content: 15.55 g, 0.500 tr oz
Silver content: 1.14 g, 0.045 tr oz
Weight: 16.966 g **Edge:** Reeded
Diameter: 25.00 mm **Die Axis:** ↑↑
Thickness: 2.20 mm **Finish:** Proof
Case: Cowhide and wood case, black suede insert, COA

DATE	DESCRIPTION	QUANTITY SOLD	ISSUE PRICE	FINISH	65	66	67	68
1976	Montreal Olympics, 14 kt	650,000	105.00	Circulation	400.	425.	450.	—
1976	Montreal Olympics, 22 kt	350,000	150.00	Proof	—	—	800.	825.

NOTE FOR COLLECTORS

Beginning with the modern issues, gold coins were offered for sale at a small premium over face value giving investors a call on gold with a limited downside risk. Investors soon realised this and purchased large quantities of coins which resulted in high mintage figures.

Currently, modern gold coins trade at their intrinsic value, or slightly higher.

QUEEN ELIZABETH II SILVER JUBILEE COMMEMORATIVE, 1977.

Following the sales success of the Olympic $100 coins the Royal Canadian Mint decided to embark upon a programme of issuing a $100 coin every year. The 1997 commemorative reverse shows a bouquet of flowers made up of the official flowers of the provinces and territories. All were issued in proof quality, with mirror fields and frosted devices and legends.

Designers and Engravers:
Obv.: Arnold Machin, RCM Staff
Rev.: Raymond Lee, Walter Ott
Composition: 91.67% Au, 8.33% Ag
Gold content: 15.55 g, 0.500 tr oz
Silver content: 1.413 g, 0.045 tr oz
Weight: 16.965 g **Edge:** Reeded
Diameter: 27.00 mm **Die Axis:** ↑↑
Thickness: 2.20 mm **Finish:** Proof
Case: Black leatherette case, maroon insert, plastic coin holder, COA

DATE	DESCRIPTION	QUANTITY SOLD	ISSUE PRICE	FINISH	PR-67 UHC	PR-68 UHC
1977	Silver Jubilee Elizabeth II	180,396	140.00	Proof	800.	825.

CANADIAN UNITY COIN, 1978.

The reverse of the proof $100 gold coin for 1978 depicts twelve Canada geese flying in formation. The image represents the ten provinces and two territories, and so promotes Canadian unity.

Designers and Engravers:
Obv.: Arnold Machin, RCM Staff
Rev.: Roger Savage, Ago Aarand
Composition: 91.67% Au, 8.33% Ag
Gold content: 15.55 g, 0.500 tr oz
Silver content: 1.413 g, 0.045 tr oz
Weight: 16.965 g **Edge:** Reeded
Diameter: 27.00 mm **Die Axis:** ↑↑
Thickness: 2.20 mm **Finish:** Proof
Case: Black leatherette case, maroon insert, plastic coin holder, COA

DATE	DESCRIPTION	QUANTITY SOLD	ISSUE PRICE	FINISH	PR-67 UHC	PR-68 UHC
1978	Canadian Unity	200,000	150.00	Proof	800.	825.

INTERNATIONAL YEAR OF THE CHILD COMMEMORATIVE, 1979.

Children playing hand in hand beside a globe adorn the reverse of the 1979 $100 gold coin struck in honour of the International Year of the Child.

Designers and Engravers:
Obv.: Arnold Machin, RCM Staff
Rev.: Carola Tietz, Victor Coté
Composition: 91.67% Au, 8.33% Ag
Gold content: 15.55 g, 0.500 tr oz
Silver content: 1.413 g, 0.045 tr oz
Weight: 16.965 g **Edge:** Reeded
Diameter: 27.00 mm **Die Axis:** ↑↑
Thickness: 2.20 mm **Finish:** Proof
Case: Brown leatherette case, brown flocked insert, plastic coin holder, COA

DATE	DESCRIPTION	QUANTITY SOLD	ISSUE PRICE	FINISH	PR-67 UHC	PR-68 UHC
1979	International Year of the Child	250,000	185.00	Proof	800.	825.

ARCTIC TERRITORIES COMMEMORATIVE, 1980.

The gold $100 coin for 1980 is a commemorative marking the 100th anniversary of the transfer of the Arctic Islands from the British Government to the Government of the Dominion of Canada. Its reverse shows an Inuk paddling a kayak near a small iceberg and has no lettering or date. The obverse features the Machin bust of Queen Elizabeth, with the legend and date.

Designers and Engravers:
Obv.: Arnold Machin, RCM Staff
Rev.: A. Marchetti, Sheldon Beveridge
Composition: 91.67% Au, 8.33% Ag
Gold content: 15.55 g, 0.500 tr oz
Silver content: 1.413 g, 0.045 tr oz
Weight: 16.965 g **Edge:** Reeded
Diameter: 27.00 mm **Die Axis:** ↑↑
Thickness: 2.20 mm **Finish:** Proof
Case: Brown leatherette case, brown flocked insert, plastic coin holder, COA

DATE	DESCRIPTION	QUANTITY SOLD	ISSUE PRICE	FINISH	PR-67 UHC	PR-68 UHC
1980	Arctic Territories	130,000	430.00	Proof	800.	825.

"O CANADA" COMMEMORATIVE, 1981.

The $100 gold coin for 1981 marks the decision of the Canadian Parliament, on July 1, 1980, to adopt the song "O Canada" as our national anthem.

Designers and Engravers:
Obv.: Arnold Machin, RCM Staff
Rev.: Roger Savage, Walter Ott
Composition: 91.67% Au, 8.33% Ag
Gold content: 15.55 g, 0.500 tr oz
Silver content: 1.413 g, 0.045 tr oz
Weight: 16.965 g **Edge:** Reeded
Diameter: 27.00 mm **Die Axis:** ↑↑
Thickness: 2.20 mm **Finish:** Proof
Case: Brown leatherette case, brown flocked insert, plastic coin holder, COA

DATE	DESCRIPTION	QUANTITY SOLD	ISSUE PRICE	FINISH	PR-67 UHC	PR-68 UHC
1981	"O Canada"	100,950	300.00	Proof	800.	825.

PATRIATION OF THE CANADIAN CONSTITUTION, 1982.

The $100 gold coin for 1982 commemorates the patriation of the Constitution of Canada. The reverse of the coin portrays this historical event by a page turning in an open book bearing the coat of arms of Canada and a maple leaf. The obverse of this coin, the seventh in the 22 karat $100 series, depicts Arnold Machin's effigy of Her Majesty Elizabeth II and the legend "100 Dollars" and "Elizabeth II."

Designers and Engravers:
Obv.: Arnold Machin, RCM Staff
Rev.: Friedrich Peter, Walter Ott
Composition: 91.67% Au, 8.33% Ag
Gold content: 15.55 g, 0.500 tr oz
Silver content: 1.413 g, 0.045 tr oz
Weight: 16.965 g **Edge:** Reeded
Diameter: 27.00 mm **Die Axis:** ↑↑
Thickness: 2.20 mm **Finish:** Proof
Case: Brown leatherette case, brown flocked insert, plastic coin holder, COA

DATE	DESCRIPTION	QUANTITY SOLD	ISSUE PRICE	FINISH	PR-67 UHC	PR-68 UHC
1982	Patriation of the Canadian Constitution	121,706	290.00	Proof	800.	825.

SIR HUMPHREY GILBERT'S LANDING IN NEWFOUNDLAND, 1983.

The $100 gold coin for 1983 commemorates Gilbert's landing in Newfoundland, where he proclaimed it England's first overseas colony. The word "CANADA" appears on the edge for the first time in Canadian coinage.

Designers and Engravers:
Obv.: Arnold Machin, RCM Staff
Rev.: John Jaciw, Walter Ott
Composition: 91.67% Au, 8.33% Ag
Gold content: 15.55 g, 0.500 tr oz
Silver content: 1.413 g, 0.045 tr oz
Weight: 16.965 g **Edge:** Reeded
Diameter: 27.00 mm **Die Axis:** ↑↑
Thickness: 2.20 mm **Finish:** Proof
Case: Brown leatherette case, brown flocked insert, plastic coin holder, COA

DATE	DESCRIPTION	QUANTITY SOLD	ISSUE PRICE	FINISH	PR-67 UHC	PR-68 UHC
1983	Gilbert's Landing in Newfoundland	83,128	310.00	Proof	800.	825.

JACQUES CARTIER'S VOYAGE OF DISCOVERY, 1984.

The $100 gold coin for 1984 commemorates Cartier's landing at Gaspé, Bonaventure in 1534. The reverse portrays a profile of Jacques Cartier and a ship of his era. Arnold Machin's effigy of Her Majesty Queen Elizabeth II is continued. The edge security lettering of 1983 was not continued in 1984.

Designers and Engravers:
Obv.: Arnold Machin, RCM Staff
Rev.: Carola Tietz, Walter Ott
Composition: 91.67% Au, 8.33% Ag
Gold content: 15.55 g, 0.500 tr oz
Silver content: 1.413 g, 0.045 tr oz
Weight: 16.965 g **Edge:** Reeded
Diameter: 27.00 mm **Die Axis:** ↑↑
Thickness: 2.20 mm **Finish:** Proof
Case: Brown leatherette case, brown flocked insert, plastic coin holder, COA

DATE	DESCRIPTION	QUANTITY SOLD	ISSUE PRICE	FINISH	PR-67 UHC	PR-68 UHC
1984	Jacques Cartier's Voyage of Discovery	67,662	325.00	Proof	800.	825.

NATIONAL PARKS CENTENARY, 1985.

The $100 gold coin of 1985 commemorates the centennial of an important part of Canada's heritage, the National Parks. The reverse of the coin portrays a bighorn sheep poised on a cliff in the Canadian Rockies.

Designers and Engravers:
Obv.: Arnold Machin, RCM Staff
Rev.: Hector Greville, Walter Ott
Composition: 91.67% Au, 8.33% Ag
Gold content: 15.55 g, 0.500 tr oz
Silver content: 1.413 g, 0.045 tr oz
Weight: 16.965 g **Edge:** Reeded
Diameter: 27.00 mm **Die Axis:** ↑↑
Thickness: 2.20 mm **Finish:** Proof
Case: Brown leatherette book type case with maple leaf emblem, beige satin interior, encapsulated coin. All enclosed in a brown plastic box

DATE	DESCRIPTION	QUANTITY SOLD	ISSUE PRICE	FINISH	PR-67 UHC	PR-68 UHC
1985	National Parks Centenary	58,520	325.00	Proof	800.	825.

INTERNATIONAL YEAR OF PEACE, 1986.

The $100 gold coin for 1986 signifies Canada's support for world peace. The reverse depicts a branch of maple leaves intertwined with a branch of olive leaves, symbols of Canada and Peace coming together. The words "Peace-Paix" forming a circle are superimposed on the design.

Designers and Engravers:
Obv.: Arnold Machin, RCM Staff
Rev.: Dora de Pédery-Hunt
Composition: 91.67% Au, 8.33% Ag
Gold content: 15.55 g, 0.500 tr oz
Silver content: 1.413 g, 0.045 tr oz
Weight: 16.965 g **Edge:** Reeded
Diameter: 27.00 mm **Die Axis:** ↑↑
Thickness: 2.20 mm **Finish:** Proof

Case: Brown leatherette book type case with maple leaf emblem, beige satin interior, encapsulated coin. All enclosed in a brown plastic box

DATE	DESCRIPTION	QUANTITY SOLD	ISSUE PRICE	FINISH	PR-67 UHC	PR-68 UHC
1986	International Year of Peace	76,255	325.00	Proof	800.	825.

XV OLYMPIC WINTER GAMES, 1987.

The $100 gold coin for 1987 commemorates the XV Olympic Winter Games held in Calgary in 1988. The reverse portrays a hand holding the Olympic Torch with a stylized flame forming an image of the Canadian Rocky Mountains. This is the second $100 gold coin to have a lettered edge. The inscription reads "XV Olympic Winter Games - XVes Jeux Olympiques D'Hiver."

Designers and Engravers:
Obv.: Arnold Machin, RCM Staff
Rev.: Friedrich Peter, Ago Aarand
Composition: 58.33% Au, 41.67% Ag
Gold content: 7.78 g, 0.250 tr oz
Silver content: 5.56 g, 0.179 tr oz
Weight: 13.338 g **Edge:** Lettered
Diameter: 27.00 mm **Die Axis:** ↑↑
Thickness: 2.15 mm **Finish:** Proof

Case: Brown leatherette book type case with maple leaf emblem, beige satin interior, encapsulated coin. All enclosed in a brown plastic box

DATE	DESCRIPTION	QUANTITY SOLD	ISSUE PRICE	FINISH	PR-67 UHC	PR-68 UHC
1987	XV Olympic Winter Games, With edge lettering	145,175	255.00	Proof	400.	425.
1987	XV Olympic Winter Games, Without edge lettering	Incl. above	255.00	Proof	425.	450.

THE BOWHEAD WHALE (BALAENA MYSTICETUS), 1988.

The $100 gold coin for 1988 celebrates a precious national treasure, the Bowhead whale. The reverse of this coin portrays a bowhead whale and her calf enclosed in a circle.

Designers and Engravers:
Obv.: Arnold Machin, RCM Staff
Rev.: Robert R. Carmichael, Ago Aarand
Composition: 58.33% Au, 41.67% Ag
Gold content: 7.78 g, 0.250 tr oz
Silver content: 5.56 g, 0.179 tr oz
Weight: 13.338 g **Edge:** Lettered
Diameter: 27.00 mm **Die Axis:** ↑↑
Thickness: 2.15 mm **Finish:** Proof

Case: Brown leatherette book type case with maple leaf emblem, beige satin interior, encapsulated coin. All enclosed in a brown plastic box

DATE	DESCRIPTION	QUANTITY SOLD	ISSUE PRICE	FINISH	PR-67 UHC	PR-68 UHC
1988	Bowhead Whale (Balaena Mysticetus)	52,239	255.00	Proof	400.	425.

SAINTE-MARIE, 1639-1989.

In 1639 the French Jesuits founded a fortified mission village near Midland, Ontario, which they named Sainte-Marie among the Hurons. 1989 was the 350th anniversary of this first self-sufficient settlement in Ontario, where one-fifth of the European population of Canada once lived.

Designers and Engravers:
Obv.: Arnold Machin, Patrick Brindley
Rev.: David Craig Ago Aarand
Composition: 58.33% Au, 41.67% Ag
Gold content: 7.78 g, 0.250 tr oz
Silver content: 5.56 g, 0.179 tr oz
Weight: 13.338 g
Diameter: 27.00 mm
Thickness: 2.15 mm
Edge: Lettered
Die Axis: ↑↑
Finish: Proof

Case: Brown leatherette book type case with maple leaf emblem, beige satin interior, encapsulated coin. All enclosed in a brown plastic box

DATE	DESCRIPTION	QUANTITY SOLD	ISSUE PRICE	FINISH	PR-67 UHC	PR-68 UHC
1989	Sainte-Marie	63,881	245.00	Proof	400.	425.

INTERNATIONAL LITERACY YEAR, 1990.

The General Assembly of the United Nations declared 1990 as the International Year of Literacy, setting the stage for the eradication of illiteracy around the world by the year 2000.

Designers and Engravers:
Obv.: Dora de Pédery-Hunt
Rev.: John Mardon , Ago Aarand, Susan Taylor
Composition: 58.33% Au, 41.67% Ag
Gold content: 7.78 g, 0.250 tr oz
Silver content: 5.56 g, 0.179 tr oz
Weight: 13.338 g
Diameter: 27.00 mm
Thickness: 2.15 mm
Edge: Lettered
Die Axis: ↑↑
Finish: Proof

Case: Brown leatherette book type case with maple leaf emblem, beige satin interior, encapsulated coin. All enclosed in a brown plastic box

DATE	DESCRIPTION	QUANTITY SOLD	ISSUE PRICE	FINISH	PR-67 UHC	PR-68 UHC
1990	International Literacy Year	49,940	245.00	Proof	400.	425.

EMPRESS OF INDIA, 1991.

This coin commemorates the 100th anniversary of the *Empress of India*'s first arrival in Vancouver from Yokohama, Japan. The Canadian Pacific's trans-Pacific Empress ships were among the world's first cruise ships.

Designers and Engravers:
Obv.: Dora de Pédery-Hunt
Rev.: Karsten Smith, S. Beveridge
Composition: 58.33% Au, 41.67% Ag
Gold content: 7.78 g, 0.250 tr oz
Silver content: 5.56 g, 0.179 tr oz
Weight: 13.338 g
Diameter: 27.00 mm
Thickness: 2.15 mm
Edge: Lettered
Die Axis: ↑↑
Finish: Proof

Case: Brown leatherette book type case with maple leaf emblem, beige satin interior, encapsulated coin. All enclosed in a brown plastic box

DATE	DESCRIPTION	QUANTITY SOLD	ISSUE PRICE	FINISH	PR-67 UHC	PR-68 UHC
1991	Empress of India	33,966	245.00	Proof	400.	425.

CITY OF MONTREAL, 350TH ANNIVERSARY, 1642-1992.

On May 17, 1642, three vessels arrived from France landing Maisonneuve and his men on an island in the St. Lawrence River. They called the island Ville-Marie which was renamed Montreal in the early 1700s.

Designers and Engravers:
Obv.: Dora de Pédery-Hunt
Rev.: S. Sherwood, A. Aarand, C. Saffioti
Composition: 58.33% Au, 41.67% Ag
Gold content: 7.78 g, 0.250 tr oz
Silver content: 5.56 g, 0.179 tr oz
Weight: 13.338 g **Edge:** Lettered
Diameter: 27.00 mm **Die Axis:** ↑↑
Thickness: 2.15 mm **Finish:** Proof

Case: Brown leatherette book type case with maple leaf emblem, beige satin interior, encapsulated coin. All enclosed in a brown plastic box

DATE	DESCRIPTION	QUANTITY SOLD	ISSUE PRICE	FINISH	PR-67 UHC	PR-68 UHC
1992	City of Montreal, 350th Anniversary	28,190	239.85	Proof	400.	425.

1893 THE ERA OF THE HORSELESS CARRIAGE, 1993.

The five vehicles pictured on the reverse of the 1993 gold coin are, clockwise from the left, the French Panhard-Levassor's Daimler, the American Duryea, the German Benz Victoria, the Simmonds Steam Carriage and, in the centre, the first Canadian built electric car, the Featherstonhaugh.

Designers and Engravers:
Obv.: Dora de Pédery-Hunt
Rev.: John Mardon, Ago Aarand, William Woodruff
Composition: 58.33% Au, 41.67% Ag
Gold content: 7.78 g, 0.250 tr oz
Weight: 13.338 g **Edge:** Lettered
Diameter: 27.00 mm **Die Axis:** ↑↑
Thickness: 2.15 mm **Finish:** Proof

Case: Brown leatherette book type case with maple leaf emblem, beige satin interior, encapsulated coin. All enclosed in a brown plastic box

DATE	DESCRIPTION	QUANTITY SOLD	ISSUE PRICE	FINISH	PR-67 UHC	PR-68 UHC
1993	The Horseless Carriage	25,971	239.85	Proof	400.	425.

THE HOME FRONT, 1994.

The 1994 $100 gold coin is part of the Remembrance and Peace Issue. The design was taken from a 1945 painting by P. Clark, entitled "Maintenance Jobs in the Hangar."

Designers and Engravers:
Obv.: Dora de Pédery-Hunt
Rev.: P. Clark, Susan Taylor, Ago Aarand
Composition: 58.33% Au, 41.67% Ag
Gold content: 7.78 g, 0.250 tr oz
Weight: 13.338 g **Edge:** Lettered
Diameter: 27.00 mm **Die Axis:** ↑↑
Thickness: 2.15 mm **Finish:** Proof

Case: Brown leatherette book type case with maple leaf emblem, beige satin interior, encapsulated coin. All enclosed in a brown plastic box

DATE	DESCRIPTION	QUANTITY SOLD	ISSUE PRICE	FINISH	PR-67 UHC	PR-68 UHC
1994	The Home Front	17,603	249.95	Proof	400.	425.

275TH ANNIVERSARY OF THE FOUNDING OF LOUISBOURG, 1995.

Louisbourg, built in 1720 as a strategic centre for the French military in North America, is commemorated on the $100.00 gold coin of 1995.

Designers and Engravers:
Obv.: Dora de Pédery-Hunt
Rev.: Lewis Parker, Sheldon Beveridge
Composition: 58.33% Au, 41.67% Ag
Gold content: 7.78 g, 0.250 tr oz
Silver content: 5.56 g, 0.179 tr oz
Weight: 13.338 g **Edge:** Lettered
Diameter: 27.00 mm **Die Axis:** ↑↑
Thickness: 2.15 mm **Finish:** Proof

Case: Brown leatherette book type case with maple leaf emblem, beige satin interior, encapsulated coin. All enclosed in a brown plastic box

DATE	DESCRIPTION	QUANTITY SOLD	ISSUE PRICE	FINISH	PR-67 UHC	PR-68 UHC
1995	275th Anniv. Founding of Louisbourg	16,916	249.95	Proof	400.	425.

100TH ANNIVERSARY OF THE FIRST MAJOR GOLD DISCOVERY IN THE KLONDIKE, 1996.

In 1896 the Gold Rush began when George and Kate Carmack, Skookum Jim and Dawson Charlie made the Klondike's first major gold find. 1996 was the last year in which $100.00 gold coins were packaged in the book-type cases.

Designers and Engravers:
Obv.: Dora de Pédery-Hunt
Rev.: John Mantha, Cosme Saffioti
Composition: 58.33% Au, 41.67% Ag
Gold content: 7.78 g, 0.250 tr oz
Silver content: 5.56 g, 0.179 tr oz
Weight: 13.338 g **Edge:** Lettered
Diameter: 27.00 mm **Die Axis:** ↑↑
Thickness: 2.15 mm **Finish:** Proof

Case: Brown leatherette book type case with maple leaf emblem, beige satin interior, encapsulated coin. All enclosed in a brown plastic box

DATE	DESCRIPTION	QUANTITY SOLD	ISSUE PRICE	FINISH	PR-67 UHC	PR-68 UHC
1996	100th Anniv. Gold Discovery in the Klondike	17,973	259.95	Proof	400.	425.

150TH ANNIVERSARY OF ALEXANDER GRAHAM BELL'S BIRTH, 1997.

The $100 gold coin of 1997 honours the creative genius of Alexander Graham Bell. He was born in Scotland in 1847. In 1874, while in Ontario, he carried out the experiments that led to the invention of the telephone. The $100 gold coin was offered for the first time with an optional case.

Designers and Engravers:
Obv.: Dora de Pédery-Hunt
Rev.: D. H. Curley, S. Beveridge
Composition: 58.33% Au, 41.67% Ag
Gold content: 7.78 g, 0.250 tr oz
Silver content: 5.56 g, 0.179 tr oz
Weight: 13.338 g **Edge:** Lettered
Diameter: 27.00 mm **Die Axis:** ↑↑
Thickness: 2.15 mm **Finish:** Proof

Case: Black suede clam type case, black suede interior, encapsulated coin

DATE	DESCRIPTION	QUANTITY SOLD	ISSUE PRICE	FINISH	PR-67 UHC	PR-68 UHC
1997	150th Anniv. of Alexander Graham Bell's Birth	14,030	254.95	Proof	400.	425.

75TH ANNIVERSARY OF THE NOBEL PRIZE FOR THE DISCOVERY OF INSULIN, 1998.

The discovery of insulin by Frederick Banting and John Macleod earned them the Nobel Prize for Physiology and Medicine in 1923.

Designers and Engravers:
Obv.: Dora de Pédery-Hunt
Rev.: Robert R. Carmichael, Stan Witten
Composition: 58.33% Au, 41.67% Ag
Gold content: 7.78 g, 0.250 tr oz
Silver content: 5.56 g, 0.179 tr oz
Weight: 13.338 g **Edge:** Lettered
Diameter: 27.00 mm **Die Axis:** ↑↑
Thickness: 2.15 mm **Finish:** Proof
Case: Black suede clam type case, black suede interior, encapsulated coin

DATE	DESCRIPTION	QUANTITY SOLD	ISSUE PRICE	FINISH	PR-67 UHC	PR-68 UHC
1998	75th Anniv. Nobel Prize Discovery Insulin	11,220	254.95	Proof	400.	425.

50TH ANNIVERSARY OF NEWFOUNDLAND'S CONFEDERATION WITH CANADA IN 1949, 1999.

The 50th anniversary of Newfoundland's union with Canada on March 31, 1949 is celebrated on the 1999 $100 gold coin.

Designers and Engravers:
Obv.: Dora de Pédery-Hunt
Rev.: J. Gale-Vaillancourt, William Woodruff
Composition: 58.33% Au, 41.67% Ag
Gold content: 7.78 g, 0.250 tr oz
Silver content: 5.56 g, 0.179 tr oz
Weight: 13.338 g **Edge:** Lettered
Diameter: 27.00 mm **Die Axis:** ↑↑
Thickness: 2.15 mm **Finish:** Proof
Case: Black suede clam type case, black suede interior, encapsulated coin

DATE	DESCRIPTION	QUANTITY SOLD	ISSUE PRICE	FINISH	PR-67 UHC	PR-68 UHC
1999	50th Anniv. Newfoundland's Confederation	10,242	254.95	Proof	400.	425.

150TH ANNIVERSARY OF THE SEARCH FOR THE NORTHWEST PASSAGE IN 1850, 2000.

The Franklin Expedition, which was lost on its voyage to discover a Northwest passage to the far East, is commemorated on the gold coin for 2000.

Designers and Engravers:
Obv.: Dora de Pédery-Hunt
Rev.: John Mardon, Stan Witten
Composition: 58.33% Au, 41.67% Ag
Gold content: 7.78 g, 0.250 tr oz
Silver content: 5.56 g, 0.179 tr oz
Weight: 13.338 g **Edge:** Lettered
Diameter: 27.00 mm **Die Axis:** ↑↑
Thickness: 2.15 mm **Finish:** Proof
Case: Metal presentation case, wooden insert, COA

DATE	DESCRIPTION	QUANTITY SOLD	ISSUE PRICE	FINISH	PR-67 UHC	PR-68 UHC
2000	150th Anniv. Search for NW Passage	10,547	254.95	Proof	400.	425.

125TH ANNIVERSARY OF THE LIBRARY OF PARLIAMENT, 2001.

The Library of Parliament is one of the most famous symbols of the Canadian Confederation. "This beautiful building is an architectural marvel, and a treasure for all Canadians to cherish."

Designers and Engravers:
Obv.: Dora de Pédery-Hunt
Rev.: R.R. Carmichael, S. Taylor, W. Woodruff
Composition: 58.33% Au, 41.67% Ag
Gold content: 7.78 g, 0.250 tr oz
Silver content: 5.56 g, 0.179 tr oz
Weight: 13.338 g **Edge:** Lettered
Diameter: 27.00 mm **Die Axis:** ↑↑
Thickness: 2.15 mm **Finish:** Proof
Case: Metal presentation case, wooden insert, COA

DATE	DESCRIPTION	QUANTITY SOLD	ISSUE PRICE	FINISH	PR-67 UHC	PR-68 UHC
2001	125th Anniv. Library of Parliament	8,080	260.95	Proof	400.	425.

COMMEMORATING CANADA'S OIL INDUSTRY, 2002.

This coin commemorates the major economic importance of oil to the Canadian economy and Canada's place as one of the major oil producers of the world. The sea of 'black gold' at the foot of the oil rig commemorates the major discovery of the Leduc oil field on February 13, 1947.

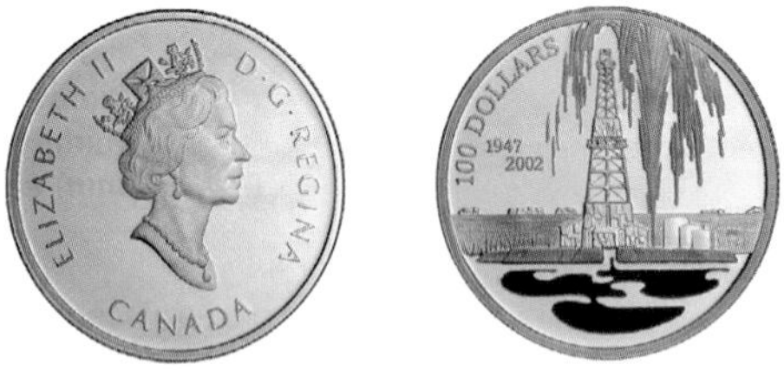

Designers and Engravers:
Obv.: Dora de Pédery-Hunt
Rev.: John Mardon, Stan Witten
Composition: 58.33% Au, 41.67% Ag
Gold content: 7.78 g, 0.250 tr oz
Silver content: 5.56 g, 0.179 tr oz
Weight: 13.338 g **Edge:** Lettered
Diameter: 27.00 mm **Die Axis:** ↑↑
Thickness: 2.15 mm **Finish:** Proof, Painted
Case: Metal presentation case, wooden insert, COA

DATE	DESCRIPTION	QUANTITY SOLD	ISSUE PRICE	FINISH	PR-67 UHC	PR-68 UHC
2002	Canada's Oil Industry	9,994	260.95	Proof	400.	425.

100TH ANNIVERSARY OF DISCOVERY OF MARQUIS WHEAT, 2003.

After 10 years of experiments, Dr. William Saunders and his sons Percy and Charles discovered the marquis wheat variety, making Canada forever known as the world's bread basket.

Designers and Engravers:
Obv.: Dora de Pédery-Hunt
Rev.: Thom Nelson, Stan Witten
Composition: 58.33% Au, 41.67% Ag
Gold content: 7.78 g, 0.250 tr oz
Silver content: 5.56 g, 0.179 tr oz
Weight: 13.338 g **Edge:** Lettered
Diameter: 27.00 mm **Die Axis:** ↑↑
Thickness: 2.15 mm **Finish:** Proof, Painted
Case: Metal presentation case, wooden insert, COA

DATE	DESCRIPTION	QUANTITY SOLD	ISSUE PRICE	FINISH	PR-67 UHC	PR-68 UHC
2003	100th Anniv. Discovery Marquis Wheat	9,993	277.95	Proof	400.	425.

50TH ANNIVERSARY OF THE COMMENCEMENT OF THE ST. LAWRENCE SEAWAY CONSTRUCTION, 2004.

The $100 gold for 2004 commemorates the commencement of the construction of the St. Lawrence Seaway. On August 10, 1954, a sod turning ceremony signalled the start of a mammoth project by Canada and the United States.

Designers and Engravers:
Obv.: Susanna Blunt, Susan Taylor
Rev.: John Mardon, José Osio
Composition: 58.33% Au, 41.67% Ag
Gold content: 7.00 g, 0.225 tr oz
Silver content: 5.00 g, 0.160 tr oz
Weight: 12.00 g **Edge:** Reeded
Diameter: 27.00 mm **Die Axis:** ↑↑
Thickness: 2.15 mm **Finish:** Proof
Case: Metal presentation case, wooden insert, COA

DATE	DESCRIPTION	QUANTITY SOLD	ISSUE PRICE	FINISH	PR-67 UHC	PR-68 UHC
2004	50th Anniv., St. Lawrence Seaway	7,454	277.95	Proof	400.	425.

130TH ANNIVERSARY OF THE SUPREME COURT OF CANADA, 2005.

On April 8, 1875, Canada's "Court of Last Resort" was founded. It has been an essential component of Canadian justice for 130 years. The 2004 $100 gold coin celebrates the 130th anniversary of the Supreme Court of Canada.

Designers and Engravers:
Obv.: Susanna Blunt, Susan Taylor
Rev.: S. Duranceau, José Osio
Composition: 58.33% Au, 41.67% Ag
Gold content: 7.00 g, 0.225 tr oz
Silver content: 5.00 g, 0.160 tr oz
Weight: 12.00 g **Edge:** Reeded
Diameter: 27.00 mm **Die Axis:** ↑↑
Thickness: 2.15 mm **Finish:** Proof, Painted
Case: Maroon plastic case, black plastic insert, encapsulated coin, COA

DATE	DESCRIPTION	QUANTITY SOLD	ISSUE PRICE	FINISH	PR-67 UHC	PR-68 UHC
2005	130th Anniv. Supreme Court Canada	5,092	289.95	Proof	400.	425.

75TH GAME, WORLD'S LONGEST HOCKEY SERIES, 2006.

The 2006 $100 gold coin celebrates the 75th anniversary of the world's longest running international hockey series between the Royal Military College in Kingston, Ontario and the Military Academy in West Point, New York.

Designers and Engravers:
Obv.: Susanna Blunt, Susan Taylor
Rev.: Tony Bianco, K. Wachelko
Composition: 58.33% Au, 41.67% Ag
Gold content: 7.00 g, 0.225 tr oz
Silver content: 5.00 g, 0.160 tr oz
Weight: 12.00 g **Edge:** Reeded
Diameter: 27.00 mm **Die Axis:** ↑↑
Thickness: 2.15 mm **Finish:** Proof, Painted
Case: Maroon plastic case, black plastic insert, encapsulated coin, COA

DATE	DESCRIPTION	QUANTITY SOLD	ISSUE PRICE	FINISH	PR-67 UHC	PR-68 UHC
2006	75th Game, World's Longest Hockey Series	5,439	329.95	Proof	400.	425.

140TH ANNIVERSARY OF THE DOMINION OF CANADA, 2007.

The 2007 $100 gold coin celebrates the 140th anniversary of the Dominion of Canada.

Designers and Engravers:
Obv.: Susanna Blunt, Susan Taylor
Rev.: Bonnie Ross, Susan Taylor
Composition: 58.33% Au, 41.67% Ag
Gold content: 7.00 g, 0.225 tr oz
Silver content: 5.00 g, 0.160 tr oz
Weight: 12.00 g **Edge:** Reeded
Diameter: 27.00 mm **Die Axis:** ↑↑
Thickness: 2.15 mm **Finish:** Proof
Case: Maroon leatherette clam style case, black flocked insert, encapsulated coin, COA

DATE	DESCRIPTION	QUANTITY SOLD	ISSUE PRICE	FINISH	PR-67 UHC	PR-68 UHC
2007	140th Anniversary, Dominion of Canada	4,453	369.95	Proof	400.	425.

200TH ANNIVERSARY, DESCENDING FRASER RIVER, 2008.

The Fraser River is named for Simon Fraser, who on behalf of the North West Company descended the river from a point in the vicinity of Prince Rupert to its mouth at Vancouver. This one hundred dollar gold coin commemorates Fraser's journey in 1808.

Designers and Engravers:
Obv.: Susanna Blunt, Susan Taylor
Rev.: John Mantha, RCM Staff
Composition: 58.33% Au, 41.67% Ag
Gold content: 7.00 g, 0.225 tr oz
Silver content: 5.00 g, 0.160 tr oz
Weight: 12.00 g **Edge:** Reeded
Diameter: 27.00 mm **Die Axis:** ↑↑
Thickness: 2.15 mm **Finish:** Proof
Case: Maroon leatherette clam style case, black flocked insert, encapsulated coin, COA

DATE	DESCRIPTION	QUANTITY SOLD	ISSUE PRICE	FINISH	PR-67 UHC	PR-68 UHC
2008	200th Anniversary, Descending Fraser River	3,089	386.95	Proof	400.	425.

10TH ANNIVERSARY OF NUNAVUT, 2009.

On April 1st, 1999, Nunavut, Canada's youngest territory, was formed. In 2009 we celebrated the 10th anniversary of its formation.

Designers and Engravers:
Obv.: Susanna Blunt, Susan Taylor
Rev.: Andrew Qappik, RCM Staff
Composition: 58.33% Au, 41.67% Ag
Gold content: 7.00 g, 0.225 tr oz
Silver content: 5.00 g, 0.160 tr oz
Weight: 12.00 g **Edge:** Reeded
Diameter: 27.00 mm **Die Axis:** ↑↑
Thickness: 2.15 mm **Finish:** Proof
Case: Maroon leatherette clam style case , black flocked insert, encapsulated coin, COA

DATE	DESCRIPTION	QUANTITY SOLD	ISSUE PRICE	FINISH	PR-67 UHC	PR-68 UHC
2009	10th Anniversary of Nunavut	2,309	509.95	Proof	500.	525.

400TH ANNIVERSARY OF THE DISCOVERY OF THE HUDSON'S BAY, 2010.

In 1610, Henry Hudson an English navigator and explorer, on his fourth voyage to discover a passage from Europe to the Far East through the Arctic passage, sailed into the world's second largest bay (Hudson's Bay).

In November 1610, Hudson's ship *Discovery* was locked in ice, and in June 1611, Hudson along with eight other crewmen was set adrift in a small boat by a mutinous crew. Hudson perished. The Hudson's Bay is named after him.

Designers and Engravers:
Obv.: Susanna Blunt, Susan Taylor
Rev.: John Mantha, RCM Staff
Composition: 58.33% Au, 41.67% Ag
Gold content: 7.00 g, 0.225 tr oz
Silver content: 5.00 g, 0.160 tr oz
Weight: 12.00 g
Edge: Reeded
Diameter: 27.00 mm
Die Axis: ↑↑
Thickness: 2.15 mm
Finish: Proof
Case: Maroon leatherette clam style case , black flocked insert, encapsulated coin, COA

DATE	DESCRIPTION	QUANTITY SOLD	ISSUE PRICE	FINISH	PR-67 UHC	PR-68 UHC
2010	400th Anniversary, Discovery of Hudson's Bay	5,000	589.95	Proof	590.	600.

Note: Presently Canadian gold coins trade at a small premium over bullion value. Please refer to the market price of gold for pricing if there is a major change in the market

ONE HUNDRED FIFTY DOLLAR GOLD COINS

ONE HUNDRED FIFTY DOLLAR GOLD HOLOGRAM COINS, 2000-2011.

2000
Obverse

2000
Year of the Dragon

2001
Obverse

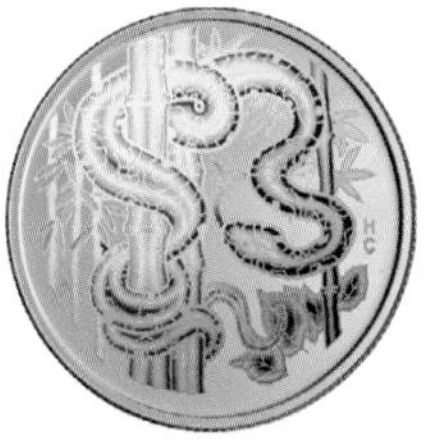

2001
Year of the Snake

2002
Obverse

2002
Year of the Horse

2003
Obverse

2003
Year of the Ram

2004
Obverse

2004
Year of the Monkey

2005
Obverse

2005
Year of the Rooster

2006
Obverse

2006
Year of the Dog

2007
Obverse

2007
Year of the Pig

2008
Obverse

2008
Year of the Rat

2009
Obverse

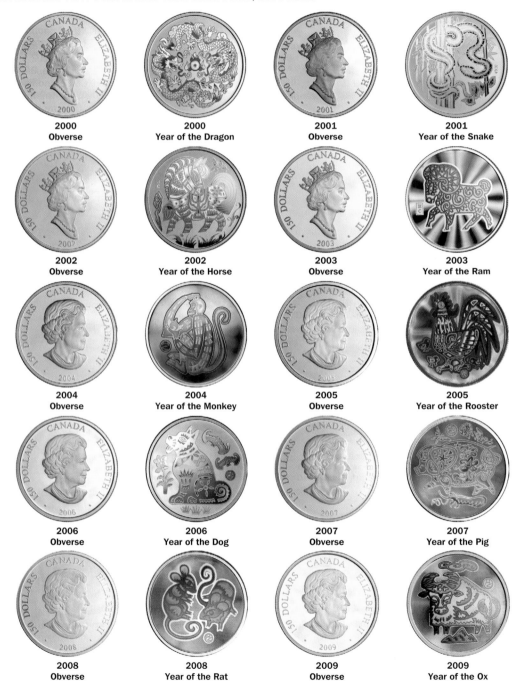

2009
Year of the Ox

ONE HUNDRED FIFTY DOLLAR GOLD HOLOGRAM COINS, 2000-2011 (cont.)

2010
Obverse

2010
Year of the Tiger

2011
Obverse

2011
Year of the Rabbit

Designers:
2000-2003 Obv.: Dora de Pédery-Hunt
2004-2011 Obv.: Susanna Blunt, Susan Taylor

Engravers:
Rev.: Harvey Chan, RCM Staff
Rev.: Harvey Chan, RCM Staff

Composition: 75.0% Au, 25.0% Ag
Gold content: 8.88 g, 0.285 tr oz
Silver content: 2.96 g, 0.095 tr oz
Weight: 11.84 g
Diameter: 28.00 mm
Thickness: 1.5 to 1.81 mm
Edge: Reeded
Die Axis: ↑↑
Finish: Proof, Hologram
Case of Issue: Gold satin case, taupe flocked insert, encapsulated coin, COA

DATE	DESCRIPTION	QUANTITY SOLD	ISSUE PRICE	FINISH	PR-67 UHC	PR-68 UHC
2000	Year of the Dragon, Hologram	8,874	388.88	Proof	1,175.	1,250.
2001	Year of the Snake, Hologram	6,571	388.88	Proof	500.	525.
2002	Year of the Horse, Hologram	6,843	388.88	Proof	500.	525.
2003	Year of the Ram, Hologram	3,927	398.88	Proof	500.	525.
2004	Year of the Monkey, Hologram	3,392	398.88	Proof	500.	525.
2005	Year of the Rooster, Hologram	3,731	398.88	Proof	500.	525.
2006	Year of the Dog, Hologram	2,609	448.88	Proof	600.	625.
2007	Year of the Pig, Hologram	826	498.95	Proof	600.	625.
2008	Year of the Rat, Hologram	582	508.95	Proof	600.	625.
2009	Year of the Ox, Hologram	486	638.88	Proof	600.	625.
2010	Year of the Tiger, Hologram	1,507	555.55	Proof	600.	625.
2011	Year of the Rabbit, Hologram	4,888	638.88	Proof	650.	675.

BLESSINGS SERIES

BLESSINGS OF WEALTH, 2009.

In China, blessings of wealth abound in a multitude of ancient symbols and artistic impressions, many of which are represented on this pure gold coin.

Designers and Engravers:
Obv.: Susanna Blunt, Susan Taylor
Rev.: Harvey Chan, RCM Staff
Composition: 99.999% Au
Gold content: 10.40 g, 0.334 tr oz
Weight: 10.40 g **Edge:** Plain
Diameter: 22.50 mm **Die Axis:** ↑↑
Thickness: 1.80 mm **Finish:** Proof
Case: Maroon leatherette clam style case, black flocked insert, encapsulated coin, COA

DATE	DESCRIPTION	QUANTITY SOLD	ISSUE PRICE	FINISH	PR-67 UHC	PR-68 UHC
2009	Blessings of Wealth	1,273	799.95	Proof	800.	825.

BLESSINGS OF STRENGTH, 2010.

The reverse design of this coin depicts a dragon and tiger to represent the blessings of bravery and strength.

Designers and Engravers:
Obv.: Susanna Blunt, Susan Taylor
Rev.: Harvey Chan, RCM Staff
Composition: 99.999% Au
Gold content: 10.40 g, 0.334 tr oz
Weight: 10.40 g **Edge:** Plain
Diameter: 22.50 mm **Die Axis:** ↑↑
Thickness: 1.80 mm **Finish:** Proof
Case: Maroon leatherette clam style case, black flocked insert, encapsulated coin, COA

DATE	DESCRIPTION	QUANTITY SOLD	ISSUE PRICE	FINISH	PR-67 UHC	PR-68 UHC
2010	Blessings of Strength	1,388	939.95	Proof	950.	975.

CLASSIC CHINESE LUNAR SERIES

CLASSIC CHINESE LUNAR SERIES. 2010-2021.

The Year of the Tiger $150 gold coin is the first in a new series of Lunar coins created by the Royal Canadian Mint, who with the Asian Business, are the sole distributors of this series.

Designers:
Obv.: Susanna Blunt
Rev.: Aries Cheung

Engravers:
Obv.: Susan Taylor
Rev.: RCM Staff

Composition: 75.0% Au, 25.0% Ag
Gold content: 8.78 g, 0.282 tr oz
Silver content: 2.92 g, 0.094 tr oz
Weight: 11.70 g
Diameter: 28.00 mm
Thickness: 1.6 mm
Edge: Reeded
Die Axis: ↑↑
Finish: Proof
Case of Issue: Singly: Gold satin-like covered case, black flocked insert, encapsulated coin, COA.
Set: Hardwood exterior with high-gloss finish and silk-screened paper. Interior has high-gloss finish in Chinese red with a silver design, wooden insert accommodates 12 coins.

Common Obverse

2010
Year of the Tiger

2011
Year of the Rabbit

DATE	DESCRIPTION	QUANTITY SOLD	ISSUE PRICE	FINISH	PR-67 UHC	PR-68 UHC
2010	Year of the Tiger	2,500	555.55	Proof	560.	585.
2011	Year of the Rabbit	2,500	638.88	Proof	650.	675.

ONE HUNDRED SEVENTY-FIVE DOLLAR GOLD COIN

100TH ANNIVERSARY OF THE OLYMPIC MOVEMENT, 1992-1996.

Commemorating the 100th anniversary of the Olympic movement in 1996, Canada and four other countries, Australia, France, Austria and Greece, issued three-coin sets, consisting of one gold and two silver coins. One set was issued each year beginning with Canada's in 1992. See page 139 for the Royal Canadian Mint silver issues. Only the Royal Canadian Mint issued coins are listed in the Standard Catalogue.

Designers:
Obv.: Dora de Pédery-Hunt
Rev.: Stewart Sherwood

Engravers:
Obv.: Dora de Pédery-Hunt
Rev.: Ago Aarand

Composition: 91.67% Au, 8.33% Cu
Gold content: 15.556 g, 0.50 tr oz
Weight: 16.97 g
Diameter: 28.00 mm
Thickness: 2.00 mm
Edge: Lettering: Citius, altius, fortius
Die Axis: ↑↑
Finish: Proof
Case of Issue: Blue clam style case, black insert, encapsulated coin, COA

DATE	DESCRIPTION	QUANTITY SOLD	ISSUE PRICE	FINISH	PR-67 UHC	PR-68 UHC
1992	100th Anniversary of the Olympic Movement	22,092	429.75	Proof	800.	825.

TWO HUNDRED DOLLAR GOLD COINS

CANADA'S FLAG SILVER JUBILEE, 1990.

The 1990 $200 dollar coin commemorates the 25th anniversary of the proclamation approving Canada's flag.

Designers and Engravers:
Obv.: Dora de Pédery-Hunt
Rev.: Stewart Sherwood, Ago Aarand
Composition: 91.67% Au, 8.33% Ag
Gold content: 15.703 g, 0.505 tr oz
Silver content: 1.427 g, 0.046 tr oz
Weight: 17.13 g **Edge:** Reeded
Diameter: 29.00 mm **Die Axis:** ↑↑
Thickness: 2.00 mm **Finish:** Proof
Case: Woven Jacquard case, black insert, encapsulated coin, COA

DATE	DESCRIPTION	QUANTITY SOLD	ISSUE PRICE	FINISH	PR-67 UHC	PR-68 UHC
1990	Canada's Flag Silver Jubilee	20,980	395.00	Proof	800.	825.

A NATIONAL PASSION, 1991.

The 1991 two hundred dollar proof gold coin was issued as a tribute to the spirit and vitality of Canadian youth and the national game of hockey.

Designers and Engravers:
Obv.: Dora de Pédery-Hunt
Rev.: Stewart Sherwood, Susan Taylor
Composition: 91.67% Au, 8.33% Ag
Gold content: 15.703 g, 0.505 tr oz
Silver content: 1.427 g, 0.046 tr oz
Weight: 17.13 g **Edge:** Reeded
Diameter: 29.00 mm **Die Axis:** ↑↑
Thickness: 2.00 mm **Finish:** Proof
Case: Woven Jacquard case, black insert, encapsulated coin, COA

DATE	DESCRIPTION	QUANTITY SOLD	ISSUE PRICE	FINISH	PR-67 UHC	PR-68 UHC
1991	A National Passion	10,215	425.00	Proof	800.	825.

NIAGARA FALLS, 1992.

The 1992 two hundred dollar gold coin was issued as a tribute to the beauty and majesty of Niagara Falls. The coin features two children playing near the falls.

Designers and Engravers:
Obv.: Dora de Pédery-Hunt
Rev.: John Mardon, Susan Taylor
Composition: 91.67% Au, 8.33% Ag
Gold content: 15.703 g, 0.505 tr oz
Silver content: 1.427 g, 0.046 tr oz
Weight: 17.13 g **Edge:** Reeded
Diameter: 29.00 mm **Die Axis:** ↑↑
Thickness: 2.00 mm **Finish:** Proof
Case: Woven Jacquard case, black insert, encapsulated coin, COA

DATE	DESCRIPTION	QUANTITY SOLD	ISSUE PRICE	FINISH	PR-67 UHC	PR-68 UHC
1992	Niagara Falls	9,465	389.65	Proof	800.	825.

ROYAL CANADIAN MOUNTED POLICE, 1993.

The 1993 issue of the two hundred dollar gold coin pays tribute to the unique contribution of the R.C.M.P. to Canadian history.

Designers and Engravers:
Obv.: Dora de Pédery-Hunt
Rev.: Stewart Sherwood, Susan Taylor
Composition: 91.67% Au, 8.33% Ag
Gold content: 15.703 g, 0.505 tr oz
Silver content: 1.427 g, 0.046 tr oz
Weight: 17.13 g **Edge:** Reeded
Diameter: 29.00 mm **Die Axis:** ↑↑
Thickness: 2.00 mm **Finish:** Proof
Case: Woven Jacquard case, black insert, encapsulated coin, COA

DATE	DESCRIPTION	QUANTITY SOLD	ISSUE PRICE	FINISH	PR-67 UHC	PR-68 UHC
1993	Royal Canadian Mounted Police	10,807	389.65	Proof	800.	825.

ANNE OF GREEN GABLES, 1994.

Issued as a tribute to the famous character Anne in the novel by Canadian writer Lucy Maud Montgomery, this is the last in the youth and heritage series.

Designers and Engravers:
Obv.: Dora de Pédery-Hunt
Rev.: Pheobe Gilman, Susan Taylor
Composition: 91.67% Au, 8.33% Ag
Gold content: 15.703 g, 0.505 tr oz
Silver content: 1.427 g, 0.046 tr oz
Weight: 17.13 g **Edge:** Reeded
Diameter: 29.00 mm **Die Axis:** ↑↑
Thickness: 2.00 mm **Finish:** Proof
Case: Woven Jacquard case, black insert, encapsulated coin, COA

DATE	DESCRIPTION	QUANTITY SOLD	ISSUE PRICE	FINISH	PR-67 UHC	PR-68 UHC
1994	Anne of Green Gables	10,655	399.95	Proof	800.	825.

THE SUGAR BUSH, 1995.

The 1995 $200 coin celebrates the time-honoured rite of spring known in Canada as "sugaring off."

Designers and Engravers:
Obv.: Dora de Pédery-Hunt
Rev.: J. D. Mantha, Sheldon Beveridge
Composition: 91.67% Au, 8.33% Ag
Gold content: 15.703 g, 0.505 tr oz
Silver content: 1.427 g, 0.046 tr oz
Weight: 17.13 g **Edge:** Reeded
Diameter: 29.00 mm **Die Axis:** ↑↑
Thickness: 2.00 mm **Finish:** Proof
Case: Woven Jacquard case, black insert, encapsulated coin, COA

DATE	DESCRIPTION	QUANTITY SOLD	ISSUE PRICE	FINISH	PR-67 UHC	PR-68 UHC
1995	The Sugar Bush	9,579	399.95	Proof	800.	825.

TRANSCONTINENTAL LANDSCAPE, 1996.

The railway, a central symbol of national life, is commemorated on the 1996 $200 gold coin.

Designers and Engravers:
Obv.: Dora de Pédery-Hunt
Rev.: Suzanne Duranceau, Cosme Saffioti
Composition: 91.67% Au, 8.33% Ag
Gold content: 15.703 g, 0.505 tr oz
Silver content: 1.427 g, 0.046 tr oz
Weight: 17.13 g **Edge:** Reeded
Diameter: 29.00 mm **Die Axis:** ↑↑
Thickness: 2.00 mm **Finish:** Proof
Case: Woven Jacquard case, black insert, encapsulated coin, COA

DATE	DESCRIPTION	QUANTITY SOLD	ISSUE PRICE	FINISH	PR-67 UHC	PR-68 UHC
1996	Transcontinental Landscape	8,047	414.95	Proof	800.	825.

HAIDA "RAVEN BRINGING LIGHT TO THE WORLD," 1997.

This coin was the first issue of a four year program, celebrating Canadian Native cultures and traditions and was available with or without a case because the mint offered a four-coin case to house the set.

Designers and Engravers:
Obv.: Dora de Pédery-Hunt
Rev.: R. Davidson, Cosme Saffioti, A. Aarand
Composition: 91.67% Au, 8.33% Ag
Gold content: 15.703 g, 0.505 tr oz
Silver content: 1.427 g, 0.046 tr oz
Weight: 17.13 g **Edge:** Reeded
Diameter: 29.00 mm **Die Axis:** ↑↑
Thickness: 2.00 mm **Finish:** Proof
Case: Metal trimmed case, black insert, encapsulated coin, COA

DATE	DESCRIPTION	QUANTITY SOLD	ISSUE PRICE	FINISH	PR-67 UHC	PR-68 UHC
1997	Haida "Raven Bringing Light to the World"	11,610	414.95	Proof	850.	875.

THE LEGEND OF THE WHITE BUFFALO, 1998.

The second issue of the four year program celebrating Canadian Native cultures and traditions.

Designers and Engravers:
Obv.: Dora de Pédery-Hunt
Rev.: Alex Janvier, Cosme Saffioti
Composition: 91.67% Au, 8.33% Ag
Gold content: 15.703 g, 0.505 tr oz
Silver content: 1.427 g, 0.046 tr oz
Weight: 17.13 g **Edge:** Reeded
Diameter: 29.00 mm **Die Axis:** ↑↑
Thickness: 2.00 mm **Finish:** Proof
Case: Metal trimmed case, black insert, encapsulated coin, COA

DATE	DESCRIPTION	QUANTITY SOLD	ISSUE PRICE	FINISH	PR-67 UHC	PR-68 UHC
1998	Legend of the White Buffalo	7,149	414.95	Proof	800.	825.

MIKMAQ BUTTERFLY, 1999.

This is the third in the four-coin series celebrating Canadian Native cultures and traditions, The coin depicts a butterfly in the traditional Mikmaq double curve, symbolic of the balance between the physical and spiritual worlds.

Designers and Engravers:
Obv.: Dora de Pédery-Hunt
Rev.: Alan Syliboy, Cosme Saffioti
Composition: 91.67% Au, 8.33% Ag
Gold content: 15.703 g, 0.505 tr oz
Silver content: 1.427 g, 0.046 tr oz
Weight: 17.13 g **Edge:** Reeded
Diameter: 29.00 mm **Die Axis:** ↑↑
Thickness: 2.00 mm **Finish:** Proof
Case: Woven Jacquard case, black insert, encapsulated coin, COA

DATE	DESCRIPTION	QUANTITY SOLD	ISSUE PRICE	FINISH	PR-67 UHC	PR-68 UHC
1999	Mikmaq Butterfly	6,510	414.95	Proof	800.	825.

MOTHER AND CHILD, 2000.

This is the fourth and last coin in the four-coin Native Cultures and Traditions series.

Designers and Engravers:
Obv.: Dora de Pédery-Hunt
Rev.: G. Arnaktauyok, Susan Taylor
Composition: 91.67% Au, 8.33% Ag
Gold content: 15.703 g, 0.505 tr oz
Silver content: 1.427 g, 0.046 tr oz
Weight: 17.13 g **Edge:** Reeded
Diameter: 29.00 mm **Die Axis:** ↑↑
Thickness: 2.00 mm **Finish:** Proof
Case: Metal trimmed case, black insert, encapsulated coin, COA

DATE	DESCRIPTION	QUANTITY SOLD	ISSUE PRICE	FINISH	PR-67 UHC	PR-68 UHC
2000	Mother and Child	7,410	414.95	Proof	800.	825.

Note: A special collector case designed by Maryanne Barkhouse for the "Canadian Native Cultures and Traditions" series was issued in 1998. The box was made of imitation stone resin, with the Arctic Fox as the central panel, and on each side an animal on which the native aboriginal depended. The four-coin case was available directly from the Mint, priced at $79.95. The complete four-coin set in case was issued at $1,600.00.

CORNELIUS KRIEGHOFF, 2001.

The 2001 $200 gold coin is the first in a four-coin series featuring Canadian art and artists. Cornelius Krieghoff's famous painting *The Habitant Farm* (1856) is featured on the reverse.

Designers and Engravers:
Obv.: Dora de Pédery-Hunt
Rev.: C. Krieghoff, Susan Taylor
Composition: 91.67% Au, 8.33% Ag
Gold content: 15.703 g, 0.505 tr oz
Silver content: 1.427 g, 0.046 tr oz
Weight: 17.13 g **Edge:** Reeded
Diameter: 29.00 mm **Die Axis:** ↑↑
Thickness: 2.00 mm **Finish:** Proof
Case: Metal trimmed case, black insert, encapsulated coin, COA

DATE	DESCRIPTION	QUANTITY SOLD	ISSUE PRICE	FINISH	PR-67 UHC	PR-68 UHC
2001	Cornelius Krieghoff, *The Habitant Farm*	5,406	412.95	Proof	800.	825.

TOM THOMPSON, 2002.

The 2002 $200 gold coin is the second coin of the four-coin series honouring Canada's famous painters. Thompson's (1877-1917) *The Jack Pine*, painted in 1916 in Algonquin Park, is one of Canada's most familiar images.

Designers and Engravers:
Obv.: Dora de Pédery-Hunt
Rev.: Tom Thompson, Susan Taylor
Composition: 91.67% Au, 8.33% Ag
Gold content: 15.703 g, 0.505 tr oz
Silver content: 1.427 g, 0.046 tr oz
Weight: 17.13 g **Edge:** Reeded
Diameter: 29.00 mm **Die Axis:** ↑↑
Thickness: 2.00 mm **Finish:** Proof
Case: Woven Jacquard case, black insert, encapsulated coin, COA

DATE	DESCRIPTION	QUANTITY SOLD	ISSUE PRICE	FINISH	PR-67 UHC	PR-68 UHC
2002	Tom Thompson, *The Jack Pine*	5,754	412.95	Proof	800.	825.

LIONEL LEMOINE FITZGERALD, 2003.

The third gold coin in the Canadian Art series features Fitzgerald's *Houses*, painted in 1929. The rural life of the small prairie towns is the theme of this magnificent painting.

Designers and Engravers:
Obv.: Dora de Pédery-Hunt
Rev.: L. L. Fitzgerald, Susan Taylor
Composition: 91.67% Au, 8.33% Ag
Gold content: 15.703 g, 0.505 tr oz
Silver content: 1.427 g, 0.046 tr oz
Weight: 17.13 g **Edge:** Reeded
Diameter: 29.00 mm **Die Axis:** ↑↑
Thickness: 2.00 mm **Finish:** Proof
Case: Metal trimmed case, black insert, encapsulated coin, COA

DATE	DESCRIPTION	QUANTITY SOLD	ISSUE PRICE	FINISH	PR-67 UHC	PR-68 UHC
2003	Lionel LeMoine Fitzgerald, *Houses*	4,118	412.95	Proof	800.	825.

ALFRED PELLAN, 2004.

The fourth and last gold coin in the Canadian Art series, Alfred Pellan's *Fragments* make him one of the most fascinating figures in Canadian Art.

Designers and Engravers:
Obv.: Susanna Blunt, Susan Taylor
Rev.: Alfred Pellan, Christie Paquet
Composition: 91.67% Au, 8.33% Ag
Gold content: 14.667 g, 0.471 tr oz
Silver content: 1.332 g, 0.043 tr oz
Weight: 16.00 g **Edge:** Reeded
Diameter: 29.00 mm **Die Axis:** ↑↑
Thickness: 1.75 mm **Finish:** Proof
Case: Metal trimmed case, black insert, encapsulated coin, COA

DATE	DESCRIPTION	QUANTITY SOLD	ISSUE PRICE	FINISH	PR-67 UHC	PR-68 UHC
2004	Alfred Pellan, *Fragments*	3,917	412.95	Proof	800.	825.

FUR TRADE, 2005.

This is the first issue in the Historical Trade Series. The fur trade in Canada was founded as an adjunct to the fishing trade. In the 16th century European fishermen who dried their catch on the shores of Newfoundland began trade with the Native people.

Designers and Engravers:
Obv.: Susanna Blunt, Susan Taylor
Rev.: John Mardon, José Osio
Composition: 91.67% Au, 8.33% Ag
Gold content: 14.667 g, 0.471 tr oz
Silver content: 1.332 g, 0.043 tr oz
Weight: 16.00 g **Edge:** Reeded
Diameter: 29.00 mm **Die Axis:** ↑↑
Thickness: 1.75 mm **Finish:** Proof
Case: Maroon plastic slide case, black plastic insert, encapsulated coin, COA

DATE	DESCRIPTION	QUANTITY SOLD	ISSUE PRICE	FINISH	PR-67 UHC	PR-68 UHC
2005	Fur Trade	3,669	489.95	Proof	800.	825.

TIMBER TRADE, 2006.

The coin which represents the timber trade in Canada is the second issue in the Historical Trade Series. Wood was the great staple of Canadian trade for much of the 19th century, built on European demand for timber which brought investment and immigration to eastern Canada.

Designers and Engravers:
Obv.: Susanna Blunt, Susan Taylor
Rev.: John Mardon, Stan Witten
Composition: 91.67% Au, 8.33% Ag
Gold content: 14.667 g, 0.471 tr oz
Silver content: 1.332 g, 0.043 tr oz
Weight: 16.00 g **Edge:** Reeded
Diameter: 29.00 mm **Die Axis:** ↑↑
Thickness: 1.75 mm **Finish:** Proof
Case: Maroon leatherette clam style case, black flocked insert; encapsulated coin, COA

DATE	DESCRIPTION	QUANTITY SOLD	ISSUE PRICE	FINISH	PR-67 UHC	PR-68 UHC
2006	Timber Trade	3,218	489.95	Proof	800.	825.

FISHING TRADE, 2007.

The fishing trade on the Grand Banks began in the 16th century when fishermen from the northwestern section of Europe landed large catches of cod. This is the third coin in the Historical Trade Series.

Designers and Engravers:
Obv.: Susanna Blunt, Susan Taylor
Rev.: John Mardon, Susan Taylor
Composition: 91.67% Au, 8.33% Ag
Gold content: 14.667 g, 0.471 tr oz
Silver content: 1.332 g, 0.043 tr oz
Weight: 16.00 g **Edge:** Reeded
Diameter: 29.00 mm **Die Axis:** ↑↑
Thickness: 1.75 mm **Finish:** Proof
Case: Maroon leatherette clam style case, black flocked insert, encapsulated coin, COA

DATE	DESCRIPTION	QUANTITY SOLD	ISSUE PRICE	FINISH	PR-67 UHC	PR-68 UHC
2007	Fishing Trade	2,137	579.95	Proof	800.	825.

AGRICULTURE TRADE, 2008.

The agriculture trade has been one of the staple industries of Canada since the 17th century. Canada is one of the world's major producers of food, particularly cereal grains and dairy products. This coin is the fourth in the Historical Trade Series.

Designers and Engravers:
Obv.: Susanna Blunt, Susan Taylor
Rev.: John Mardon, RCM Staff
Composition: 91.67% Au, 8.33% Ag
Gold content: 14.667 g, 0.471 tr oz
Silver content: 1.332 g, 0.043 tr oz
Weight: 16.00 g **Edge:** Reeded
Diameter: 29.00 mm **Die Axis:** ↑↑
Thickness: 1.75 mm **Finish:** Proof
Case: Maroon leatherette clam style case, black flocked insert, encapsulated coin, COA

DATE	DESCRIPTION	QUANTITY SOLD	ISSUE PRICE	FINISH	PR-67 UHC	PR-68 UHC
2008	Agriculture Trade	1,951	619.95	Proof	800.	825.

COAL MINING TRADE, 2009.

The fifth coin in the Historical Trade Series represents the coal mining industry. Coal was first discovered by the French settlers in the late 1600s along the Nova Scotia coast. It soon became a valuable resource used both by the military and civilians.

Designers and Engravers:
Obv.: Susanna Blunt, Susan Taylor
Rev.: John Mardon, RCM Staff
Composition: 91.67% Au, 8.33% Ag
Gold content: 14.667 g, 0.471 tr oz
Silver content: 1.332 g, 0.043 tr oz
Weight: 16.00 g **Edge:** Reeded
Diameter: 29.00 mm **Die Axis:** ↑↑
Thickness: 1.75 mm **Finish:** Proof, Painted
Case: Maroon leatherette clam style case, black flocked insert, encapsulated coin, COA

DATE	DESCRIPTION	QUANTITY SOLD	ISSUE PRICE	FINISH	PR-67 UHC	PR-68 UHC
2009	Coal Mining Trade	2,241	849.95	Proof	850.	875.

FIRST CANADIAN OLYMPIC GOLD MEDAL ON HOME SOIL, 2010.

This coin was issued to commemorate the first Olympic gold medal to be won by a Canadian in a Canadian hosted Olympic Games. The gold medal was won by Alexandre Bilodeau in the men's mogul event at the Vancouver 2010 Olympic Winter Games.

Designers and Engravers:
Obv.: Susanna Blunt, Susan Taylor
Rev.: Bonnie Ross, RCM Staff
Composition: 91.67% Au, 8.33% Ag
Gold content: 14.667 g, 0.471 tr oz
Silver content: 1.332 g, 0.043 tr oz
Weight: 16.00 g **Edge:** Reeded
Diameter: 29.00 mm **Die Axis:** ↑↑
Thickness: 1.75 mm **Finish:** Proof
Case: Black leatherette display case, black flocked insert, encapsulated coin, COA

DATE	DESCRIPTION	QUANTITY SOLD	ISSUE PRICE	FINISH	PR-67 UHC	PR-68 UHC
2010	First Canadian Olympic Gold Medal on Home Soil	2,010	989.95	Proof	1,100.	1,125.

PETROLEUM AND OIL TRADE, 2010.

This is the sixth coin in the Historical Trade Series. The design combines the iconic oil plume with other elements representing turn-of-the-century oil exploration, production, storage and transportation to create a telling montage of the early days of Canada's oil trade.

Designers and Engravers:
Obv.: Susanna Blunt, Susan Taylor
Rev.: John Mardon, RCM Staff
Composition: 91.67% Au, 8.33% Ag
Gold content: 14.667 g, 0.471 tr oz
Silver content: 1.332 g, 0.043 tr oz
Weight: 16.00 g
Edge: Reeded
Diameter: 29.00 mm
Die Axis: ↑↑
Thickness: 1.75 mm
Finish: Proof, Painted
Case: Maroon leatherette clam style case, black flocked insert, encapsulated coin, COA

DATE	DESCRIPTION	QUANTITY SOLD	ISSUE PRICE	FINISH	PR-67 UHC	PR-68 UHC
2010	Petroleum and Oil Trade	4,000	999.95	Proof	1,000.	1,025.

TWO HUNDRED FIFTY DOLLAR GOLD COIN

DOG SLED TEAM, 2006.

Designers and Engravers:
Obv.: Susanna Blunt, Susan Taylor
Rev.: Arnold Nogy, José Osio
Composition: 58.33% Au, 41.67% Ag
Gold content: 26.25 g, 0.844 tr oz
Silver content: 18.75 g, 0.603 tr oz
Weight: 45.00 g
Diameter: 40.00 mm
Thickness: 2.90 mm
Edge: Reeded
Die Axis: ↑↑
Finish: Proof
Case: Maroon leatherette clam style case, black flocked insert, encapsulated coin, COA

DATE	DESCRIPTION	QUANTITY SOLD	ISSUE PRICE	FINISH	PR-67 UHC	PR-68 UHC
2006	Dog Sled Team	953	1,089.95	Proof	1,350.	1,400.

Note: An identical design is utilized on the $30 silver coin for 2006, see page 173.

THREE HUNDRED DOLLAR GOLD COINS (Large Size, 50mm)

TRIPLE CAMEO PORTRAITS OF QUEEN ELIZABETH II, 2002.

This 14 karat gold coin bears the triple cameo portraits of Queen Elizabeth II on the obverse: 1953-1964 portrait by Mary Gillick; 1965-1989 portrait by Arnold Machin; 1990-2003 portrait by Dora de Pédery-Hunt.

Designers:
Obv.: Dora de Pédery-Hunt
Rev.: Sheldon Beveridge, Cosme Saffioti

Engravers:
Obv.: Stan Witten
Rev.: Cosme Saffioti

Composition: 58.33% Au, 41.67% Ag
Gold content: 35.00 g, 1.125 tr oz
Silver content: 25.00 g, 0.804 tr oz
Weight: 60.00 g
Diameter: 50.00 mm

Thickness: 2.5 mm
Edge: Reeded
Die Axis: ↑↑
Finish: Proof / Bullion

Case of Issue: Purple laminated wooden case, cream insert, encapsulated coin, COA, black / gold outer case

DATE	DESCRIPTION	QUANTITY SOLD	ISSUE PRICE	FINISH	PR-67 UHC	PR-68 UHC
2002 (1952-)	Triple Cameo Portraits	999	1,095.95	Proof	1,800.	1,850.

Note: Coins on pages 220 and 221 illustrated smaller than actual size.

GREAT SEAL OF CANADA, 2003.

The Royal Seal, or Great Seal of Canada, is the official stamp used to bring the Queen's authority to any documents produced on her behalf.

2003 Obverse

2003 Reverse
Designer: RCM Staff
Engraver: RCM Staff

QUADRUPLE CAMEO PORTRAITS, 2004.

The four coinage portraits of Queen Elizabeth II are featured on the Obverse of the $300 coin for 2004. Each is struck in 24kt gold.

2004 Obverse

2004 Reverse
Designer: Christie Paquet
Engraver: Christie Paquet

Designers:
Obv.: Susanna Blunt
Rev.: See coin

Engravers:
Obv.: Susan Taylor
Rev.: See coin

Composition: 58.33% Au, 41.67% Ag
Gold content: 35.00 g, 1.125 tr oz
Silver content: 25.00 g, 0.804 tr oz
Weight: 60.00 g
Diameter: 50.00 mm

Thickness: 2.5 mm
Edge: Reeded
Die Axis: ↑↑
Finish: Proof / Bullion

Case of Issue: Black leatherette case, RCM plaque, black flocked insert, encapsulated coin, COA, black and gold outer case

DATE	DESCRIPTION	QUANTITY SOLD	ISSUE PRICE	FINISH	PR-67 UHC	PR-68 UHC
2003	Great Seal of Canada	998	1,099.95	Proof	1,800.	1,850.
2004	Quadruple Cameo Portraits	998	1,099.95	Proof	1,800.	1,850.

VIGNETTES OF THE TWENTY-FIVE CENT FRACTIONAL NOTES OF THE DOMINION OF CANADA, 2005-2007.

These coins commemorate the vignettes which appear on the Dominion of Canada twenty-five cent fractional note issues of 1870, 1900 and 1923.

2005-2007
Common Obverse

2005 The 1870 Shinplaster
Vignette of Britannia
Designer: R. R. Carmichael
Engraver: José Osio

2006 The 1900 Shinplaster
Vignette of Britannia
Designer: RCM Staff
Engraver: RCM Staff

2007 The 1923 Shinplaster
Vignette of Britannia
Designer: Robert-Ralph Carmichael
Engraver: Christie Paquet

Designers:
Obv.: See illustration
Rev.: See coin

Engravers:
Obv.: Susan Taylor
Rev.: See coin

Composition: 58.33% Au, 41.67% Ag
Gold content: 35.00 g, 1.125 tr oz
Silver content: 25.00 g, 0.804 tr oz
Weight: 60.00 g
Diameter: 50.00 mm
Thickness: 2.5 mm
Edge: Reeded
Die Axis: ↑↑
Finish: Proof / Bullion
Case of Issue: Black leatherette case, RCM plaque, black flocked insert, encapsulated coin, COA, black and gold outer case

DATE	DESCRIPTION	QUANTITY SOLD	ISSUE PRICE	FINISH	PR-67 UHC	PR-68 UHC
2005	1870 Shinplaster Vignette of Britannia	994	N/A	Proof	1,800.	1,850.
2006	1900 Shinplaster Vignette of Britannia	947	1,295.95	Proof	1,800.	1,850.
2007	1923 Shinplaster Vignette of Britannia	778	1,440.95	Proof	1,800.	1,850.

Note: Coins illustrated smaller than actual size.

CRYSTAL SNOWFLAKE SERIES, 2006 and 2010

Designers:
Obv.: Susanna Blunt
Rev.: Konrad Wachelko

Engravers:
Obv.: Susan Taylor
Rev.: Konrad Wachelko

Composition: 58.33% Au, 41.67% Ag
Gold content: 35.00 g, 1.125 tr oz
Silver content: 25.00 g, 0.804 tr oz
Weight: 60.00 g
Diameter: 50.00 mm
Thickness: 2.5 mm
Edge: Reeded
Die Axis: ↑↑
Finish: Proof with Swarovski crystal elements
Case of Issue: Maroon leatherette clam style case, black flocked insert, encapsulated coin, COA

CRYSTAL SNOWFLAKE, 2006.

CRYSTAL SNOWFLAKE, 2010.

DATE	DESCRIPTION	QUANTITY SOLD	ISSUE PRICE	FINISH	PR-67 UHC	PR-68 UHC
2006	Crystal Snowflake	998	1,520.95	Proof	1,800.	1,850.
2010	Crystal Snowflake	750	2,295.95	Proof	2,300.	2,350.

Note: Coins illustrated smaller than actual size.

80TH BIRTHDAY OF QUEEN ELIZABETH II, 2006

80TH BIRTHDAY OF QUEEN ELIZABETH II, 2006.

Designers:
Obv.: Susanna Blunt
Rev.: See coin

Engravers:
Obv.: Susan Taylor
Rev.: See coin

Composition: 58.33% Au, 41.67% Ag
Gold content: 35.00 g, 1.125 tr oz
Silver content: 25.00 g, 0.804 tr oz
Weight: 60.00 g
Diameter: 50.00 mm
Thickness: 2.5 mm
Edge: Reeded
Die Axis: ↑↑
Finish: Proof, Enamelled
Case of Issue: Maroon leatherette clam style case, black flocked insert, encapsulated coin, COA

DATE	DESCRIPTION	QUANTITY SOLD	ISSUE PRICE	FINISH	PR-67 UHC	PR-68 UHC
2006 (1926-)	80th Birthday Elizabeth II, Enamelled	1,000	1,520,95	Proof	1,800.	1,850.

Note: Coin illustrated smaller than actual size.

VANCOUVER 2010 OLYMPIC WINTER GAMES, 2007-2009

OLYMPIC IDEALS, 2007.

COMPETITION, 2008.

Designers:
Obv.: Susanna Blunt
Rev.: Laurie McGaw, David Craig

Engravers:
Obv.: Susan Taylor
Rev.: 2007: Susan Taylor, José Osio
2008: Susan Taylor, Christie Paquet

Composition: 58.33% Au, 41.67% Ag
Gold content: 35.00 g, 1.125 tr oz
Silver content: 25.00 g, 0.804 tr oz
Weight: 60.00 g
Diameter: 50.00 mm

Thickness: 2.5 mm
Edge: Reeded
Die Axis: ↑↑
Finish: Proof

Case of Issue: Black leatherette case, black flocked insert, encapsulated coin, COA

DATE	DESCRIPTION	DATE OF ISSUE	QUANTITY SOLD	ISSUE PRICE	FINISH	PR-67 UHC	PR-68 UHC
2007	Olympic Ideals	Feb. 23, 2007	953	1,499.95	Proof	1,800.	1,850.
2008	Competition	Feb. 20, 2008	334	1,599.95	Proof	1,800.	1,850.

Note: Coins illustrated smaller than actual size.

VANCOUVER 2010 OLYMPIC WINTER GAMES, 2007-2009 (cont.).

FRIENDSHIP, 2009.

Designers:
Obv.: Susanna Blunt
Rev.: Laurie McGaw, David Craig

Engravers:
Obv.: Susan Taylor
Rev.: Susan Taylor, José Osio

Composition: 58.33% Au, 41.67% Ag
Gold content: 35.00 g, 1.125 tr oz
Silver content: 25.00 g, 0.804 tr oz
Weight: 60.00 g
Diameter: 50.00 mm
Thickness: 2.5 mm
Edge: Reeded
Die Axis: ↑↑
Finish: Proof
Case of Issue: Black leatherette case, black flocked insert, encapsulated coin, COA

DATE	DESCRIPTION	DATE OF ISSUE	QUANTITY SOLD	ISSUE PRICE	FINISH	PR-67 UHC	PR-68 UHC
2009	Friendship	Feb. 18, 2009	880	1,999.95	Proof	2,000.	2,100.

Note: Coin illustrated smaller than actual size.

PROVINCIAL COATS OF ARMS SERIES, 2008-2010

PROVINCIAL COATS OF ARMS SERIES, 2008-2010.

Designers:
Obv.: Susanna Blunt
Rev.: Reproduction of official Coat of Arms

Engravers:
Obv.: Susan Taylor
Rev.: RCM Staff

Composition: 58.33% Au, 41.67% Ag
Gold content: 35.00 g, 1.125 tr oz
Silver content: 25.00 g, 0.804 tr oz
Weight: 60.00 g
Diameter: 50.00 mm
Thickness: 2.5 mm
Edge: Reeded
Die Axis: ↑↑
Finish: Proof
Case of Issue: Maroon leatherette clam style case, black flocked insert, encapsulated coin, COA

Common Obverse
With RCM Logo

2008
Newfoundland and Labrador

2008
Alberta

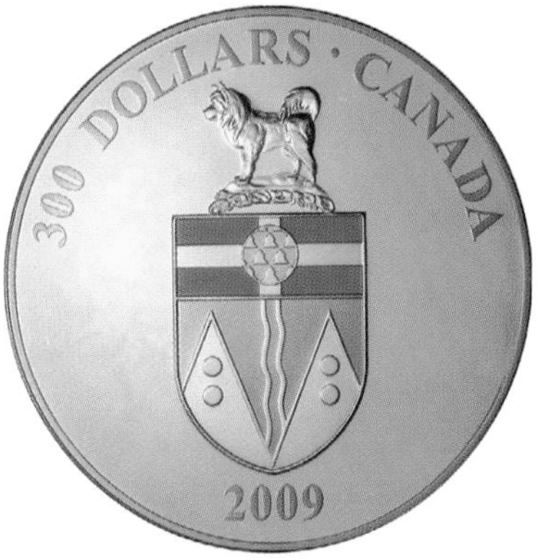

2009
Yukon Territory

DATE	DESCRIPTION	QUANTITY SOLD	ISSUE PRICE	FINISH	PR-67 UHC	PR-68 UHC
2008	Newfoundland and Labrador	472	1,541.95	Proof	1,800.	1,850.
2008	Alberta	344	1,631.95	Proof	1,800.	1,850.
2009	Yukon Territory	325	1,949.95	Proof	2,000.	2,100.

Note: Coins illustrated smaller than actual size.

PROVINCIAL COATS OF ARMS SERIES, 2008-2010 (cont.).

Designers:
Obv.: Susanna Blunt
Rev.: Reproduction of official Coat of Arms

Engravers:
Obv.: Susan Taylor
Rev.: RCM Staff

Composition: 58.33% Au, 41.67% Ag
Gold content: 35.00 g, 1.125 tr oz
Silver content: 25.00 g, 0.804 tr oz
Weight: 60.00 g
Diameter: 50.00 mm
Thickness: 2.5 mm
Edge: Reeded
Die Axis: ↑↑
Finish: Proof
Case of Issue: Maroon leatherette clam style case, black flocked insert, encapsulated coin, COA

Common Obverse
Without RCM Logo

2009
Prince Edward Island

2010
British Columbia

2010
New Brunswick

DATE	DESCRIPTION	QUANTITY SOLD	ISSUE PRICE	FINISH	PR-67 UHC	PR-68 UHC
2009	Prince Edward Island	236	1,949.95	Proof	2,000.	2,050.
2010	British Columbia	500	2,249.95	Proof	2,250.	2,300.
2010	New Brunswick	500	2,249.95	Proof	2,250.	2,300.

Note: Coins illustrated smaller than actual size.

MOON MASKS, 2008-2009

FOUR SEASONS MOON MASK, 2008.

SUMMER MOON MASK, 2009.

Designers:
Obv.: Susanna Blunt
Rev.: Jody Broomfield

Engravers:
Obv.: Susan Taylor
Rev.: RCM Staff

Composition: 58.33% Au, 41.67% Ag
Gold content: 35.00 g, 1.125 tr oz
Silver content: 25.00 g, 0.804 tr oz
Weight: 60.00 g
Diameter: 50.00 mm
Thickness: 2.5 mm
Edge: Reeded
Die Axis: ↑↑
Finish: Proof, Enamelled
Case of Issue: Maroon leatherette clam style case, black flocked insert, encapsulated coin, COA

DATE	DESCRIPTION	QUANTITY SOLD	ISSUE PRICE	FINISH	PR-67 UHC	PR-68 UHC
2008	Four Seasons Moon Mask	544	1,559.95	Proof	1,800.	1,850.
2009	Summer Moon Mask	N/A	1,723.95	Proof	1,800.	1,850.

Note: Coins illustrated smaller than actual size.

THREE HUNDRED DOLLAR GOLD COINS (Small Size 40mm)

WELCOME FIGURE (DZUNUK'WA) TOTEM POLE, 2005.

Dzunuk'wa is a giant, hairy, black-bodied, big-breasted, wide-eyed female monster. She is physically strong enough to tear down large trees, spiritually powerful enough to resurrect the dead and possesses magical treasures and great wealth.

Designers and Engravers:
Obv.: Susanna Blunt, Susan Taylor
Rev.: Dr. Richard Hunt, RCM Staff
Composition: 58.33% Au, 41.67% Ag
Gold content: 26.25 g, 0.844 tr oz
Silver content: 18.75 g, 0.603 tr oz
Weight: 45.0 g
Diameter: 40.0 mm
Thickness: 3.0 mm
Edge: Reeded
Die Axis: ↑↑
Finish: Proof
Case: Maroon leatherette clam style case, black flocked insert, encapsulated coin, COA

DATE	DESCRIPTION	QUANTITY SOLD	ISSUE PRICE	FINISH	PR-67 UHC	PR-68 UHC
2005	Welcome Figure Totem Pole	948	1,199.95	Proof	1,350.	1,400.

Note: An identical design is utilized on the $30 silver coin for 2005, see page 173.

CANADIAN ACHIEVEMENT SERIES, 2005-2008

120TH ANNIVERSARY OF THE INTERNATIONAL IMPLEMENTATION OF STANDARD TIME, 2005.

In 1885 Sir Sandford Fleming's system of standard time was implemented, dividing the world into 24 time zones. These are the first coins in the Canadian Achievements series.

Designers and Engravers:
Obv.: Susanna Blunt, Susan Taylor
Rev.: Bonnie Ross, Stan Witten
Composition: 58.33% Au, 41.67% Ag
Gold content: 26.25 g, 0.844 tr oz
Silver content: 18.75 g, 0.603 tr oz
Weight: 45.0 g
Diameter: 40.0 mm
Edge: Reeded
Thickness: 3.0 mm
Die Axis: ↑↑
Finish: Proof, Colourised
Case of Issue: Anodized gold-coloured aluminum box with cherry wood stained side panels, encapsulated coin, COA

Pacific Time 4:00

Mountain Time 5:00

Central Time 6:00

Eastern Time 7:00

Atlantic Time 8:00

Newfoundland Time 8:30

DATE	DESCRIPTION	QUANTITY SOLD	ISSUE PRICE	FINISH	PR-67 UHC	PR-68 UHC
2005	Pacific Time 4:00	200	999.95	Proof	1,350.	1,400.
2005	Mountain Time 5:00	200	999.95	Proof	1,350.	1,400.
2005	Central Time 6:00	200	999.95	Proof	1,350.	1,400.
2005	Eastern Time 7:00	200	999.95	Proof	1,350.	1,400.
2005	Atlantic Time 8:00	200	999.95	Proof	1,350.	1,400.
2005	Newfoundland Time 8:30	200	999.95	Proof	1,350.	1,400.

Note: It is reported in the 2006 Mint Report that a total of 1,199 coins were issued, however, it did not stipulate which coin was short struck.

CANADIAN ACHIEVEMENT SERIES CONTINUED, 2005-2008

FIFTH ANNIVERSARY OF CANADARM, 2006.

This is the second coin in the Canadian Achievements series.

Designers and Engravers:
Obv.: Susanna Blunt, Susan Taylor
Rev.: Cecily Mok, Cecily Mok
Composition: 58.33% Au, 41.67% Ag
Gold content: 26.25 g, 0.844 tr oz
Silver content: 18.75 g, 0.603 tr oz
Weight: 45.0 g
Diameter: 40.0 mm
Thickness: 3.0 mm
Edge: Reeded
Die Axis: ↑↑
Finish: Proof, Decal
Case: Maroon leatherette clam style case, black flocked insert, encapsulated coin. COA

PANORAMIC PHOTOGRAPHY IN CANADA, NIAGARA FALLS, 2007.

This is the third coin in the Canadian Achievements series.

Designers and Engravers:
Obv.: Susanna Blunt, Susan Taylor
Rev.: Chris Jordison, RCM Staff
Composition: 58.33% Au, 41.67% Ag
Gold content: 26.25 g, 0.844 tr oz
Silver content: 18.75 g, 0.603 tr oz
Weight: 45.0 g
Diameter: 40.0 mm
Thickness: 3.0 mm
Edge: Reeded
Die Axis: ↑↑
Finish: Proof, Hologram
Case: Maroon leatherette clam style case, black flocked insert, encapsulated coin, COA

IMAX©, 2008.

This is the last coin in the Canadian Achievements series.

Designers and Engravers:
Obv.: Susanna Blunt, Susan Taylor
Rev.: IMAX©, RCM Staff
Composition: 58.33% Au, 41.67% Ag
Gold content: 26.25 g, 0.844 tr oz
Silver content: 18.75 g, 0.603 tr oz
Weight: 45.0 g
Diameter: 40.0 mm
Thickness: 3.0 mm
Edge: Reeded
Die Axis: ↑↑
Finish: Proof, Hologram
Case: Maroon leatherette clam style case, black flocked insert, encapsulated coin, COA

DATE	DESCRIPTION	QUANTITY SOLD	ISSUE PRICE	FINISH	PR-67 UHC	PR-68 UHC
2006	5th Anniversary Canadarm, Decal	581	1,089.95	Proof	1,950.	2,000.
2007	Panoramic Photography, Niagara Falls, Hologram	551	1,111.95	Proof	1,350.	1,400.
2008	IMAX©, Hologram	252	1,228.95	Proof	1,350.	1,400.

THREE HUNDRED FIFTY DOLLAR GOLD COINS

PROVINCIAL FLORAL SERIES, 1998-2010.

Begun in 1998 and issued annually, the $350 gold coin bears either a national or provincial flower.

Designers:
Obv.: Dora de Pédery-Hunt
Rev.: See coin

Engravers:
Obv.: Dora de Pédery-Hunt
Rev.: See coin

Composition: 99.999% Au
Gold content: 38.05 g, 1.222 tr oz
Weight: 38.05 g
Diameter: 34.00 mm
Thickness: 3.2 mm
Edge: Reeded
Die Axis: ↑↑
Finish: Proof
Cases of Issue: 1998-2003: Anodized gold-coloured aluminum box with cherry wood stained side panels, encapsulated coin, COA
2004-2006: Maroon plastic display case, black plastic insert, encapsulated coin, COA
2007-2009: Maroon leatherette clam style case, black flocked insert, encapsulated coin, COA

1998
90th Anniversary of the Royal Canadian Mint

Obv.: 1998

Designer: Pierre Leduc
Engraver: Ago Aarand

1999
The Golden Slipper
Prince Edward Island's Floral Emblem

Obv.: 1999

Designer: Henry Purdy
Engraver: José Osio

2000
Pacific Dogwood
British Columbia's Floral Emblem

Obv.: 2000

Designer: Caren Heine
Engraver: José Osio

2001
The Mayflower
Nova Scotia's Floral Emblem

Obv.: 2001

Designer: Bonnie Ross
Engraver: Susan Taylor

DATE	DESCRIPTION	QUANTITY SOLD	ISSUE PRICE	FINISH	PR-67 UHC	PR-68 UHC
1998	90th Anniversary of the Royal Canadian Min	1,999	999.99	Proof	1,950.	2,000.
1999	The Golden Slipper, P.E.I.	1,990	999.99	Proof	1,950.	2,000.
2000	The Pacific Dogwood, B.C.	1,971	999.99	Proof	1,950.	2,000.
2001	The Mayflower, N.S.	1,988	999.99	Proof	1,950.	2,000.

PROVINCIAL FLORAL SERIES, 1998-2010 (cont.).

Designers:
Obv.: Dora de Pédery-Hunt
Rev.: See coin

Engravers:
Obv.: Dora de Pédery-Hunt
Rev.: See coin

Composition: 99.999% Au
Gold content: 38.05 g, 1.222 tr oz
Weight: 38.05 g
Diameter: 34.00 mm
Thickness: 3.2 mm
Edge: Reeded
Die Axis: ↑↑
Finish: Proof
Cases of Issue: 1998-2003: Anodized gold-coloured aluminum box with cherry wood stained side panels, encapsulated coin, COA
2004-2006: Maroon plastic display case, black plastic insert, encapsulated coin, COA
2007-2009: Maroon leatherette clam style case, black flocked insert, encapsulated coin, COA

2002
The Wild Rose
Alberta's Flora Emblem

Obv.: 2002

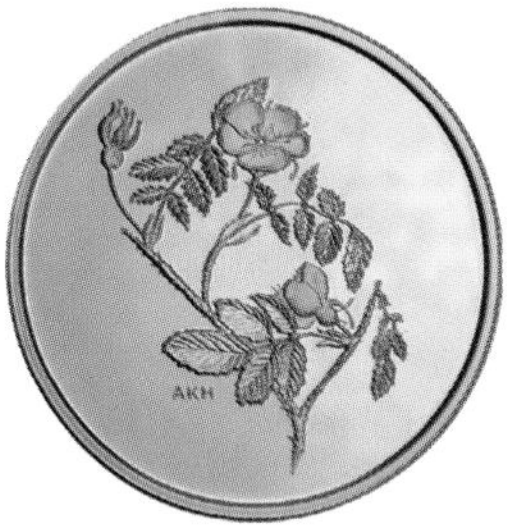

Designer: Dr. A. K. Hellum
Engraver: William Woodruff

2003
The White Trillium
Ontario's Floral Emblem

Obv.: 2003

Designer: Pamela Stagg
Engraver: William Woodruff

DATE	DESCRIPTION	QUANTITY SOLD	ISSUE PRICE	FINISH	PR-67 UHC	PR-68 UHC
2002	The Wild Rose, Alberta	2,001	1,099.99	Proof	1,950.	2,000.
2003	The White Trillium, Ontario	1,865	1,099.99	Proof	1,950.	2,000.

PROVINCIAL FLORAL SERIES, 1998-2010 (cont.).

In 2004 the weight was decreased from 38.05 to 35.00 grams.

Designers:
Obv.: Susanna Blunt
Rev.: See coin

Engravers:
Obv.: Susan Taylor
Rev.: See coin

Composition: 99.999% Au
Gold content: 35.00 g, 1.125 tr oz
Weight: 35.00 g
Diameter: 34.00 mm
Thickness: 2.75 mm
Edge: Reeded
Die Axis: ↑↑
Finish: Proof
Cases of Issue: 1998-2003: Anodized gold-coloured aluminum box with cherry wood stained side panels, encapsulated coin, COA
2004-2006: Maroon plastic display case, black plastic insert, encapsulated coin, COA
2007-2009: Maroon leatherette clam style case, black flocked insert, encapsulated coin, COA

2004
The Fireweed
Yukon Territory's Floral Emblem

Obv.: 2004

Des.: Catherine Ann Deer
Eng.: William Woodruff

2005
The Western Red Lily
Saskatchewan's Floral Emblem

Obv.: 2005

Designer: Chris Jordison
Engraver: José Osio

2006
The Iris Versicolor
Quebec's Floral Emblem

Obv.: 2006

Designer: Susan Taylor
Engraver: Susan Taylor

2007
Purple Violet
New Brunswick's Floral Emblem

Obv.: 2007

Designer: Sue Rose
Engraver: William Woodruff

DATE	DESCRIPTION	QUANTITY SOLD	ISSUE PRICE	FINISH	PR-67 UHC	PR-68 UHC
2004	The Fireweed, Yukon Territory	1,836	1,099.95	Proof	1,950.	2,000.
2005	Western Red Lily, Saskatchewan	1,634	1,295.99	Proof	1,950.	2,000.
2006	Iris Versicolor, Quebec	1,995	1,295.95	Proof	1,950.	2,000.
2007	Purple Violet, New Brunswick	1,392	1,520.95	Proof	1,950.	2,000.

PROVINCIAL FLORAL SERIES, 1998-2010 (cont.).

Designers:
Obv.: Susanna Blunt
Rev.: See coin

Engravers:
Obv.: Susan Taylor
Rev.: See coin

Composition: 99.999% Au
Gold content: 35.00 g, 1.125 tr oz
Weight: 35.00 g
Diameter: 34.00 mm
Thickness: 2.75 mm
Edge: Reeded
Die Axis: ↑↑
Finish: Proof
Cases of Issue: 1998-2003: Anodized gold-coloured aluminum box with cherry wood stained side panels, encapsulated coin, COA
2004-2006: Maroon plastic display case, black plastic insert, encapsulated coin, COA
2007-2009: Maroon leatherette clam style case, black flocked insert, encapsulated coin, COA

2008
Purple Saxifrage
Nunavut's Floral Emblem

Obv.: 2008

Designer: Celia Godkin
Engraver: RCM Mint

2009
Pitcher Plant
Newfoundland and Labrador's Floral Emblem

Obv.: 2009

Designer: Celia Godkin
Engraver: RCM Mint

2010
Prairie Crocus
Manitoba's Floral Emblem

Obv.: 2010

Designer: Celia Godkin
Engraver: RCM Mint

DATE	DESCRIPTION	QUANTITY SOLD	ISSUE PRICE	FINISH	PR-67 UHC	PR-68 UHC
2008	Purple Saxifrage, Nunavut	1,313	1,675.95	Proof	1,950.	2,000.
2009	Pitcher Plant, Newfoundland and Labrador	1,003	2,149.95	Proof	2,150.	2,200.
2010	Prairie Crocus, Manitoba	1,400	2,599.95	Proof	2,600.	2,650.

FIVE HUNDRED DOLLAR GOLD COINS

60TH WEDDING ANNIVERSARY OF QUEEN ELIZABETH AND PRINCE PHILIP, 2007.

This is the first gold coin (.9999) weighing five ounces with a $500 denomination to be produced by the Royal Canadian Mint. The coin celebrates the sixtieth wedding anniversary of HM Queen Elizabeth II and HRH Prince Philip, Duke of Edinburgh. The shields are from their respective Coats of Arms and the mascots on the State vehicles in which they travel.

Designers:
Obv.: Susanna Blunt
Rev.: Steve Hepburn

Engravers:
Obv.: Susan Taylor
Rev.: RCM Staff

Composition: 99.99% Au
Gold content: 155.76 g, 5.01 tr oz
Weight: 155.76 g
Diameter: 60.00 mm
Thickness: N/A
Edge: Reeded
Die Axis: ↑↑
Finish: Proof
Case of Issue: Black clam style case, black insert, encapsulated coin, COA

DATE	DESCRIPTION	QUANTITY SOLD	ISSUE PRICE	FINISH	PR-67 UHC	PR-68 UHC
2007 (1947-)	60th Wedding Anniversary Queen / Prince Philip	198	5,999.95	Proof	8,000.	8,250.

Note: 1. An identical design is utilized on the $250 silver coin for 2007, see page 177.
2. Coin illustrated smaller than actual size.
3. Images courtesy of the Royal Canadian Mint.

100TH ANNIVERSARY OF THE ROYAL CANADIAN MINT, 2008

This coin was issued to commemorate the 100th anniversary of the Ottawa Mint (Royal Canadian Mint) which was opened January 2nd, 1908.

150TH ANNIVERSARY OF THE START OF CONSTRUCTION OF THE PARLIAMENT BUILDINGS, 2009

Construction of the Parliament Buildings began in December 1859, and was completed in the summer of 1866.

Designers:
Obv.: Susanna Blunt
Rev.: RCM Staff

Engravers:
Obv.: Susan Taylor
Rev.: RCM Staff

Composition: 99.99% Au
Gold content: 156.5 g, 5.03 tr oz
Weight: 156.05 g
Diameter: 60.00 mm
Thickness: N/A
Edge: Reeded
Die Axis: ↑↑
Finish: Proof
Case of Issue: Black clam style case, black insert, encapsulated coin, COA

DATE	DESCRIPTION	QUANTITY SOLD	ISSUE PRICE	FINISH	PR-67 UHC	PR-68 UHC
2008	100th Anniversary of the Royal Canadian Mint	248	8,159.95	Proof	8,000.	8,250.
2009	150th Anniv. Start Construction Parliament Buildings	77	10,199.95	Proof	10,100.	10,200.

Note:
1. Identical designs are utilized on the $250 silver coins for 2008 and 2009, see page 178.
2. Coins illustrated smaller than actual size.
3. Quantity sold numbers are current to the 2009 Royal Canadian Mint Report, and will possibly change with the release of the 2010 report.
4. Images of the 150th Anniversary of the Start of Construction of the Parliament Buildings coin courtesy of the Royal Canadian Mint.

75TH ANNIVERSARY OF THE FIRST BANK NOTES ISSUED BY THE BANK OF CANADA, 2010

The reverse design on this coin is a reproduction of the central vignette that appears on the $500 bank note of 1935, a seated woman with a sickle, surrounded by the fruits of harvest, symbolising fertility.

Designers:
Obv.: Susanna Blunt
Rev.: Steve Hepburn

Engravers:
Obv.: Susan Taylor
Rev.: RCM Staff

Composition: 99.99% Au
Gold content: 156.50 g, 5.03 tr oz
Weight: 156.50 g
Diameter: 60.15 mm
Thickness: N/A
Edge: Reeded
Die Axis: ↑↑
Finish: Proof
Case of Issue: Red leatherette clam style case, black insert, encapsulated coin, COA

DATE	DESCRIPTION	QUANTITY SOLD	ISSUE PRICE	FINISH	PR-67 UHC	PR-68 UHC
2010	75th Anniversary of the First Bank of Canada Notes	200	9,495.95	Proof	9,500.	9,600.

Note: 1. An identical design is utilized on the $250 silver coin for 2010, see page 179.
2. Coin illustrated smaller than actual size.
3. Images courtesy of the Royal Canadian Mint.

TWO THOUSAND FIVE HUNDRED DOLLAR GOLD COINS

VANCOUVER 2010 OLYMPIC WINTER GAMES, 2007-2010

EARLY CANADA, 2007.

TOWARDS CONFEDERATION, 2008.

Designers:
Obv.: Susanna Blunt
Rev.: Stan Witten

Engravers:
Obv.: Susan Taylor
Rev.: Stan Witten

Composition: 99.99% Au
Gold content: 1,000.0 g, 32.15 tr oz
Weight: 1,000 g (1 kilo)
Diameter: 101.6 mm
Thickness: N/A
Edge: Plain
Die Axis: ↑↑
Finish: Proof
Case of Issue: Black display case, encapsulated coins, COA, 2010 Olympic Winter Games theme sleeve.

DATE	DESCRIPTION	DATE OF ISSUE	QUANTITY SOLD	ISSUE PRICE	FINISH	PR-67 UHC	PR-68 UHC
2007	Early Canada	Feb. 23, 2007	20	36,000.	Proof	48,000.	48,250.
2008	Towards Confederation	Feb. 20, 2008	20	49,000.	Proof	48,000.	48,250.

Note: 1. Identical designs are utilized on the $250 silver coins for 2007 and 2008, see page 180.
2. Coins illustrated smaller than actual size.
3. Images courtesy of the Royal Canadian Mint.

VANCOUVER 2010 OLYMPIC WINTER GAMES, 2007-2010 (cont.)

THE CANADA OF TODAY, 2009.

SURVIVING THE FLOOD, 2009.

Designers:
Obv.: Susanna Blunt
Rev.: Design Team of the Vancouver Organizing Committee for the 2010 Olympic and Paralympic Games

Engravers:
Obv.: Susan Taylor
Rev.: RCM Staff

Composition: 99.99% Au
Gold content: 1,000.0 g, 32.15 tr oz
Weight: 1,000 g (1 kilo)
Diameter: 101.6 mm
Thickness: N/A
Case of Issue: Black display case, encapsulated coins, COA

Edge: Plain
Die Axis: ↑↑
Finish: Proof

DATE	DESCRIPTION	DATE OF ISSUE	QUANTITY SOLD	ISSUE PRICE	FINISH	PR-67 UHC	PR-68 UHC
2009	The Canada of Today	Apr. 15, 2009	50	54,000.	Proof	48,000.	48,250.
2009	Surviving The Flood	Nov. 21, 2009	40	49,000.	Proof	48,000.	48,250.

Note: 1. Identical designs are utilized on the $250 silver coins for 2009, see page 181.
2. Coins illustrated smaller than actual size.
3. Images courtesy of Gatewest Coins.

VANCOUVER 2010 OLYMPIC WINTER GAMES, 2010 (cont.)

THE EAGLE, 2010.

The eagle, an important First Nations symbol, represents power, peace and prestige.

Designers:
Obv.: Susanna Blunt
Rev.: Xwa lac tun (Ricky Harry)

Engravers:
Obv.: Susan Taylor
Rev.: RCM Staff

Composition: 99.99% Au
Gold content: 1,000.0 g, 32.15 tr oz
Weight: 1,000 g (1 kilo)
Diameter: 101.6 mm
Thickness: N/A
Edge: Plain
Die Axis: ↑↑
Finish: Proof
Case of Issue: Black display case, black flocked insert, encapsulated coin, COA

DATE	DESCRIPTION	DATE OF ISSUE	QUANTITY SOLD	ISSUE PRICE	FINISH	PR-67 UHC	PR-68 UHC
2010	The Eagle	Nov. 19, 2009	20	49,000	Proof	49,000.	49,250.

Note: 1. An identical design is utilized on the $250 silver coins for 2010, see page 182.
2. Coin illustrated smaller than actual size.
3. Images courtesy of Gatewest Coins.

125TH ANNIVERSARY BANFF NATIONAL PARK

125TH ANNIVERSARY OF BANFF NATIONAL PARK, 2010.

Designers:
Obv.: Susanna Blunt
Rev.: Tony Bianco

Engravers:
Obv.: Susan Taylor
Rev.: RCM Staff

Composition: 99.99% Au
Gold content: 1000.0 g, 32.15 tr oz
Weight: 1,000.0 g (1 kilo)
Diameter: 101.6 mm
Thickness: N/A
Edge: Plain
Die Axis: ↑↑
Finish: Proof
Case of Issue: Black clam style case, black insert, encapsulated coin, COA

DATE	DESCRIPTION	QUANTITY SOLD	ISSUE PRICE	FINISH	PR-67 UHC	PR-68 UHC
2010	125th Anniversary Banff National Park	25	57,000	Proof	57,000.	57,250.

Note: 1. An identical design is utilized on the $250 silver coins for 2010, see page 183.
2. Coin illustrated smaller than actual size.
3. Images courtesy of the Royal Canadian Mint.

PALLADIUM COINS

FIFTY DOLLAR PALLADIUM COINS

BIG AND LITTLE BEAR CONSTELLATIONS, 2006.

Each coin has been crafted with a special laser effect to illustrate the position of Big Bear and Little Bear constellations above a conceptual Canadian forest, as they would appear when viewed from the nation's capital during each of the four seasons.

Common Obverse

Designers and Engravers:
Obv.: Susanna Blunt, Susan Taylor
Rev.: Colin Mayne, RCM Staff
Composition: 99.95% Pl
Palladium content: 31.144 g, 1.00 tr oz
Weight: 31.16 g
Diameter: 34.00 mm
Thickness: 3.50 mm
Edge: Reeded
Die Axis: ↑↑
Finish: Specimen; Laser effect
Case: Maroon clam style case; black flocked insert, encapsulated coin, COA

Spring

Summer

Autumn

Winter

DATE	DESCRIPTION	QUANTITY SOLD	ISSUE PRICE	FINISH	SP-66	SP-67
2006	Spring	300	849.95	Specimen	1,000.	1,100.
2006	Summer	300	849.95	Specimen	1,000.	1,100.
2006	Autumn	300	849.95	Specimen	1,000.	1,100.
2006	Winter	300	849.95	Specimen	1,000.	1,100.

PLATINUM COINS

THREE HUNDRED DOLLAR PLATINUM COINS

PREHISTORIC ANIMALS SERIES, 2007-2010

This series of platinum coins highlights the prehistoric animals which roamed the North American continent thousands of years ago.

Designers:
Obv.: Susanna Blunt
Rev.: 2007-2009: RCM Staff
2010: Kerri Burnett

Engravers:
Obv.: Susan Taylor
Rev.: RCM Staff
RCM Staff

Composition: 99.95% Pt
Platinum content: 31.14 g, 1.00 tr oz
Weight: 31.16 g
Diameter: 30.00 mm
Thickness: 2.6 mm
Edge: Reeded
Die Axis: ↑↑
Finish: Proof
Case of Issue: Maroon leatherette clam style case, black flocked insert, encapsulated coin, COA

Obverse 2007-2008
With RCM Logo

2007
Woolly Mammoth

2008
Scimitar Cat

Obverse 2009-2010
Without RCM Logo

2009
Steppe Bison

2010
Ground Sloth

DATE	DESCRIPTION	QUANTITY SOLD	ISSUE PRICE	FINISH	PR-67 UHC	PR-68 UHC
2007	Woolly Mammoth	287	2,999.95	Proof	3,000.	3,100.
2008	Scimitar Cat	200	3,419.95	Proof	3,000.	3,100.
2009	Steppe Bison	197	2,999.95	Proof	3,000.	3,100.
2010	Ground Sloth	200	2,999.95	Proof	3,000.	3,100.

COLLECTOR SETS

NOTES ON COLLECTOR SETS MINTAGES

1. For some sets the mintage was pre-announced as a maximum number of sets to be issued. In other cases the mintage was open-ended with the issue period a function of time. In the pricing tables for sets the mintage number denotes the number of sets sold. The final number is usually only available after a second year of RCM Reports.
2. Within the set listings are sets with different finishes and compositions. Currently the four main finish categories are Uncirculated, Brilliant Uncirculated, Specimen and Proof. Usually, these sets contain exact design copies of the circulating business strike coins, but there are a few exceptions when commemorative coins are involved.
3. For a complete explanation on finishes, see page xxiv in the introduction.

COLLECTOR CARDS FOR CIRCULATION COINAGE, 2004-2010

2004 "Lest We Forget" The Poppy Coin Collector Card

2005 Terry Fox Coin Collector Card

DATE	DESCRIPTION	QUANTITY SOLD	ISSUE PRICE	FINISH	MS-65
2004	**"Lest We Forget" Poppy Coin Collector Card** to hold Standard 5 coins, Poppy 25¢	N/A	Free	—	5.
2004	**400th Anniversary First French Settlement Collector Card** to hold Standard 5 coins, Île Sainte-Croix 5¢	N/A	Free	—	5.
2005	**"Canada Celebrates Peace" Victory Anniversary Collector Card** to hold Standard 5 coins, 1945-2005 Victory 5¢	N/A	Free	—	5.
2005	**Year of the Veteran Collector Card** to hold Standard 5 coins, Veteran 25¢	N/A	Free	—	5.
2005	**Terry Fox Coin Collector Card** to hold Standard 5 coins, Terry Fox $1	N/A	Free	—	5.
2005	**Creating a Future Without Breast Cancer 25-Cent Collector Card** to hold Standard 5 coins, Breast Cancer 25¢	N/A	Free	—	5.
2010	**11-sided Red Maple Vancouver 2010 Olympic Winter Games Display Card** to hold 10 Olympic and 2 Paralympic 25¢ coins; 2008 Loon Dance $1; and 2010 Inukshuk $1	104,400	4.95	—	5.

COLLECTOR CARDS FOR CIRCULATION COINAGE, 2004-2010 (cont.)

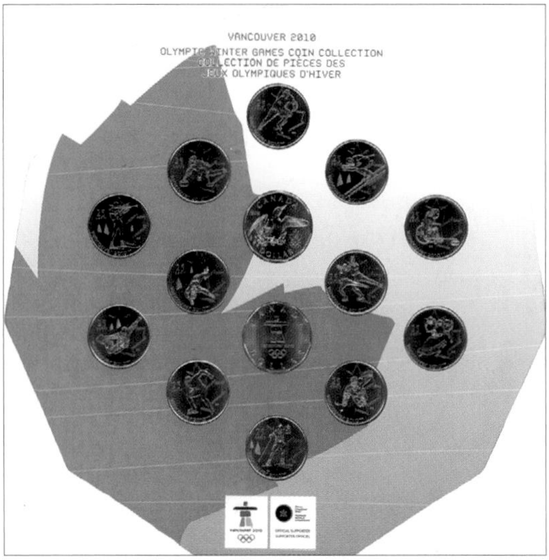

11-sided Red Maple Vancouver 2010 Olympic Winter Games Display Card

Remembrance Day Collector Card

DATE	DESCRIPTION	QUANTITY SOLD	ISSUE PRICE	FINISH	MS-65
2010	**11-sided Red Maple Vancouver 2010 Olympic Winter Games Display Card** holding 10 Olympic and 2 Paralympic 25¢; 2008 Loon Dance $1; 2010 Inukshuk $1	164,295	29.95	Circulation	20.
2010	**Vancouver 2010 Olympic Winter Games Collector Card**, to hold 10 Olympic and 2 Paralympic 25¢; 2008 Loon Dance $1; 2010 Inukshuk $1	N/A	Free	—	5.
2010	**Remembrance Day Collector Card** contains the 2010 25¢ Remembrance Day coin, two die-cut holes to hold the 2004 and 2008 25¢ Poppy coins; Postage paid postcard	N/A	9.95	Circulation	10.

CIRCULATION COIN COLLECTION CARDS, 2007-2010

VANCOUVER 2010 OLYMPIC WINTER AND PARALYMPIC GAMES

The Vancouver 2010 Olympic and Paralympic Winter Games coins consisting of 12 twenty-five cent pieces and two one dollar coins were issued as sets in four different scenic card holders with plastic sleeves.

Vancouver Landscape Coin Collector Card

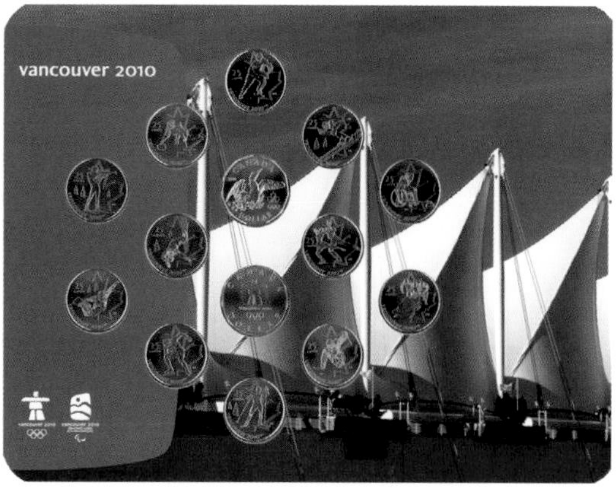

Vancouver City Coin Collector Card

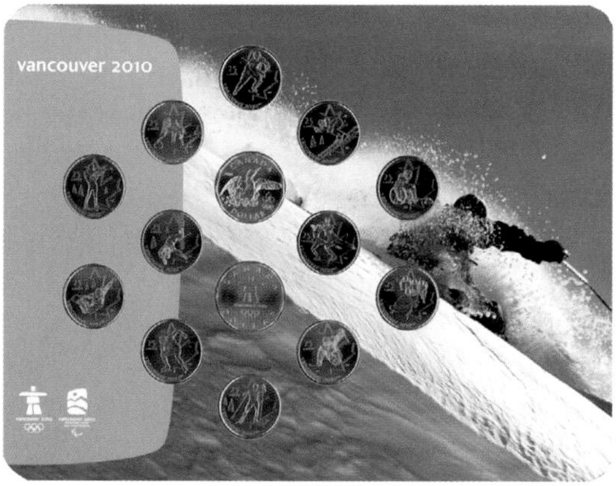

Vancouver Skier Coin Collector Card

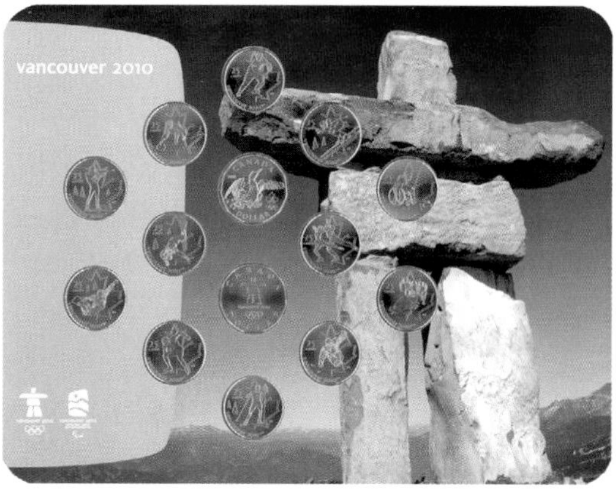

Inukshuk Collector Coin Card

DATE	DESCRIPTION	QUANTITY SOLD	ISSUE PRICE	FINISH	MS-65
2007-2010	**Vancouver Landscape** display card holding 10 Olympic and 2 Paralympic 25¢ coins; $1 Loon Dance, $1 Inukshuk	26,743	29.95	Circulation	20.
2007-2010	**Vancouver City** display card holding 10 Olympic and 2 Paralympic 25¢ coins; $1 Loon Dance, $1 Inukshuk	14,752	29.95	Circulation	20.
2007-2010	**Vancouver Skier** display card holding 10 Olympic and 2 Paralympic 25¢ coins; $1 Loon Dance, $1 Lucky Loonie	32,367	29.95	Circulation	20.
2007-2010	**Inukshuk** display card holding 10 Olympic and 2 Paralympic 25¢ coins; $1 Loon Dance, $1 Inukshuk	79,220	29.95	Circulation	25.

CIRCULATION COIN COLLECTION CARDS, 2010 (cont.)

Each card contains six coins (1¢, 5¢, 10¢, 25¢, $1 and $2) in circulation finish.

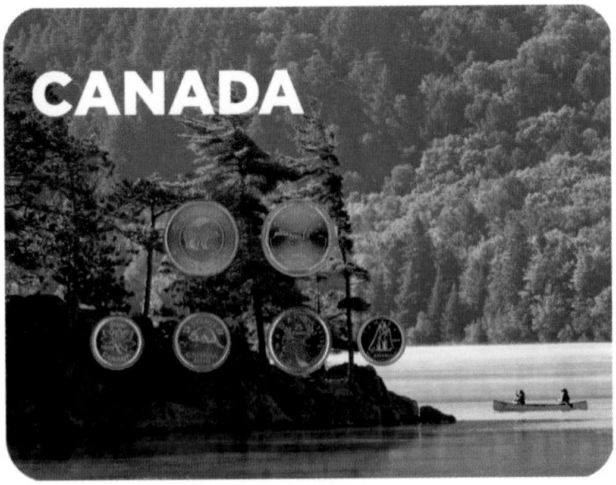

Canoe Coin Collection Card

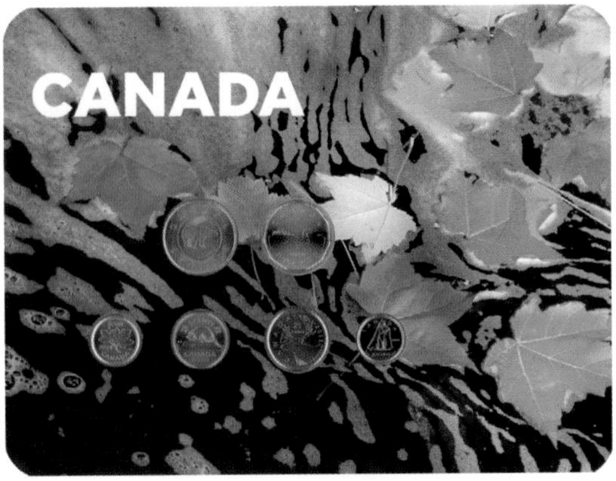

Maple Leaves Coin Collection Card

Polar Bear Coin Collection Card

RCMP Collection Coin Card

DATE	DESCRIPTION	QUANTITY SOLD	ISSUE PRICE	FINISH	MS-65
2010	Canoe Coin Collection Card	N/A	19.95	Circulation	20.
2010	Maple Leaves Coin Collection card	N/A	19.95	Circulation	20.
2010	Polar Bear Coin Collection Card	N/A	19.95	Circulation	20.
2010	RCMP Coin Collection Card	N/A	19.95	Circulation	20.

PROOF-LIKE SETS 1954-1967

SIX COIN SILVER PROOF-LIKE SETS, 1954-1960

1953 saw the first use of the white cardboard six-coin holder that in 1954 became the package for public sale of sets. The holder with the coins included was wrapped in cellophane. The finish on the coins offered acquired the name proof-like.

1954-1959

In 1960 the white cardboard holders appeared with a Royal Canadian Mint domicile. Three varieties of stamps exist. A sealed wooden box containing 250 proof-like sets was available directly from the Mint in 1960.

ROYAL CANADIAN MINT
320 SUSSEX DRIVE
OTTAWA 2, ONTARIO.

Stamp One

ROYAL CANADIAN MINT
OTTAWA CANADA

Stamp Two

ROYAL CANADIAN MINT
OTTAWA CANADA

Stamp One

DATE	QUANTITY SOLD	ISSUE PRICE	FINISH	PL-65
1954 NSF	3,000	2.50	Proof-like	1,500.
1954 SF	Included	2.50	Proof-like	725.
1955	6,300	2.50	Proof-like	500.
1955 ARN	Included	2.50	Proof-like	675.
1956	6,500	2.50	Proof-like	300.
1957	11,862	2.50	Proof-like	200.
1957 1WL	Included	2.50	Proof-like	250.
1958	18,259	2.50	Proof-like	150.
1959	31,577	3.00	Proof-like	75.
1960	64,097	3.00	Proof-like	60.

NOTES ON 1954 TO 1960 PROOF-LIKE SETS

1. The 1954 No Shoulder Fold designation applies only to the one cent coin; the balance of the coins (5) are of the Shoulder Fold variety.
2. Proof-like-65 prices are for sets in their original packaging.
3. The single denomination proof-like coins have now been incorporated into the pricing tables in the circulating coinage section of Volume One.

SIX COIN SILVER PROOF-LIKE SETS, 1961-1967

In 1961 a new system of packaging sets was introduced. The six coins were heat sealed between two layers of pliofilm which was embossed with the words ROYAL CANADIAN MINT. The set was then inserted in an envelope along with an explanatory card.

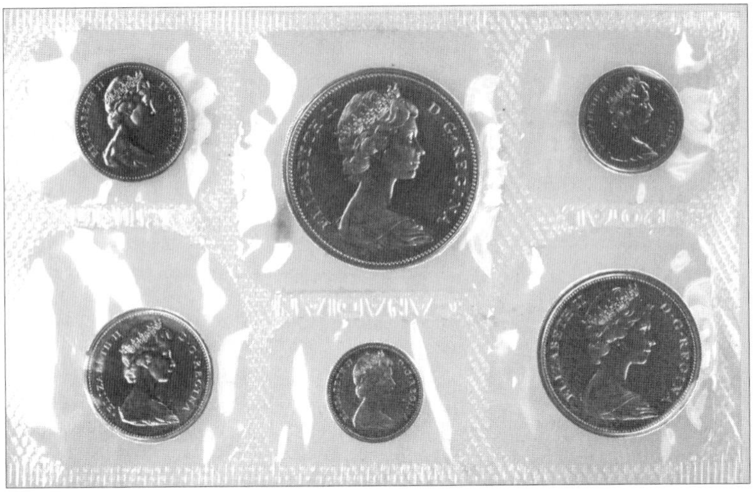

1961-1967

DATE	QUANTITY SOLD	ISSUE PRICE	FINISH	PL- 65
1961	98,373	3.00	Proof-like (PL)	50.
1962	200,950	3.00	Proof-like (PL)	40.
1963	673,006	3.00	Proof-like (PL)	40.
1964	1,653,162	3.00	Proof-like (PL)	40.
1965 Type 1	2,904,352	4.00	Proof-like (PL)	40.
1965 Type 2	Included	4.00	Proof-like (PL)	40.
1966 LB	672,514	4.00	Proof-like (PL)	40.
1967	963,714	4.00	Proof-like (PL)	40.

NOTES ON 1961 TO 1967 PROOF-LIKE SETS

1. The 1961 set, which of course was the first set packaged in the pliofilm, did not come without problems. The one cent coin was prone to discolouring, making a brilliant, red PL-65 cent a scarcity.
2. Only Types One, Small Bead, Pointed 5 and Type 2, Small Bead, Blunt 5, 1965 silver dollars were used in the assembly of proof-like sets for that year.
3. The following variety combinations will be found in the 1965 proof-like sets.
   - **A.** Type 1 dollar with Type 1 cent
   - **B.** Type 1 dollar with Type 3 cent
   - **C.** Type 2 dollar with Type 1 cent
   - **D.** Type 2 dollar with Type 3 cent
4. Since they were not officially released, no 1966 small bead dollars were issued in proof-like sets.

BRILLIANT UNCIRCULATED SETS, 1968-2010

SIX COIN NICKEL BRILLIANT UNCIRCULATED SETS, 1968-1987

This is a continuation of the sets previously offered, except that the 10 cents through one dollar coins were now nickel in composition. Naturally, the one cent and five cents remained the same, and the pliofilm packaging continued. The outer envelope was white with blue printing. The finish on the coins in the sets was brilliant uncirculated: brilliant relief on brilliant background.

In 1977 the quality of the pliofilm sets began to improve, probably as a result of purchase of numismatic presses in 1972 to produce Canada's first officially recognized proof coins for the Montreal Olympic sets. The finish on the coins in the sets was now advertised by the Royal Canadian Mint as brilliant relief against a brilliant background. In 1980 the Mint's marketing department began a restructuring of the selection of coins offered to collectors. The old issue of Proof-like sets (not a term recognized by the R.C.M.) was officially replaced by a new issue called "The Brilliant Uncirculated Set." This set featured one coin of each denomination issued for circulation in Canada. The quality improvement which began in 1977 continued with the 1981 introduction of a confirmed finish on the pliofilm set of "brilliant relief on brilliant background."

In 1985 the Mint experimented with a clear hard plastic package to replace the soft pliofilm package used in previous years. As it did not prove to be practical the experimental package was not adopted. 1987 was the last year the nickel voyageur dollar was used in the brilliant uncirculated sets.

Pliofilm packaging, 1968-1987

1968 NICKEL DOLLAR VARIETIES IN SETS

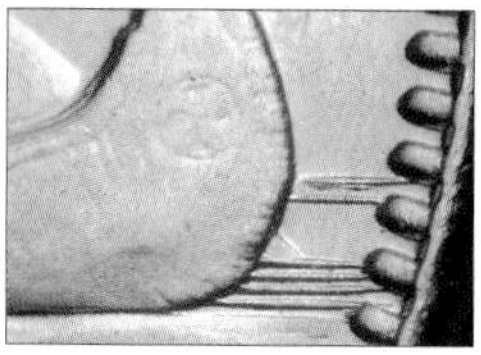

Normal Island

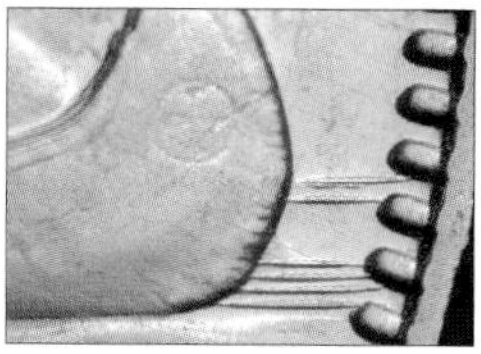

Small Island (S Is)

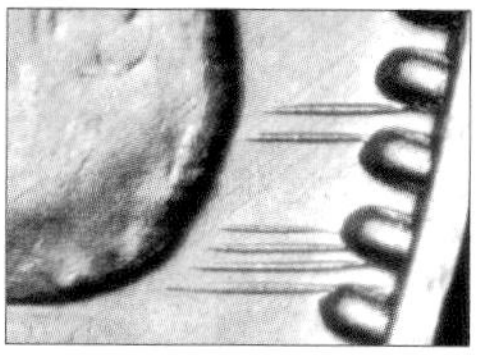

No Island (N Is)

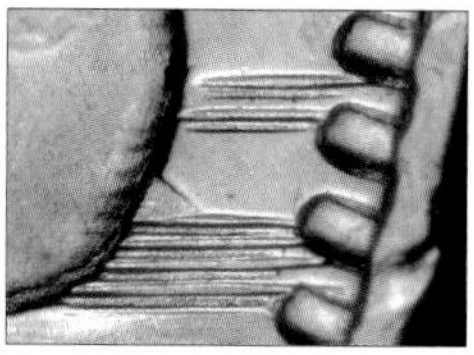

1968 Double Waterlines Doubled Die (DD)

DATE	QUANTITY SOLD	ISSUE PRICE	FINISH	MS-65
1968	521,641	4.00	BU	6.
1968 S. Is.	Included	4.00	BU	17.
1968 No Is.	Included	4.00	BU	15.
1968 DD	Included	4.00	BU	60.
1969	326,203	4.00	BU	7.
1970	349,120	4.00	BU	8.
1971	253,311	4.00	BU	8.
1972	224,275	4.00	BU	8.

1973 TWENTY-FIVE CENT VARIETIES IN SETS

1973 Large Bust
Beads near rim

1973 Reverse

1973 Small Bust
Beads far
from rim

1974 and 1977 NICKEL DOLLAR VARIETIES IN SETS

1974 Double Yoke
Doubled Die, Variety 1

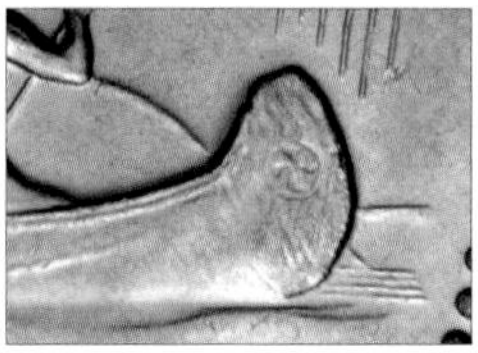

1977 Full Water Lines

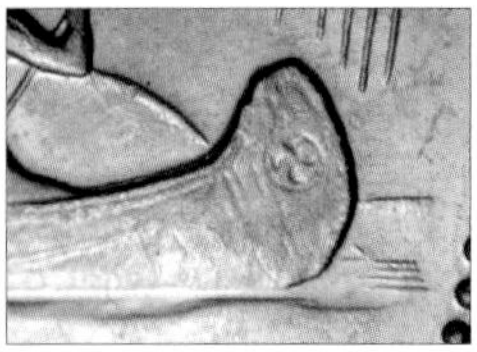

1977 Short Water Lines

DATE	QUANTITY SOLD	ISSUE PRICE	FINISH	MS-65
1973 L.B.	243,695	4.00	BU	375.
1973 S.B.	Included	4.00	BU	9.
1974	213,589	5.00	BU	8.
1974 Var. 1	Included	5.00	BU	600.
1975	197,372	5.00	BU	8.
1976	171,737	5.15	BU	8.
1977	225,307	5.15	BU	9.
1977 SWL	Included	5.15	BU	15.

1978 FIFTY CENT VARIETIES IN SETS

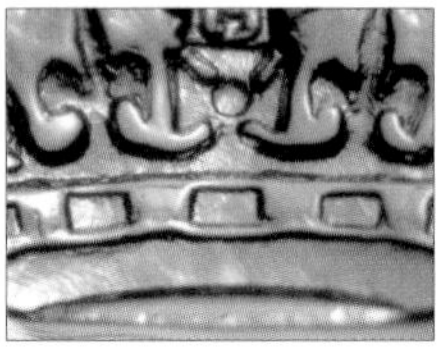

1978 Reverse
Square Jewels (SJ)

1978 Reverse
Round Jewels (RJ)

DATE	QUANTITY SOLD	ISSUE PRICE	FINISH	MS-65
1978 SJ	260,000	5.25	BU	8.
1978 RJ	Included	5.25	BU	20.
1979 BL	187,624	6.25	BU	8.
1979 Ptd	Included	6.25	BU	9.
1980	169,390	8.00	BU	8.
1981	186,250	5.00	BU	8.
1982	203,287	5.00	BU	8.
1983	190,838	5.00	BU	9.
1984	181,415	5.00	BU	9.
1985 Pliofilm	173,924	6.95	BU	10.
1985 Plastic	Included	N/A	BU	40.
1986	167,338	6.95	BU	10.
1987	212,136	6.95	BU	10.

SIX COIN NICKEL BRILLIANT UNCIRCULATED SETS, 1988-1996

In 1987 the nickel Voyageur dollar was retired and in 1988 the bronze Loon dollar was introduced into the Brilliant Uncirculated Set. The finish on the coins in these sets was brilliant relief on a brilliant background.

In 1989 the pliofilm heat sealing dies were modified. The embossed words ROYAL CANADIAN MINT were removed from the dies and replaced with the Circle M logo.

In 1996 the finish on the coins was changed to brilliant relief against a parallel lined background. This finish was first developed for the bullion maple leaf program, and used in 1981 on the Specimen sets issued by the Mint for that year.

DATE	QUANTITY SOLD	ISSUE PRICE	FINISH	MS-65
1988	182,048	6.95	BU	10.
1989	158,636	7.70	BU	15.
1990	170,791	7.70	BU	15.
1991	147,814	8.50	BU	40.
1992	217,597	9.50	BU	18.
1993	171,680	9.50	BU	9.
1993 CNA	Included	9.50	BU	25.
1994	141,676	9.75	BU	13.
1995	143,892	9.75	BU	13.
1996	120,217	11.95	Specimen	40.

NOTES FOR COLLECTORS

1. The 1993 CNA set is packaged in a commemorative envelope.
2. The 1996 Brilliant Uncirculated set contains the 5¢ Near Six 6 variety, see Volume One (65th edition), page 101 for details.

SEVEN COIN NICKEL BRILLIANT UNCIRCULATED SETS WITH SPECIMEN FINISH, 1997

In 1997 the two dollar Polar Bear coin was added to the set. In mid-1997 the Royal Canadian Mint transferred production of the Brilliant Uncirculated Sets to the Winnipeg mint. The Ottawa and Winnipeg issues of 1997 can be distinguished by the method of packaging, and by the finish on the two dollar coins. Those produced in Ottawa have a brilliant, or shiny, polar bear, whereas on coins produced at Winnipeg, the bear has a frosted appearance. They coins are indicated by (O) for Ottawa and (W) for Winnipeg in the listings. No mint marks appear on 1997-dated coins. The finishes on both sets (1997) are technically equal, being Brilliant Relief on Parallel Lined background.

1997 Ottawa Brilliant Uncirculated Set with Specimen Finish
The $1.00 Loon is at top right with the $2.00 (shiny) Polar Bear at top centre

1997 Winnipeg Brilliant Uncirculated Set with Specimen Finish
The $1.00 Loon is at top left with the $2.00 (frosted) Polar Bear at top centre

DATE	DESCRIPTION	QUANTITY SOLD	ISSUE PRICE	FINISH	SP-65
1997 (O)	Loon/Polar Bear	174,692	13.95	Specimen	15.
1997 (W)	Loon/Polar Bear	Included	13.95	Specimen	12.

SEVEN COIN NICKEL BRILLIANT UNCIRCULATED SETS, 1998-2000

In 1998 the finish on the coins returned to a brilliant relief with a brilliant background, and this was continued until 2000. To distinguish the sets produced at the Winnipeg mint in 1998, a "W" was added to all coins from the one cent through to the two dollar coin. This is the first time the Canadian mint placed a mint mark on Canadian coins. When the set production was moved back to Ottawa, in mid-1998, the coins were struck without a mint mark. In 2000, the mint mark appeared again as set production was moved back to the Winnipeg mint. The packaging of the sets in transparent plastic film was continued, and 2000 was the last year of issue for sets containing pure nickel coinage. The Winnipeg mint mark 'W' is found on the obverse, to the lower left of the portrait.

"W" Mint Mark

DATE	DESCRIPTION	QUANTITY SOLD	ISSUE PRICE	FINISH	MS-65
1998	Loon/Polar Bear	145,439	13.95	BU	25.
1998 W	Loon/Polar Bear	Included	13.95	BU	30.
1999	Loon/Polar Bear	117,318	13.95	BU	20.
1999	Loon/Nunavut	74,821	13.95	BU	20.
1999	Loon/Nun. Mule	Included	13.95	BU	325.
2000	Loon/Knowledge	186,985	15.95	BU	20.
2000 W	Loon/Polar Bear	Included	15.95	BU	20.

Note: See page 109 for the listing and explanation of the 1999 Nunavut Mule.

FIVE COIN MULTI-PLY PLATED STEEL TEST SET FOR 1999

This set is a Royal Canadian Mint test token set (TTS-3); see Volume One (65th edition), page 263, for a complete listing.

SEVEN COIN MULTI-PLY PLATED STEEL BRILLIANT UNCIRCULATED SETS, "P" COMPOSITION MARK, 2001-2006

The first issue of the new multi-ply plated steel, brilliant uncirculated sets took place in 2001. Five coins, one cent through fifty cents, all carried the new composition mark "P". The $1.00 and $2.00 coins did not; they were struck on the standard planchets for those denominations. The finish on the multi-ply plated steel coins is brilliant relief on a brilliant background, continuing from the 2000 nickel sets.

In 2002, to commemorate the Golden Jubilee of Queen Elizabeth II, the Mint issued double dated (1952-2002) plated steel coinage for circulation. These coins were used in the collectors' sets, and are identical to those of the previous year except for the double dates. Special Edition Jubilee Sets are found on page 260.

Mid year 2003 the tiara portrait of Elizabeth II, which had been used since 1990, was replaced with the new uncrowned portrait by Susanna Blunt. The first set with this portrait was issued in 2004.

DATE	DESCRIPTION	QUANTITY SOLD	ISSUE PRICE	FINISH	MS-65
2001P	Loon/Bear	115,897	15.95	BU	20.
2002P (1952-)	Loon/Bear	100,467	15.95	BU	20.
2003P	Loon/Bear	94,126	15.95	BU	30.
2004P	Loon/Bear	96,847	15.95	BU	30.
2005P	Loon/Bear	114,650	15.95	BU	20.
2006P (1996-)	Loon/Bear	93,361	15.95	BU	30.

Note: The 2006 Brilliant Uncirculated set contains the 10th anniversary two dollar coin, double dated 1996-2006.

SEVEN COIN MULTI-PLY PLATED STEEL BRILLIANT UNCIRCULATED SETS, MAPLE LEAF LOGO, 2007-2010

Two thousand and seven saw the first use of coins carrying the new Royal Canadian Mint logo (Circle M) in brilliant uncirculated sets.

Also in 2007, two different pairs of dies were used to strike the ten cent pieces. One pair has an obverse die carrying a small, far logo and reverse die with a curved 7. The other pair has an obverse die carrying a large, near logo and a reverse die with a straight 7

In 2009 brilliant uncirculated sets were assembled in two locations, the Mint in Ottawa and an outside contractor. Sets assembled within the Mint have the Circle M logo embossed into the pliofilm packaging, while sets assembled by the contractor do not.

Ten Cents 2007 Obverse: Small, Far RCM Logo

Ten Cents 2007 Reverse: Curved 7

Ten Cents 2007 Obverse: Large, Near RCM Logo

Ten Cents 2007 Reverse: Straight 7

DATE	DESCRIPTION	QUANTITY SOLD	ISSUE PRICE	FINISH	MS-65
2007	Standard 7 coins, Small RCM Logo / Curved 7	45,733	21.95	BU	30.
2007	Standard 7 coins, Large RCM Logo / Straight 7	Incl. above	21.95	BU	125.
2008	Standard 7 coins	42,833	21.95	BU	20.
2009	Standard 7 coins, with RCM logo embossed into pliofilm	37,980	22.95	BU	23.
2009	Standard 7 coins, without RCM logo embossed into pliofilm	Incl. above	22.95	BU	23.
2009	Standard 7 coins, without RCM logo; World Money Fair, Berlin, Germany	1,000	50.00	BU	50.
2010	Standard 7 coins	55,000	23.95	BU	25.

NOTES FOR COLLECTORS

1. In the description column of the pricing table the use of the word "standard" refers to the everyday denominations in use for daily transactions.
2. While the 2007 ten-cent coin with the Large, Near RCM Logo obverse and the Straight 7 Reverse is a relatively common coin, the rarity factor changes when it is struck with a Brilliant Uncirculated finish, and is packaged in a Brilliant Uncirculated set.
3. The 2009 Brilliant Uncirculated sets sold at the World Money Fair in Berlin, Germany, included a certificate of authenticity for the Fair. The set was issued in a limited edition of 1,000.

SEVEN COIN NICKEL CUSTOM SETS 1971-1975

The custom set contains one coin of each denomination, with an extra cent to show the obverse. The finish of the coins is identical to the corresponding year of brilliant uncirculated, brilliant relief on a brilliant background.

Cases: **1971:** Coins in black vinyl-covered case with Canada's coat of arms and the word "CANADA" stamped in gold on the top.

1972-1973: As 1971, except the outer case is red.

1974-1975: As 1971, except the outer case is maroon.

1973 Custom Set

DATE	DESCRIPTION	QUANTITY SOLD	ISSUE PRICE	FINISH	MS-65
1971		33,517	6.50	BU	10.
1972		38,198	6.50	BU	10.
1973	Large Bust 25¢	49,376	6.50	BU	375.
1973	Small Bust 25¢	Included	6.50	BU	10.
1974		44,296	8.00	BU	10.
1975		36,581	8.00	BU	10.

Note: For illustrations of the large and small bust varieties of the 1973 twenty-five cent coin see page 254.

SPECIAL EDITION BRILLIANT UNCIRCULATED SETS, 2002-2010

QUEEN ELIZABETH II, DIADEM PORTRAIT, GOLDEN JUBILEE, 1952-2002

The Special Edition Brilliant Uncirculated Set of 1952-2002 contains the Golden Jubilee 50-cent piece and the 1952-2002 Canada Day 25-cent coin; the balance of the coins are the regular double-dated Jubilee 1952-2002P issue.

Golden Jubilee, 1952-2002

DATE	DESCRIPTION	QUANTITY SOLD	ISSUE PRICE	FINISH	MS-65
2002P (1952-)	Diadem Portrait Obverse	49,869	15.95	BU	20.

QUEEN ELIZABETH II, MATURE PORTRAIT, 2003

In mid-year 2003, the "Diadem Portrait" of Queen Elizabeth, by Dora de Pédery-Hunt, was replaced by a more mature portrait by Susanna Blunt. The Special Edition Brilliant Uncirculated Set of 2003 contains the seven circulating denominations, with the new effigy of Queen Elizabeth II. This set was struck at the Winnipeg Mint, and naturally carries the mint mark W (WP). The lower denominations, one cent to fifty cents also carry the composition mark "P."

Mature Portrait Obverses

Mint and Composition Mark

DATE	DESCRIPTION	QUANTITY SOLD	ISSUE PRICE	FINISH	MS-65
2003WP	Mature Portrait Obverse	71,142	15.95	BU	30.

CENTENARIES OF ALBERTA AND SASKATCHEWAN, 2005

This Special Edition Brilliant Uncirculated Set was issued to commemorate the centenaries of both Alberta and Saskatchewan. It contains two commemorative twenty-five cent coins, one depicting an oil derrick (Alberta), the other the Western Meadowlark (Saskatchewan). The balance of the coins are the regular 2005P issue.

Alberta and Saskatchewan 100th Anniversary Set

Alberta Centenary 25¢ Coin

Saskatchewan Centenary 25¢ Coin

DATE	DESCRIPTION	QUANTITY SOLD	ISSUE PRICE	FINISH	MS-65
2005P	Centenaries of Alberta and Saskatchewan	N/A	15.95	BU	20.

10TH ANNIVERSARY OF THE TWO DOLLAR COIN, RCM LOGO, 2006

The Special Edition Brilliant Uncirculated Set of 2006 contains the "Churchill" two dollar coin. The obverse of all coins in this set feature the unique Royal Canadian Mint logo that was introduced to Canadian circulating coins in 2006.

10th Anniversary of the Two Dollar Coins

Churchill Two Dollar Coin

DATE	DESCRIPTION	QUANTITY SOLD	ISSUE PRICE	FINISH	MS-65
2006	10th Anniversary; Churchill two dollar coin	31,636	19.95	BU	20.

VANCOUVER 2010 WINTER OLYMPIC GAMES, 2007-2008

Over the four years, 2007-2010, all Vancouver 2010 twenty-five cent coins, plus the two bronze one dollar coins, were incorporated into Special Edition Brilliant Uncirculated Sets.

2007 Vancouver 2010 Olympic Winter Games

2007 Vancouver Logo Obverse

Wheelchair Curling Reverse

Vancouver Logo Mule

The Vancouver Olympic obverse was paired with the Paralympic Wheelchair Curling reverse to form a mule which is found only in the 2007 Vancouver Olympic Winter Games Special Edition Set.

2008 Vancouver 2010 Olympic Winter Games

Note For Collectors

The 2007 Special Edition Brilliant Uncirculated Set contains the 10-cent variety:
Small, Far Logo Obverse / Curved 7 Reverse

DATE	DESCRIPTION	QUANTITY SOLD	ISSUE PRICE	FINISH	MS-65
2007	Standard 5 coins 1¢, 5¢, 10¢, 50¢ and $2; 5 x 25¢ Alpine Skiing, Biathlon, Curling, Ice Hockey, Wheelchair Curling, $1 Loon Dance; (11 coins)	28,852	23.95	BU	30.
2007	As above, but with the Mule 25¢ Vancouver Logo Obverse paired with the Wheelchair Curling Reverse	Included	23.95	BU	450.
2008	Standard 5 coins 1¢, 5¢, 10¢, 50¢ and $2; 4 x 25¢ Bobsleigh, Figure Skating,, Freestyle Skiing, Snow Boarding;, $1 Loon Dance; (10 coins)	16,471	23.95	BU	30.

VANCOUVER 2010 OLYMPIC WINTER GAMES, 2009-2010

The Golden Moments Set commemorates the Olympic gold medals won by the Men's and Women's Hockey Teams in 2002, and Cindy Klassen's gold medal of 2006. These quarters have the partial maple leaf painted red.

2009 Vancouver 2010 Olympic Winter Games

2010 Golden Moments Special Edition Set

DATE	DESCRIPTION	QUANTITY SOLD	ISSUE PRICE	FINISH	MS-65
2009	Standard 5 coins 1¢, 5¢, 10¢, 50¢ and $2; 3 x 25¢ Cross Country Skiing, Ice Sledge Hockey, Speed Skating, $1 Loon Dance; (9 coins)	11,313	23.95	BU	25.
2010	Standard 5 coins 1¢, 5¢, 10¢, 50¢ and $2; 3 x 25¢ Painted Men's Ice Hockey 2002, Painted Women's Ice Hockey 2002, Painted Speed Skating, Cindy Klassen; $1 Inukshuk; (9 coins)	8,564	27.95	BU	30.

2010 SPECIAL EDITION UNCIRCULATED SET

This 8-coin set features the standard 1¢, 5¢, 10¢, 50¢ and $2 coins, but also includes the 2010 25¢ Remembrance Day Poppy coin, and two one-dollar coins which commemorate the 100th Anniversary of the Royal Canadian Navy, and the Saskatchewan Roughriders Centennial. The set is shrink wrapped in clear plastic.

25¢ Remembrance Day Poppies

$1 Royal Canadian Navy

$1 Saskatchewan Roughriders

DATE	DESCRIPTION	QUANTITY SOLD	ISSUE PRICE	FINISH	MS-65
2010	Special Edition Uncirculated Set	15,000	25.95	Uncirculated	30.

BABY GIFT SETS, 1995-2010

BUNDLE OF JOY / TINY TREASURES

NICKEL BRILLIANT UNCIRCULATED SETS, 1995-2000.

First issued in 1995, the brilliant uncirculated set of coins was specially packaged for the gift market using the six coins from the brilliant uncirculated set of that year. In 1997 this set was expanded to include the two dollar polar bear coin. In 1998 the name changed from Bundle of Joy to Tiny Treasures Brilliant Uncirculated sets. In the same year the packaging of the sets of Tiny Treasures changed from card displays to clear plastic display units. The movement of set production to Winnipeg and back to Ottawa that occurred in 1998 also affected the Oh! Canada! and Tiny Treasures sets. In 2000 production of the sets occurred in both the Ottawa and Winnipeg mints.

1997 Bundle of Joy Set

DATE	DESCRIPTION	QUANTITY SOLD	ISSUE PRICE	FINISH	MS-65
1995	Standard 6 coins; Folder	36,443	19.95	BU	15.
1996	Standard 6 coins; Folder	56,618	19.95	BU	15.
1997	Standard 7 coins; Folder	55,199	21.95	BU	15.
1998	Standard 7 coins; Display case	46,139	21.95	BU	20.
1998W	Winnipeg Mint, 7 coins; Display case	12,625	21.95	BU	20.
1999	Standard 7 coins; Display case	67,694	21.95	BU	20.
2000	Standard 7 coins; Display case	82,964	21.95	BU	22.
2000W	Winnipeg Mint, 7 coins; Display case	Included	21.95	BU	22.

TINY TREASURES

MULTI-PLY PLATED STEEL BRILLIANT UNCIRCULATED SETS, 2001-2003.

As with the Brilliant Uncirculated sets of 2001, the nickel coinage of the previous year was replaced with the new patented multi-ply plated steel coins. In the 2002 set all coins bore the double dates 1952-2002 to commemorate the 50th anniversary of Her Majesty Queen Elizabeth II's accession to the throne. Two thousand and three was the last year of issue for the Tiny Treasures sets.

2002 Tiny Treasures Set

DATE	DESCRIPTION	QUANTITY SOLD	ISSUE PRICE	FINISH	MS-65
2001P	Standard 7 coins; Display case	52,085	22.95	BU	25.
2002P (1952-)	Standard 7 coins; Display case	51,491	22.95	BU	25.
2003P	Standard 7 coins; Display case	43,197	22.95	BU	25.

BABY GIFT SETS

MULTI-PLY PLATED STEEL BRILLIANT UNCIRCULATED SETS, 2004-2005.

With the revamping of the Gift Sets in 2004, a name change took place, Tiny Treasures become Baby Gift Sets.

DATE	DESCRIPTION	QUANTITY SOLD	ISSUE PRICE	FINISH	MS-65
2004P	Standard 7 coins; Folder	53,726	19.95	BU	20.
2005P	Standard 7 coins; Folder	42,245	19.95	BU	20.

BABY GIFT SETS (cont.)

MULTI-PLY PLATED STEEL UNCIRCULATED SETS, 2004-2010.

Beginning in 2006 the finish on the coins in these sets was changed to uncirculated. The uncirculated sets were struck and assembled at the Winnipeg Mint, however, they do not carry the "W" mint mark.

In 2007 the Caribou design on the twenty-five cent coin was replaced with a coloured design. The ten cent coins contained in the 2007 Birthday Gift Sets are the Large, Near Logo obverse / Straight 7 reverse variety.

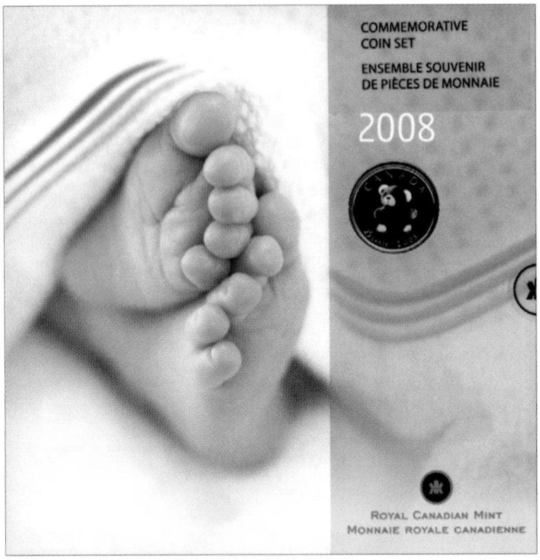

2008 Commemorative Coin Set

2009 Baby Gift Set

DATE	DESCRIPTION	QUANTITY SOLD	ISSUE PRICE	FINISH	MS-65
2006P	Standard 7 coins; Folder	33,786	19.95	Uncirculated	20.
2007	Standard 6 coins; Coloured 25¢ Rattle; Folder	30,090	19.95	Uncirculated	20.
2008	Standard 6 coins; Coloured 25¢ Teddy Bear; Folder	29,819	19.95	Uncirculated	20.
2009	Standard 6 coins; Coloured 25¢ Teddy Bear and Blanket; Folder	25,182	19.95	Uncirculated	25.
2010	Standard 6 coins; Coloured 25¢ Baby Carriage; Folder	N/A	19.95	Uncirculated	20.

Note: For the coloured designs of the twenty-five cent coins contained in the sets of 2007-2010 see pages 22 and 23.

BIRTHDAY GIFT SETS, 2004-2008

MULTI-PLY PLATED STEEL BRILLIANT UNCIRCULATED SETS, 2004-2005.

The Baby Gift Set was first introduced in 2004. The finish on these seven-coin sets is brilliant uncirculated.

2006 Birthday Gift Set

2008 Commemorative Coin Set

DATE	DESCRIPTION	QUANTITY SOLD	ISSUE PRICE	FINISH	MS-65
2004P	Standard 7 coins; Folder	N/A	19.95	BU	20.
2005P	Standard 7 coins; Folder	20,227	19.95	BU	20.

MULTI-PLY PLATED STEEL UNCIRCULATED SETS, 2006-2008.

Beginning in 2006 the finish on the coins contained in the Baby Gift Sets was uncirculated. The uncirculated sets were struck and assembled at the Winnipeg Mint, however, they do not carry the "W" mint mark.

In 2007 the Caribou design on the twenty-five cent coin was replaced with a coloured design. The ten cent coins contained in the 2007 Birthday Gift Sets are the Large, Near Logo obverse / Straight 7 reverse variety.

For 2008 the set carried the name "Commemorative Coin Set."

The Birthday Gift Set was discontinued in 2009 and replaced by the Cards With Coins series, see page 24.

DATE	DESCRIPTION	QUANTITY SOLD	ISSUE PRICE	FINISH	MS-65
2006P	Standard 7 coins; Folder	11,984	19.95	Uncirculated	20.
2007	Standard 6 coins; Coloured 25¢ Balloons; Folder	12,547	19.95	Uncirculated	20.
2008	Standard 6 coins; Coloured 25¢ Party Hat; Folder	11,366	19.95	Uncirculated	20.

Note: For the coloured design of the twenty-five cent coins contained in the sets of 2007-2008, see page 22.

CONGRATULATIONS / GRADUATION GIFT SETS, 2004-2008

MULTI-PLY PLATED STEEL BRILLIANT UNCIRCULATED SETS, 2004-2005.

This gift set in 2004 was directed at the school or college graduation market. By 2006 the scope was broadened to a Congratulations Gift Set. The Graduation Sets have a brilliant uncirculated finish, while the Congratulations Gift Sets have an uncirculated finish.

2005 Graduation Gift Set

2008 Congratulations Gift Set

DATE	DESCRIPTION	QUANTITY SOLD	ISSUE PRICE	FINISH	MS-65
2004P	Graduation Set, Standard 7 coins; Folder	22,094	19.95	BU	20.
2005P	Graduation Set, Standard 7 coins; Folder	12,411	19.95	BU	20.

MULTI-PLY PLATED STEEL UNCIRCULATED SETS, 2006-2008.

Beginning in 2006 the finish on the coins in these sets was changed to uncirculated. The uncirculated sets were struck and assembled at the Winnipeg Mint, however, they do not carry the "W" mint mark.

The ten cent coins contained in the 2007 Congratulations Gift Sets are the Large, Near Logo obverse / Straight 7 reverse variety.

These sets were discontinued in 2009 and replaced by the Cards With Coins Series, see page 24.

DATE	DESCRIPTION	QUANTITY SOLD	ISSUE PRICE	FINISH	MS-65
2006P	Congratulations Set, Standard 7 coins; Folder	9,428	19.95	Uncirculated	20.
2007	Congratulations Set, Standard 6 coins; Coloured 25¢ Fireworks; Folder	9,571	19.95	Uncirculated	20.
2008	Congratulations Set, Standard 6 coins; Coloured 25¢ Trophy; Folder	6,821	19.95	Uncirculated	20.

Note: For the coloured designs of the twenty-five cent coins contained in the sets of 2007-2008, see page 22.

HOLIDAY GIFT SETS, 2004-2010

MULTI-PLY PLATED STEEL, BRILLIANT UNCIRCULATED SETS, 2004-2005.

In 2004 the Royal Canadian Mint introduced a new Holiday Gift Set to their product line. This set was issued in a colourful Season's Greetings folder and included a coloured twenty-five cent coin in place of the standard Caribou design. The finish on all coins is Brilliant Uncirculated.

2005 Holiday Gift Set

2008 Holiday Gift Set

DATE	DESCRIPTION	QUANTITY SOLD	ISSUE PRICE	FINISH	MS-65 NC
2004P	Standard 6 coins; Coloured 25¢ Santa Claus; Folder	22,094	19.95	BU	40.
2005P	Standard 6 coins; Coloured 25¢ Christmas Stocking; Folder	72,831	19.95	BU	20.

MULTI-PLY PLATED STEEL, UNCIRCULATED SETS 2006-2010.

In 2006 the finish on all coins contained in these sets was changed to uncirculated.

The ten cent coins contained in the 2007 Holiday Gift Sets are the Large, Near Logo obverse / Straight 7 reverse variety.

DATE	DESCRIPTION	QUANTITY SOLD	ISSUE PRICE	FINISH	MS-65 NC
2006P	Standard 6 coins; Coloured 25¢ Santa in Sleigh and Reindeer; Folder	99,258	19.95	Uncirculated	20.
2007	Standard 6 coins; Coloured 25¢ Christmas Tree; Folder	66,267	19.95	Uncirculated	20.
2008	Standard 6 coins; Coloured 25¢ Santa, Folder	42,344	19.95	Uncirculated	20.
2009	Standard 6 coins; Coloured 25¢ Santa, Three Maple Leaves; Folder	32,967	19.95	Uncirculated	20.
2010	Standard 6 coins; Coloured 25¢ Santa, Christmas Tree; Folder	N/A	19.95	Uncirculated	20.

Note: For the coloured designs of the twenty-five cent coins contained in the sets of 2004-2010, see page 17.

NHL TEAM GIFT SETS, UNCIRCULATED, 2006-2009

MULTI-PLY PLATED STEEL, UNCIRCULATED SETS, 2006-2009.

These sets were introduced for the 2005-2006 hockey season with only three Canadian NHL teams being represented: Montreal Canadiens, Ottawa Senators and the Toronto Maple Leafs. Each set contained the standard six coins, 1¢, 5¢, 10¢, 50¢, $1 and $2, with the twenty-five cent Caribou design being replaced by a coloured NHL team logo. For the 2006-2007 season all six Canadian NHL teams were represented.

In the Fall of 2008 the sets issued for the 2008-2009 season had the twenty-five cent Caribou design as one of the standard 6 coins, but the loon design on the one dollar coin was replaced by a coloured team jersey logo.

The finish on all sets is uncirculated.

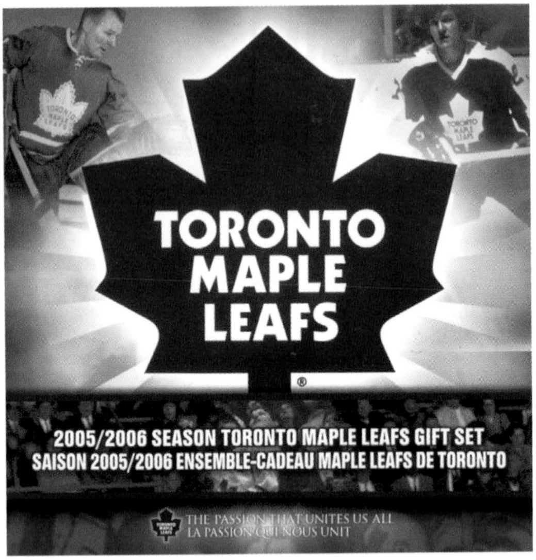

2005-2006 Season
Toronto Maple Leafs

2006-2007 Season
Toronto Maple Leafs

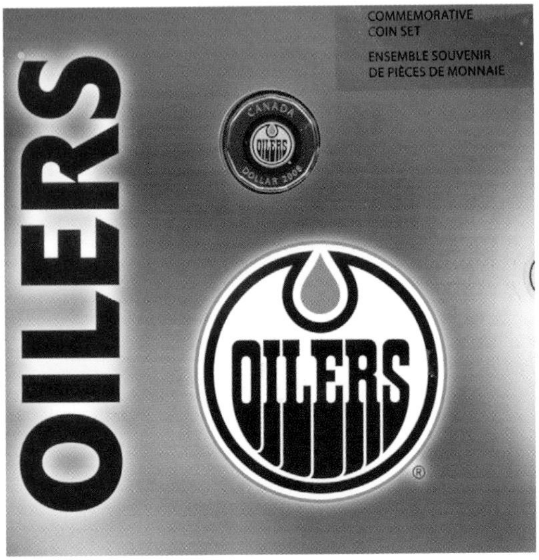

2007-2008 Season
Edmonton Oilers

2008-2009 Season
Calgary Flames

MULTI-PLY PLATED STEEL, UNCIRCULATED SETS, 2006-2009, PRICING TABLE.

DATE	DESCRIPTION	QUANTITY SOLD	ISSUE PRICE	FINISH	MS-65
2006P	Montreal Canadiens, Standard 6 coin set; Coloured 25¢	11,765	24.95	Uncirculated	20.
2006P	Ottawa Senators; Standard 6 coin set; Coloured 25¢	Included	24.95	Uncirculated	20.
2006P	Toronto Maple Leafs; Standard 6 coin set; Coloured 25¢	Included	24.95	Uncirculated	20.
2007	Calgary Flames; Standard 6 coins; Coloured 25¢	1.082	24.95	Uncirculated	20.
2007	Edmonton Oilers; Standard 6 coins; Coloured 25¢	2,214	24.95	Uncirculated	20.
2007	Montreal Canadiens; Standard 6 coins; Coloured 25¢	4,091	24.95	Uncirculated	20.
2007	Ottawa Senators; Standard 6 coin set; Coloured 25¢	2,474	24.95	Uncirculated	20.
2007	Toronto Maple Leafs; Standard 6 coin set; Coloured 25¢	5,365	24.95	Uncirculated	20.
2007	Vancouver Canucks; Standard 6 coin set; Coloured 25¢	1,526	24.95	Uncirculated	20.
2008	Calgary Flames; Standard 6 coins; Coloured $1	N/A	24.95	Uncirculated	25.
2008	Edmonton Oilers; Standard 6 coins; Coloured $1	N/A	24.95	Uncirculated	25.
2008	Montreal Canadiens; Standard 6 coins; Coloured $1	N/A	24.95	Uncirculated	25.
2008	Ottawa Senators; Standard 6 coin set; Coloured $1	N/A	24.95	Uncirculated	25.
2008	Toronto Maple Leafs; Standard 6 coin set; Coloured $1	N/A	24.95	Uncirculated	25.
2008	Vancouver Canucks; Standard 6 coin set; Coloured $1	N/A	24.95	Uncirculated	25.
2009	Calgary Flames; Standard 6 coins; Coloured $1	382	24.95	Uncirculated	25.
2009	Edmonton Oilers; Standard 6 coins; Coloured $1	472	24.95	Uncirculated	25.
2009	Montreal Canadiens; Standard 6 coins; Coloured $1	4,857	24.95	Uncirculated	25.
2009	Ottawa Senators; Standard 6 coin set; Coloured $1	387	24.95	Uncirculated	25.
2009	Toronto Maple Leafs; Standard 6 coin set; Coloured $1	1,328	24.95	Uncirculated	25.
2009	Vancouver Canucks; Standard 6 coin set; Coloured $1	794	24.95	Uncirculated	25.

NOTES

1. For the coloured designs of the twenty-five cent coins used in the NHL Team Gift Sets see page 21.
2. For the coloured designs of the one dollar coins used in the NHL Team Gift Sets see pages 98-101.
3. The “Quantity Sold” numbers may or may not be reported in a single year, but may carry over to the following year. The collector must wait a year or two before the final numbers are known.
4. No “Quantity Sold” number was listed in the 2008 Royal Canadian Mint Report for the 2008 issue of NHL Team Gift Sets.
5. The 2007 NHL Team Gift Sets contain the Large, Near Logo obverse / Straight 7 reverse variety ten cent coin.

OH! CANADA! GIFT SETS, 1994-2010

BRILLIANT UNCIRCULATED SETS, 1994-2000

First issued in 1994, this set included the bronze dollar plus the other five denominations for that year. In 1997 this set was expanded to include the two dollar polar bear coin. In 1998 the packaging of the Oh! Canada! Gift Sets changed from card displays to clear plastic display units. The coins in the Oh! Canada! set are identical in finish to those of the corresponding year of the Brilliant Uncirculated Set.

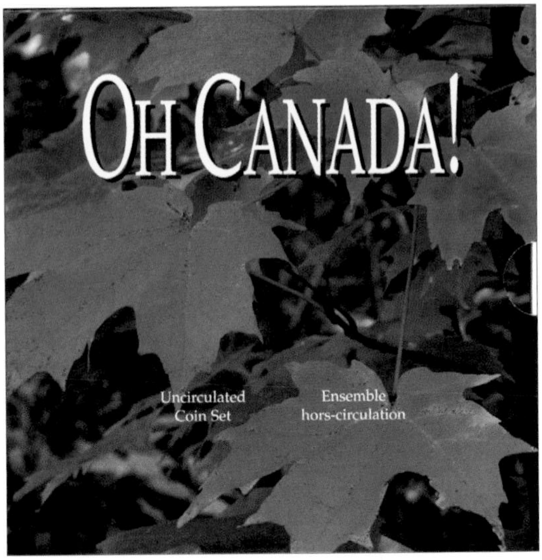

1997 Oh! Canada! Gift Set with Flying Loon Dollar

DATE	DESCRIPTION	QUANTITY SOLD	ISSUE PRICE	FINISH	MS-65
1994	Standard 6 coins	18,794	16.95	BU	15.
1995	Standard 5 coins, Peacekeeping dollar	50,927	16.95	BU	12.
1996	Standard 6 coins	31,083	16.95	BU	20.
1997	Standard 6 coins, Flying Loon dollar	84,124	21.95	Specimen	50.
1998	Standard 7 coins	42,710	21.95	BU	25.
1998W	Winnipeg Mint, 7 coins	24,792	21.95	BU	20.
1999	Standard 7 coins	82,754	21.95	BU	25.
2000	Standard 7 coins	107,884	21.95	BU	20.
2000W	Standard 7 coins	Included	21.95	BU	20.

MULTI-PLY PLATED STEEL BRILLIANT UNCIRCULATED SETS, 2001-2005.

In 2001 the five subsidiary coins of the Oh! Canada! set were replaced by the five multi-ply plated steel coins.

In the 2002 set all coins bear the double dates 1952-2002 to commemorate the 50th anniversary of Her Majesty Queen Elizabeth II's accession to the throne.

Beginning in 2004 the coins carried the new Susanna Blunt effigy of Queen Elizabeth II. The coins in the "Oh Canada!" set were identical in finish to coins of the Brilliant Uncirculated Set of that year.

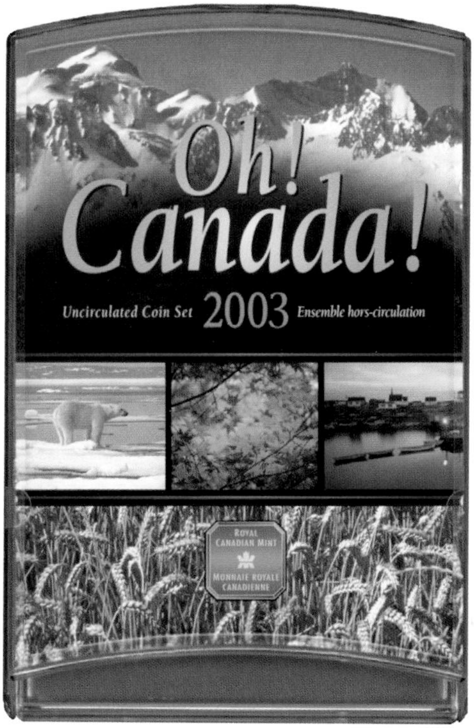

2003 Oh! Canada! Gift Set

DATE	DESCRIPTION	QUANTITY SOLD	ISSUE PRICE	FINISH	MS-65
2001P	Standard 7 coins	66,726	22.95	BU	25.
2002P (1952-)	Standard 7 coins, Double Date	61,484	22.95	BU	25.
2003P	Standard 7 coins	51,146	23.95	BU	25.
2004P	Standard 7 coins	53,111	23.95	BU	25.
2005P	Standard 7 coins	40,890	19.95	BU	20.

MULTI-PLY PLATED STEEL UNCIRCULATED SET, 2006.

In 2006 the finish on all coins contained in these sets was changed to uncirculated. This was also the last year the composition mark "P" would be seen on coins in the sets.

DATE	DESCRIPTION	QUANTITY SOLD	ISSUE PRICE	FINISH	MS-65
2006P	Standard 7 coins	28,213	19.95	Uncirculated	22.

MULTI-PLY PLATED STEEL UNCIRCULATED SETS, 2007-2010.

Starting in 2007 several changes were made to the Oh! Canada! set. All coins now carried the Royal Canadian Mint logo on the obverse, and the Caribou design on the twenty-five cent coin was replaced by a coloured design. For the coloured designs of the twenty-five cent coins of 2007-2010, see page 22 and 23.

2008 Oh! Canada! Gift Set

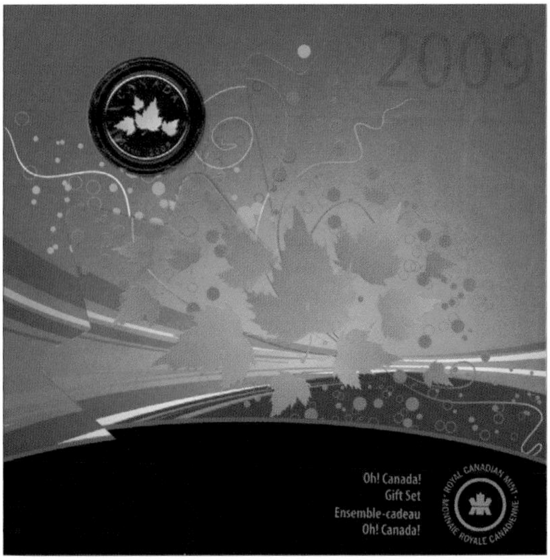

2009 Oh! Canada! Gift Set

DATE	DESCRIPTION	QUANTITY SOLD	ISSUE PRICE	FINISH	MS-65
2007	Standard 6 coins, Coloured 25¢ Maple Leaf; Folder	24,096	19.95	Uncirculated	20.
2008	Standard 6 coins, Coloured 25¢ Canadian Flag; Folder	30,567	19.95	Uncirculated	22.
2009	Standard 6 coins, Coloured 25¢ Four Maple Leaves; Folder	14,451	19.95	Uncirculated	20.
2010	Standard 6 coins, Coloured 25¢ Three Maple Leaves; Folder	N/A	19.95	Uncirculated	20.

Note: The ten cent coins contained in the 2007 Oh! Canada! sets are the Large, Near Logo obverse / Straight 7 reverse variety.

WEDDING GIFT SETS, 2004-2010

MULTI-PLY PLATED STEEL UNCIRCULATED SETS, 2004-2006.

The Gift Set line was expanded in 2004 to include a Wedding set, which included the seven standard circulating denominations housed in a colourful wedding folder. The finish on these sets is uncirculated.

2004 Wedding Gift Set

2008 Wedding Gift Set

DATE	DESCRIPTION	QUANTITY SOLD	ISSUE PRICE	FINISH	MS-65 NC
2004P	Standard 7 coin set; Folder	18,660	19.95	Uncirculated	20.
2005P	Standard 7 coin set; Folder	11,597	19.95	Uncirculated	20.
2006P	Standard 7 coin set; Folder	8,012	19.95	Uncirculated	20.

MULTI-PLY PLATED STEEL UNCIRCULATED SETS, 2007-2010.

In 2007 the standard twenty-five cent Caribou design was replaced with a coloured design which changed each year. The finish on this set is uncirculated. The ten cent coins contained in the 2007 Oh! Canada! sets are the Large, Near Logo obverse / Straight 7 reverse variety.

The Wedding Gift Set was not issued in 2009, it was replaced by the Cards With Coins series (see page 24), however it was reintroduced in 2010.

For the coloured designs of the twenty-five cent Wedding coins of 2007, 2008 and 2010, see page 22 and 23.

DATE	DESCRIPTION	QUANTITY SOLD	ISSUE PRICE	FINISH	MS-65 NC
2007	Standard 6 coins; Coloured 25¢ Bouquet; Folder	10,687	19.95	Uncirculated	20.
2008	Standard 6 coins; Coloured 25¢ Wedding Cake; Folder	7,404	19.95	Uncirculated	20.
2010	Standard 6 coins; Coloured 25¢ Heart and Roses; Folder	N/A	19.95	Uncirculated	20.

MISCELLANEOUS GIFT SETS, 1983-2007

Sets issued between 1983 and 2001 have a brilliant uncirculated finish, while sets from 2006 forward have an uncirculated finish.

2006 Québec Winter Carnival Gift Set

DATE	DESCRIPTION	QUANTITY SOLD	ISSUE PRICE	ISSUER	FINISH	MARKET VALUE
1983	British Royal Mint, Standard 6 coins	N/A	N/A	RCM,BRM	BU	100.
1998	Canadian Imperial Bank of Commerce,"Oh! Canada!" Set; Standard 7 coins	N/A	21.95	RCM	BU	15.
2001P	Canada 2001 Set, Standard 7 coins; Medallion	N/A	N/A	RCM	BU	15.
2001P	"OH! CANADA!", Banff, Standard 7 coins	500	22.95	RCM	BU	15.
2001P	"OH! CANADA!", Calgary, Standard 7 coins	500	22.95	RCM	BU	15.
2001P	"OH! CANADA!", Halifax, Standard 7 coins	500	22.95	RCM	BU	15.
2001P	"OH! CANADA!", Montreal, Standard 7 coins	500	22.95	RCM	BU	15.
2001P	"OH! CANADA!", Niagara Falls, Standard 7 coins	500	22.95	RCM	BU	15.
2001P	"OH! CANADA!", Quebec City, Standard 7 coins	500	22.95	RCM	BU	15.
2001P	"OH! CANADA!", R.C.M., Standard 7 coins	500	22.95	RCM	BU	15.
2001P	"OH! CANADA!", St. John's, Standard 7 coins	500	22.95	RCM	BU	15.
2001P	"OH! CANADA!", Vancouver, Standard 7 coins	500	22.95	RCM	BU	15.
2001P	"OH! CANADA!", Whistler, Standard 7 coins	500	22.95	RCM	BU	15.
2006P	QUEBEC WINTER CARNIVAL; Standard 6 coins; Colourised 25¢ "Bonhomme"; Festive folder	8,200	19.95	RCM	Uncirculated	25.
2007	Calendar Coin Set, Standard 7 coins	5,264	29.95	RCM	Uncirculated	30.

Note: 1. For the coloured design of the Quebec Winter Carnival twenty-five cent coin, see page 19.
2. The 2007 Calendar Coin Set contains the Large, Near Logo obverse / Straight 7 reverse.

VANCOUVER 2010 WINTER OLYMPIC AND PARALYMPIC GAMES COIN AND STAMP SETS, 2010

These sets were issued in conjunction with Canada Post in three versions: gold, silver and bronze.

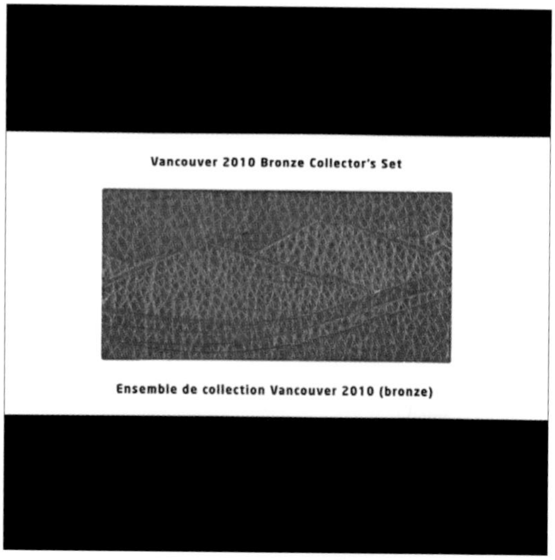

Bronze Collector Set

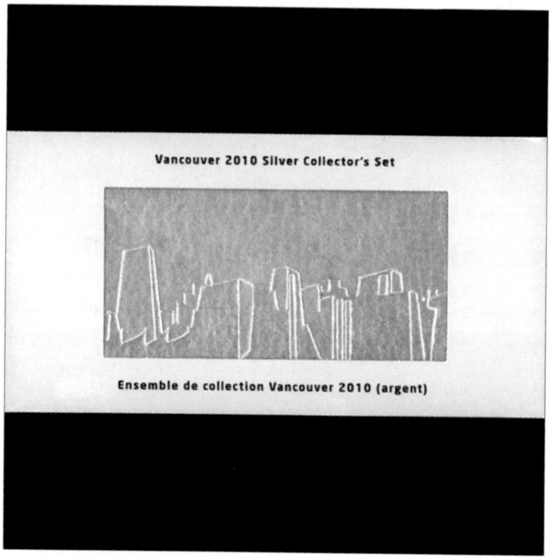

Silver Collector Set

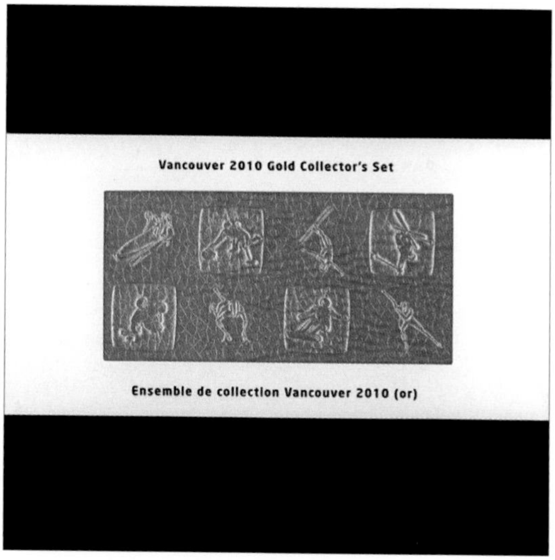

Gold Collector Set

DATE	DESCRIPTION	QUANTITY SOLD	ISSUE PRICE	FINISH	MS-65
2010	**Vancouver 2010 Emblems and Mascots Set, Bronze Collector Set**, Three 50¢ Mascot coins, Vancouver 2010 Souvenir Sheet of five Mascot theme stamps, 2 bronze lapel pins	16,000	49.95	Uncirculated	60.
2010	**Vancouver 2010 Winter Games Sports Set, Silver Collector Set**, Five painted 25¢ coins, Bobsleigh, Curling, Free Style Skiing, Ice Sledge Hockey, Snowboarding; Vancouver 2010 Souvenir Sheet of five Olympic theme stamps; 2 silver lapel pins	16,000	49.95	Uncirculated	60.
2010	**Vancouver 2010 Logo Set, Gold Collector Set**, Bronze Inukshuk dollar, Nickel painted Inukshuk dollar, 50¢ Inukshuk lenticular coin; Vancouver 2010 Souvenir Sheet of two stamps (Whistler and Vancouver)2 gold plated pins.	16,000	49.95	Uncirculated	75.

SPECIMEN SETS, 1970-2010

SIX COIN SPECIMEN SET, 1970

In 1968 the Royal Canadian Mint began to study the feasibility of offering for sale six-coin specimen sets to the public. The 1967 specimen set was extremely successful and opened the way for expanded offerings. Trial cases were prepared and a small number of specimen nickel and bronze coins of the years 1968 and 1969 were struck. These coins were not made available to the public.

In 1970 the Royal Canadian Mint provided special specimen sets to Prime Minister Pierre Trudeau for presentation purposes during his trip to China that year. A quantity of specimen sets in narrow cases were made up. After Trudeau's trip, some of these sets were sold to the public for $13 each. The total quantity of 1970 specimen sets issued in Canada is believed to be fewer than 1,000 and the only way 1970 specimen coins were available was in these sets. When the Mint made specimen sets available to the public starting in 1971, they were housed in larger, seven-coin cases. These sets are listed under prestige sets 1971-1980 on page 282.

In the early 1970's empty narrow specimen cases became available. The coins that could be housed in them were taken from prestige sets of the year.

Finish: Specimen, Brilliant relief on brilliant background

DATE	DESCRIPTION	FINISH	SP-65
1970	Specimen set in black case	Specimen	700.

SEVEN COIN CUSTOM SPECIMEN SETS, 1976-1980

With the end of the 1976 Montreal Olympic Coin program, and with a new numismatic production facility now in place, the Mint staff turned their attention to improving the quality of their numismatic product line. The quality of the custom sets was upgraded to specimen. The packaging remained constant except for the modifications listed below.

Finish: Specimen, Brilliant relief on a parallel lined background

Cases: **1976-1978:** Coins in maroon vinyl-covered case with Canada's coat of arms and the word "CANADA" stamped in gold on the top.

1979-1980: As 1977, except a gold maple leaf replaces the coat of arms and "CANADA"

DATE	DESCRIPTION	QUANTITY SOLD	ISSUE PRICE	FINISH	SP-66
1976	Voyageur	28,162	8.15	Specimen	15.
1977	Voyageur	44,198	8.15	Specimen	15.
1977 SWL	Voyageur	Included	8.15	Specimen	20.
1978 SJ 50¢	Voyageur	41,000	8.75	Specimen	15.
1978 RJ 50¢	Voyageur	Included	8.75	Specimen	20.
1979 RD Bust	Voyageur	31,174	10.75	Specimen	15.
1979 PT Bust	Voyageur	Included	10.75	Specimen	15.
1980	Voyageur	41,447	12.50	Specimen	15.

SIX COIN SPECIMEN SETS, 1981-1996

1981 saw the first officially stated issue of specimen coinage. The package was redesigned, and the coins were marketed as being of specimen quality. The number of coins in the set was reduced to six. The finish on the coins from 1981 to 1995 was brilliant relief on a brilliant background, and in 1996 was changed to brilliant relief against parallel lined background.

Finish: **1981-1995:** Specimen, Brilliant relief on a brilliant background
1996: Specimen, Brilliant relief on a parallel lined background
Cases: **1981-1987:** Blue leatherette, booklet type (103 mm x 141 mm), inside a hinged blue plastic frame housing, six encapsulated coins. All enclosed in a silver box.
1988-1996: Blue leatherette, wallet type, (96 mm x 153 mm) silver stamped mint crest, inside clear plastic frame with blue plastic insert. All enclosed in a silver sleeve.

DATE	DESCRIPTION	QUANTITY SOLD	ISSUE PRICE	FINISH	SP-66
1981	Voyageur	71,300	10.00	Specimen	15.
1982	Voyageur	62,298	11.50	Specimen	15.
1983	Voyageur	60,329	12.75	Specimen	15.
1984	Voyageur	60,030	12.95	Specimen	15.
1985	Voyageur	61,533	12.95	Specimen	15.
1986	Voyageur	67,152	12.95	Specimen	15.
1987	Voyageur	74,441	14.00	Specimen	15.
1988	Loon	70,205	14.00	Specimen	15.
1989	Loon	66,855	16.95	Specimen	20.
1990	Loon	76,611	17.95	Specimen	20.
1991	Loon	68,552	17.95	Specimen	40.
1992 (1967-)	Loon	78,328	18.95	Specimen	25.
1993	Loon	77,351	18.95	Specimen	18.
1994	Loon	75,973	19.25	Specimen	18.
1995	Loon	77,326	19.25	Specimen	20.
1996	Loon	62,125	19.25	Specimen	25.

SEVEN COIN SPECIMEN SETS, 1997-2000

In 1997 the two dollar coin was added to the set, raising the number of coins to seven. The set continued as specimen quality with the packaging being revised in 1998.

Finish: **1997-2000:** Specimen, Brilliant relief on a parallel lined background
Cases: **1997:** Blue leatherette, wallet type, (96 mm x 153 mm) silver stamped mint crest, inside clear plastic frame with blue plastic insert. All enclosed in a silver sleeve.
1998-2000: Green leatherette outer cover with RCM logo. All enclosed in a multicoloured box.

DATE	DESCRIPTION	QUANTITY SOLD	ISSUE PRICE	FINISH	SP-66
1997	Flying Loon/Bear	97,595	26.95	Specimen	50.
1998	Loon/Bear	67,697	26.95	Specimen	25.
1999	Loon/Bear	46,786	26.95	Specimen	25.
1999	Loon/Nunavut	45,104	26.95	Specimen	40.
2000	Loon/Bear	87,965	34.95	Specimen	25.
2000	Loon/Bears	Included	34.95	Specimen	40.

SEVEN COIN MULTI-PLY PLATED STEEL SPECIMEN SETS, 2001-2010

The 2002 specimen set is a double anniversary set issued to commemorate the Golden Jubilee of Queen Elizabeth II, and the 15th anniversary of the Loon dollar coin which was introduced in 1987. This is the only set which contains the "Family of Loons" one dollar coin.

The 2004 issue carries the new uncrowned effigy of Queen Elizabeth II, by Susanna Blunt. In 2006 only the $2 coin carried the double date (1996-2006) which commemorated the tenth anniversary of the "Toonie."

From 2007 to 2009 all coins that comprise the specimen set carried the Royal Canadian Mint logo, but in 2010 the logo was discontinued.

In 2010 the finish used on specimen coinage was changed. The earlier finish, in use since 1996, was a variety of that used by the Bullion Department on their maple leaf coinage. However, this finish was surfacing on giftware coinage, so it is thought the time had arrived to again make specimen set coinage a distinct finish, brilliant relief on the obverse portrait and reverse design, with a frosted relief of the legends and date, all on a lined matte background.

The one dollar "Bird Series" that began in 1997 with the Flying Loon was continued to 2010 with the Northern Harrier. For design illustrations of these coins see pages 92-95.

Finish: **2001-2009:** Specimen, Brilliant relief on a raised lined background.
2010: Specimen, Brilliant relief on obverse portrait and reverse design, frosted relief on legends and date, all on a laser lined background

Cases: Maroon leatherette display case, RCM Logo, 7-hole black insert encased in clear plastic black shipping box.

DATE	DESCRIPTION	QUANTITY SOLD	ISSUE PRICE	FINISH	SP-66
2001P	Loon/Bear	54,613	39.95	Specimen	25.
2002P (1952-)	Loon Family/Bear	67,672	39.95	Specimen	25.
2003P	Loon/Bear	41,640	39.95	Specimen	35.
2004P	Canada Goose/Bear	46,493	44.95	Specimen	45.
2005P	Tufted Puffin/Bear	39,818	39.95	Specimen	50.
2006P	Snowy Owl/Bear	39,935	44.95	Specimen	50.
2007	Trumpeter Swan/Bear	27,056	45.95	Specimen	60.
2008	Common Eider/Bear	21,227	45.95	Specimen	60.
2009	Great Blue Heron/Bear	21,677	47.95	Specimen	60.
2010	Northern Harrier/Bear	N/A	49.95	Specimen	60.

Note: The ten cent coins contained in the 2007 specimen sets are the Small, Far Logo obverse / Curved 7 reverse variety.

SPECIAL EDITION SPECIMEN SETS, 1967 and 2010

100TH ANNIVERSARY OF CONFEDERATION, 1867-1967

In 1967 the Royal Canadian Mint produced two special cased coin sets to mark the 100th anniversary of Confederation. The silver medallion set in the red leather-covered case contained one each of the 1¢ to $1 (proof-like finish) and a sterling silver medallion designed and modelled by Thomas Shingles. The gold presentation set contained a $20 gold coin and one each of the 1¢ to $1, all of specimen finish. This set was housed in a black leather presentation case.

DATE	DESCRIPTION	QUANTITY SOLD	ISSUE PRICE	FINISH		SET PRICE	
1967	Medallion	72,463	12.00	Proof-like	—	50.	—
1967	Gold	337,687	40.00	Specimen	850.	—	—

SPECIAL EDITION "YOUNG WILDLIFE" SPECIMEN SET, 2010

A new series in specimen sets was introduced in 2010, one in which the $2.00 coin will carry an image of the "young wildlife" of Canada. The first in the series are a pair of Lynx Kittens. See page 112 for an image.

A "finish" ten cent mule is found in the 2010 Lynx Specimen Set. The coin has an obverse with a brilliant relief on a raised lined background (2009 finish), and a reverse with a brilliant relief on the legend and date, with a lined matte finish background (2010 finish).

TEN CENT "FINISH" MULE

10¢ Obverse with 2009 Specimen Finish

10¢ Reverse with 2010 Specimen Finish

10¢ Finish Mule Actual Size

Finish: Specimen, Brilliant relief on obverse portrait and revere design, frosted relief on legends and date, all on a laser lined background

Case: Maroon leatherette clam style case, RCM logo, 7-hole black insert in clear plastic, multicoloured box.

DATE	DESCRIPTION	QUANTITY SOLD	ISSUE PRICE	FINISH	SP-66	SP-67
2010	Specimen set with standard 2010 Specimen Finish	15,000	49.95	Specimen	50.	50.
2010	Specimen set with 'Finish' Mule ten cent coin	Included	49.95	Specimen	450.	550.

SPECIAL NOTE ON FINISHES

It is very important to understand the different finishes the Royal Canadian Mint uses on their various issues. These finishes are altered from time-to-time as the Mint develops new products.

For example, the brilliant relief against a parallel lined background finish first used on bullion coins was carried forward in 1996 to be used on the coins contained in the specimen set.

In 2006 this finish was used on giftware coins such as the twenty-five cent coin issued to celebrate the 80th birthday of Queen Elizabeth II.

Now, in 2010, we have a new specimen finish (brilliant relief against a laser-lined background) which is used for the coins contained in the specimen set. There are now two different specimen finishes being utilised on Canadian coinage.

Circulation, uncirculated, and brilliant uncirculated (proof-like) finishes are another very confusing mixture of finishes, see page xxiv for a further explanation.

PRESTIGE SETS, 1971-1980

SEVEN COIN PRESTIGE SETS 1971-1980

When it was first introduced in 1971, the prestige set (double dollar set) contained two nickel dollars, with the second nickel dollar being used to display the obverse. This was also true for the 1972 set; however, from 1973 on the second nickel dollar was replaced with a silver dollar. The coins in the prestige sets were of specimen quality until 1980, and proof quality thereafter.

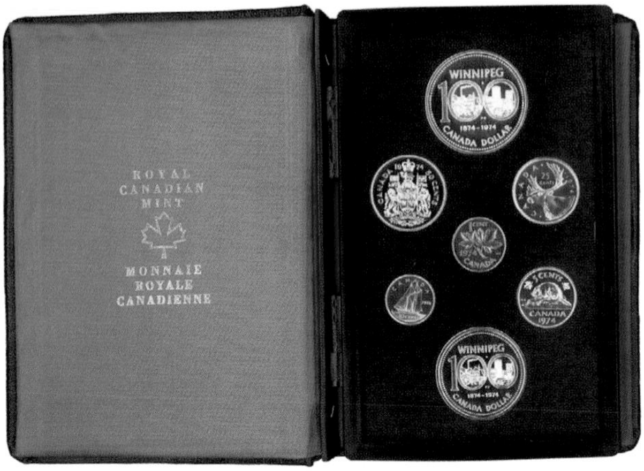

1974 Prestige Set

Finish: **1971-1980:** Specimen, Brilliant relief on a brilliant background

Cases: **1971-1973:** Crest of Canada; black leather, book type with clasp. Red satin inside red flocked 7-hole stationary display - coloured flocked jackets.

1974-1978: Crest of Canada; black leather, book type with clasp. Red satin inside, hinged black plastic 7-hole display - coloured flocked jackets.

1979-1980: Maple Leaf; black cardboard box, book type with clasp. Red satin inside, hinged black plastic 7-hole display - coloured flocked jackets.

DATE	DESCRIPTION	QUANTITY SOLD	ISSUE PRICE	FINISH	SP-66
1971	B.C./B.C.	66,860	12.00	Specimen	20.
1972	Voyageur/Voyageur	36,349	12.00	Specimen	45.
1973 LB 25¢	P.E.I./R.C.M.P.	119,891	12.00	Specimen	350.
1973 SB 25¢	P.E.I./R.C.M.P.	Included	12.00	Specimen	25.
1974	Winnipeg/Winnipeg	85,230	15.00	Specimen	20.
1975	Voyageur/Calgary	97,263	15.00	Specimen	22.
1976	Voyageur/Parliament	87,744	16.00	Specimen	22.
1977	Voyageur/Jubilee	142,577	16.00	Specimen	20.
1977 SWL	Voyageur/Jubilee	Included	16.00	Specimen	25.
1978 SJ	Voyageur/Edmonton	147,000	16.50	Specimen	20.
1978 RJ	Voyaguer/Edmonton	Included	16.50	Specimen	35.
1979	Voyageur/Griffon	155,698	18.50	Specimen	25.
1980	Voyageur/Polar Bear	162,875	36.00	Specimen	30.

Note: For images of the large bust (LB) and small bust (SB) varieties of 1973, see page 254. For an image of the 1977 short water line (SWL) variety see page 254. For and image of the 1978 square jewels (SJ) and round jewels (RJ) varieties see page 254.

PROOF SETS, 1981-2010

SEVEN COIN PROOF SETS 1981-1996

In the product reorganization of 1981 the prestige set of previous years was upgraded to proof quality.

Beginning in 1996 the five cent, ten cent, twenty-five cent and fifty cent coins were struck on sterling silver planchets (92.5% Ag and 7.5% Cu). All other specifications remained the same. The composition of the one cent, one dollar and two dollar coins remained unchanged.

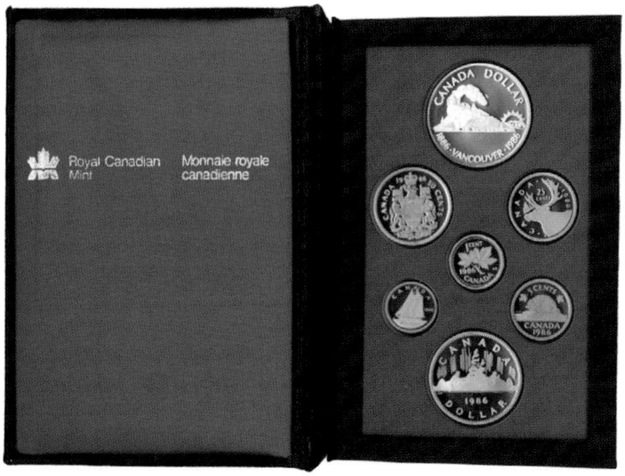

1986 Proof Set

Finish: **1981-1996:** Proof, Frosted relief against a mirror background

Cases: **1981-1985:** Maple Leaf; black cardboard box, book type with clasp. Red satin inside, hinged black plastic 7-hole display - coloured flocked jackets.

1986-1995: Maple leaf; black plastic box, wallet type. Red satin inside, hinged black plastic 7-hole display - coloured flocked jackets.

1996: Mint logo; dark green leather case with black plastic 8-hole insert, green interior, outer box

DATE	DESCRIPTION	QUANTITY SOLD	ISSUE PRICE	FINISH	PR-67 UHC
1981	Voyageur/Train	199,000	36.00	Proof	30.
1982	Voyageur/Skull	180,908	36.00	Proof	25.
1983	Voyageur/Games	166,779	36.00	Proof	28.
1984	Voyageur/Toronto	161,602	40.00	Proof	28.
1985	Voyageur/Parks	153,950	40.00	Proof	28.
1986	Voyageur/Vancouver	176,224	40.00	Proof	28.
1987	Voyageur/Davis Strait	175,686	43.00	Proof	28.
1988	Loon/Ironworks	175,259	43.00	Proof	30.
1989	Loon/MacKenzie	154,693	46.95	Proof	35.
1990	Loon/Kelsey	158,068	48.00	Proof	45.
1991	Loon/Frontenac	131,888	48.00	Proof	75.
1992	Loon/Stagecoach	147,061	49.75	Proof	40.
1993	Loon/Hockey	143,065	49.75	Proof	40.
1994	Loon/Dogsled Team	104,485	50.75	Proof	45.
1995	Loon/Hudson's Bay	101,560	50.75	Proof	40.
1996	Loon/McIntosh	112,835	66.25	Proof	55.

EIGHT COIN PROOF SETS, 1997-2010

In 1997 the two dollar coin was added to the set, raising the total to eight coins. The two dollar coin, following the practice established in 1996, was made of sterling silver with a gold plated centre. The one cent coin up to and including 2003, was not of the multi-ply plated steel, but of bronze composition.

Mid year 2003 the tiara portrait of Elizabeth II, which had been in use since 1990, was replaced with the new uncrowned portrait by Susanna Blunt. The first proof set with the new portrait was dated 2004.

The 2008 proof set was the first set to feature a commemorative dollar selectively gold plated on the reverse and rim.

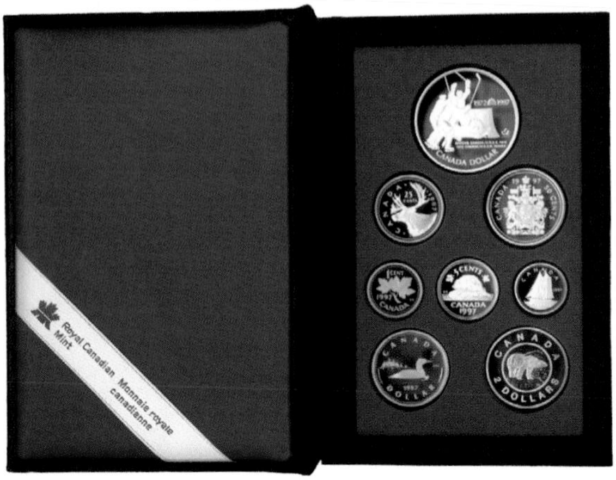

1997 Proof Set

Finish: **1997-2010:** Proof, frosted relief against a mirror background
Cases: **1997-2010:** Mint logo; dark green leather case with black plastic 8-hole insert, green interior with outer box

DATE	DESCRIPTION	QUANTITY SOLD	ISSUE PRICE	FINISH	PR-67 UHC
1997	Loon/Hockey/Bear	113,647	79.95	Proof	65.
1997	CNA Edition signed Cournoyer / Ferguson	N/A	N/A	Proof	125.
1997	ANA Edition, signed Gilbert / Park	N/A	N/A	Proof	110.
1998	Loon/R.C.M.P./Bear	93,632	79.95	Proof	90.
1999	Loon/Juan Perez/Bear	95,113	79.95	Proof	110.
2000	Loon/Discovery/Bear	90,921	79.95	Proof	100.
2001	Loon/Ballet/Bear	74,194	81.95	Proof	70.
2001	ANA Edition	750	69.95	Proof	200.
2001	CNA Edition	N/A	89.95	Proof	100.
2002 (1952-)	Loon/Queen Elizabeth II/Bear	65,315	81.95	Proof	90.
2002 (1952-)	ANA Edition	500	69.95	Proof	115.
2003	Loon/Cobalt/Bear	62,007	81.95	Proof	85.
2003	ANA Edition	500	74.95	Proof	115.
2004	Loon/French Settlement/Bear	57,614	83.92	Proof	110.
2004	ANA Edition	500	74.95	Proof	120.
2004	CNA Edition	250	74.95	Proof	120.
2005	Loon/Flag (gold plated) /Bear	63,562	81.95	Proof	125.
2005	CNA Edition	197	74.95	Proof	135.
2006 (1996-)	Loon/Victoria Cross (gold plated) /Bear	53,822	84.95	Proof	135.
2006	CNA Edition	200	84.95	Proof	145.
2007	Loon/Thayendanegea (gold plated)/Bear	37,413	89.95	Proof	125.
2008	Loon/Quebec City (gold plated)/Bear	38,630	89.95	Proof	115.
2009	Loon/First Flight (gold plated)/Bear	27,549	99.95	Proof	115.
2009	RCNA Edition	200	99.95	Proof	125.
2010	Loon/Corvette (gold plated)/Bear	N/A	109.95	Proof	110.

Note: 1. ANA and CNA sets must contain a numbered Certificate of Authenticity.
2. The ten cent coins contained in the 2007 proof sets are the Small, Far Logo obverse / Curved 7 reverse variety.

SPECIAL ISSUE PROOF SETS, 1994-2010

90th ANNIVERSARY OF THE ROYAL CANADIAN MINT, 1908-1998

Issued to commemorate the 90th Anniversary of the Royal Canadian Mint, this five coin set features the same reverse designs as the original 1908 coins, except for the double date 1908-1998. The set was issued in two finishes, matte and mirror proof. The matte one cent coin does not carry the country of origin, "Canada." This error was corrected on the mirror proof cent.

1¢ Matte Issue Without CANADA

1¢ Mirror Issue With CANADA

Designers:
Obv.: Dora de Pédery-Hunt
Rev.: Ago Aarand

Engravers:
Obv.: Dora de Pédery-Hunt
Rev.: 1¢ – G. W. DeSaulles
5¢, 10¢, 25¢, 50¢ – W. H. J. Blakemore

1¢ Mirror Issue

5¢ Mirror Issue

10¢ Mirror Issue

25¢ Mirror Issue

50¢ Mirror Issue

1¢ Matte Issue

5¢ Matte Issue

10¢ Matte Issue

25¢ Matte Issue

50¢ Matte Issue

Finish: Proof, matte or mirror
Case of Issue: Burgundy leather clam style case, RCM Mint logo, white lining, five-hole plastic insert, COA Matte set with bronze logo on case. Mirror set with nickel logo on the case

COIN	COMPOSITION	WEIGHT	DIAMETER	EDGE	DIE AXIS
1¢	Copper plated, 92.5% Ag, 7.5% Cu	5.90	25.30	Plain	↑↑
5¢	92.5% Ag, 7.5% Cu	1.30	15.25	Reeded	↑↑
10¢	92.5% Ag, 7.5% Cu	2.50	17.90	Reeded	↑↑
25¢	92.5% Ag, 7.5% Cu	5.80	23.50	Reeded	↑↑
50¢	92.5% Ag, 7.5% Cu	11.80	29.60	Reeded	↑↑

DATE	DESCRIPTION	QUANTITY SOLD	ISSUE PRICE	FINISH	PR-67 UHC	PR-68 UHC
1998 (1908-)	Without "CANADA" on 1¢	24,893	99.00	Matte proof	75.	—
1998 (1908-)	With "CANADA" on 1¢	18,376	99.00	Mirror proof	65.	—

SPECIAL LIMITED EDITION PROOF SETS, 1994-1995

First issued in 1994, these proof sets were limited to 50,000. They contained the silver dollar commemorative, along with the bronze/nickel commemorative of the year. The other five coins are the same as contained in the proof set of that year.

Finish: Proof, frosted relief against a mirror background

Case: Burgundy display case, wallet type, dated on spine with year of issue. Interior: White satin with brown plastic display frame - burgundy plastic box.

DATE	DESCRIPTION	QUANTITY SOLD	ISSUE PRICE	FINISH	PR-67 UHC	PR-68 UHC
1994	Remembrance/Dog Team Patrol	49,222	59.50	Proof	50.	—
1995	Peacekeeping/Hudson's Bay	49,802	66.95	Proof	50.	—

SPECIAL LIMITED EDITION PROOF SETS, 2002-2003

The Special Edition Proof Set, 1952-2002, contains the 2002 commemorative dollar (22kt gold plated), the two dollar 24kt gold plated inner core, and the 2002 fifty cent commemorative. The balance of the coins are as the regular issue.

The Special Edition Proof Set, 1953-2003, carries the laureate portrait of Queen Elizabeth II, first issued in 1953. This set commemorates Queen Elizabeth II's Coronation in 1953, and her Jubilee in 2003, with the double dates 1953-2003.

Finish: Proof, frosted relief against a mirror background

DATE	DESCRIPTION	QUANTITY SOLD	ISSUE PRICE	FINISH	PR-67 UHC	PR-68 UHC
2002 (1952-)	Accession	33,490	99.95	Proof	125.	—
2003 (1953-)	Coronation	21,537	99.95	Proof	125.	—

PREMIUM GIFT BABY AND WEDDING, STERLING SILVER PROOF SETS, 2006-2008

These sets contain a commemorative sterling silver loon dollar and a commemorative medallion; the balance of the coins are the regular proof set issue.

2006 Premium Gift Baby Proof Set

2006 Premium Gift Baby Proof Set

Finish: Proof, frosted relief, against mirror background **Case of Issue:** Leatherette folder

DATE	DESCRIPTION	QUANTITY SOLD	ISSUE PRICE	FINISH	PR-67 UHC	PR-68 UHC
2006	Sterling Silver Loon, Lullaby Loonie, Teddy Bear Medallion	3,863	79.95	Proof	65.	—
2007	Sterling Silver "Gold Plated Rattle", Baby Medallion	1,911	89.95	Proof	65.	—
2007	Sterling Silver Loon, Wedding Medallion	849	89.95	Proof	90.	—
2008	Sterling Silver Loon, Baby Medallion	1,168	99.95	Proof	100.	—
2008	Sterling Silver Loon, Wedding Medallion	508	99.95	Proof	100.	—

SPECIAL LIMITED EDITION PROOF SET, 2010

Canada's first circulating silver dollar was introduced in 1935 featuring Emanuel Hahn's classic Voyageur design. This special edition proof set, with four other coins carrying the 1935 design commemorates the 75th anniversary of our famous dollar.

2010 REVERSES

One Cent

Five Cents

Ten Cents

Twenty-Five Cents

One Dollar

Finish: Proof, frosted relief against a mirror background

DATE	DESCRIPTION	QUANTITY SOLD	ISSUE PRICE	FINISH	PR-67 UHC	PR-68 UHC
2010 (1935-)	75th Anniv, of the Voyageur Dollar	5,000	159.95	Proof	200.	—

PROOF PLATINUM SETS

In 1990 the Royal Canadian Mint entered the luxury market for high quality collector coins. While the proof platinum sets are scarce their value is linked to the market price of platinum. The value of these sets was based on a $1,750. Canadian market price for platinum.

CANADIAN WILDLIFE SERIES, 1990-1994.

1990-1994 Obverse

Physical and chemical specifications:

	$300	$150	$75	$30
Denomination:	**$300**	**$150**	**$75**	**$30**
Weight (oz);	1.000	.500	.250	.100
Diameter (mm):	30.0	25.0	20.0	16.0
Thickness (mm):	2.60	2.12	1.65	1.08

Composition: 99.95% Pt

Platinum content:

Grams	31.10	15.55	7.75	3.10
Troy ounces	1.00	0.50	0.25	0.10

Edge: Reeded
Die Axis: ↑↑
Finish: Proof
Case of Issue: 1992-1994: Walnut case, black suede four hole insert, encapsulated, COA.

POLAR BEARS PLATINUM SET 1990.

Canada's "Monarch of the North" has been transferred by Robert Bateman from the sparkling Arctic environment to the gleaming surfaces of pure platinum coins.

$300 **$150** **$75** **$30**

Designers:
Obv.: Dora de Pédery-Hunt
Rev.: Robert Bateman
Engravers:
Obv.: Dora de Pédery-Hunt
Rev.: $300 - Terry Smith
$150 - William Woodruff
$ 75 - Ago Aarand
$ 30 - Sheldon Beveridge

DATE	DESCRIPTION	QUANTITY SOLD	ISSUE PRICE	FINISH	PR-67 UHC	PR-68 UHC
1990	Polar Bears, 4-coin set	2,629	1,990.00	Proof	3,600.	—

SNOWY OWLS PLATINUM SET 1991.

This is the second set in the series of proof platinum coins dedicated to Canadian wildlife.

$300 **$150** **$75** **$30**

Designers:
Obv.: Dora de Pédery-Hunt
Rev.: Glen Loates
Engravers:
Obv.: Dora de Pédery-Hunt
Rev.: $300 - Sheldon Beveridge
$150 - Ago Aarand
$ 75 - Terry Smith
$ 30 - William Woodruff

DATE	DESCRIPTION	QUANTITY SOLD	ISSUE PRICE	FINISH	PR-67 UHC	PR-68 UHC
1991	Snowy Owls, 4-coin set	1,164	1,990.00	Proof	3,600.	—

COUGARS PLATINUM SET 1992.

This is the third set in the series of proof platinum coins dedicated to Canadian wildlife.

$300 $150 $75 $30

Designers:
Obv.: Dora de Pédery-Hunt
Rev.: George McLean
Engravers:
Obv.: Dora de Pédery-Hunt
Rev.: $300 - Ago Aarand, Cosme Saffioti
$150 - Susan Taylor
$ 75 - Sheldon Beveridge
$ 30 - Ago Aarand

DATE	DESCRIPTION	QUANTITY SOLD	ISSUE PRICE	FINISH	PR-67 UHC	PR-68 UHC
1992	Cougars, 4-coin set	1,081	1,955.00	Proof	3,600.	—

ARCTIC FOXES PLATINUM SET 1993.

This is the fourth set in the series of proof platinum coins dedicated to Canadian wildlife.

$300 $150 $75 $30

Designers:
Obv.: Dora de Pédery-Hunt
Rev.: Claudio D'Angelo
Engravers:
Obv.: Dora de Pédery-Hunt
Rev.: $300 - Susan Taylor
$150 - Sheldon Beveridge
$ 75 - Ago Aarand
$ 30 - Ago Aarand

DATE	DESCRIPTION	QUANTITY SOLD	ISSUE PRICE	FINISH	PR-67 UHC	PR-68 UHC
1993	Arctic Foxes, 4-coin set	1,033	1,955.00	Proof	3,600.	—

SEA OTTERS PLATINUM SET 1994.

This is the fifth and last set in the series of proof platinum coins dedicated to Canadian wildlife.

$300 $150 $75 $30

Designers:
Obv.: Dora de Pédery-Hunt
Rev.: Ron S. Parker
Engravers:
Obv.: Dora de Pédery-Hunt
Rev.: $300 - Sheldon Beveridge
$150 - William Woodruff
$ 75 - Terry Smith
$ 30 - Susan Taylor

DATE	DESCRIPTION	QUANTITY SOLD	ISSUE PRICE	FINISH	PR-67 UHC	PR-68 UHC
1994	Sea Otters, 4-coin set	766	1,995.00	Proof	3,600.	—

ENDANGERED WILDLIFE SERIES, 1995-2004

1995-2004 Obverse

Specifications: See page 288
Case of Issue:
1/10 oz coin: Leather display case, encapsulated coin
½ oz coin: Mahogany case, encapsulated coin
Set, 4 coins: Mahogany case, inside green satin, coins individually encapsulated

CANADA LYNX PLATINUM SET, 1995.

This is the first set in the series of proof platinum coins commemorating Canada's endangered wildlife.

$300

$150

$75

$30

Designers:
Obv.: Dora de Pédery-Hunt
Rev.: Michael Dumas
Engravers:
Obv.: Dora de Pédery-Hunt
Rev.: $300 - Susan Taylor
$150 - Cosme Saffioti
$ 75 - Stan Witten
$ 30 - Ago Aarand

DATE	DESCRIPTION	QUANTITY SOLD	ISSUE PRICE	FINISH	PR-67 UHC	PR-68 UHC
1995	30 Dollars	620	179.95	Proof	200.	225.
1995	150 Dollars	226	599.95	Proof	1,000.	1,100.
1995	Canada Lynx, 4-coin set	682	1,950.00	Proof	3,600.	—

PEREGRINE FALCON PLATINUM SET 1996.

This is the second set in the series of proof platinum coins commemorating Canada's endangered wildlife.

$300

$150

$75

$30

Designers:
Obv.: Dora de Pédery-Hunt
Rev.: Dwayne Harty
Engravers:
Obv.: Dora de Pédery-Hunt
Rev.: $300 - Sheldon Beveridge
$150 - Stan Witten
$ 75 - Cosme Saffioti
$ 30 - Ago Aarand

DATE	DESCRIPTION	QUANTITY SOLD	ISSUE PRICE	FINISH	PR-67 UHC	PR-68 UHC
1996	30 Dollars	910	179.95	Proof	200.	225.
1996	150 Dollars	196	599.95	Proof	1,000.	1,100.
1996	Peregrine Falcon, 4-coin set	675	2,095.95	Proof	3,600.	—

WOOD BISON PLATINUM SET, 1997.

This is the third set in the series of proof platinum coins commemorating Canada's endangered wildlife.

$300 $150 $75 $30

Designers:
Obv.: Dora de Pédery-Hunt
Rev.: Chris Bacon
Engravers:
Obv.: Dora de Pédery-Hunt
Rev.: $300 - Sheldon Beveridge
$150 - William Woodruff
$ 75 - Stan Witten
$ 30 - Ago Aarand

DATE	DESCRIPTION	QUANTITY SOLD	ISSUE PRICE	FINISH	PR-67 UHC	PR-68 UHC
1997	30 Dollars	469	179.95	Proof	200.	225.
1997	150 Dollars	116	599.95	Proof	1,000.	1,100.
1997	Wood Bison, 4-coin set	413	1,950.00	Proof	3,600.	—

GREY WOLF PLATINUM SET, 1998.

This is the fourth set in the series of proof platinum coins commemorating Canada's endangered wildlife.

$300 $150 $75 $30

Designers:
Obv.: Dora de Pédery-Hunt
Rev.: Kerri Burnett
Engravers:
Obv.: Dora de Pédery-Hunt
Rev.: $300 - Sheldon Beveridge
$150 - Cosme Saffioti
$ 75 - William Woodruff
$ 30 - A. Aarand, J. Osio

DATE	DESCRIPTION	QUANTITY SOLD	ISSUE PRICE	FINISH	PR-67 UHC	PR-68 UHC
1998	30 Dollars	664	179.95	Proof	200.	225.
1998	150 Dollars	194	599.95	Proof	1,000.	1,100.
1998	Grey Wolf, 4-coin set	661	2,095.00	Proof	3,600.	—

MUSKOX PLATINUM SET, 1999.

This is the fifth set in the series of proof platinum coins commemorating Canada's endangered wildlife.

$300

$150

$75

$30

Designers:
Obv.: Dora de Pédery-Hunt
Rev.: Mark Hobson
Engravers:
Obv.: Dora de Pédery-Hunt
Rev.: $300 -William Woodruff
$150 - Stan Witten
$ 75 - Cosme Saffioti
$ 30 - Sheldon Beveridge

DATE	DESCRIPTION	QUANTITY SOLD	ISSUE PRICE	FINISH	PR-67 UHC	PR-68 UHC
1999	30 Dollars	999	179.95	Proof	200.	225.
1999	Muskox, 4-coin set	495	2,095.95	Proof	3,600.	—

PRONGHORN PLATINUM SET, 2000.

This is the sixth set in the series of proof platinum coins commemorating Canada's endangered wildlife.

$300

$150

$75

$30

Designers:
Obv.: Dora de Pédery-Hunt
Rev.: Mark Hobson
Engravers:
Obv.: Dora de Pédery-Hunt
Rev.: $300 - José Osio
$150 - Susan Taylor
$ 75 - Stan Witten
$ 30 - William Woodruff

DATE	DESCRIPTION	QUANTITY SOLD	ISSUE PRICE	FINISH	PR-67 UHC	PR-68 UHC
2000	Pronghorn, 4-coin set	599	2,095.95	Proof	3,600.	—

HARLEQUIN DUCK PLATINUM SET 2001.

This is the seventh set in the series of proof platinum coins commemorating Canada's endangered wildlife.

$300

$150

$75

$30

Designers:
Obv.: Dora de Pédery-Hunt
Rev.: C. Saffioti, S. Taylor
S. Witten

Engravers:
Obv.: Dora de Pédery-Hunt
Rev.: $300 - Stan Witten
$150 - Susan Taylor
$ 75 - Cosme Saffioti
$ 30 - Susan Taylor

DATE	DESCRIPTION	QUANTITY SOLD	ISSUE PRICE	FINISH	PR-67 UHC	PR-68 UHC
2001	Harlequin Duck, 4-coin set	448	2,395.95	Proof	3,600.	—

GREAT BLUE HERON PLATINUM SET 2002.

This is the eighth set in the series of proof platinum coins commemorating Canada's endangered wildlife.

$300

$150

$75

$30

Designers:
Obv.: Dora de Pédery-Hunt
Rev.: John-Luc Grondin

Engravers:
Obv.: Dora de Pédery-Hunt
Rev.: $300 - Stan Witten
$150 - Susan Taylor
$ 75 - Stan Witten
$ 30 - José Osio

DATE	DESCRIPTION	QUANTITY SOLD	ISSUE PRICE	FINISH	PR-67 UHC	PR-68 UHC
2002	Great Blue Heron, 4-coin set	344	2,495.95	Proof	3,600.	—

ATLANTIC WALRUS PLATINUM SET 2003.

This is the ninth set in the series of proof platinum coins commemorating Canada's endangered wildlife.

$300 $175 $75 $30

Designers:
Obv.: Dora de Pédery-Hunt
Rev.: Pierre Leduc
Engravers:
Obv.: Dora de Pédery-Hunt
Rev.: $300 - Susan Taylor
$150 - José Osio
$ 75 - Stan Witten
$ 30 - Stan Witten

DATE	DESCRIPTION	QUANTITY SOLD	ISSUE PRICE	FINISH	PR-67 UHC	PR-68 UHC
2003	Atlantic Walrus, 4-coin set	365	2,995.95	Proof	3,600.	—

GRIZZLY BEAR PLATINUM SET 2004.

This is the tenth and last set in the Endangered Wildlife proof platinum series, and it commemorates Canada's Great Grizzly bears.

$300 $150 $75 $30

Designers:
Obv.: Susanna Blunt
Rev.: Kerri Burnett
Engravers:
Obv.: Susan Taylor
Rev.: $300 - José Osio
$150 - José Osio
$ 75 - José Osio
$ 30 - José Osio

DATE	DESCRIPTION	QUANTITY SOLD	ISSUE PRICE	FINISH	PR-67 UHC	PR-68 UHC
2004	Grizzly Bear, 4-coin set	380	2,995.95	Proof	3,600.	—

MAPLE LEAF BULLION COINS

GUIDE AND INDEX TO MAPLE LEAF BULLION COINS

The following categories were generated to divide the maple leaf bullion coins into a frame work for listing. These coins needed a logical listing order due to the many special effects that are used with them. It appears that special effects are first tested on maple leaf bullions coins before they are used on general collector coins..

The only criteria for a coin to be listed in this section is that the reverse must carry the bullion designation of weight or fineness.

GOLD MAPLE LEAFS

INTRODUCTION

In 1979 the Canadian Government introduced a gold bullion coin to compete with similar coins issued by other countries (such as the Krugerrand of South Africa). From 1979 to 1981 only the 50 dollar coin (Maple Leaf) in the one troy ounce size was produced. The Maple Leaf during this period was issued with a gold fineness of .999. During November 1982 the range of the gold Maple Leaf bullion coins being offered was expanded to three sizes. Now included in the offering were the five dollar or 1/10 maple and the ten dollar or ¼ maple. With the addition of the two fractional Maple Leafs all sizes were upgraded in gold content to .9999 fine. July of 1986 saw the offering range expanded once again to include the 20 dollar or ½ maple. All four coins are produced from .9999 fine gold and are legal tender coinage of Canada. In 1988 the Royal Canadian Mint, again expanding their bullion program, introduced five new coins; four platinum (1/10, ¼, ½ and one maple) and one silver (one maple). In 1990 the reverse hub of the one ounce gold Maple Leaf was re-engraved, enhancing veins in the maple leaf design. Other changes included a more slender stem on the maple leaf and wider spacing of the letters in the legend "Fine Gold 1 oz Or Pur." In 1993 the Royal Canadian Mint added to the series of bullion coin by issuing a 1/20 of an ounce ($1.00) size in gold and platinum. Again in 1994 the $2.00 denomination was added to the bullion coin series (1/15 of an ounce) in both platinum and gold. The $2.00 - 1/15 Maple denomination was discontinued in 1995.

The original finish developed by the Mint in 1979 for the Maple Leaf Gold Program was "The Bullion Finish," a brilliant relief on a parallel lined background.

FINISHES USED ON MAPLE LEAF COINS

Bullion: Brilliant relief against a parallel lined background
Coloured
Hologram

Specimen: Brilliant relief on a satin background
(Reverse proof) Coloured
Hologram

Proof: Frosted relief against a mirror background
Coloured
Hologram

PRIVY MARKS ON BULLION COINS

1999 marked the 20th anniversary of the Maple Leaf program. To commemorate this event a privy mark was incorporated into the design of all regular issue Maple Leafs.

A special issue of maple leafs was produced for January 1st, 2000. These were given a double date, 1999-2000, and a Fireworks privy mark.

To celebrate the millennium year, the privy mark added to all maple leaf denominations was "Fireworks" above the numerals 2000.

1999
20 YEARS ANS

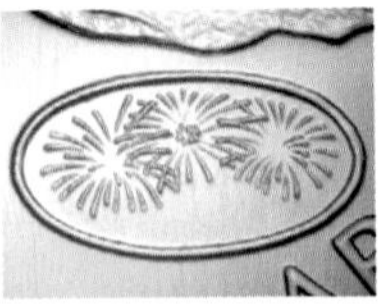

1999-2000
Fireworks

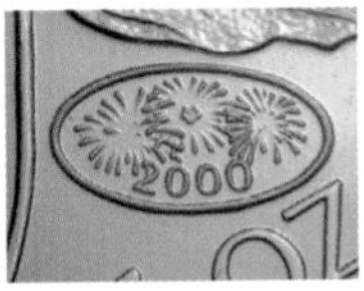

2000
Fireworks 2000

GOLD MAPLE LEAF SPECIFICATIONS

CHARACTERISTICS	.50¢ = 1/25 oz	$1 =1/20 oz	$2 = 1/15 oz	$5 = 1/10 oz	$10. = 1/4 oz	$20 = 1/2 oz	$50 = 1 oz
Fineness (1979-1982)	—	—	—	—	—	—	99.90%
Fineness (1982 to date)	99.99%	99.99%	99.99%	99.99%	99.99%	99.99%	99.99%
Weight (grams)	1.244	1.555	2.074	3.110	7.776	15.552	31.1035
Diameter (mm)	13.92	14.1	15.0	16.0	20.0	25.0	30.0
Thickness (mm)	0.63	0.92	0.98	1.22	1.70	2.23	2.93
Edge	Reeded	Reeded	Reeded	Reeded	Reeded	Reeded	Reeded
Die Axis	↑↑	↑↑	↑↑	↑↑	↑↑	↑↑	↑↑
Finish	Bullion	Bullion	Bullion	Bullion	Bullion	Bullion	Bullion

GOLD MAPLE LEAF OBVERSES

Tiara Portrait
1979-1989

Royal Diadem Portrait
1990-2003

Uncrowned Portrait
2004-2010

GOLD MAPLE LEAF REVERSES

.999 Fine
1979-1982

.9999 Fine
1983-1989

.9999 Fine
Re-engraved Leaf
1990-2010

		Designers	Engravers:
Obv.:	1979-1989	Arnold Machin	Walter Ott
	1990-2003	Dora de Pédery-Hunt	Dora de Pédery-Hunt
	2004-2010	Susanna Blunt	Susan Taylor
Rev.:	1979-1982	Walter Ott	R.C.M. Staff
	1983-1989	Walter Ott	R.C.M. Staff
	1990-2010	Walter Ott	R.C.M. Staff

GOLD MAPLE LEAFS

BULLION ISSUES

Finish: Bullion, Brilliant relief against a parallel lined background

MINTAGES:

The production (quantity minted) of regular issue gold maple leaf bullion coins is on a demand basis. As coins are ordered by the distributors they are struck and shipped by the Mint.

	QUANTITIES SOLD				
DATE	$1 = 1/20 oz	$5 = 1/10oz	$10 = 1/4oz	$20 = 1/2oz	$50 = 1oz
1979	N/I	N/I	N/I	N/I	1,000,000
1980	N/I	N/I	N/I	N/I	1,215,000
1981	N/I	N/I	N/I	N/I	863,000
1982	N/I	184,000	246,000	N/I	883,000
1983	N/I	224,000	130,000	N/I	695,000
1984	N/I	226,000	355,200	N/I	1,098,000
1985	N/I	476,000	607,200	N/I	1,747,500
1986	N/I	483,000	879,200	386,400	1,093,500
1987	N/I	459,000	376,800	332,800	978,000
1988	N/I	412,000	380,000	521,600	800,500
1989	N/I	539,000	328,800	259,200	856,000
1990	N/I	476,000	253,600	174,400	815,000
1991	N/I	322,000	166,400	96,200	290,000
1992	N/I	384,000	179,600	116,000	368,900
1993	37,080	248,630	158,452	99,492	321,413
1994	78,860	313,150	148,792	104,766	180,357
1995	85,920	294,890	127,596	103,162	208,729
1996	56,520	179,220	89,148	66,246	143,682
1997	59,720	188,540	98,104	63,354	478,211
1998	44,260	301,940	85,472	65,366	593,704
1999	62,820	709,920	98,928	64,760	627,067
1999-2000	Included	Included	Included	Included	Included
2000	31,280	52,970	31,688	24,404	86,375
2001	20,720	63,470	35,168	26,556	138,878
2002	17,140	45,020	42,940	28,706	344,883
2003	3,890	26,940	23,228	23,470	194,631
2004	9,880	33,480	18,296	13,160	253,978
2005	10,220	30,380	25,748	20,052	281,647
2006	19,340	40,960	25,964	21,138	209,937
2007	17,900	21,300	17,004	13,476	189,462
2008	15,740	38,510	34,368	28,782	710,718
2009	39,020	227,670	71,268	54,506	1,011,235
2010	N/A	N/A	N/A	N/A	N/A

PRICING:

Buying and selling prices are based on the interday spot price of bullion plus a small percentage premium for the striking and handling. The smaller the unit the larger the percentage premium charged on buying; however, in later selling the premium could very well disappear.

With gold at $1,425.00 per troy ounce during the first week of December 2010 the approximate selling price for the following coins was:

1 oz - One Maple - $1,500.
½ oz - Half Maple - $750.
¼ oz - Quarter Maple - $385.
1/10 oz - One Tenth Maple - $160.
1/15 oz - One Fifteenth Maple, see page 300
1/20 oz - One Twentieth Maple - $95.

Note: N/I denotes Not Issued.

GOLD MAPLE LEAF SPECIAL ISSUES

SPECIAL ISSUE SINGLES

FIFTY CENTS

FIFTY CENT (1/25 ounce) ISSUES, 2004-2010.

The1/25 oz gold coin is the smallest ever produced by the Royal Canadian Mint.

COMMON SPECIFICATIONS

Designers:
Obv.: Susanna Blunt
Rev.: See illustration

Engravers:
Obv.: Susan Taylor
Rev.: See illustration

Composition: 99.99% Au
Gold content: 1.27 g, 0.041 tr oz
Weight: 1.27 g
Diameter: 13.92 mm
Thickness: 0.63 mm
Edge: Reeded
Die Axis: ↑↑
Finish: Proof
Case of Issue: 2004: Maroon leatherette case, black flocked insert, encapsulated coin, COA
2005-2006: Maroon plastic slide case, black plastic insert, encapsulated coin, COA
2007-2009: Maroon leatherette clam style case, black flocked insert, encapsulated coin, COA

2004
25th Anniversary of the Gold Maple Leafs

Des. and Engr.: José Osio

Actual Size

2005
70th Anniversary Voyageur Design by Emanuel Hahn

Des.: E. Hahn
Engr.: RCM Staff

Actual Size

2006
Cowboy

Des.: M. Grant
Engr.: S. Witten

Actual Size

2007
The Wolf

Des. and Engr.:
W. Woodruff

Actual Size

DATE	DESCRIPTION	QUANTITY SOLD	ISSUE PRICE	FINISH	PR-67 UHC	PR-68 UHC
2004	Majestic Moose, 25th Anniv. Gold Maple Leafs	24,992	69.95	Proof	185.	195.
2005	70th Anniversary of Voyageur Design	13,933	69.95	Proof	125.	135.
2006	Cowboy	13,524	69.95	Proof	125.	135.
2007	The Wolf	12,514	81.95	Proof	125.	135.

FIFTY CENT (1/25 ounce) ISSUES, 2004-2010 (cont.).

2008
de Havilland Beaver

Des.: P. Mossman
Engr.: RCM Staff

Actual Size

2009
Red Maple Leaves

Des.: W. Woodruff
Engr.: RCM Staff

Actual Size

2010
Royal Canadian Mounted Police

Des.: Janet Griffin-Scott
Engr.: RCM Staff

Actual Size

DATE	DESCRIPTION	QUANTITY SOLD	ISSUE PRICE	FINISH	PR-67 UHC	PR-68 UHC
2008	de Havilland Beaver	13,526	85.95	Proof	125.	135.
2009	Red Maple Leaves	11,854	99.95	Proof	125.	135.
2010	Royal Canadian Mounted Police	14,000	109.95	Proof	110.	125.

TWO DOLLAR COIN

TWO DOLLAR (1/15 ounce) BULLION ISSUE, 1994.

Issued 1994 as a new addition to the line of bullion coins offered by the Royal Canadian Mint, the two dollar (1/15 troy ounce) coin was not a success and was discontinued in 1995. It is a one year type and for this reason popular.

Photograph not available at press time

Designers and Engravers:
Obv.: Dora de Pédery-Hunt
Rev.: Walter Ott, RCM Staff
Composition: 99.99% Au
Gold content: 1.244 g, 0.040 tr oz
Weight: 1.244 g
Diameter: 13.92 mm
Thickness: 0.63 mm
Edge: Reeded
Die Axis: ↑↑
Finish: Bullion
Case: Mylar pouch

DATE	DESCRIPTION	QUANTITY SOLD	ISSUE PRICE	FINISH	MS-65	MS-66
1994	$2 (1/15 oz), Bullion Issue	3,540	BV	Bullion	475.	525.

TEN DOLLAR COIN

TEN DOLLARS, PIEDFORT MAPLE LEAF, 2010.

This ten dollar gold maple leaf was issued in a set of two coins, the second being a five dollar silver maple, see page 322.

Actual Size

Designers and Engravers:
Obv.: Susanna Blunt, Susan Taylor
Rev.: RCM Staff
Composition: 99.999% Au
Gold content: 6.25 g, 0.20 tr oz
Weight: 6.25 g
Diameter: 15.9 mm
Thickness: 1.93 mm
Edge: Reeded
Die Axis: ↑↑
Finish: Bullion
Case: Maroon leatherette clam style case, black flock insert, encapsulated coin(s), COA

DATE	DESCRIPTION	QUANTITY SOLD	ISSUE PRICE	FINISH	MS-65	MS-66
2010	$10 Gold Piedfort Maple Leaf	3,000	N.I.I.	Bullion	600.	625.
2010	Piedfort Set, $10 Gold and $5 Silver	3,000	679.95	Bullion	675.	700.

FIFTY DOLLAR COINS

FIFTY DOLLARS (1 ounce), 10TH ANNIVERSARY OF THE MAPLE LEAF BULLION COINS, 1989.

To commemorate the 10th anniversary of the maple leaf bullion coin program in 1989 the Royal Canadian Mint issued a series of proof quality silver, gold and platinum coins individually and in sets. The single coins and sets were packaged in solid maple wood presentation cases with brown velvet liners.

Designers and Engravers:
Obv.: Arnold Machin, Walter Ott
Rev.: Walter Ott, RCM Staff
Composition: 99.99% Au
Gold content: 31.10 g, 1.00 tr oz
Weight: 31.1035 g, 1oz
Diameter: 30.00 mm **Edge:** Reeded
Thickness: 2.93 mm **Die Axis:** ↑↑
Finish: Proof
Case of Issue: Maple wood case, black flocked insert, encapsulated coin, COA

DATE	DESCRIPTION	QUANTITY SOLD	ISSUE PRICE	FINISH	PR-67 UHC	PR-68 UHC
1989	$50 (1 oz) 10th Anniv. of Maple Leaf Coins	6,817	BV	Proof	1,550.	1,575.

FIFTY DOLLARS (1 ounce), 125TH ANNIVERSARY OF THE R.C.M.P. 1997.

In 1997 the Royal Canadian Mint issued a $50.00 gold (1 oz .9999 fine) coin with a guaranteed value of U.S. $310.00 in effect until January 1st, 2000. Since that date the coin has traded at the market price of gold bullion.

Designer: Ago Aarand
Engraver: Stan Witten
Composition: 99.99% Au
Gold content: 31.10 g, 1.00 tr oz
Weight: 31.1035 g, 1 oz
Diameter: 30.00 mm **Edge:** Plain, 10-sided
Thickness: 3.25 mm **Die Axis:** ↑↑
Finish: Bullion
Case of Issue: Black card folder

DATE	DESCRIPTION	QUANTITY SOLD	ISSUE PRICE	FINISH	MS-65	MS-66
1997	$50 (1 oz) 125th Anniv. R.C.M.P.	12,913	310. USF	Bullion	1,550.	1,575.

FIFTY DOLLARS (1 ounce), 25TH ANNIVERSARY OF THE GOLD MAPLE LEAF COIN, 2004.

A special commemorative design for the one ounce maple celebrating Canada's 25 years as a world leader in bullion coin production was issued in 2004, at the A.N.A. World's Fair of Money.

Designers and Engravers:
Obv.: Susanna Blunt, Susan Taylor
Rev.: Stan Witten, Stan Witten
Composition: 99.99% Au
Gold content: 31.10 g, 1.00 tr oz
Weight: 31.1035 g, 1 oz
Diameter: 30.00 mm **Edge:** Reeded
Thickness: 2.93 mm **Die Axis:** ↑↑
Finish: Bullion
Case of Issue: Mylar pouch

DATE	DESCRIPTION	QUANTITY SOLD	ISSUE PRICE	FINISH	MS-65	MS-66
2004	$50 (1 oz) 25th Anniv. Gold Maple Leaf	10,000	BV	Bullion	1,550.	1,575.

FIFTY DOLLARS (1 ounce), TEST MAPLE LEAF, FIVE 9'S GOLD, 2005.

This was a production test for "five 9's" fineness of the one ounce maple leaf. Of the six hundred pieces which were produced, two hundred were melted, and four hundred were released, sealed in Mylar pouches.

Designers and Engravers:
Obv.: Susanna Blunt, Susan Taylor
Rev.: Walter Ott, RCM Staff
Composition: 99.999% Au
Gold content: 31.10 g, 1.00 tr oz
Weight: 31.1035 g, 1 oz
Diameter: 30.0 mm
Edge: Reeded
Thickness: 2.93 mm
Die Axis: ↑↑
Finish: Bullion
Case: Mylar pouch

DATE	DESCRIPTION	QUANTITY SOLD	ISSUE PRICE	FINISH	MS-65	MS-66
2005	$50 (1 oz) .99999	400	BV	Bullion	2,750.	2,850.

VANCOUVER 2010 OLYMPIC WINTER GAMES

FIFTY DOLLARS (1 ounce), VANCOUVER 2010 WINTER OLYMPIC GAMES, 2008-2010

Designers:
Obv.: Susanna Blunt
Rev.: 2008, 2010 RCM Staff
2009 Xwa lac tun (Ricky Harry)

Engravers:
Rev.: Susan Taylor
Rev.: RCM Staff

Composition: 99.99% Au
Gold content: 31.10 g, 1.00 tr oz
Weight: 31.1035 g, 1 oz
Diameter: 30.0 mm
Thickness: 2.93 mm

Edge: Reeded
Die Axis: ↑↑
Finish: Bullion; Bullion, Painted

Cases: Singly: Mylar pouch
Coloured Set: Maple wood box, black flocked insert, encapsulated coins, COA

2008 MAPLE LEAF AND VANCOUVER 2010 OLYMPIC LOGO

2009 THUNDERBIRD

2010 HOCKEY PLAYER

DATE	DESCRIPTION	QUANTITY SOLD	ISSUE PRICE	FINISH	MS-65	MS-66
2008	$50 (1oz) Maple Leaf and 2010 Logo	75,876	BV	Bullion	1,550.	1,575.
2008	$50 (1oz) Maple Leaf and 2010 Logo, Painted	200	2,000.	Bullion	2,200.	2,250.
2009	$50 (1oz) Thunderbird	74,124	BV	Bullion	1,550.	1,575.
2009	$50 (1oz) Thunderbird, Painted	200	2,000.	Bullion	2,200.	2,250.
2010	$50 (1oz) Hockey Player	N/A	BV	Bullion	1,550.	1,575.
2010	$50 (1oz) Hockey Player, Painted	200	2,000.	Bullion	2,200.	2,250.
—	3 coin set, 2008, 2009, 2010, Painted	200	5,999.95	Bullion	6,000.	—

TWO HUNDRED DOLLAR COINS

TWO HUNDRED DOLLARS (1 ounce), MAPLE LEAF, FIVE 9'S GOLD, 2007-2009.

Testing was continued of the five 9's gold concept first started in 2005, however the test coins were now offered to the numismatic market.

The issue of 2007 was offered with and without a privy mark.

2007 Obverse

2007 Reverse

2007 Obverse

2007 Reverse With Privy Mark

2008 Obverse

2008 Reverse

2009 Obverse

2009 Reverse

Designers:
Obv.: Susanna Blunt
Rev.: 2007: Stan Witten
2008: G. E. Kruger-Gray

Composition: 99.999% Au
Gold content: 31.10 g, 1.00 tr oz
Weight: 31.1035 g, 1 oz
Diameter: 30.0 mm
Thickness: 2.75 mm

Engravers:
Obv.: Susan Taylor
Rev.: 2007: Stan Witten
2008: G. E. Kruger-Gray

Edge: 2007: Plain, Interrupted serrations
2008: Interrupted serrations
Die Axis: ↑↑
Finish: Bullion

Case of Issue: 1. Maroon clam style case, black flocked insert, encapsulated maple leaf, COA
2. Card capsule

DATE	DESCRIPTION	QUANTITY SOLD	ISSUE PRICE	FINISH	MS-65	MS-66
2007	$200 (1 oz) 99.999 gold	30,848	BV	Bullion	1,550.	1,575.
2007	$200 (1 oz) 99.999 gold, with Privy Mark	595	1,899.95	Bullion	3,000.	3,250.
2008	$200 (1 oz) 99.999 gold	27,476	BV	Bullion	1,550.	1,575.
2009	$200 (1 oz) 99.999 gold	13,765	BV	Bullion	1,550.	1,575.

ONE MILLION DOLLAR GOLD COIN

This coin was issued May 3, 2007, as a promotional item for a new line of five 9's (99.999% fine gold) maple leaf gold coins. The million dollar gold coin being the largest and heaviest minted attracted buyers from all over the world. The Canadian Mint received orders for five coins. The 3,215 troy ounce coin is produced by casting, engraving and hand polishing. The reverse design of the million dollar maple leaf is very similar to the five dollar (2006) silver maple, see page 331.

Designers:
Obv.: Susanna Blunt
Rev.: Stan Witten
Composition: 99.999% Au
Gold content: 100 kilos, 3,215 tr oz
Weight: 100 kilos
Diameter: 53.0 cm
Thickness: 3.0 cm

Engravers:
Obv.: Stan Witten
Rev.: RCM Staff

Edge: Plain
Die Axis: ↑↑
Finish: Bullion

DATE	DESCRIPTION	QUANTITY SOLD	ISSUE PRICE	FINISH	PR-67 UHC	PR-68 UHC
2007	One Million Dollar Coin, 3,215 tr oz	5	BV	Bullion	—	—

Note: 1. The last recorded sale of this coins was $4,300,250. at auction on June 25th, 2010. It was auctioned by Dorotheum of Vienna, Austria, at their headquarters.
2. Coin illustrated smaller than actual size.

GOLD MAPLE LEAF SPECIAL ISSUES

SPECIAL ISSUE SETS

10TH ANNIVERSARY OF THE GOLD MAPLE LEAF COIN, 1979-1989.

The three sets detailed below were issued for the tenth anniversary of the maple leaf bullion program.

THREE-COIN SET **(1 oz gold, silver and platinum maple leafs)**

1 oz Gold Maple Leaf

1 oz Silver Maple Leaf

1 oz Platinum Maple Leaf

THREE-COIN SET **(1oz silver, 1/10 oz gold and platinum maple leafs)**

1 oz Silver Maple Leaf

1/10 oz Gold Maple Leaf

1/10 oz Platinum Leaf

FOUR-COIN SET **(1 oz, 1/2 oz, 1/4 oz, 1/10 oz platinum maple leafs**

1 oz Platinum Maple Leaf

½ oz Platinum Maple Leaf

¼ oz Platinum Maple Leaf

1/10 oz Platinum

10TH ANNIVERSARY OF THE GOLD MAPLE LEAF COIN, 1979-1989 (cont.).

Designers:
Obv.: Arnold Machin
Rev.: Walter Ott

Engravers:
Obv.: Walter Ott
Rev.: RCM Staff

Specifications: Gold: See page 297
Platinum: See page 314
Silver: See page 319

Finish: Proof

Case of Issue: Maple wood presentation box, black flocked insert, encapsulated coin, COA

DATE	DESCRIPTION	QUANTITY SOLD	ISSUE PRICE	FINISH	PR-67 UHC	PR-68 UHC
1989	3-coin set: 1oz gold, 1oz silver, 1oz platinum	3,966	1,795.00	Proof	3,400.	3,500.
1989	3-coin set: 1/10 oz gold, 1/10 oz platinum, 1 oz silver	10,000	195.00	Proof	400.	425.
1989	4-coin gold set: 1, ½, ¼, 1/10 oz maples	6,998	1,395.00	Proof	2,900.	—

GOLD MAPLE LEAFS WITH PRIVY MARKS

PRIVY MARK SINGLES

GOLD MAPLE LEAF PRIVY MARKS.

In 1997, the Royal Canadian Mint began adding privy marks to specific gold maple leaf denominations to commemorate special events. These privy mark maples were commissioned by different organizations and struck by the Royal Canadian Mint.

$5 — 1/10 oz Maple Leaf Privy Marks

1997 $5
Family

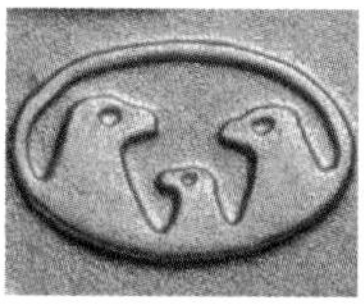

1998
Eagles $5

$10 — ¼ oz Maple Leaf Privy Marks

2000 $10
Expo
Hannover

2001 $10
Basle Coin Fair

2005 $10
Liberation
Royal Dutch Mint

2005-2006 $10
M7 Privy Mark

DATE	DENOMINATION	CASE OF ISSUE	QUANTITY SOLD	ISSUE PRICE	FINISH	SP-66	SP-67
1997	$5, Family (1/10 oz)	Plastic case	100,730	N/A	Specimen	175.	200.
1998	$5, Eagles (1/10 oz)	Plastic case	51,440	N/A	Specimen	175.	200.
2000	$10, Expo (¼ oz)	N/A	1,000	N/A	Specimen	575.	625.
2001	$10, Basle (¼ oz)	N/A	750	N/A	Specimen	750.	800.
2005	$10, Liberation (¼ oz)	N/A	500	€299	Specimen	375.	400.
2005	$10, M7 (¼ oz)	Wooden display case	600	N/A	Specimen	375.	400.
2006	$10, M7 (¼ oz)	Mylar pouch	1,093	N/A	Specimen	375.	400.

PRIVY MARK SETS

GOLD MAPLE LEAF PRIVY MARK SET, 2001.

Each of the five coins in this set carries the bow of a Viking ship as a privy mark. The maples in this set are: 1 oz, ½ oz, ¼ oz, 1/10 oz and 1/20 oz.

Designers:
Obv.: Dora de Pédery-Hunt
Rev.: Walter Ott

Engravers:
Obv.: Dora de Pédery-Hunt
Rev.: RCM Staff

Specifications: See page 297
Finish: Specimen (reverse proof)
Case of Issue: Red mahogany wooden case, black insert, encapsulated coins, green velour with metal trim box.

2001 Viking Privy Mark

DATE	DESCRIPTION	PRIVY MARK	QUANTITY SOLD	ISSUE PRICE	FINISH	SP-66	SP-67
2001	$1.00 (1/20 oz)	Viking	850	N.I.I.	Specimen	95.	100.
2001	$5.00 (1/10 oz)	Viking	850	N.I.I.	Specimen	175.	185.
2001	$10.00 (¼ oz)	Viking	850	N.I.I.	Specimen	400.	425.
2001	$20.00 (½ oz)	Viking	850	N.I.I.	Specimen	800.	850.
2001	$50.00 (1 oz)	Viking	850	N.I.I.	Specimen	1,550.	1,600.
2001	5 coin set	Viking	850	N/A	Specimen	2,825.	—

COLOURED SETS

20TH ANNIVERSARY OF THE MAPLE LEAF PROGRAM, 1979-1999.

This limited edition five-coin set, (1 oz, ½ oz, ¼ oz, 1/10 oz and 1/20 oz) struck by the Royal Canadian Mint and coloured in Balerna, Switzerland, was issued with a mintage of 500. They are the first coloured Canadian coins.

Designers:
Obv. Dora de Pédery-Hunt
Rev.: Walter Ott

Specifications: See page 297

Engravers:
Obv.: Dora de Pédery-Hunt
Rev.: RCM Staff

Finish: Bullion, Coloured

Case of Issue: Wooden maple display case, black leatherette sleeve, black flocked insert, encapsulated coins, COA, red and gold outer box.

1979-1999
Privy Mark

DATE	DESCRIPTION	PRIVY MARK	QUANTITY SOLD	ISSUE PRICE	FINISH	MS-65	MS-66
1999	$1.00 (1/20 oz)	20 Years / ans	500	N.I.I.	Bullion	100.	110.
1999	$5.00 (1/10 oz)	20 Years / ans	500	N.I.I.	Bullion	185.	200.
1999	$10.00 (¼ oz)	20 Years / ans	500	N.I.I.	Bullion	425.	450.
1999	$20.00 (½ oz)	20 Years / ans	500	N.I.I.	Bullion	850.	900.
1999	$50.00 (1 oz)	20 Years / ans	500	N.I.I.	Bullion	1,600.	1,650.
1999	5 coin set	20 Years / ans	500	N/A	Bullion	3,000.	—

Note: For the Vancouver 2010 Winter Olympic Coloured Set see page 304.

GOLD MAPLE LEAFS HOLOGRAM ISSUES

HOLOGRAM SINGLES AND SETS

TEN DOLLARS (¼ ounce), GOLD MAPLE LEAF HOLOGRAM 2001.

A distinctive maple leaf design appears as a high resolution dot matrix hologram, which is struck directly into the coin.

Designers and Engravers:
Obv.: Susanna Blunt, Susan Taylor
Rev.: Walter Ott, RCM Staff
Composition: 99.99% Au
Gold content: 7.775 g, 0.25 tr oz
Weight: 7.776 g
Diameter: 20.0 mm **Edge:** Reeded
Thickness: 1.70 mm **Die Axis:** ↑↑
Finish: Specimen (reverse proof), Hologram
Case of Issue: Wooden presentation case

DATE	DESCRIPTION	QUANTITY SOLD	ISSUE PRICE	FINISH	SP-66	SP-67
2001	$10 (¼ oz)	14,614	195.00	Specimen	450.	475.

GOLD MAPLE LEAF HOLOGRAM SETS 1999, 2001 and 2009.

The Hologram gold maple leaf set of 1999 was the first official issue of hologram coins in Canada. The five coins in this set are: 1oz, ½oz, ¼oz, 1/10 oz and 1/20 oz. All coins carry identical designs.

The 2009 thirtieth anniversary hologram set was issued with 4 coins; 1oz, ¼oz, 1.20oz and 1/20 oz maples.

Obv. $50 (1 oz)

Rev. $50 (1 oz)

Designers and Engravers:
Obv.: Dora de Pédery-Hunt
Rev.: Walter Ott, RCM Staff
Specifications: See page 297
Finish: Bullion, Hologram
Case of Issue: Presentation case

DATE	DESCRIPTION	QUANTITY SOLD	ISSUE PRICE	FINISH	MS-65	MS-66
1999	20th Anniversary, 5 coin set	500	1,995.00	Bullion	3,000.	—
2001	5 coin set	600	1,995.00	Bullion	3,000.	—
2009	30th Anniversary, 4 coin set	739	N/A	Bullion	3,000.	—

GOLD MAPLE LEAF BIMETALLIC ISSUES

BIMETALLIC SETS

25TH ANNIVERSARY OF THE GOLD MAPLE LEAF, 1979-2004.

To celebrate 25 years as an international standard in bullion coins, a new bimetallic maple leaf set was issued. The six-coin set is the first to include the 1/25 oz maple leaf denomination. Each coin is double-dated 1979-2004, and the 1 ounce coin features a 25 year commemorative privy mark.

1979-2004
Privy Mark

DOLLAR VALUES AND FINE OUNCE SPECIFICATIONS

CHARACTERISTICS	.50¢ = 1/25oz	$1 = 1/20oz	$5 = 1/10oz	$10 =1/4oz	$20 = 1/2oz	$50 = 1oz
Composition						
Ring - fine silver	99.99%	99.99%	99.99%	99.99%	99.99%	99.99%
Core - fine gold	99.99%	99.99%	99.99%	99.99%	99.99%	99.99%
Weight (grams)	1.270	1.581	3.136	7.802	15.589	31.650
Diameter (mm)	16.00	18.03	20.00	25.00	30.00	36.07
Thickness (mm)	N/A	N/A	N/A	N/A	N/A	N/A
Edge:	Plain	Plain	Plain	Plain	Plain	Plain
Die Axis	↑↑	↑↑	↑↑	↑↑	↑↑	↑↑

Designers and Engravers: RCM Staff
Finish: Bullion
Case: Black leather presentation case, black velour insert, encapsulated coins, COA

DATE	DESCRIPTION	PRIVY MARK	QUANTITY SOLD	ISSUE PRICE	FINISH	MS-65	MS-66
2004 (1979-)	$1.00 (1/20 oz)	None	801	N.I.I.	Bullion	100.	110.
2004 (1979-)	$5.00 (1/10 oz)	None	801	N.I.I.	Bullion	185.	200.
2004 (1979-)	$10.00 (¼ oz)	None	801	N.I.I.	Bullion	425.	450.
2004 (1979-)	$20.00 (½ oz)	None	801	N.I.I.	Bullion	850.	900.
2004 (1979-)	$50.00 (1 oz)	20 Years	801	N.I.I.	Bullion	1,600.	1,650.
2004 (1979-)	6 coin set	20 Years	801	2,495.95	Bullion	3,000.	—

PLATINUM MAPLE LEAFS

BULLION ISSUES

Obverse 1988-1989

Obverse 1990-1999

Obverse 2009-2010

Platinum Maple Leaf Reverse

Designers: See page 297
Finish: Bullion

Engravers: See page 296
Case of Issue: Mylar pouch

PLATINUM MAPLE LEAF SPECIFICATIONS

CHARACTERISTICS	$1 = 1/20oz	$2 = 1/15oz	$5 = 1/10oz	$10 = 1/4oz	$20 = 1/2oz	$50 = 1oz
Fineness	99.95%	99.95%	99.95%	99.95%	99.95%	99.95%
Weight (grams)	1.555	2.074	3.110	7.776	15.552	31.1035
Diameter (mm)	14.10	15.00	16.00	20.00	25.00	30.00
Thickness (mm)	0.92	0.94	1.01	1.50	2.02	2.52
Edge	Reeded	Reeded	Reeded	Reeded	Reeded	Reeded
Die Axis	↑↑	↑↑	↑↑	↑↑	↑↑	↑↑

MINTAGES

The production of platinum maple leafs was on an order basis, unlike the production of coinage for circulation where the Mint will anticipate the number of coins required to fulfill the needs of the economy. Maple leafs are not struck unless ordered.

	QUANTITIES SOLD				
DATE	$1 = 1/20oz	$5 = 1/10oz	$10 = 1/4oz	$20 = 1/2oz	$50 - 1oz
1988	N/I	46,000	87,200	23,600	26,000
1989	N/I	18,000	3,200	4,800	10,000
1990	N/I	9,000	1,600	2,600	31,900
1991	N/I	13,000	7,200	5,600	31,900
1992	N/I	16,000	11,600	12,800	40,500
1993	2,120	14,020	8,048	6,022	17,666
1994	4,260	19,190	9,456	6,710	36,245
1995	460	8,940	6,524	6,308	25,829
1996	1,640	8,820	6,160	5,490	62,273
1997	1,340	7,050	4,552	3,990	25,480
1998	2,000	5,710	3,816	5,486	10,403
1999	4,000	4,080	2,092	788	3,248
2009	N/I	N/I	N/I	N/I	33,000
2010	N/I	N/I	N/I	N/I	N/A

PRICING

Buying and selling prices are based on the interday spot price of platinum plus a small percentage premium for striking and handling. The smaller the unit the larger the percentage premium charged on buying; however, in later selling the premium could very well disappear.

NOTE FOR COLLECTORS

1. No platinum bullion coins were produced between 2000 and 2008.
2. N/I indicates Not Issued.

ONE AND TWO DOLLAR COINS

TWO DOLLAR (1/15 ounce) BULLION ISSUE, 1994, and ONE DOLLAR (1/20 OUNCE), 1995.

Issued 1994 as a new addition to the line of bullion coins offered by the Royal Canadian Mint, the two dollar (1/15 troy ounce) coin was not a success and was discontinued in 1995. It is a one year type and for this reason is popular.

The 1995 one dollar (1/20 ounce) has an extremely small mintage of 460 coins. Even so, the slightest demand will affect the price without regard for the market price of platinum.

1994 Obv.
$2 (1/15oz)

1994 Rev.
$2 (1/15 oz)

1995 Obv.
$1 (1/20 oz)

1995 Rev.
$1 (1/20 oz)

Designers and Engravers:
See page 297
Specifications: See page 314
Finish: Bullion
Case: Mylar pouch

DATE	DESCRIPTION	QUANTITY SOLD	ISSUE PRICE	FINISH	MS-65	MS-66
1994	$2 (1/15 oz), Bullion Issue	600	BV	Bullion	1,000.	1,200.
1995	$1 (1/20 oz), Bullion Issue	460	BV	Bullion	1,250.	1,350.

PLATINUM MAPLE LEAF SPECIAL ISSUES

SPECIAL ISSUE SETS

10TH ANNIVERSARY OF MAPLE LEAF BULLION COINS, 1989.

This four-coin proof platinum set was issued to commemorate the 10th anniversary of the first maple leaf coins issued in 1979.

Obv. $50 (1 oz)

Rev. $50 (1oz)

Designers and Engravers:
Obv.: Arnold Machin, Walter Ott
Rev.: Walter Ott
Specifications: See page 314
Finish: Proof
Case of Issue: Wooden maple presentation case, black flocked insert, encapsulated coin, COA

Obv. $20 (½ oz)

Rev. $20 (½ oz)

Obv. $10 (¼ oz)

Rev. $10 (¼oz)

Obv. $5 (1/10 oz)

Rev. $5 (1/10 oz)

DATE	DESCRIPTION	QUANTITY SOLD	ISSUE PRICE	FINISH	PR-67 UHC	PR-68 UHC
1989	4 coin set, (1 oz, ½ oz, ¼ oz, 1/10 oz)	1,999	1,995.	Proof	3,250.	—

POLAR BEAR ISSUE, 1999.

In 1999 the Royal Canadian Mint issued a special set of platinum Maple Leafs at the request of a distributor, MTB Bank. They are legal tender coins issued in five denominations with the same specifications as the bullion issues but with a polar bear reverse design. The reverse design is a modification of the two dollar polar bear reverse by Brent Townsend.

Obv. $20 (½ oz)

Rev. $20 (½oz)

Designers and Engravers:
Obv.: Dora de Pédery-Hunt
Rev.: Brent Townsend, Ago Aarand
Specifications: See page 314
Finish: Bullion, Brilliant relief against a parallel lined background
Case of Issue: N/A

DATE	DESCRIPTION	QUANTITY SOLD	ISSUE PRICE	FINISH	MS-65	MS-66
1999	$1.00 (1/20 oz)	1999	N/A	Bullion	100.	110.
1999	$5.00 (1/10 oz)	1999	N/A	Bullion	200.	210.
1999	$10.00 (¼ oz)	500	N/A	Bullion	500.	525.
1999	$20.00 (½ oz)	1999	N/A	Bullion	1,000.	1,050.
1999	$50.00 (1 oz)	1999	N/A	Bullion	1,950.	2,000.
1999	Set of 5 coins	500	N/A	Bullion	3,650.	—

HOLOGRAM SETS

PLATINUM MAPLE LEAF PROOF HOLOGRAM FIVE-COIN SET, 2002.

In this set the distinctive maple leaf appears as a high-resolution dot matrix hologram which has been struck directly onto regular issues of each of the five coins. The five coins are struck with the same specifications and denominations as the regular issues of 1988-1999.

Designers and Engravers:
Obv.: Dora de Pédery-Hunt
Rev.: RCM Staff
Specifications: See page 314
Finish: Specimen (reverse proof), Brilliant relief on a satin background, Hologram
Case of Issue: Red mahogany wooden case, black insert, encapsulated coins, green velour with metal trim box.

DATE	DESCRIPTION	QUANTITY SOLD	ISSUE PRICE	FINISH	MS-65	MS-66
2002	$1.00 (1/20 oz)	500	N.I.I.	Specimen	100.	110.
2002	$5.00 (1/10 oz)	500	N.I.I.	Specimen	200.	210.
2002	$10.00 (¼ oz)	500	N.I.I.	Specimen	500.	525.
2002	$20.00 (½ oz)	500	N.I.I.	Specimen	1,000.	1,050.
2002	$50.00 (1 oz)	500	N.I.I.	Specimen	1,950.	2,000.
2002	Set of 5 coins	500	2,895.95	Specimen	3,650.	—

PALLADIUM MAPLE LEAFS

BULLION ISSUES

FIFTY DOLLARS (1 ounce) PALLADIUM MAPLE LEAF, 2005-2010.

Designers and Engravers:
Obv.: Susanna Blunt, Susan Taylor
Rev.: Walter Ott, RCM Staff
Composition: 99.95% Pl
Platinum content: 31.10 g, 1.00 tr oz
Weight: 31.1035 g
Diameter: 30.00 mm **Edge:** Reeded
Thickness: 2.93 mm **Die Axis:** ↑↑
Finish: Bullion
Case of Issue: Mylar pouch

DATE	DESCRIPTION	QUANTITY SOLD	ISSUE PRICE	FINISH	MS-65	MS-66
2005	$50 (1 oz) 99.99%	62,919	BV	Bullion	850.	900.
2006	$50 (1 oz)	68,707	BV	Bullion	850.	900.
2007	$50 (1 oz)	15,415	BV	Bullion	850.	900.
2008	$50 (1 oz)	9,694	BV	Bullion	850.	900.
2009	$50 (1 oz)	40,000	BV	Bullion	850.	900.
2010	$50 (1oz)	N/A	BV	Bullion	850.	900.

SPECIAL ISSUES

EXPERIMENTAL FINISH TEST PALLADIUM MAPLES, 2005.

In 2005 the Royal Canadian Mint conducted tests on palladium planchets. Planchets with the Royal Canadian Mint logo A were finished outside mint facilities, and planchets with the Royal Canadian Mint logo B were finished inside the Mint. Test results showed little variation in the manufacture, resulting in the internal planchets being used in the production of palladium maple leafs.

Reverse Privy Mark "A"

Privy Mark "A"

Reverse Privy Mark "B"

Privy Mark "B"

Designers:
Obv.: Susanna Blunt
Rev.: Walter Ott

Engravers:
Obv.: Susan Taylor
Rev.: RCM Staff

Composition: 99.95% Pl
Platinum content: 31.10 g, 1.00 tr oz
Weight: 31.1035 g
Diameter: 30.00 mm
Thickness: 2.93 mm
Edge: Reeded
Die Axis: ↑↑
Finish: Bullion, Brilliant relief against a parallel lined background

DATE	DESCRIPTION	QUANTITY SOLD	ISSUE PRICE	FINISH	MS-65	MS-66
2005	Royal Mint Privy Mark "A"	146	1,300.00	Bullion	3,500.	3,750.
2005	Royal Mint Privy Mark "B"	144	1,300.00	Bullion	3,500.	3,750.

SILVER MAPLE LEAFS

BULLION ISSUES

The first silver one ounce maple leaf was issued in 1988. The design is a continuation of that first conceived for the gold maples in 1979. The 1999-2000, and the 2000-dated silver maple leaf $5.00 coins carry the fireworks privy mark for 1999-2000, and the millennium privy mark for 2000.

SILVER MAPLE LEAF SPECIFICATIONS

CHARACTERISTICS	$1 = 1/20 oz	$2 = 1/10 oz	$3 = ¼ oz	$4 = ½ oz	$5 = 1 oz
Fineness	99.99%	99.99%	99.99%	99.99%	99.99%
Weight (grams)	1.555	3.110	7.776	15.552	31.1035
Diameter (mm)	16.00	20.00	27.00	34.00	38.00
Thickness (mm)	1.10	1.30	1.80	2.10	3.15
Edge	Reeded	Reeded	Reeded	Reeded	Reeded
Die Axis	↑↑	↑↑	↑↑	↑↑	↑↑

FIVE DOLLAR or ONE OUNCE MAPLES

Obverses

Tiara Portrait
1988-1989

Royal Diadem Portrait
1990-2003

Uncrowned Portrait
2004-2010

Reverse

1988-2010

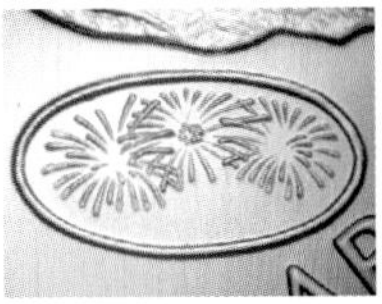

Dated 1999-2000
"Fireworks"

Dated 2000
"Fireworks 2000"

The two privy marks illustrated appear on all silver maple leafs for that particular year.

Designers and Engravers:

1988-1989: Obv.: Arnold Machin, Walter Ott — Rev.: Walter Ott, R.C.M. Staff
1989-2003: Obv.: Dora de Pédery Hunt — Rev.: Walter Ott, R.C.M. Staff
2004-2010: Obv.: Susanna Blunt, Susan Taylor — Rev.: Walter Ott, R.C.M. Staff

Finish: Bullion, Brilliant relief against a parallel lined background

Cases of Issue: 1988-1998: (A) Single coin sealed in clear Mylar pouch
(B) Plastic tubes of 20 coins
1999-2010: (A) Sealed singly in clear Mylar pouches, in strips of 10 coins
(B) Plastic tubes of 25 coins

SILVER MAPLE LEAFS

BULLION ISSUES

PRICING: Please remember that silver maple leaf prices are linked to the price of silver and may be priced higher, or lower, than prices shown depending on market conditions. Unlike gold and platinum maple leafs, silver leafs do experience a collector demand which will result in price differentials between dates. The price is affected by the total mintage and the pattern of distribution during year of issue.

SILVER MAPLE LEAF SPECIFICATIONS

DATE	PRIVY MARKS	QUANTITY SOLD	ISSUE PRICE	FINISH	MS-65	MS-66	MS-67
1988		1,062,000	BV	Bullion	40.	45.	60.
1989		3,332,200	BV	Bullion	40.	45.	60.
1990		1,708,800	BV	Bullion	40.	45.	60.
1991		644,300	BV	Bullion	40.	45.	60.
1992		343,800	BV	Bullion	40.	45.	60.
1993		889,946	BV	Bullion	40.	45.	60.
1994		1,133,900	BV	Bullion	40.	45.	60.
1995		326,244	BV	Bullion	45.	50.	60.
1996		250,445	BV	Bullion	60.	75.	100.
1997		100,970	BV	Bullion	50.	60.	85.
1998		591,359	BV	Bullion	40.	45.	75.
1999		1,229,442	BV	Bullion	40.	45.	75.
1999-2000	Fireworks	Included	BV	Bullion	45.	50.	75.
2000	Fireworks 2000	403,652	BV	Bullion	45.	50.	75.
2001		398,563	BV	Bullion	45.	50.	75.
2002		576,196	BV	Bullion	45.	50.	75.
2003		684,750	BV	Bullion	40.	45.	60.
2004		680,925	BV	Bullion	40.	45.	60.
2005		955,694	BV	Bullion	40.	45.	60.
2006		2,464,727	BV	Bullion	40.	45.	60.
2007		3,526,052	BV	Bullion	40.	45.	60.
2008		7,909,161	BV	Bullion	40.	45.	60.
2009		9,727,592	BV	Bullion	40.	45.	60.
2010		N/A	BV	Bullion	40.	45.	60.

NOTES FOR COLLECTORS

1 Silver maple leafs are priced based on the world market price for silver, plus a small premium on the day the transaction takes place. Premiums will vary depending on the size of the transaction.
2. The packaging of silver maple leafs changed in 2009 from single coins in mylar pouches to twenty-five coin packaged in plastic tubes. In 2010 the silver maple leafs were available again in mylar pouches or plastic tubes of twenty-five.
3. The silver maple leafs listed in the table above are priced at a silver market value of $30.00 an ounce. Market changes, up or down, will necessitate a price revision.

SILVER MAPLE LEAF SPECIAL ISSUES

SINGLES

ONE DOLLAR, (½ ounce) SILVER WOLF, 2006.

Designers and Engravers:
Obv.: Susanna Blunt, Susan Taylor
Rev.: W. Woodruff, W. Woodruff
Composition: 99.99% Ag
Weight: 15.552 g, ½ oz
Diameter: 34.00 mm
Edge: Reeded
Thickness: 2.10 mm
Die Axis: ↑↑
Finish: Bullion
Case of Issue: Mylar Pouch

DATE	DESCRIPTION	QUANTITY SOLD	ISSUE PRICE	FINISH	MS-65	MS-66	MS-67
2006	$1 (½ oz), Silver Wolf	106,800	BV	Bullion	25.	30.	50.

FIVE DOLLARS (1 ounce), 10TH ANNIVERSARY OF MAPLE LEAF BULLION COINS, 1989.
Issued in 1989 in proof finish to commemorate the 10th anniversary of the introduction of the maple leaf in 1979.

Designers and Engravers:
Obv.: Arnold Machin
Rev.: Walter Ott, RCM Staff
Composition: 99.99% Ag
Weight: 31.1035 g, 1 oz
Diameter: 38.00 mm
Thickness: 3.15 mm
Edge: Reeded
Die Axis: ↑↑
Finish: Bullion
Case of issue: Maple wood presentation box, black flocked insert, encapsulated coins, COA, outer maple leaf printed box.

DATE	DESCRIPTION	QUANTITY SOLD	ISSUE PRICE	FINISH	PR-67 UHC	PR-68 UHC
1989	$5 (1 oz) 10th Anniv. Maple Leaf coins	29,999	39.00	Proof	70.	85.

FIVE DOLLARS (1 ounce), 20TH ANNIVERSARY OF THE SILVER MAPLE LEAF, 1988-2008.
This bullion coin was issued to commemorate the 20th anniversary of the silver maple leaf which was introduced in 1988.

Designers and Engravers:
Obv.: Arnold Machin
Rev.: RCM Staff
Composition: 99.99% Ag
Weight: 31.3035 g, 1 oz
Diameter: 38.00 mm
Thickness: 3.15 mm
Edge: Reeded
Die Axis: ↑↑
Finish: Bullion, Selectively gold plated
Case: Maroon leatherette clam style case, black flocked insert, encapsulated coin, COA

DATE	DESCRIPTION	QUANTITY SOLD	ISSUE PRICE	FINISH	MS-65	MS-66	MS-67
2008	$5 (1 oz), 20th Anniv. of the Silver Maple Leaf	9,998	74.95	Bullion	100.	110.	150.

FIVE DOLLARS (1 ounce), PIEDFORT MAPLE LEAF, 2010.

Designers and Engravers:
Obv.: Susanna Blunt, Susan Taylor
Rev.: RCM Staff
Composition: 99.99% Au
Silver content: 31.39 g, 1.01 tr oz
Weight: 31.39 g
Diameter: 34.0 mm
Edge: Reeded
Thickness: 4.00 mm
Die Axis: ↑↑
Finish: Bullion
Case: Maroon leatherette clam style case, black flock insert, encapsulated coin(s), COA

DATE	DESCRIPTION	QUANTITY SOLD	ISSUE PRICE	FINISH	MS-65	MS-66
2010	$5 Silver Piedfort Maple Leaf	6,000	79.95	Bullion	100.	125.
2010	Piedfort Set, $10 gold and $5 Silver	3,000	679.95	Bullion	675.	700.

FIVE DOLLARS (1 ounce), WOLF, 2011.

This is the first in a six-coin Canadian Wildlife Series which will be issued over a three year period beginning in 2011. The Timber Wolf first appeared as the reverse design on the 2006 half-ounce silver maple and, then again in 2007 on the gold fifty cent issue.

Designers and Engravers:
Obv.: Susanna Blunt, Susan Taylor
Rev.: William Woodruff, RCM Staff
Composition: 99.99% Au
Silver content: 31.11 g, 1.00 tr oz
Weight: 31.11 g
Diameter: 38.0 mm
Edge: Reeded
Thickness: 3.00 mm
Die Axis: ↑↑
Finish: Bullion
Case: Mylar pouch

DATE	DESCRIPTION	QUANTITY SOLD	ISSUE PRICE	FINISH	MS-65	MS-66
2011	$1 (1 oz), Wolf	N/A	BV	Bullion	40.	45.

FIVE DOLLARS (1 ounce), VANCOUVER 2010 WINTER OLYMPIC GAMES, 2008-2010.

Designers:
Obv.: Susanna Blunt
Rev.: 2008, 2010 RCM Staff; 2009 Xwa lac tun (Ricky Harry)

Engravers:
Rev.: Susan Taylor
Rev.: RCM Staff

Composition: 99.99% Ag
Weight: 31.1035 g, 1 oz
Diameter: 38.0 mm
Thickness: 3.15 mm
Cases: Singly: Mylar pouch
Coloured Set: Maple wood box, black flocked insert, encapsulated coins, COA

Edge: Reeded
Die Axis: ↑↑
Finish: 1. Bullion; 2. Bullion, Selectively gold plated, 3. Bullion, Gilt

2008 MAPLE LEAF AND VANCOUVER 2010 OLYMPIC LOGO

2009 THUNDERBIRD

2010 HOCKEY PLAYER

DATE	DESCRIPTION	QUANTITY SOLD	ISSUE PRICE	FINISH	MS-65	MS-66	MS-67
2008	$5 (1oz) 2010 Logo	937,839	BV	Bullion	40.	45.	60.
2008	$5 (1oz) 2010 Logo, Selectively gold plated	N/A	N.I.I.	Bullion	125.	135.	—
2009	$5 (1oz) Thunderbird	569,048	BV	Bullion	40.	45.	60.
2009	$5 (1oz) Thunderbird, Selectively gold plated	N/A	N.I.I.	Bullion	125.	135.	—
2010	$5 (1oz) Hockey Player	N/A	BV	Bullion	40.	45.	60.
2010	$5 (1oz) Hockey Player, Selectively gold plated	N/A	N.I.I.	Bullion	125	135.	—
2010	$5 (1oz) Hockey Player, Gold plated	N/A	71.95	Bullion	75.	80.	100.
—	3-Coin Set, Selectively gold plated	4,000	199.95	Bullion	200.	—	—

Note: Images illustrated smaller than actual size.

TWENTY DOLLARS (1 ounce), SAMBRO ISLAND LIGHTHOUSE, 2004.

This silver maple was issued to commemorate the oldest working lighthouse in North America. Sambro Lighthouse has guided ships in and out of Halifax Harbour for over 200 years.

Designers, and Engravers:
Obv.: Susanna Blunt, Susan Taylor
Rev.: Hedley Doty. William Woodruff
Composition: 99.99% Ag
Weight: 31.1035 g, 1 oz
Diameter: 38.0 mm
Edge: Reeded
Thickness: 3.15 mm
Die Axis: ↑↑
Finish: Proof, Frosted relief against a mirror background
Case of Issue: Maroon leatherette clam style case, black insert, encapsulated coin, COA

DATE	DESCRIPTION	QUANTITY SOLD	ISSUE PRICE	FINISH	PR-67 UHC	PR-68 UHC
2004	$20 Sambro Island Lighthouse	18,476	69.95	Proof	60.	70.

Note: See page 335 for Sambro Island Lighthouse derivative.

TWENTY DOLLARS (1 ounce), TORONTO ISLAND LIGHTHOUSE, 2005.

The Toronto Island Lighthouse built in 1809 on Gibraltar Point, on what is now Toronto Island, guided ships into the Port of York (Toronto). It is the oldest existing lighthouse on the Great Lakes.

Designers and Engravers:
Obv.: Susanna Blunt, Susan Taylor
Rev.: Brian Hughes, William Woodruff
Composition: 99.99% Ag
Weight: 31.1035 g, 1 oz
Diameter: 38.0 mm
Edge: Reeded
Thickness: 3.15 mm
Die Axis: ↑↑
Finish: Proof, Frosted relief against a mirror background
Case of Issue: Maroon plastic display case, black plastic insert, encapsulated coin, COA

DATE	DESCRIPTION	QUANTITY SOLD	ISSUE PRICE	FINISH	PR-67 UHC	PR-68 UHC
2005	$20 Toronto Island Lighthouse	14,006	69.95	Proof	60.	70.

FIFTY DOLLARS (10 ounces), 10TH ANNIVERSARY OF THE SILVER MAPLE LEAF, 1998.

In 1998 the Royal Canadian Mint issued the 10 ounce silver maple leaf in celebration of the 10th anniversary of the silver maple leaf bullion coin. This coin is the largest legal tender Canadian coin ever produced, and is accompanied by a sterling silver plaque of authenticity. This coin is shown smaller than its actual size.

Designers:
Obv.: Dora de Pédery-Hunt
Rev.: RCM Staff

Engravers:
Obv.: Dora de Pédery-Hunt
Rev.: RCM Staff

Composition: 99.99% Ag
Silver content: 311.0 g, 10.00 tr oz
Weight: 311.04 g, 10 oz
Diameter: 65.0 mm
Thickness: 11 mm

Edge: Lettered, 10th Anniversary 10e Anniversaire
Die Axis: ↑↑
Finish: Reverse proof
Nominal Value: $50.00

Case of Issue: Black leather case with silver "Royal Canadian Mint" plaque, black flock lining, encapsulated coin, Sterling silver certificate of authenticity

DATE	DESCRIPTION	QUANTITY SOLD	ISSUE PRICE	FINISH	MS-65	MS-66
1998	$50 (10 oz), 10th Anniv. Silver Maple Leaf	13,533	200.00	Proof	600.	650.

SILVER MAPLE LEAF SPECIAL ISSUES

SETS

ARCTIC FOX FINE SILVER COIN SET, 2004.

The first fractional fine silver coins feature wildlife designs that were originally created for platinum proof coins. The Arctic Fox first appeared on the Platinum proof coins of 1993.

Designers and Engravers:
Obv.: S. Blunt, S. Taylor
Rev.: Claude D'Angelo
Rev.: $5 – Susan Taylor
$4 – Sheldon Beveridge
$3 – Ago Aarand
$2 – Ago Aarand

Specifications: See page 319

Finish: Proof, Frosted relief against a mirror background

Case of Issue: Black case, multicoloured outer sleeve

DATE	DESCRIPTION	QUANTITY SOLD	ISSUE PRICE	FINISH	PR-67 UHC	PR-68 UHC
2004	Arctic Fox, 4-coin set	14,566	89.95	Proof	100.	—

CANADA LYNX FINE SILVER COIN SET, 2005.

The Canada Lynx first appeared on the platinum proof coins of 1995.

Designers and Engravers:
Obv.: S. Blunt, S. Taylor
Rev.: Michael Dumas
Rev.: $5 – Susan Taylor
$4 – Cosme Saffioti
$3 – Stan Witten
$2 – Ago Aarand

Specifications: See page 319

Finish: Proof, Frosted relief against a mirror background

Case of Issue: N/A

DATE	DESCRIPTION	QUANTITY SOLD	ISSUE PRICE	FINISH	PR-67 UHC	PR-68 UHC
2005	Canada Lynx, 4-coin set	7,942	89.95	Proof	100.	—

Note: Arctic Fox and Canadian Lynx coins are illustrated smaller than actual size.

SILVER MAPLE LEAFS WITH PRIVY MARKS

SINGLES

FIVE DOLLAR (1 ounce), SILVER MAPLE LEAFS WITH PRIVY MARKS, 1998-2009.

Beginning in 1998 the Royal Canadian Mint started a special issue of the $5.00 - 1 oz silver Maple Leafs. Privy marks were added to the reverses, commemorating special events for each year. For Designers, Engravers see page 297 and for Specifications see page 319.

1998 Titanic
Dillon - Gage

1998 Tiger
MTB Bank

1998 R.C.M.P.
Post Office

1908-1998 Anniv.
R.C.M.

1999 Rabbit
MTB Bank

2000 Dragon
MTB Bank

2000 Expo Hanover
R.C.M.

2001 Snake
R.C.M.

2002 Horse
R.C.M.

2003 Sheep
R.C.M.

2004 Monkey
R.C.M.

2004 D-Day
R.C.M.

2004 Desjardins
R.C.M.

2005 Rooster
R.C.M.

2005 Liberation of the Netherlands
R.D.M.

2005 V.E. Day
R.C.M.

2005 VJ Day
R.C.M.

2006
Year of Dog

2007
Year of the Pig

2007, 2008, 2009
Fabulous 12

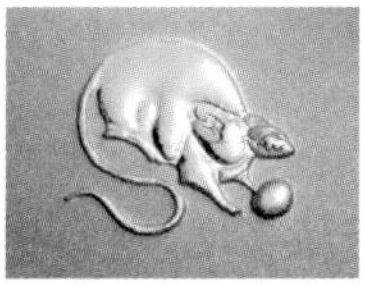

2008
Year of the Rat

2008
Brandenburg Gate

2009
Year of the Ox

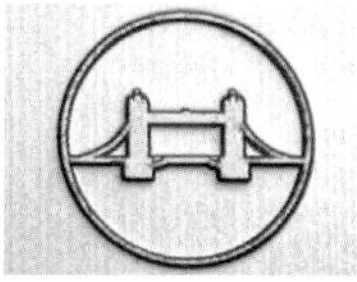

2009
Tower Bridge

FIVE DOLLAR (1 ounce), SILVER MAPLE LEAFS WITH PRIVY MARKS, 1998-2009, PRICING TABLE.

DATE	DESCRIPTION	CASE OF ISSUE	QUANTITY SOLD	ISSUE PRICE	FINISH	66	67
1998	Titanic	Mylar pouch	26,000	N/A	Specimen	65.	75.
1998	Tiger	Mylar pouch	25,000	N/A	Specimen	85.	95.
1998	R.C.M.P.	Mylar pouch	25,000	N/A	Specimen	75.	85.
1998	90th Anniv.	Mylar pouch	13,025	N/A	Specimen	60.	70.
1999	Rabbit	Mylar pouch	25,000	N/A	Specimen	70.	80.
2000	Dragon	Mylar pouch	25,000	N/A	Specimen	70.	80.
2000	Expo	Mylar pouch	15,000	N/A	Specimen	125.	135.
2001	Snake	Mylar pouch	25,000	N/A	Specimen	90.	100.
2002	Horse	Mylar pouch	25,000	N/A	Specimen	60.	70.
2003	Sheep	Mylar pouch	25,000	N/A	Specimen	60.	70.
2004	Monkey	Mylar pouch	25,000	N/A	Specimen	55.	65.
2004	D-Day	Red display	11,698	39.95	Specimen	75.	85.
2004	Desjardins	Red display	15,000	39.95	Bullion	90.	100.
2005	Rooster	Mylar pouch	15,000	24.95	Specimen	55.	65.
2005	Liberation	Mylar pouch	3,500	E45.95	Specimen	150.	160.
2005	VE Day	Mylar pouch	6,998	49.95	Specimen	85.	98.
2005	VJ Day	Mylar pouch	6,998	49.95	Specimen	90.	100.
2006	Year of the Dog	Mylar pouch	10,000	24.95	Specimen	50.	60.
2007	Year of the Pig	Mylar pouch	8,000	29.95	Specimen	50.	60.
2007	Fabulous 12	Mylar pouch	5,000	39.95	Specimen	75.	85.
2008	Fabulous 12	Mylar pouch	5,000	N/A	Specimen	100.	110.
2008	Year of the Rat	Mylar pouch	8,000	24.95	Specimen	45.	55.
2008	Brandenburg Gate	Mylar pouch	50,000	39.95	Specimen	55.	65.
2009	Year of the Ox	Mylar pouch	8,000	23.95	Specimen	45.	55.
2009	Tower Bridge	Mylar pouch	75,000	34.95	Bullion	55.	65.
2009	Fabulous 12	Mylar pouch	5,000	N/A	Specimen	75.	85.

NOTES

1. A specimen finish on a bullion coin is also known as a reverse proof — a brilliant relief on a matte or satin background.
2. The method of packaging may vary from the normal mylar pouch to red or black flocked clam style cases, depending on the distributor.
3. The Fabulous 12 silver maple leaf with the “F12” privy mark commemorates the twelve winning coin designs of the 2007 Berlin Money Fair.

MINT LOGO SET

ROYAL CANADIAN MINT LOGO SET, 2004.

This five coin set carries the Royal Canadian Mint logo on each coin.

$5 (1oz) Obverse

$5 (1oz) Reverse

Designers and Engravers:
Obv.: Susanna Blunt, Susan Taylor
Rev.: RCM Staff

Specifications: See page 319
Finish: Specimen (reverse proof)
Case of Issue: Dark blue leatherette clam style case, black insert, encapsulated coin, COA, silver sleeve

Logo

$4 (1/2 oz) Reverse

$3 (1/4 oz) Reverse

$2 (1/10 oz) Reverse

$1 (1/20 oz) Reverse

DATE	DESCRIPTION	QUANTITY SOLD	ISSUE PRICE	FINISH	SP-66	SP-67
2004	Set of 5 coins	13,859	99.95	Specimen	100.	—

SPECIAL PRIVY SET

FIVE DOLLARS (1 ounce) SILVER MAPLE LEAFS, ZODIAC PRIVY MARK SET, 2004.

This twelve coin set was struck by the Royal Canadian Mint, and issued by Universal Coins of Ottawa. Each coin carries one of the twelve signs of zodiac as a privy mark.

Aries

Taurus

Gemini

Cancer

Leo

Virgo

Libra

Scorpio

Sagittarius

Capricorn

Aquarius

Pisces

Designers:
Obv.: Susanna Blunt
Rev.: RCM Staff

Engravers:
Obv.: Susan Taylor
Rev.: RCM Staff

Composition: 99.99% Ag
Weight: 31.1035 g, 1 oz
Diameter: 38.0 mm
Finish: Specimen (reverse proof)
Case of Issue: Singly: Mylar pouch
Set: Red 12-hole case

Thickness: 3.15 mm
Edge: Reeded
Die Axis: ↑↑

DATE	DESCRIPTION	QUANTITY SOLD	ISSUE PRICE	FINISH	SP-66	SP-67
2004	Set of 12 coins	5,000	368.88	Specimen	750.	—
2004	Single coin	Included	39.95	Specimen	65.	75.

COLOURED SILVER MAPLES

SINGLE COINS

FIVE DOLLARS (1 ounce), SILVER MAPLE LEAFS, COLOURED COIN SERIES, 2001-2007.

2001-2003 Obverse
Designer and Engraver:
Dora de Pédery-Hunt

2001 Autumn
Designer: Debbie Adams
Engraver: Unknown

2002 Spring
Designer: Unknown
Engraver: Unknown

2003 Summer
Designer and Engraver:
Stan Witten

2004-2007 Obverse
Designer: Susanna Blunt
Engraver: Susan Taylor

2004 Winter
Designer and Engraver:
Stan Witten

2005 Bigleaf Maple
Designer and Engraver:
Stan Witten

2006 Silver Maple
Designer and Engraver:
Stan Witten

2007 Obverse
Designer: Susanna Blunt
Engraver: Susan Taylor

2007 Sugar Maple
Designer: Stan Witten
Engraver: Stan Witten

Designers and Engravers: See illustrations above
Specifications: See page 319
Finish: Bullion, colourised
Case of Issue: 2001-2004: Dark green clam case, black flocked insert, encapsulated coin, COA
2005-2007: Maroon plastic slide case, black plastic insert, encapsulated coin, COA

DATE	DESCRIPTION	QUANTITY SOLD	ISSUE PRICE	FINISH	MS-65	MS-66	MS-67
2001	Autumn	49,709	34.95	Bullion	60.	70.	85.
2002	Spring	29,509	34.95	Bullion	65.	75.	95.
2003	Summer	29,416	34.95	Bullion	60.	70.	85.
2004	Winter	26,763	34.95	Bullion	75.	85.	100.
2005	Bigleaf Maple	21,233	39.95	Bullion	60.	70.	95.
2006	Silver Maple	14,157	45.95	Bullion	125.	135.	150.
2007	Sugar Maple	11,495	49.95	Bullion	125.	135.	150.

Note: Images illustrated smaller than actual size.

SILVER MAPLE LEAFS WITH HOLOGRAMS

SINGLE COINS

FIVE DOLLARS (1 ounce), "MAPLE OF GOOD FORTUNE" HOLOGRAM, 2001, 2003 and 2005.

First issued in 2001, the $5 Maple Leaf coin carries a privy mark of Chinese characters, meaning Maple of Good Fortune, or Hope, as part of the hologram.

2001 Obverse

2001 Reverse

Privy Mark 2001

2003 Obverse

2003 Reverse

Privy Mark 2003

2005 Obverse

2005 Reverse

Privy Mark 2005

Designers:
2001, 2003: Obv.: Dora de Pédery-Hunt
Rev.: RCM Staff
2005: Obv.: Susanna Blunt
Rev.: RCM Staff

Specifications: See page 319

Finish: Specimen (reverse proof), hologram

Case of Issue: Red clam oval case, taupe flocked insert, encapsulated coin, COA

Engravers:
Obv.: Dora de Pédery-Hunt
Rev.: RCM Staff
Obv.: Susan Taylor
Rev.: RCM Staff

Case of Issue: Mylar pouch

DATE	DESCRIPTION	QUANTITY SOLD	ISSUE PRICE	FINISH	SP-66	SP-67
2001	Good Fortune	29,817	59.99	Specimen	85.	100.
2003	Good Fortune	29,731	39.99	Specimen	80.	90.
2005	Good Fortune	19,888	39.95	Specimen	90.	100.

SILVER MAPLE LEAFS WITH HOLOGRAMS

SINGLE COINS

FIVE DOLLARS (1 ounce), 15TH ANNIVERSARY OF THE ONE DOLLAR LOON, 2002.

These maple leaf coins were struck to commemorate the 15th anniversary of the one dollar loon coin issued in 1987. The reverse design on this coin depicts a male loon flapping its wings in the "Loon Dance" protecting its nest from intruders.

Designers and Engravers:
Obv.: Dora de Pédery-Hunt
Rev.: RCM Staff
Composition: 99.99% Ag
Weight: 31.1035 g, 1 oz
Diameter: 38.0 mm
Edge: Reeded
Thickness: 3.15 mm
Die Axis: ↑↑
Finish: Specimen (reverse proof), Hologram
Case of Issue: Black leatherette clam case, hunter green interior, encapsulated coin, COA

DATE	DESCRIPTION	QUANTITY SOLD	ISSUE PRICE	FINISH	SP-66	SP-67
2002	$5 (1 oz) 15th Anniv. of One Dollar Loon	29,970	39.95	Specimen	125.	135.

FIVE COIN SETS

15TH ANNIVERSARY OF THE SILVER MAPLE, 2003.

These maple leaf coins were struck to commemorate the 15th anniversary of the silver maple leaf, 1988-2003. At the time, this five coin set contained two new denominations for Canadian coinage, a $3 and a $4 coin. All coins are struck with a maple leaf hologram.

$5 (1oz) Obverse

$5 (1oz) Reverse

Designers and Engravers:
Obv.: Dora de Pédery-Hunt
Rev.: RCM Staff
Specifications: See page 319
Finish: Bullion, Hologram
Case of Issue: Red wooden case, black flocked insert, encapsulated coin, COA silver outer box

$4 (1/2 oz) Reverse

$3 (1/4 oz) Reverse

$2 (1/10 oz) Reverse

$1 (1/20 oz) Reverse

DATE	DESCRIPTION	QUANTITY SOLD	ISSUE PRICE	FINISH	MS-65	MS-66	MS-67
2003	Set of 5 coins, 15th Anniv. Silver Maple	28,947	149.95	Bullion	150.	—	—

SILVER MAPLE LEAF SETS

$5 SILVER MAPLE LEAF WITH PROOF SETS, 2001.

Three varieties of silver maples (colourised, hologram and regular) were combined with seven proof coins, 1¢ to $2, of the 2001 Proof Set to form the following Premium Proof sets:

DATE	DESCRIPTION	QUANTITY SOLD	ISSUE PRICE	ISSUER	FINISH	MARKET VALUE
2001	**Proof Set 2001.** Seven proof coins. Reverse proof hologram, silver maple leaf	3,000	150.00	RCM	PR-67, SP-66	175.
2001	**Proof Set 2001**. Seven proof coins. Reverse proof privy snake, silver maple leaf	Included	100.00	RCM	PR-67, MS-65	150.
2001	**Proof Set 2001**. Seven proof coins and a colourised 2001 silver maple leaf	Included	75.00	RCM	PR-67, MS-65	100.

SILVER MAPLE LEAF DERIVATIVES

DATE	DESCRIPTION	QUANTITY SOLD	ISSUE PRICE	ISSUER	FINISH	MARKET VALUE
1998	**125th Anniv. of R.C.M.P.**, Silver maple with R.C.M.P. privy mark. Souvenir sheet. Dark blue presentation case. COA. Booklet	25,000	47.95	RCM, CP	SP-66	75.
2004	**Sambro Island**. Framed image and twenty dollar coin	N/A	249.00	RCM	PR-67	100.

$2,500 Gold Coin
The 125th Anniversary of Banff National Park